Marketing in the New Asia

Edited by
Siew Meng Leong
Swee Hoon Ang
Chin Tiong Tan

Singapore • Boston • Burr Ridge, IL • Dubuque, IA • Madison, WI
New York • San Francisco • St. Louis • Bangkok • Bogotá • Caracas
Kuala Lumpur • Lisbon • London • Madrid • Mexico City • Milan
Montreal • New Delhi • Santiago • Seoul • Sydney • Taipei • Toronto

McGraw Hill

McGraw-Hill
A Division of The McGraw-Hill Companies

Marketing in the New Asia

Copyright © 2001 by McGraw-Hill Book Co. – Singapore. All rights reserved. No part of this publication may be reproduced or distributed in any form or by any means, or stored in a data base or retrieval system, without the prior written permission of the publisher.

1 2 3 4 5 6 7 8 9 10 LG ANL 05 04 03 02 01

Cover photograph: © Daniel Aubry / Imagefinder

When ordering this title, use ISBN 0-07-118467-8

Printed in Singapore

Contents

Preface		v
About the Editors		vi
1	Marketing in the Year 2000: An International Perspective	1
2	Competing in Asia Pacific: Understanding the Rules of the Game	27
3	The Asian Apocalypse: Crisis Marketing for Consumers and Businesses	55
4	Marketers and the External Environment: The Indonesian Experience	83
5	Asian Youth and Implications for Marketing Strategies: Changes and Differences in Consumption Attitudes and Lifestyle Values	98
6	Asian Culture and the Global Consumer	115
7	The Effects of Language on Marketing: A Comparison of the Use of Chinese and English Idioms in Print Advertisements	125
8	The Power of Money: A Cross-cultural Analysis of Business-related Beliefs	137
9	Culture, Customers, and Contemporary Communism: Vietnamese Marketing Management under *Doi Moi*	159

⑩	Strategic Alliances in China: Negotiating the Barriers	182
⑪	East vs. West: Strategic Marketing Management Meets the Asian Networks	199
⑫	Business-to-Business Marketing in Asia Pacific: The Telecommunications Competitiveness of Regional Economies	216
⑬	Assessing National Competitive Superiority: An Importance–Performance Matrix Approach	228
⑭	Managing Brands for the Long Run: Brand Reinforcement and Revitalization Strategies	243
⑮	Chinese Consumers' Perception of Alpha-numeric Brand Names	272
⑯	Asia's Growing Service Sector	289
⑰	New vs. Old: The Rise of Full-service Superstores and the Demise of Traditional Wet Markets	312
⑱	E-tailing in Asia Pacific: A BCG Perspective	327
⑲	Ethical Issues across Cultures: Managing the Differing Perspectives of China and the U.S.A.	340
⑳	Take a Conservative Approach When Entering the China Market	364

PREFACE

With the dawn of the new millennium, Asia appears to have recovered from the depths of an economic and social crisis in the late 1990s. Marketing in and to the region, however, remains as challenging as ever. Greater competition and more sophisticated consumers make for a tougher operating environment for businesses. Yet, opportunities also abound with the trend toward deregulation, online channels, and less socialist governance structures.

These issues are addressed in the 20 articles that we have assembled for this book. The articles are organized into four sections paralleling the 1999 edition of Kotler, Ang, Leong, and Tan's *Marketing Management: An Asian Perspective*—Understanding Marketing Management, Analyzing Marketing Opportunities, Developing Marketing Strategies, and Planning Marketing Programs.

While most articles were culled from a variety of scholarly and professional sources, five were written specifically for this book. Several articles discuss issues from a pan-regional perspective, while others furnish country-specific coverage of such markets as China and Vietnam. Likewise, both consumer and industrial buyer behaviors and marketing practices receive attention.

Collectively, this selection of articles should provide the requisite insights for marketing survival and success in postcrisis Asia. Although our primary target audience remain students taking marketing management courses at both undergraduate and MBA levels, the articles are also appropriate for managers as they focus on the practical aspects of marketing in the region.

We wish to thank the authors who contributed their work to this book, the publishers who granted us permission to use the articles, the staff at McGraw-Hill (notably Lee Ming Ang) who so professionally put together the finished product, and our faculties and families for their continued support of our research.

About the Editors

SIEW MENG LEONG is Professor at the Faculty of Business Administration, National University of Singapore. He received his MBA and Ph.D. in business administration at the University of Wisconsin, Madison. He has published in *Journal of Marketing, Journal of Marketing Research, Journal of Consumer Research, Journal of International Business Studies*, and other international journals and conference proceedings. His research focuses on consumer behavior, sales management, and marketing research. Professor Leong is editor of the *Asian Journal of Marketing* and serves on the editorial boards of the *Journal of Marketing Communications* and *Marketing Education Review*. He has consulted for such clients as Coopers & Lybrand, Economic Development Board of Singapore, Hagemeyer Electronics, Johnson & Johnson Medical, Malayan Bank, Motorola Electronics, Singapore Pools, Singapore Telecom, and Wisma Atria.

SWEE HOON ANG is Associate Professor at the Faculty of Business Administration, National University of Singapore. She received her Ph.D. degree in marketing at the University of British Columbia. She has written for journals and conferences, including *Journal of Advertising, Psychology and Marketing, Journal of World Business*, and *Long Range Planning*. Her research and teaching interests are in advertising, consumer behavior, and services marketing. Professor Ang has consulted for companies including Johnson & Johnson Medical and Tiger Medical Balm; and conducted executive training for Nokia and Port of Singapore Authority.

CHIN TIONG TAN is Provost and Professor at Singapore Management University. He received his Ph.D. degree in marketing at Pennsylvania State University. He has published in *Journal of Consumer Research, Journal of International Business Studies, International Marketing Review, European Journal of Marketing*, and other international journals and conference proceedings. Professor Tan sits on the editorial boards of several international journals, and is also on the boards of several companies and committees of government agencies. He is the Academic Advisor to Singapore Airlines' Management Development Centre and has consulted internationally for companies like Acer Computer, Altron Group, Inchcape, Singapore Telecom, Standard Chartered Bank, and Swiss Bank Corporation.

Professors Leong, Ang, and Tan are coauthors of *Marketing Management: An Asian Perspective* and *Cases in Marketing Management and Strategy: An Asia-Pacific Perspective*.

Marketing in the Year 2000

An International Perspective

Siew Meng Leong and Chin Tiong Tan

This paper reports the result of a survey of 170 corporate-level executives from the United States, Europe, and Japan regarding the business environment and marketing strategies in the year 2000. Findings indicate a strong consensus concerning the globalization of business activities although market fragmentation may provide opportunities for more customized marketing programs. Marketing's pivotal status in the organization is affirmed and the most important marketing mix elements were found to be product and price. Several cross-regional differences in expectations were also obtained. Implications of the findings are discussed.

INTRODUCTION

Profiling the future of marketing has been a recent focal point of inquiry in the discipline. This interest extends beyond the conventional anticipation of the future environment which has always been a part of the process of strategic marketing planning. The challenge is to seek views of expert, high-level executives and respected scholars to predict

---

The authors thank Jeannie Teoh for her research assistance, William Stoever and Joseph Cote for their helpful comments, and the Singapore Economic Development Board for their cooperation in data collection. This research was funded by a grant from the National University of Singapore to the second author.

Reprinted from *Research in Marketing*, Vol. 11, pp. 195–220. Copyright 1992, with permission from JAI Press.

future trends and developments in the discipline (Laczniak and Lusch, 1986; Laczniak et al., 1977; Lazer et al., 1989; Lusch et al., 1976; Udell et al., 1976).

Clearly, these efforts will assist marketers to develop ideas about the future—the objective of the American Marketing Association's Commission on Marketing in the year 2000. However, one possible shortcoming of these studies is their exclusive focus on the views of American executives and academics to the neglect of foreign marketers. As several authors have commented (Bartels, 1983; Garda, 1988), the emergence of global markets and international competition demands a "de-domestication" of research and perspective. The broadening of marketing's horizons to encompass international, comparative, and cross-cultural dimensions is therefore essential.

To this end, the research reported in this paper provides an international perspective to the prediction of trends in the business environment and marketing strategy. Specifically, the views of American, Japanese, and European senior executives are incorporated and comparisons made of expectations regarding marketing in the year 2000. According to Ohmae's (1987) concept of the triad market, North America, Japan, and Europe are the most important and largest markets of today and the future. Moreover, most major multinational corporations (MNCs) are headquartered in these regions.

The organization of the remainder of this paper is as follows. The next section provides the methodology employed in the study and its rationale. Next, the survey results are presented. In particular, executives' perceptions of the business environment in the year 2000 are first depicted. Subsequently, trends in the orientation and status of marketing and its management are delineated. Implications of the research findings are then discussed.

Method

Sample

A major consideration of research in future trends is that respondents be willing and able to provide the necessary information (cf. Campbell, 1955). Past attempts have involved leaders in the futures literature (e.g., Naisbitt, 1982; Toffler, 1971, 1980). Noted experts within the field including senior advertising and marketing managers (Bogart, 1985; Laczniak and Lusch, 1986), leading academics (Laczniak et al.,

1977), and chief executive officers (Lazer et al., 1989) have also been approached.

Clearly, respondents in this study should be executives of sufficiently high corporate standing to possess the likely expertise and bird's eye view necessary to provide an informed, integrated perspective of marketing in the year 2000. To ensure sample comparability across countries, such executives are likely to hod job titles of at least manager, vice president, or their equivalent. Moreover, they should represent multinational corporations with worldwide interests. Finally, they should provide input almost simultaneously so that enhanced comparability is possible within a given time frame (Sekaran, 1983).

One opportunity presented itself that enabled these criteria to be satisfied. A global strategies conference was organized in October 1988 by the Singapore Economic Development Board. Top officers of MNCs around the world were invited to Singapore to participate in the three-day seminar. Some 170 executives—85 from the United States, 47 from Japan, and 38 from 9 European countries (Denmark [3 respondents], Finland [1], France [3], Holland [1], Norway [1], Sweden [4], Switzerland [8], the United Kingdom [8], and West Germany [9]) participated at the meeting and formed the sample for this study. Table 1-1 contains the sample profile characteristics.

As Table 1-1 indicates, the respondents held senior management positions within the 135 organizations they represented. Indeed, the modal organization title held was managing director or general manager. In nearly 96 percent of the cases, respondents were involved in overseeing or were responsible for the corporate planning function of their organization. Executives also hailed from a cross-section of industries out of which 16 percent were service-oriented and the remainder manufacturing-based. All organizations were large concerns as indicated by average annual sales in 1987 of about $6,000 million with the number of employees averaging approximately 36,000. Sales of American firms represented in the survey averaged $4,452 million compared to $9,375 million and $5,408 million for Japanese and European organizations respectively. More than 90 percent were well-known companies on the Fortune Industrial, International, and Service 500 lists. All had corporate interests in at least three continents—North America, Europe, and Asia. The number of employees average about 34,200, 20,200, and 64,200 for American, Japanese, and European corporations respectively.

TABLE 1-1
Sample characteristics

Characteristic	Percentage
Industry category	
Electrical/electronics	25.7
Computers	12.5
Metals/metal products	10.6
Chemicals	9.2
Transportation equipment	4.7
Rubber/plastics	3.3
Petroleum refining	2.6
Food/beverage	2.6
Scientific/photographic equipment	2.0
Printing/publishing	2.0
Pharmaceuticals	1.3
Other manufacturing	7.9
Services (financial, medical, telecommunications, etc.)	15.9
Size of organization (number of employees)	
Less than 1,000	13.4
1,000–9,999	40.1
10,000–49,999	24.8
50,000–99,999	12.1
100,000 and above	9.6
Sales ($ million)	
Less than $100	9.7
$100–999	36.6
$1,000–4,999	27.6
$5,000–9,999	8.9
$10,000 and above	17.2
Organization title/rank	
CEO/president/chairman/partner	10.1
Managing director/general manager	53.2
Director/deputy managing director	11.9
Vice president	16.0
Manager/senior manager	4.8
Other (financial controller, consultant, etc.)	4.0

Measurement

A survey questionnaire was designed to collect responses from participants regarding their perceptions of marketing in the year 2000. A set of 24 statements was generated based on prior research in the futures and functional literature cited previously. The items related to evaluation of the business situation in the year 2000 followed by perceptions of marketing in general and then each of the components of the marketing mix. This is similar to the approach employed in the Lacznaik and Lusch (1986; Lacznaik et al., 1977; Lusch et al., 1976; Udell et al., 1976) studies as well as the schema used by Lazer et al. (1989) to categorize the information from interviews of chief executives. Respondents indicated their extent of agreement to statements on five-point Likert-type scales. Following this, respondents provided rankings of various marketing and corporate activities in the year 2000. Sample profile data was also collected.

The survey was administered prior to the start of the conference. The questionnaire was contained in the registration package and participants were requested to complete it before the first session. Only one version of the survey—in English—was prepared. Professional interpreters thoroughly briefed on the contents of the instrument were on hand to render translation assistance if needed. None was found necessary. The questionnaire took about 15 to 20 minutes to complete.

Results

Tables 1-2 through 1-8 contain the results of the survey.[1] Where ratings are concerned, higher scores reflect stronger agreement. The tables also contain information on the overall percentage of respondents indicating either agreement or strong agreement for all statements. In terms of rankings, lower scores reflect higher rankings. All pairwise comparisons across respondent subsamples were conducted at the .05 level of significance based on mean ratings and rankings. Only statistically significant differences are displayed.

Business Environment in the Year 2000

Two general aspects of the business environment in the year 2000 were explored. First, respondents indicated their extent of agreement to nine statements pertaining to environmental conditions facing marketers in the year 2000 (see Table 1-2). Next, respondents provided rankings in

---
[1] The possible problem of multiple responses from the same organization over-representing a particular corporate point of view was investigated by re-running the analysis based on the responses of the most senior-level respondent from each organization. The results yielded no statistically significant differences in mean ratings and rankings for the statements studied.

TABLE 1-2
Business environment in the year 2000

Statement	Total % agree/ strongly agree	Overall mean	U.S. mean	Japan mean	Europe mean	Significant differences
1. Companies will become more global in their production, distribution, and marketing systems as domestic markets become more saturated.	98.8	4.65	4.69	4.51	4.70	US > J
2. Companies must learn to operate as if the world were one large market—ignoring superficial regional and national differences.	81.8	4.14	4.24	4.00	4.11	NS
3. The state of business and professional ethics will have become an international issue of debate.	76.5	3.88	3.81	3.87	4.05	NS
4. Government legislation regulating consumer/marketing practices will have increased.	67.6	3.60	3.62	3.43	3.76	E > J
5. Several regulated industries will become less regulated as more reliance is placed on competitive forces to protect the public interest.	62.7	3.61	3.60	3.57	3.68	NS
6. Corporate cultures of excellent companies will be very different from those of excellent companies today.	48.8	3.19	3.18	3.15	3.26	NS
7. Natural resources will become less important with technological developments in agriculture, materials science, etc.	47.6	2.88	2.91	2.74	3.00	NS
8. The world's markets will have become more protectionist.	35.9	3.02	3.07	2.94	3.03	NS
9. Corporate research and development budgets will decrease as the pace of technological change slows down.	8.9	2.11	2.12	2.26	1.89	J > E

respect of the importance of six geographical regions for corporate activities in the year 2000 (Table 1-3).

Environmental trends

Several significant findings emerge from Table 1-2. First and foremost, there was almost univocal agreement that companies will become more global in orientation (99 percent) and consider the world as one large market (82 percent). Indeed, only about 36 percent of respondents felt that the world's markets would become more protectionist by that time. Interestingly, American executives agreed more strongly than their Japanese counterparts that increased globalization in production, distribution, and marketing would occur.

Second, there was a somewhat lower consensus regarding government and legal influences in the year 2000. Most respondents (68 percent) believed that there was a trend toward increased regulation of consumer/marketing practices. In particular, European executives felt more strongly on this point than Japanese respondents. One reason for this may be that the state of business and professional ethics would have become an international issue of debate. Approximately 77 percent of all respondents concurred with this statement. However, there would not be universal erection of increased legal restrictions. Specifically, almost 63 percent of respondents thought that several regulated industries would be more deregulated as greater reliance would be placed on competitive forces to protect the public interest. Executives were nearly divided on the corporate cultures of excellent companies of the future vis-à-vis those at present. Nearly 49 percent held the position that differences in corporate cultures would arise, 17 percent were neutral and 35 percent thought excellent companies in the year 2000 would not have different corporate cultures from those of today.

Finally, the potential impact of technology was explored. Only a small minority (9 percent) anticipated that the pace of technology would slow down and lead to a decrease in corporate research and development budgets. Nearly 79 percent expected otherwise. Japanese executives, in particular, disagreed more strongly on this issue than their European counterparts. Despite technological advancements, only about 48 percent of executives believed that natural resources will become less important in the year 2000.

Regional importance

From Table 1-3, the results showed that North America will be the most important region for corporate activities in the year 2000. However, Asia emerged as a close runner-up with a mean ranking of 1.95 versus 1.92 for North America. Europe was a clear third (2.42). Fourth was Latin America (4.51), with the Middle East fifth (4.66), and Africa (5.55) last.

Rankings were consistent for the last three regions across the three respondent subsamples. However, the ordering was slightly different in respect of the three most important ones. In particular, only American executives believed North America to be the most important region for corporate activities in the year 2000 followed by Asia and Europe. Indeed, it was the heavy weightage of the American subsample that boosted North America to first place. For Japanese executives, Asia ranked first ahead of North America and Europe. European respondents placed Europe in front of Asia with North America in third place.

Given these differences, it can be expected that several subsample variations in importance rankings be found. Thus, American executives ranked North America higher than their European counterparts while Japanese executives believed Asia as being more important than both American and European executives. Finally, both American and European executives considered Europe as being more important than their Japanese counterparts, with European executives furnishing a statistically significant higher ranking than the Americans as well.

TABLE 1-3
Importance of geographic regions for corporate activities in the year 2000

Region	Overall	U.S.	Japan	Europe	Significant differences
North America	1.92	1.81	1.81	2.27	US > E
Asia	1.95	2.01	1.62	2.22	J > US; J > E
Europe	2.42	2.48	2.83	1.78	US > J; E > US; E > J
Latin America	4.51	4.44	4.64	4.49	NS
Middle East	4.66	4.67	4.64	4.65	NS
Africa	5.55	5.53	5.55	5.59	NS

Mean importance ranking

Marketing in the Year 2000

Marketing orientation

Table 1-4 contains the reactions of executives to six statements pertaining to marketing in general in the year 2000. The highest level of agreement (94 percent) was reached for the statement regarding companies paying greater attention to consumer needs. Executives also widely anticipated that marketers will work more closely with other functional departments (91 percent) and that the societal marketing concept will be more widely practiced (88 percent). However, the Japanese executives felt more strongly that the role of marketing will focus increasingly on enhancing the quality of life in society compared to American executives.

TABLE 1-4
Marketing orientation in the year 2000

Statement	Total % agree/ strongly agree	Overall mean	U.S. mean	Japan mean	Europe mean	Significant differences
1. Companies will pay greater attention to consumer needs.	94.1	4.43	4.33	4.49	4.58	NS
2. Marketers will work together more with other functional departments in the firm to achieve total company objectives.	90.6	4.17	4.08	4.23	4.29	NS
3. The role of marketing will increasingly focus on enhancing the quality of life in society.	88.2	4.18	4.01	4.40	4.26	J > US
4. There will be increased fragmentation in the marketplace thus requiring more sophisticated ways of segmenting the market.	77.6	3.91	3.81	3.87	4.16	E > US
5. Marketers will concentrate their efforts more on profits than on sales volume.	59.4	3.61	3.36	3.89	3.80	J > US; E > US

Most interestingly, while executives had pointed to increased globalization, most (78 percent) also thought that there will be increased market fragmentation requiring more sophisticated segmentation techniques to be employed. Executives were more equivocal on the remaining two issues. Nearly 60 percent expected marketers to focus more on profits than on sales volume. On this statement, both Japanese and European executives were in firmer agreement than American respondents.

Marketing's status

Respondents also furnished their rankings of the importance of various functions in the year 2000 (Table 1-5, Panel A), the likelihood of chief executives coming from a particular background (Table 1-5, Panel B), the importance of the individual marketing mix elements (Table 1-6), and the importance of eight types of marketing research (Table 1-7).

Table 1-5 clearly suggests that marketing will be the key functional

TABLE 1-5
Marketing's status in the year 2000

A. Importance of corporate activities in the year 2000

Activity	Overall	U.S.	Japan	Europe	Significant differences
Marketing	1.75	1.56	2.13	1.68	US > J; E > J
Production	2.36	2.30	2.12	2.74	US > E; J > E
Personnel	2.71	2.99	2.36	2.53	J > US; E > US
Finance	3.18	3.16	3.30	3.06	NS

B. CEO background in the year 2000

Background	Overall	U.S.	Japan	Europe	Significant differences
Marketing	1.82	1.67	2.13	1.78	US > J
Finance	3.18	3.11	3.78	2.58	US > J; E > J
Engineering	3.31	3.27	3.00	3.81	J > E
Production	3.81	3.68	3.91	3.97	NS
Computer science	5.32	5.12	5.32	5.75	NS
Personnel	6.04	6.71	4.89	6.03	J > US; E > US; J > E
Accounting/taxation	6.19	6.21	6.34	5.97	NS
Legal	6.24	6.17	6.53	6.03	NS

area of an enterprise in the year 2000. Its mean ranking of 1.75 heads that of production (2.36) and personnel (2.71). Surprisingly, finance (3.18) was rated least importance despite the current focus on mergers and acquisitions. Both American and European executives attached greater importance to marketing activities than the Japanese. In contrast, American and Japanese executives perceived production as being more important than Europeans. Finally, Japanese and European executives gave personnel greater weight than the Americans.

Confirmatory evidence of marketing's status as the prime function of a commercial enterprise is that chief executive officers in the year 2000 are ranked as being most likely to have a marketing background (mean ranking 1.82). Significantly, while several differences in rank ordering across nationalities appeared, none concerned marketing, which American, Japanese, and European respondents all considered as the background CEOs in the year 2000 were most likely to have.

However, American executives accorded a higher mean ranking to marketing than Japanese respondents. Overall, marketing was followed by finance, engineering, and production. Computer science, personnel, accounting/taxation, and law occupied the lower half of the rankings.

Status of the 4Ps

Respondents' ranking of the relative status of the marketing mix components (see Table 1-6) indicates that product was overall most important followed by price, distribution, and promotion. No statistically significant differences in mean rankings were obtained across the three subsamples. Indeed, except for the Japanese executives who perceived promotion to be slightly more important than distribution, the rank ordering was consistent across respondents.

TABLE 1-6

Importance of marketing mix elements in the year 2000

Element	Overall	U.S.	Japan	Europe	Significant differences
Product	1.37	1.38	1.32	1.42	NS
Price	2.72	2.74	2.70	2.68	NS
Distribution	2.93	2.90	3.06	2.84	NS
Promotion	3.01	3.05	2.91	3.05	NS

Importance of types of marketing research

Of the eight types of marketing research covered in the survey, product research ranked as overall most important. This was followed by consumer research, market intelligence gathering, competitive behavior, pricing, segmentation, channels, and advertising research (see Table 1-7). American respondents furnished a higher ranking for product research than Europeans, while both Japanese and European respondents considered consumer research as being more important than American executives. No statistically significant differences in mean importance rankings were found for the other six types of marketing research.

TABLE 1-7
Importance of types of marketing research in the year 2000

Element	Overall	U.S.	Japan	Europe	Significant differences
Product	2.70	2.38	2.67	3.37	US > E
Consumer behavior	2.80	3.26	2.43	2.29	J > US; E > US
Market intelligence	3.38	3.26	3.48	3.50	NS
Competitive behavior	4.30	4.25	4.50	4.18	NS
Pricing	4.98	4.95	4.77	5.29	NS
Segmentation	5.55	5.62	5.67	5.26	NS
Channels	6.08	6.15	6.17	5.82	NS
Advertising	6.19	6.05	6.07	6.61	NS

Marketing Mix in the Year 2000

Table 1-8 (Panels A through D) contain respondents' evaluation of product, pricing, promotion, and distribution management respectively in the year 2000.

Product

Consistent with earlier results reported, 93 percent of the respondents agreed that new product development will assume even greater importance in the firm. Most (82 percent) also felt that global brands will become more prominent in the marketplace. In this connection, both American and European executives agreed more strongly than their Japanese counterparts. There was also general consensus

TABLE 1-8
Marketing mix in the year 2000

Statement	Total % agree/ strongly agree	Overall mean	U.S. mean	Japan mean	Europe mean	Significant differences
A. Product management in the year 2000						
1. New product development will assume even greater importance in the firm.	93.0	4.23	4.16	4.34	4.24	NS
2. Global brands will become more prominent in the marketplace.	82.3	3.98	4.06	3.74	4.08	US > J; E > J
3. Postpurchase services (e.g., maintenance, warranties, etc.) will become the new bases for product competition.	74.7	3.88	3.80	3.91	4.03	NS
4. Basic product quality will become more important than styling, packaging, and other secondary features.	57.0	3.51	3.49	3.70	3.32	J > E
5. There will be increased emphasis on the marketing of manufactured goods rather than on services.	17.1	2.71	2.62	3.02	2.53	J > US; J > E
B. Pricing in the year 2000						
1. Companies will have to become more creative in their pricing policies, shifting from traditional cost-based pricing.	80.6	3.90	3.91	3.83	3.97	NS
2. Pricing strategies to achieve long-term corporate objectives rather than short-term gains will be widely used.	79.4	3.83	3.78	3.96	3.79	NS

TABLE 1-8 (CONT.)

Statement	Total % agree/ strongly agree	Overall mean	U.S. mean	Japan mean	Europe mean	Significant differences
3. Differential cost structures of companies in different countries producing similar products will cause greater problems in price setting.	51.2	3.35	3.40	3.43	3.16	NS
4. Dumping and other predatory pricing practices will become more common.	23.0	2.84	2.85	2.68	3.00	NS
5. There will be increased governmental rules and regulations on pricing practices.	17.7	2.64	2.72	2.51	2.61	NS
C. Promotional strategies in the year 2000						
1. Global promotional activities (e.g., international trade shows and exhibitions) will be more widely used.	78.1	3.85	3.75	4.11	3.74	J > US; J > E
2. Sales management and personal selling will increase in importance.	72.2	3.70	3.58	3.89	3.71	J > US
3. The trend toward giant global advertising agencies will continue.	70.0	3.69	3.71	3.77	3.55	NS
4. Broadcast media advertising (e.g., TV and radio) will be more important than print media advertising (e.g., newspapers and magazines).	63.9	3.60	3.55	3.68	3.61	NS
5. Advertising themes will become more standardized around the world.	47.4	3.25	3.27	3.34	3.11	NS

TABLE 1-8 (CONT.)

Statement	Total % agree/ strongly agree	Overall mean	U.S. mean	Japan mean	Europe mean	Significant differences
D. Distribution channels in the year 2000						
1. Companies will increasingly employ different distribution methods to reach different markets.	87.0	3.98	3.96	3.91	4.08	NS
2. The length of marketing channels will be shortened as less reliance is placed on traditional intermediaries (e.g., wholesalers, retailers, and brokers).	74.0	3.76	3.74	3.81	3.74	NS
3. There will be an increased reliance on global rather than domestic distribution systems.	72.2	3.77	3.89	3.79	3.47	US > E
4. Direct marketing and telemarketing will increasingly replace traditional distribution and promotional methods.	68.7	3.69	3.68	3.68	3.71	NS
5. There will be continued growth in the use of vertical integrated marketing systems (e.g., franchising, single ownership of channels).	53.9	3.56	3.62	3.51	3.47	NS

(75 percent agreement) that postpurchase services would become the new bases for competition. However, only 57 percent of respondents thought that basic product quality will become more important than styling, packaging, and other secondary product features, albeit Japanese executives expressed stronger agreement than European respondents on this issue. Finally, only 17 percent of respondents

believed that there will be an increased emphasis on the marketing of manufactured goods rather than services. Japanese executives felt more strongly about this trend than either American or European respondents.

Pricing

No statistically significant differences in perception were found across the three respondents subsamples with regard to pricing practices in the year 2000. The highest level of agreement (81 percent) was found in respect of the need for more creative pricing policies and a shift from traditional cost-based practices. An almost equivalent level of concurrence (80 percent) was found for the use of pricing strategies to focus on achieving long-term rather than short-term corporate goals. Respondents were more equivocal with regard to the effects of differential cost structures. About 51 percent agreed that such structures of companies operating in different countries producing similar products will aggravate problems in price setting, while 22 percent either disagreed or strongly disagreed. Significantly, only 23 percent of respondents thought that dumping and other predatory pricing practices would be more prevalent in the year 2000. This sentiment tallies with the earlier finding indicating protectionist tendencies would not be prevalent. Finally, only about 18 percent of respondents believed that there will be increased governmental control on pricing practices.

Promotion

The trend toward globalization received qualified support in the case of promotion strategies in the year 2000. Some 78 percent of respondents agreed with the statement that global promotional activities (e.g., international trade shows and exhibitions) will be more widely employed. Japanese executives tended to concur more strongly than American and European executives on this point. The present trend toward giant global advertising agencies is also likely to continue (70 percent agreement). However, only 47 percent of respondents felt that there would be more use of standardized advertising themes worldwide. In terms of advertising media, nearly 64 percent of respondents felt that broadcast media (e.g., TV and radio) would be more important than print media (e.g., newspapers and magazines). No subsample differences were found on these three items. Last, some 72 percent of respondents agreed that sales management and personal selling will increase in importance in the year 2000. Japanese executives believed this more strongly than their American counterparts.

Distribution

The use of multiple channels for different target markets was strongly affirmed given an 87 percent overall agreement rate. The use of more direct channels is also evident given that 69 percent of respondents who thought that direct and telemarketing will increasingly replace traditional methods of distribution and promotion. Moreover, 74 percent of respondents felt that the length of marketing channels will be shorter as less reliance is placed on traditional intermediaries. Less univocal support (54 percent) was obtained for the statement that there will be continued growth of vertical marketing systems in the year 2000. However, most (72 percent) respondents believed that more emphasis would be placed on global rather than domestic distribution systems. American executives felt more strongly on this issue than European respondents.

Discussion

Several implications for the future of marketing and marketing strategy will now be discussed. They center on the major findings of the study that (1) there will be greater globalization of business activity, (2) companies will become more socially responsible and marketing oriented, (3) product and price will become more important to successful marketing management although promotion and distribution practices will also witness change, and (4) differences across American, European, and Japanese executives exist in predicting particular trends in the business environment and in marketing strategy. These subsample differences will be incorporated in the discussion of the other implications.

Globalization Implications

Ever since the publication of Levitt's (1983) provocative thesis, many scholars have debated the nature of global marketing and its associated connotation of offering globally standardized products (see, e.g., Chakravarthy and Perlmutter, 1985; Daniels, 1987; Martenson, 1987; Rau and Preble, 1987; Simmonds, 1985). The findings of our survey provide qualified support for Levitt's position. Executives from the three regions appear to endorse his position that companies must operate "as if the world were one large market—ignoring superficial regional and national differences" (1983: 92). In addition, they anticipated that global brands will become more prominent in the marketplace, that international trade shows and exhibitions will be more widely used, that more giant global advertising agencies will be established, and that greater reliance would be placed on global rather than domestic distribution systems.

Further integration of the world's economy also appears to contribute toward global marketing practices. Counter to the present tendency against free trade (Ohmae, 1987), executives did not believe that the world's market would become more protectionist (cf. Lazer et al., 1989). Deregulation of certain industries, the saturation of domestic markets, and the international concern over the state of business and professional ethics will help create a more globalized competitive environment. They will compel companies to become more global in their operations and philosophy.

Finally, technological developments do not appear to be slowing down. Such advances are likely to affect global communication patterns. The pervasive effects of broadcast media advertising will be accentuated and the use of direct and telemarketing will receive added impetus from advances in information technology and telecommunications. The notion of a "global village" seems very plausible by the year 2000. Already, interactive television with home shopping facilities is being test marketed (*Advertising Age*, 1989).

Levitt (1983: 94) argues that "technology has homogenized the globe. Even small local segments have their global equivalents everywhere and become subject to global competition." However, Ohmae (1987) asserts that as information access becomes important in modern societies, it fragments markets into individualized segments while the overall needs of the world population become increasingly homogeneous. Executives surveyed in this study believed that such market fragmentation would necessitate the development of more sophisticated bases of segmentation. This is in accord with the view that traditional methods of international segmentation founded on nationality and ethnicity are outmoded (Cunningham and Green, 1984; Levitt, 1983). An example of the new generation of segmentation approaches may be Kale and Sudharshan's (1987) method of strategically equivalent segmentation which recognizes and aggregates consumers who may cross national boundaries but nevertheless would respond similarly to a firm's marketing mix.

Despite these expectations, globalization may not equally affect all aspects of marketing. In particular, less than half of executives surveyed were of the opinion that advertising themes would become more standardized worldwide in the year 2000. Ironically, it was in the area of advertising which initially spawned the customization-standardization debate in marketing practices (Ryans, 1969). Clearly, executives were cognizant of differences in language, media, and government regulations (cf. *New York Times*, November 13, 1985). Nonetheless, the continued amalgamation of advertising agencies worldwide points to the creation of holding companies for groups of merged agencies. These promise greater efficiency, more specialization, enhanced coordination of international campaigns, and increased global service (Terpstra, 1987; Wells et al., 1989).

Last, certain regional differences in expectations also emerged in respect of specific aspects of the globalization trend. Most noteworthy was the finding that American executives expressed stronger agreement that globalization of production, distribution, and marketing would occur than their Japanese counterparts. American executives also expected more global distribution systems to emerge than their European counterparts. However, Japanese more than American and European executives anticipated increased global promotional activities such as trade shows and exhibitions. Overall, the findings indicate that American enterprise is losing its alleged insularity and becoming more international in marketing orientation.

On importance of geographical regions for corporate activities, the results generally support the notion of a World Triad advanced by Ohmae (1987). The most important regions anticipated by executives in the year 2000 were North America, Europe, and Asia. The other three areas surveyed lagged far behind these regions in corporate importance. Clearly, our findings suggest that economic progress would continue to come from these three regions in the future.

Interestingly, however, differences emerged when the sample was decomposed for analysis. A regional bias seemed evident to the extent that executives from each region rated their own as being the most important for their corporate activities in the year 2000. Hence, it may be implied that while companies will become more global in outlook, their principal focus would still be within their own regions. One plausible reason for this may be that executives believed their corporations' primary operating base and major sphere of strategic influence resides within their region.

The findings also show that executives were most divergent in respect of their evaluation of Europe's importance for their corporations in the year 2000. Statistically significant differences in rankings emerged between European and American respondents as well as between American and Japanese respondents. It seems that the establishment of a unified market in 1992 provides most opportunities for European corporations although American firms will also be focusing their efforts in this continent (Tulley, 1988). It would appear that the Japanese would prefer to accord Asia a higher priority in the year 2000. European, and particularly American, executives apparently perceived fewer opportunities in the Asia Pacific nations despite their current economic ascendency (Kraar, 1988).

Implications for Corporate Outlook

Executives surveyed were divided over the nature of corporate cultures that will be effective in the year 2000. Some anticipated changes whereas others did not. This may be attributed to the diverse industry backgrounds of respondents. However, two aspects appear to meet with more univocal acceptance. First, companies will appear to be more societally conscious, and second, there will be greater emphasis placed on marketing in the year 2000. Two expected environmental trends—one legislative and the other ethical—seem to contribute to greater corporate social responsibility in the year 2000. In particular, executives believed that there will be increased regulation over consumer and marketing practices. Curiously, European more than Japanese respondents thought this would be the case—a finding contrary to the expectations of free trade with the opening up of a unified European market in 1992. Second, consistent with other results (Lazer et al., 1989), ethical issues will assume greater proportions internationally. This may encourage companies to embrace the societal marketing concept more readily.

Executives fully endorsed marketing's greater role in the corporation in the year 2000. This is congruent with the results of previous surveys using strictly American samples (Laczniak and Lusch, 1986; Yeskey and Burnett, 1986). Marketing ranked highest both in terms of corporate importance and likelihood of chief executive officer background. While executives of all three regions considered marketing to have first priority, American executives accorded it higher status than their Japanese counterparts. This may not be too surprising given that "Japanese companies operate almost entirely without marketing departments or market research of the kind so prevalent in the West" (Levitt, 1983: 99). Indeed, for Japanese executives to opine their CEOs of the future are most likely to come from a marketing (rather than technical) background represents a fundamental shift in philosophy.

Further evidence of this direction is the increased attention to be paid to consumer needs and the high ranking of consumer research—second only to product research—found in the survey. The latter result contrasts with the little attention CEOs in the Lazer et al. (1989) study paid to consumer behavior. It appears that consumers of the future will become even more sophisticated, demanding, and conscious of their rights (McKenna, 1988) and thus will have to be studied closely.

Moreover, executives believed that close coordination will be needed between marketing and other organizational functions. This suggests that a greater corporate market orientation will be achieved in the year 2000. Such inter-functional interaction should bring about a total customer focus and sharing of information on important buying influences across departments (Shapiro, 1988). As such, respondents did not appear to share Kotler's (1986) view that the responsibilities of nonmarketing executives may be impinged upon by marketers exercising their power to accomplish corporate objectives. Instead, there was a strong preference for cooperation and working together between marketing and other functional areas in the year 2000.

One possible outcome of this more intimate interfacing may be the shift from the goal of market share dominance to one of maximizing total corporate profitability. Nearly 60 percent of respondents believed that efforts will be concentrated toward profits rather than sales. Surprisingly, it was the Japanese who felt most strongly about this—a finding not intuitively obvious given their well-known approach of market penetration. European executives also agreed more firmly than their American counterparts on this issue, perhaps reflecting the latter's emphasis on short-run results.

Marketing Management Implications

Executives considered product and price to be the more important components of marketing strategy. This is consistent with Levitt's (1983) view that effective world competitors must offer high-quality products at low cost. In particular, they felt that new product development will be vital and accorded product research first priority among the eight research areas surveyed. This finding is similar to those of Lazer et al. (1989) and Laczniak and Lusch (1986). This may be attributable to the escalation of global competition and acceleration in technological advancements in the year 2000. It is consistent with expectations of a growing internationalization of product development and further shortening of product life cycles (Terpstra, 1987).

Executives provided mixed views on the issue of intrinsic improvements in product quality over secondary features such as styling and packaging. Japanese respondents expressed stronger agreement on this issue than European executives which may reflect their firmer belief that technology will have a greater impact on businesses in the year 2000. Only a handful of executives surveyed felt that manufactured goods would be more important than services. This suggests that the growth in the service sector will continue globally. Canton (1984) has argued that manufacturers explore opportunities in the service economy by capitalizing on their existing assets, resources, and knowledge. To the extent that 84 percent of executives surveyed were manufacturing-based, the possibility that the new competition will be offering enhanced postpurchase services appears to be acknowledged, particularly among the Europeans and Americans (cf. Laczniak and Lusch, 1986).

Pricing would need to be more creative as global production may complicate traditional cost-based approaches. Executives felt that pricing would be used to achieve more strategic long-run corporate objectives rather than as a short-term tactical weapon. These findings are in accord with those of Lazer et al. (1989) who argue that longer time frames and different bases may be used to establish cost/price relationships for many products. To the extent that Japanese more than American executives in this survey believed that efforts be focused on profit rather than sales goals, it appears that they have a longer pricing horizon than their American counterparts.

Executives surveyed were optimistic that there would be no increases in government controls over pricing and that dumping and other predatory pricing practices would not increase. This is in line with their expectations of there being no increased pressure on protectionist policies. Perhaps executives realize that in the long run, low-cost producers can overcome such policies regardless of where their manufacturing bases are located (Levitt, 1983).

Beyond the impact of global advertising and sales promotion activities discussed earlier, executives believed that personal selling and sales force management will be more important in the year 2000. This may be because of their intelligence gathering capability as well as problem solving role given the need to get closer to customers and provide a total package of services to them (cf. Lazer et al., 1989). Complex product innovations also need to be effectively communicated to customers—a task well suited to the sales force of tomorrow. Technological developments (e.g., international 800 telephone numbers and video sales presentations) may enhance sales force effectiveness by enabling closer customer contact and allowing for uniformly high quality of presentations in different markets (Terpstra, 1987). Interestingly, it may be the Japanese who lead the way in this direction. The Japanese executives surveyed concurred more strongly than their American counterparts regarding the importance of the sales function.

Finally, distribution will also appear to be going through a metamorphosis in the year 2000. Reliance will be placed on multiple channels to more precisely match the requirements and characteristics of different market segments. There will also be increased emphasis on improving productivity via direct and shorter marketing channels. Once again, developments in telecommunications and transportation technology may facilitate this trend. Customer preference for quick delivery (e.g., fresh food) may also impel the establishment of shorter channels of distribution (Lazer et al., 1989).

However, respondents were more equivocal regarding the growth of vertical marketing systems. Clearly, VMSs afford greater manufacturer control in distribution. Yet, they also bring responsibilities, commitment, and attendant risks (Ahmed, 1977). These internalized channel configurations were favored in the 1970s for reaching foreign markets as firms largely preferred to act alone rather than rely on joint ventures and licensing arrangements (Terpstra, 1987). With the recent successes of strategic alliances involving companies of different nationalities (Kotler, 1986), managers are likely to be more confident of employing alternative distribution arrangements in the year 2000. The belief that a wider variety of channels will become evident as global distribution systems evolve implies a probable increase in using international cooperative ventures, licensing agreements, management contracts, and consortia for market entry and service arrangements. That European executives agree somewhat less strongly than their American counterparts regarding the globalization of the distribution function may be due to the planned establishment of a free market in Europe in 1992. As such, their focus may be slightly more regional given the abundant opportunities afforded by a truly European Common Market.

Conclusion

Long-range forecasting is generally a hazardous task. Respondents are prone to employ current trends as overweighted anchors to predict future developments. The executives surveyed in our study do envisage several contemporary environmental and marketing directions to prevail in the year 2000. Most notable among these is the continued globalization of the world's economy as well as many aspects of the marketing mix. Yet, they also foresee that certain future developments (e.g., less protectionism, fewer charges of predatory pricing practices) that run counter to present tendencies. The strong consensus on many issues by executives of such diverse national and industrial backgrounds also engenders confidence in the predictions rendered.

To conclude on an optimistic note, marketers have been known to be highly critical of themselves and the profession to which they belong. The enhanced role of marketing as predicted by this international sample of senior-level executives augurs well for the discipline and its practitioners. Perhaps this is the time to discard self-flagellation tendencies and work toward achieving marketing's status as the window to the world.

References

Advertising Age (1989). Ten categories to watch in 1989. 60 (January 2): 14.

Ahmed, A.A. (1977). Channel control in international markets. *European Journal of Marketing*, 11 (4): 327–36.

Bartels, R. (1983). Is marketing defaulting its responsibilities? *Journal of Marketing*, 49 (Fall): 32–35.

Bogart, L. (1985). War of the words: Advertising in the year 2010. *Across the Board*, 22 (January): 21–28.

Campbell, D.T. (1955). The informant in quantitative research. *American Journal of Sociology*, 60: 339–42.

Canton, I.D. (1984). Learning to love the service economy. *Harvard Business Review*, 62 (May–June): 89–97.

Chakravarthy, B.S. and H.V. Perlmutter (1985). Strategic planning for a global business. *Columbia Journal of World Business*, 18 (Summer): 3–10.

Cunningham, W. and R. Green (1984). From the editor. *Journal of Marketing*, 48 (Winter): 9–10.

Daniels, J.D. (1987). Bridging national and global marketing strategies through regional operations. *International Marketing Review*, 4 (Autumn): 29–44.

Garda, R.A. (1988). Comment. *Journal of Marketing*, 52 (October): 32–41.

Kale, S.H. and S. Sudharshan (1987). A strategic approach to international segmentation. *International Marketing Review*, 4 (Summer): 60–70.

Kotler, P. (1986). Megamarketing. *Harvard Business Review*, 64 (March–April): 117–24.

Kraar, L. (1988). The new powers of Asia. *Fortune* (international edition), 117 (March 28): 40–46.

Laczniak, G.R. and R.F. Lusch (1986). Environment and strategy in 1995: A survey of high-level executives. *Journal of Consumer Marketing*, 3 (Spring): 27–45.

Laczniak, G.R., R.F. Lusch, and J.G. Udell (1977). Marketing in 1985: A view from the ivory tower. *Journal of Marketing*, 41 (October): 47–56.

Lazer, W., P.A. LaBarbera, J. MacLachlan, and A.E. Smith (1989). Moving marketing plans toward the year 2000. Working paper, College of Business, Florida Atlantic University.

Levitt, T. (1983). The globalization of markets. *Harvard Business Review*, 61 (May–June): 92–102.

Lusch, R.F., J.G. Udell, and G.R. Laczniak (1976). The future of marketing strategy. *Business Horizons*, 19 (December): 56–64.

Martenson, R. (1987). Is standardization of marketing feasible in culture-bound industries? A European case study. *International Marketing Review*, 4 (Autumn): 7–17.

McKenna, R. (1988). Marketing in an age of diversity. *Harvard Business Review*, 66 (September–October): 88–95.

Naisbitt, J. (1982). *Megatrends: Ten New Directions Transforming Our Lives*. New York: Warner Books.

New York Times (1985). Global marketing debated. Advertising Column, November 13.

Ohmae, K. (1987). The triad world view. *Journal of Business Strategy*, 7 (Spring): 8–19.

Rau, P. and J.F. Preble (1987). Standardization of marketing strategy by multinationals. *International Marketing Review*, 4 (Autumn): 18–28.

Ryans, J.K., Jr. (1969). Is it too soon to put a tiger in every tank? *Columbia Journal of World Business*, 4 (March–April): 69–75.

Sekaran, U. (1983). Methodological and theoretical issues and advancements in cross-cultural research. *Journal of International Business Studies*, 14 (Fall): 61–74.

Shapiro, B.P. (1988). What the hell is "market oriented"? *Harvard Business Review*, 66 (November–December): 119–25.

Simmonds, K. (1985). Global strategy: Achieving the geocentric ideal. *International Marketing Review*, 2 (Spring): 8–17.

Terpstra, V. (1987). The evolution of international marketing. *International Marketing Review*, 4 (Summer): 47–59.

Toffler, A. (1971). *Future Shock*. New York: Bantam Books.

Toffler, A. (1980). *The Third Wave*. New York: William Morrow.

Tulley, S. (1988). Europe gets ready for 1992. *Fortune* (international edition), 117 (February): 64–68.

Udell, J.G., G.R. Laczniak, and R.F. Lusch (1976). The business environment of 1985. *Business Horizons*, 19 (June): 45–54.

Wells, W., J. Burnett, and S. Moriarty (1989). *Advertising: Principles and Practice*. Englewood Cliffs, NJ: Prentice Hall.

Yeskey, D.P. and C.D. Burnett (1986). A marketing outlook for U.S. businesses. *Journal of Business Strategy*, 7 (Fall): 5–12.

COMPETING IN ASIA PACIFIC

Understanding the Rules of the Game

Philippe Lasserre and Jocelyn Probert

> *One of the major issues Western companies face when doing business in the Asia Pacific region is how to approach the competitive situation. What are the criteria on which business decisions should be made? And what is the role of government, customers, and competitors in the Asian business environment?*
>
> *The INSEAD Euro-Asia Centre has sought to clarify some of these issues by surveying managers working in the region. We first conducted a survey in 1992 and reported the results in Long Range Planning in 1994 (Lasserre and Probert, 1994). We decided in the autumn of 1996 to repeat the survey to see how perceptions have changed.*[1]

....

Philippe Lasserre is Professor of Strategy and Management at INSEAD Euro-Asia Centre, Fontainebleau, France. Jocelyn Probert is a Research Analyst at INSEAD Euro-Asia Centre, Fontainebleau, France.

Reprinted from *Long Range Planning*, Vol. 31, No. 1, pp. 30–50. Copyright 1998, with permission from Elsevier Science.

[1] A note on the methodology: A total of 294 European and American managers responded to the survey which was sent to Western companies operating in the Asia Pacific region. Of these replies, 285 were valid. The response rate of 26.7 percent was high for this type of survey. By country, replies were broken down as follows: China 47; Hong Kong 36; India 7; Indonesia 18; Japan 36; South Korea 27; Malaysia 18; the Philippines 10; Singapore 44; Taiwan 14; Thailand 23; Vietnam 5. India and Vietnam were included for the first time in the 1996 survey. Also noticeable was the sharp increase in responses from China (up from 10 in the 1992 survey), reflecting the surge of activity there in recent years. Most respondents have spent at least five years in the region—the average is 8.5 years—and the vast majority have business experience in at least two Asian countries. The data tend to contradict the common perception that expatriates serve only two or three years in a posting. This suggests our executives have a certain familiarity with the issues and challenges posed by the daily operating environment.

> The survey results largely confirm the findings of our earlier study, underlining the continued importance of relationships, the difficulty of making Western business rules work, and the need to make long-term commitments both to investments and to relationships. In other words, Western multinationals and their expatriate managers must alter their Western business approach if they are to make the most of Asian business opportunities and adjust the nuances of their Asian business approach to satisfy the special attributes and preferences of each country.

INTRODUCTION

Since the survey described here was conducted, four Southeast Asian countries—Thailand, the Philippines, Indonesia, Malaysia—have experienced a currency and financial crisis during the summer of 1997. In South Korea some large conglomerates are on the verge of bankruptcy. These events are not contradictory to the results of the survey. In fact our respondents agreed with the proposition that in those countries financial and business risks are higher than in Europe or in the United States. In fact this survey may help to understand some of the reasons of the crisis: an opportunistic approach to business, as opposed to a planned approach, leading to speculation, corruption, high government interference, and imitative behavior are factors that characterize the business context of those countries and which are at the back of the financial crisis. China may also experience some kind of "deballooning" of its quasi-anarchic expansion. No doubt growth rates will suffer. However, there is no reason to be pessimistic about the business opportunities in the Asia Pacific region. By knowing more about business context and practices, Western managers will be better equipped to deal with the challenges of this region. Our survey wants to contribute to this understanding.

GOVERNMENT RELATIONS

"Government" can mean different things in different countries. In the present context the word is generally understood to include the bureaucratic establishment which administers the rules of the game. In some countries this bureaucracy is more powerful than the government—Japan would be an example—while in others the government and the bureaucracy are hardly distinguishable, whatever the theoretical distinction may be—Vietnam and China fall into this category.

The need to maintain smooth and regular contacts with government is an important factor in business throughout the region. Hong Kong has always been the exception but whether it will remain so in the future is hard to say. It is worth noting that in China managers are among the strongest believers in the need for smooth contacts. Broadly speaking, the newly industrialized economies (NIEs) seem to require less interaction between government officials and business managers than do the ASEAN nations, but even in the NIEs it cannot be ignored.

The countries where government interference is perceived to be particularly strong are obvious: Vietnam, South Korea, China, Indonesia, and India (Figure 2-1). Although the "business raj" ended when India introduced a more liberal regime for foreign investment in 1991, the business community continues to face mountains of red tape. Noteworthy since this survey was conducted in 1992 is the positive shift in attitudes in the Philippines: the Ramos government has clearly taken a more hands-off approach to business in recent years.

FIGURE 2-1

There is a high level of government interference in business

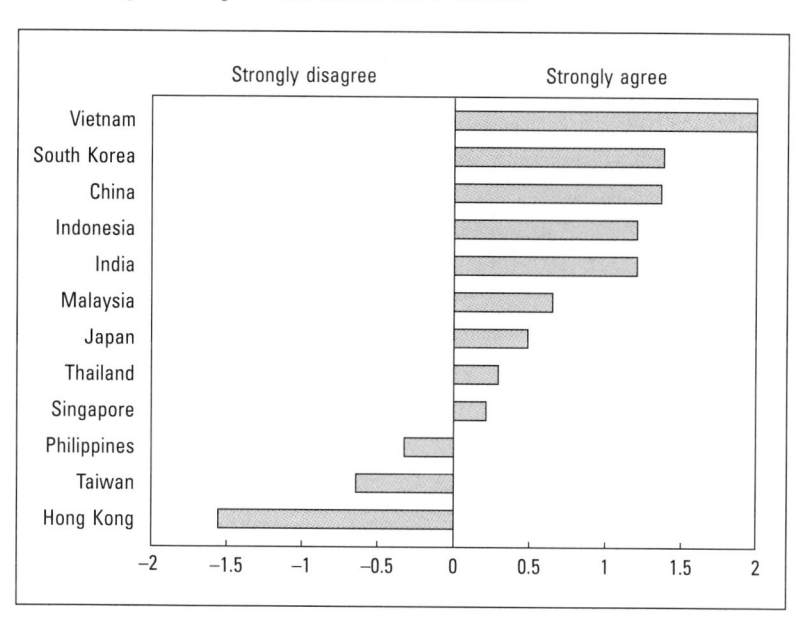

Most countries are perceived to discriminate against foreign investors in some way, whatever the intentions declared in their investment laws (Figure 2-2). Even Singapore is now perceived to be tilting the balance in favor of local firms. In China, too, observers note more advantages for local firms: the result perhaps of the withdrawal of various import duty incentives and preferential tax rates for foreign businesses, while at the same time the government remains reluctant—or unable—to reform the state-owned enterprise sector.

"Playing politics," however, is a less important weapon of competition in most countries than "marketing mix" (Figure 2-3). Government or bureaucratic influence only goes so far and the growing sophistication of consumers is likely to encourage this trend. The two relative newcomers to the foreign investment and trade scene, Vietnam and India, have yet to reach this stage. Meanwhile, the importance of "marketing mix" in Indonesia during 1996 has taken a back seat as major business decisions (such as the national car project) have been awarded to groups closely connected with President Suharto. Opinion remains divided over the wisdom of being closely associated with any particular Suharto family member.

FIGURE 2-2

The government grants some preferential advantages to local firms over foreign ones

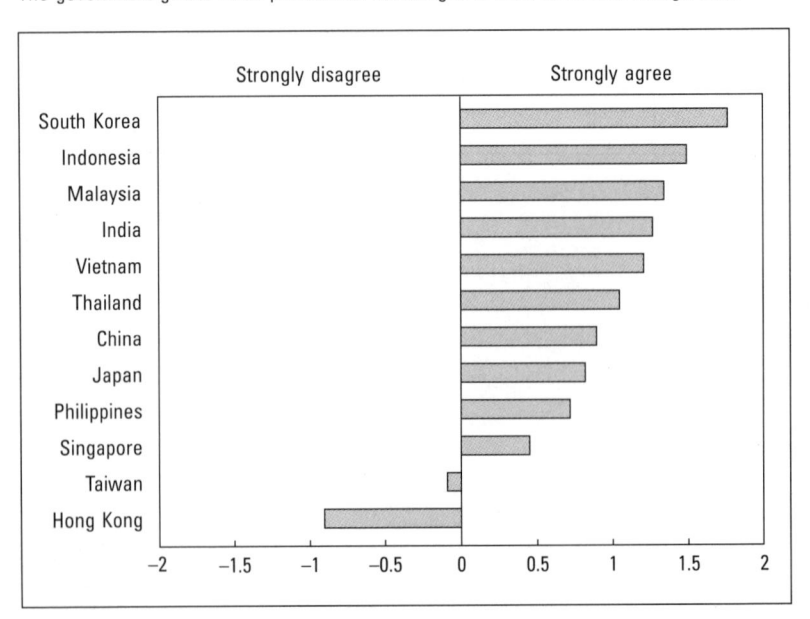

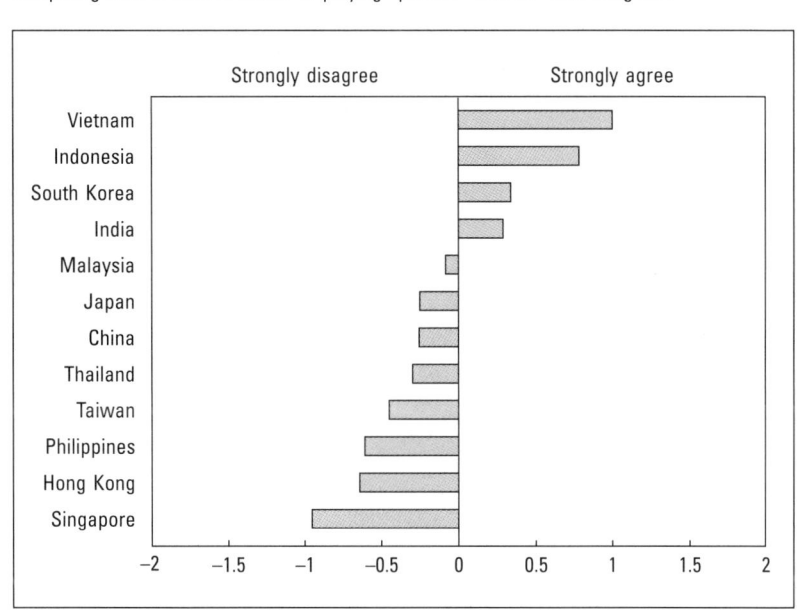

FIGURE 2-3
Competing here is more a matter of playing "politics" than of "marketing mix"

Country	Value
Vietnam	1.0
Indonesia	0.8
South Korea	0.3
India	0.3
Malaysia	-0.05
Japan	-0.3
China	-0.3
Thailand	-0.4
Taiwan	-0.5
Philippines	-0.6
Hong Kong	-0.7
Singapore	-1.0

Strongly disagree ← → Strongly agree

Indonesia has moved into prime position as the country of corruption (Figure 2-4). India and Vietnam also score badly, reflecting the current transitional status from closed business environment to a more free-ranging atmosphere: today's opportunities for economic rent-seeking may be different but are still at least as juicy. The difference between the two countries is that high-level corruption is probably more endemic in India than in Vietnam. The extent of petty and sometimes aggressive bribe-taking means that companies determined to behave honestly must resign themselves to slower progress on their projects and to the potential loss of business. Both Thailand and South Korea have lost government ministers and officials to corruption scandals in 1996–97.

Disturbingly, in only three out of twelve countries—Japan, Hong Kong, and Singapore—is corruption not seen to be an important factor. In 1992, six out of ten countries were perceived to be relatively clean. It is interesting to note that respondents in Japan continue to believe that business-related corruption is not significant, even though politicians and, increasingly, bureaucrats are regularly shown to have accumulated illicit wealth. Some observers expect Hong Kong's record on corruption to deteriorate once the territory returns to China.

FIGURE 2-4
Corruption plays a major role in doing business

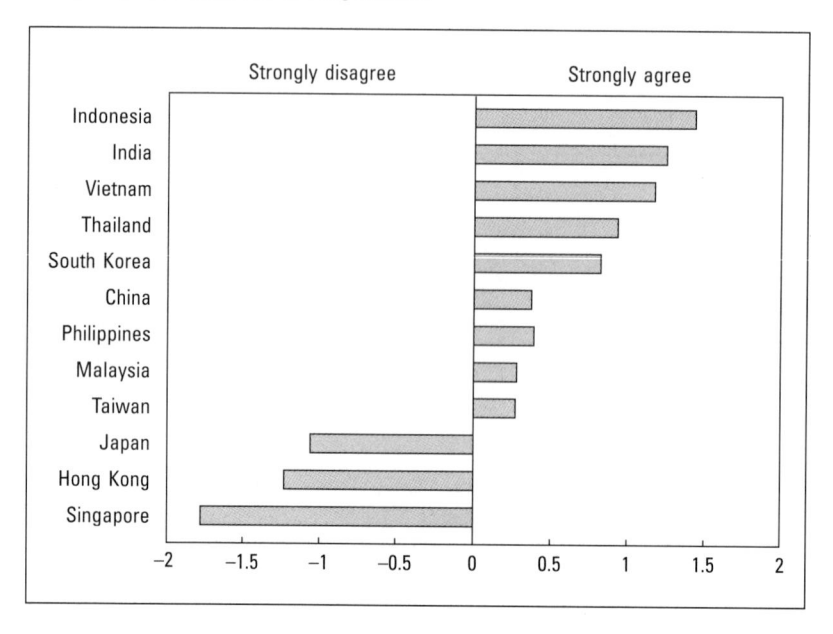

Country	Value
Indonesia	1.5
India	1.3
Vietnam	1.2
Thailand	1.0
South Korea	0.9
China	0.4
Philippines	0.4
Malaysia	0.3
Taiwan	0.3
Japan	-1.0
Hong Kong	-1.3
Singapore	-1.8

A separate survey conducted by the Euro-Asia Centre in the autumn of 1996, which asked expatriate managers which issues they personally found difficult to deal with during their assignment, singled out India, Indonesia, Vietnam, and Thailand as the places where corrupt officials caused problems; and India, Indonesia, and (marginally) Thailand where private sector corruption created difficulties.

BUSINESS RULES

There is general agreement that European or American rules of business cannot simply be transposed to the Asian region, but managers are relatively optimistic about the ability of Westerners eventually to understand the way of business in the countries to which they have been assigned, even in countries reputed to be "hard" like China and Vietnam (Figure 2-5). Expatriates in most countries in the region expect to come to understand how business is done locally and expect to achieve that understanding by amending their own, familiar Western business rules. The ability of the manager to interpret business practices in the country of his or her assignment—and the ability of

Figure 2-5
Coping with business rules

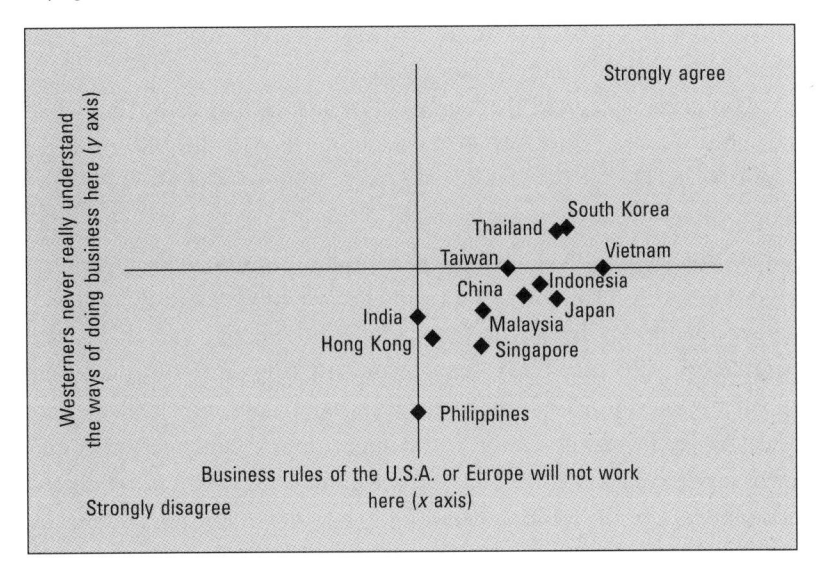

[Chart: y-axis labeled "Westerners never really understand the ways of doing business here (y axis)"; x-axis labeled "Business rules of the U.S.A. or Europe will not work here (x axis)"; corners labeled "Strongly agree" (upper right) and "Strongly disagree" (lower left). Country positions: South Korea, Vietnam, Thailand, Taiwan, China, Indonesia, Japan, India, Malaysia, Hong Kong, Singapore, Philippines.]

the head office subsequently to absorb the signals given by the country manager—determines the extent to which Western business methods are amended to meet local requirements and expectations.

In South Korea, Thailand, and Vietnam, however, business methods seem altogether unclear. There seems to be a better chance that the Western approach to business will work in the Philippines, India, and Hong Kong. India rates relatively well overall, even though the current wave of investment is fairly new (ignoring the fact that some Western multinationals [MNCs] retained their presence in the country since independence), which suggests that many Westerners feel the Indian way of doing business is closer to Western methods than to what is generally understood to be the "Asian way."

A slightly different picture of perceived environmental difficulties emerged from our parallel survey on expatriates. Questioned about local managerial styles, Western executives tended to encounter more difficulty in South Korea and Japan, and to a lesser extent in Thailand, than anywhere else. Expatriate managers also have difficulty in finding reliable sources of information. Comprehension of an unfamiliar business milieu requires good quality data (and a certain sensitivity to local customs) on which to base the decoding exercise. Sufficiently reliable information seems to be available only in Hong Kong,

Singapore, and Japan. We should note, however, that although the information is generally available in Japan, the fact that expatriates still find difficulties with the local managerial style suggests that the decoding exercise is more problematic.

It is generally agreed that successful results in Asia come only after a lengthy period, although there are opportunities for shorter-term benefits in Hong Kong and Malaysia (Figure 2-6). Corporate headquarters of Western firms would do well to take note. The fluid investment environment makes Vietnam, China, and India long-term propositions for the average MNC, and both South Korea and Japan are known for the loyalty of the population to domestic, well-established companies. The need for long-term thinking and for planning apparently do not necessarily go hand in hand: Taiwan, Thailand, and Malaysia see increasing reason to be opportunistic compared with our 1992 survey results (Figure 2-7). On the other hand, a far greater degree of confidence in the business community has turned our respondents in the Philippines into firm advocates of planning.

Firms in every country in the region seem to pose a challenge to Western firms by avidly imitating their product or commercial moves

FIGURE 2-6

Successful results do not come immediately but a long time after the initial investment has been made

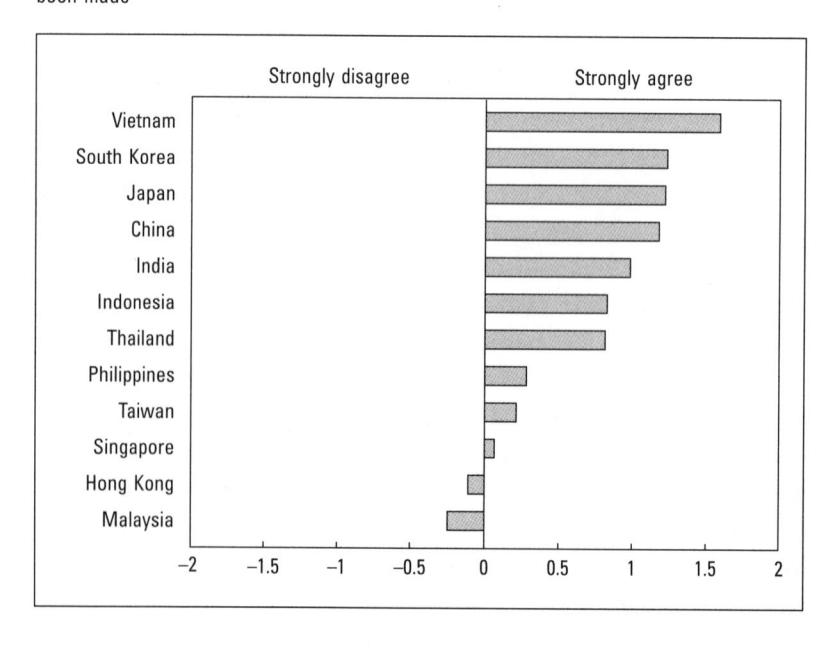

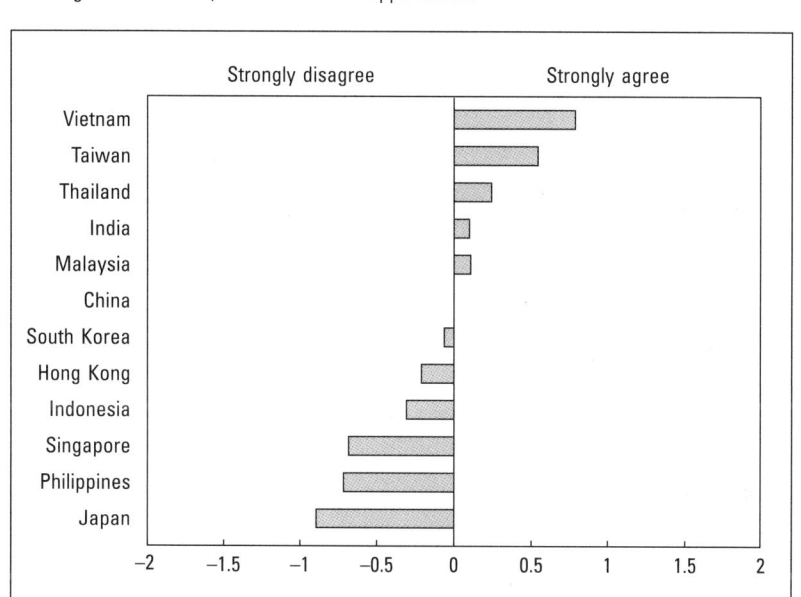

FIGURE 2-7
Planning does not work, one needs to be opportunistic

Country	Value
Vietnam	~0.75
Taiwan	~0.55
Thailand	~0.25
India	~0.1
Malaysia	~0.1
China	~0
South Korea	~-0.05
Hong Kong	~-0.25
Indonesia	~-0.4
Singapore	~-0.65
Philippines	~-0.75
Japan	~-0.9

(Strongly disagree ← → Strongly agree; scale -2 to 2)

(Figure 2-8). No company can afford to introduce a product or a concept to an Asian market and then sit back and wait for the profits to roll in. If an idea catches consumers' imaginations, local firms will rapidly bring to market competing offers and some may not infringe the original company's intellectual property rights. Counterfeiting is not a major issue in Japan, but intense competition from skilled domestic firms ensures that no product remains completely unique for long. China and Thailand, on the other hand, are not the only Asian countries to risk the wrath of Western firms for their inability or unwillingness to act strongly against counterfeiting.

SOCIAL BEHAVIOR

The handling of disputes or crises may be a tricky issue for a company even in its home market. In Asia, where the spotlight tends to be trained rapidly on foreign companies suffering labor or product problems, issues can quickly become more acute. The most effective way to seek resolution, even of person to person disputes, is by indirect communication with the opposite party through a trusted intermediary (Figure 2-9). This gives both sides the opportunity to

36 | Competing in Asia Pacific

FIGURE 2-8
One is imitated almost immediately

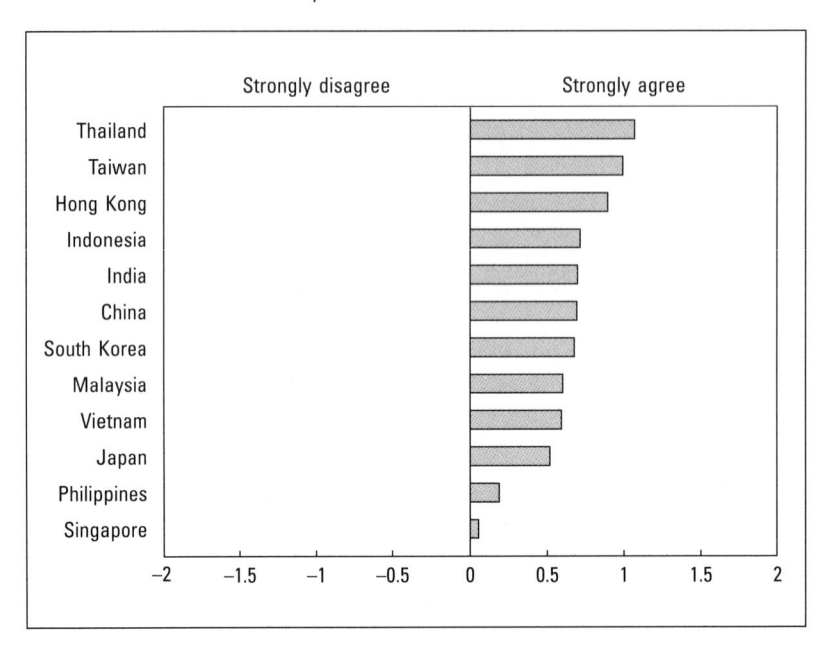

Country	Value
Thailand	~1.1
Taiwan	~1.0
Hong Kong	~0.85
Indonesia	~0.75
India	~0.7
China	~0.7
South Korea	~0.7
Malaysia	~0.6
Vietnam	~0.6
Japan	~0.5
Philippines	~0.2
Singapore	~0.05

Strongly disagree — Strongly agree (scale −2 to 2)

FIGURE 2-9
Indirect communication is the best way to solve a dispute or a crisis

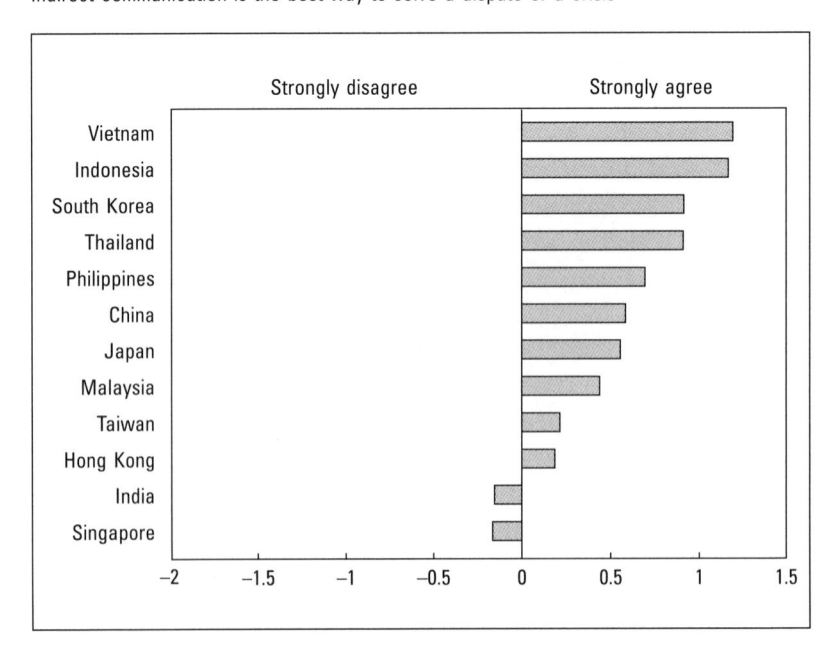

Country	Value
Vietnam	~1.2
Indonesia	~1.15
South Korea	~0.9
Thailand	~0.9
Philippines	~0.65
China	~0.55
Japan	~0.5
Malaysia	~0.4
Taiwan	~0.2
Hong Kong	~0.15
India	~−0.1
Singapore	~−0.15

Strongly disagree — Strongly agree (scale −2 to 1.5)

reach a mutually acceptable compromise without causing loss of "face." Legal recourse is generally not a suitable method of trying to solve a problem: it brings the details of the dispute into the public domain, public opinion is most likely to side with the local party, and in any case in several countries the legal system is either not well enough developed or is painfully slow. The only countries where managers can see some grounds for a direct approach to a problem are Singapore and India, both of which have strong legalistic foundations. It is interesting to note that Hong Kong, which we previously discovered to be in the same category, is moving in favor of indirect communication.

Overt displays of anger are widely considered unacceptable (Figure 2-10). This is probably true for most countries of the world, but in Asia the rules of social behavior clearly forbid one party to cause another to lose face. However, it is incorrect to assume that local managers never show anger to their employees: in China, Japan, South Korea, and Vietnam, workers are able to "take" anger, particularly if there is a sense that it is justifiable. In the "soft" countries of Thailand, Indonesia, and Malaysia (and in the latter two places managers must

FIGURE 2-10
Overt display of anger is unacceptable and can work against companies whose managers express dissatisfaction with anger

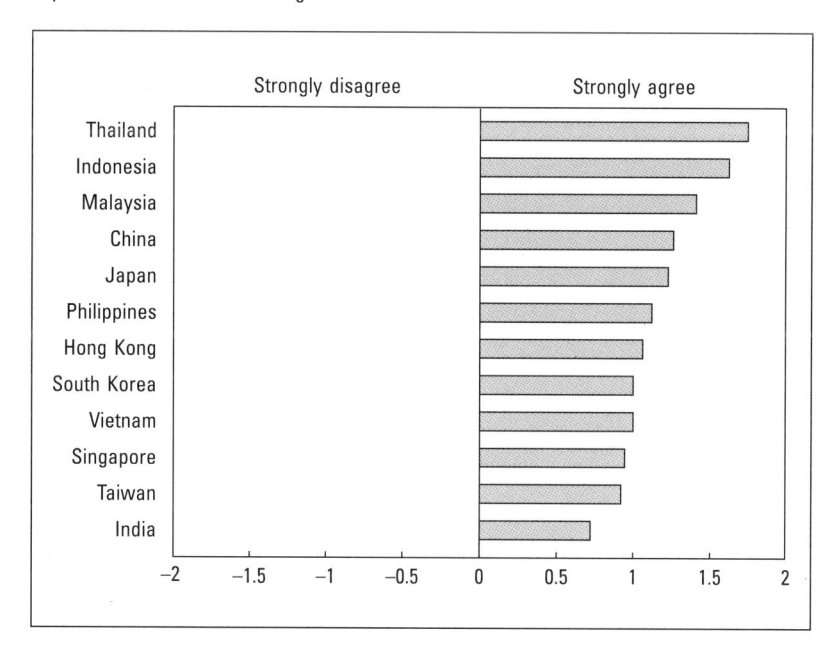

be aware of all sorts of different sensibilities), overt anger is not acceptable. In India, although it may be impolite to express anger, the concept of "face" is not the same as in countries farther east.

The rules of society also require companies and managers to take a paternalistic interest in employees, for example by arranging suitable marriages for staff members, providing loans to employees to pay for festival celebrations, and helping relatives of workers to find jobs. Western managers mostly do not believe they can match the paternalistic responsibilities of their local counterparts (Figure 2-11), except in countries at the "Western" end of the Asian business spectrum where less is expected. Anyway, expatriate managers may not wish to cultivate paternalistic relationships with employees and in joint ventures would leave such "business" to the local partner to fulfill. Nevertheless, except in the Westernized business communities of Singapore and Hong Kong, most managers agree that it is the duty of the boss to take an interest in the personal life of employees.

Relationships

The issue of relationships and relationship building is crucial for business in Asia (Figure 2-12). It is, of course, an important aspect of business management in other parts of the world but enough qualified observers have commented on its importance in Asia for us to feel certain that it is particularly significant in Asia.

Business relationships based on trust are essential but throughout the region are difficult and time consuming to build (Figure 2-13). The time required to allow relationships to develop is commonly underestimated at corporate headquarters, which tend to be more used to transaction-based business relationships. The message from this survey is that even though Singapore has consciously sought out multinationals—and these have in many ways influenced the business environment—and Hong Kong has a long (though more passive) history of multinational presence, both city-states nevertheless still require a healthy degree of "long-termism" and a "softer" approach to business transactions than is commonly found in the Anglo-Saxon model.

Ethnic, family or other informal networks such as school, university or military academy alumni groups are a potentially difficult aspect of the relationship issue for an expatriate manager to handle. "Old school tie" or regimental networks are of course not unknown in Europe or

Competing in Asia Pacific | 39

FIGURE 2-11
Local employers and managers have paternalistic responsibilities which are difficult for Western managers to emulate

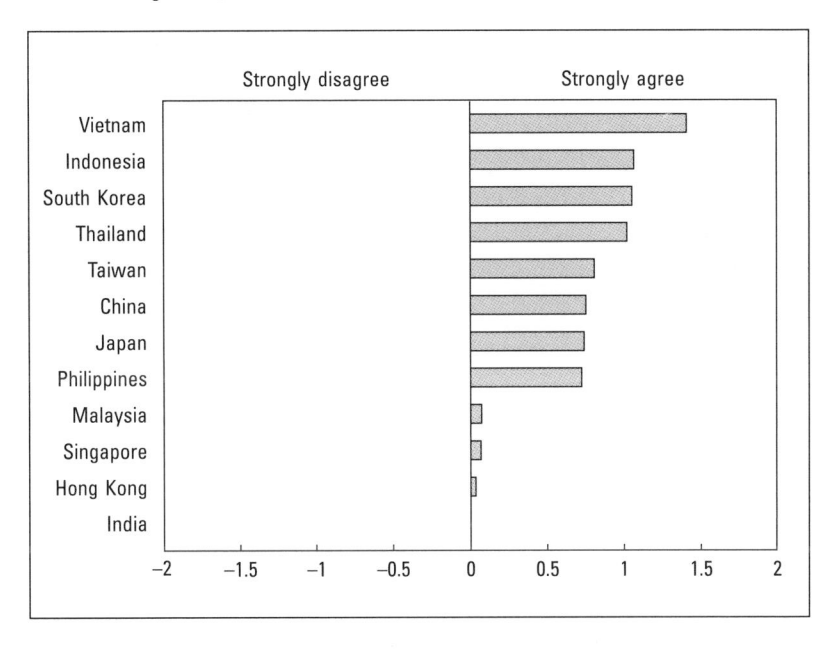

```
                Strongly disagree      Strongly agree
Vietnam                                          ████████ 1.4
Indonesia                                     ██████ 1.05
South Korea                                   ██████ 1.05
Thailand                                      █████ 1.0
Taiwan                                       ████ 0.8
China                                        ████ 0.75
Japan                                        ████ 0.75
Philippines                                  ████ 0.7
Malaysia                                     0.05
Singapore                                    0.05
Hong Kong                                    0
India
         -2    -1.5    -1    -0.5    0    0.5    1    1.5    2
```

FIGURE 2-12
In order to be successful one needs to build up a network of "contacts"

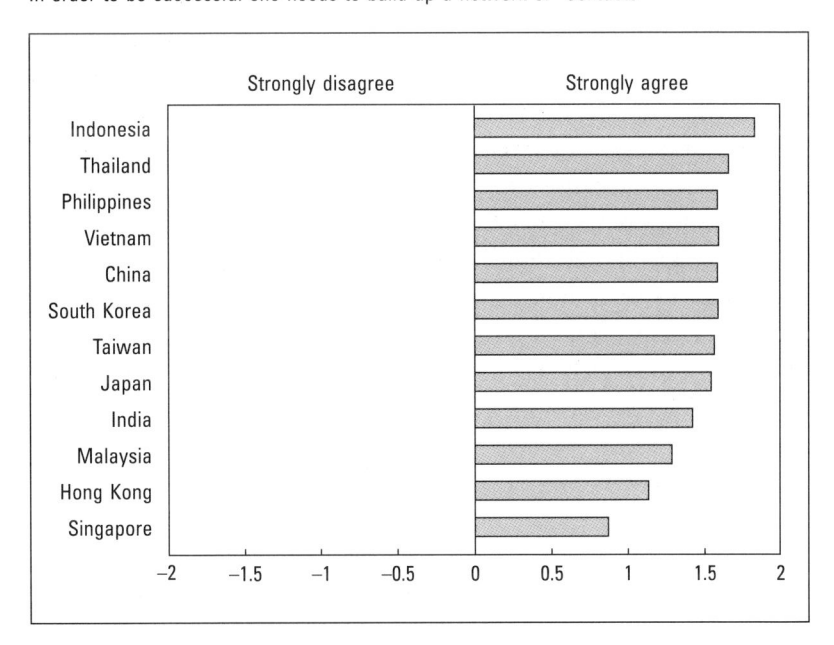

```
                Strongly disagree      Strongly agree
Indonesia                                          ████████████ 1.8
Thailand                                           ███████████ 1.65
Philippines                                        ██████████ 1.6
Vietnam                                            ██████████ 1.6
China                                              ██████████ 1.6
South Korea                                        ██████████ 1.6
Taiwan                                             ██████████ 1.55
Japan                                              █████████ 1.5
India                                              ████████ 1.4
Malaysia                                           ███████ 1.3
Hong Kong                                          ██████ 1.15
Singapore                                          █████ 0.9
         -2    -1.5    -1    -0.5    0    0.5    1    1.5    2
```

Figure 2-13
Business relationships based on trust are essential but difficult and time consuming to build

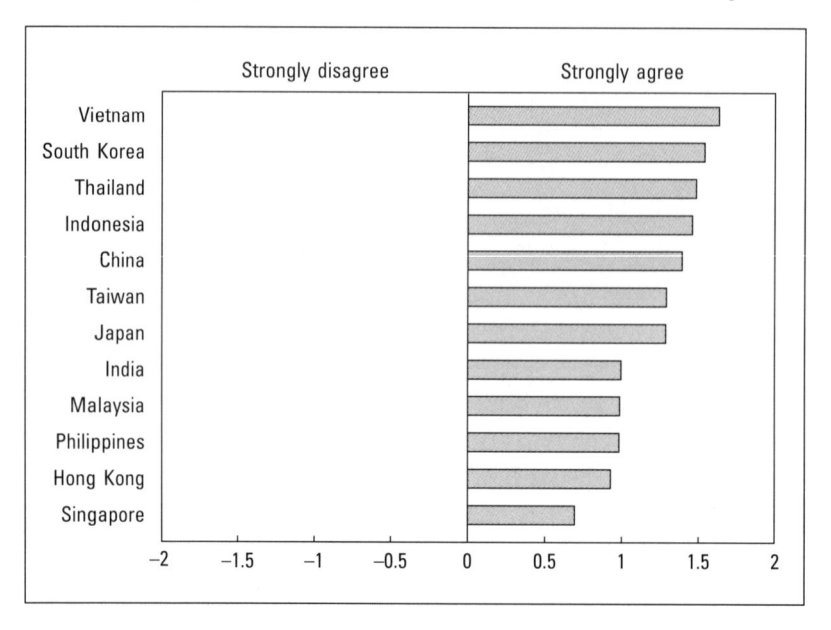

Country	Value
Vietnam	~1.65
South Korea	~1.5
Thailand	~1.45
Indonesia	~1.45
China	~1.4
Taiwan	~1.3
Japan	~1.3
India	~1.0
Malaysia	~1.0
Philippines	~1.0
Hong Kong	~0.9
Singapore	~0.65

the United States, but in many Asian countries their activities can be much more pervasive and not simply confined (as it often is in the West) to helping former classmates or their offspring find a job. Membership of, for example, a particular class of graduates from a Thai or South Korean military academy implies a host of closely shared experiences and values and the consequent responsibilities that will remain constantly with a person. An appeal from one business person to another on the basis of such network membership is hard to ignore, however unwelcome it may be. Foreign managers, who inevitably have no such ethnic or educational links in the region, must struggle longer and harder to break down the barriers to entry (Figure 2-14).

All the same, you have to "know who you are dealing with" in all countries of the region (Figure 2-15): to be aware of the affiliations and contacts of business counterparts. A local partner may be technically competent but may not have, for example, the right mix of connections to guide a business project smoothly through the bureaucratic maze. This is less of an issue in the mature economies of Japan and Singapore—both countries where technical expertise is also valued.

Relationships in Asia tend to be built on "softer" criteria than those one finds in Western business circles, and personal relationships

Competing in Asia Pacific | 41

FIGURE 2-14
When doing business it is extremely difficult to break into ethnic or classmate informal networks

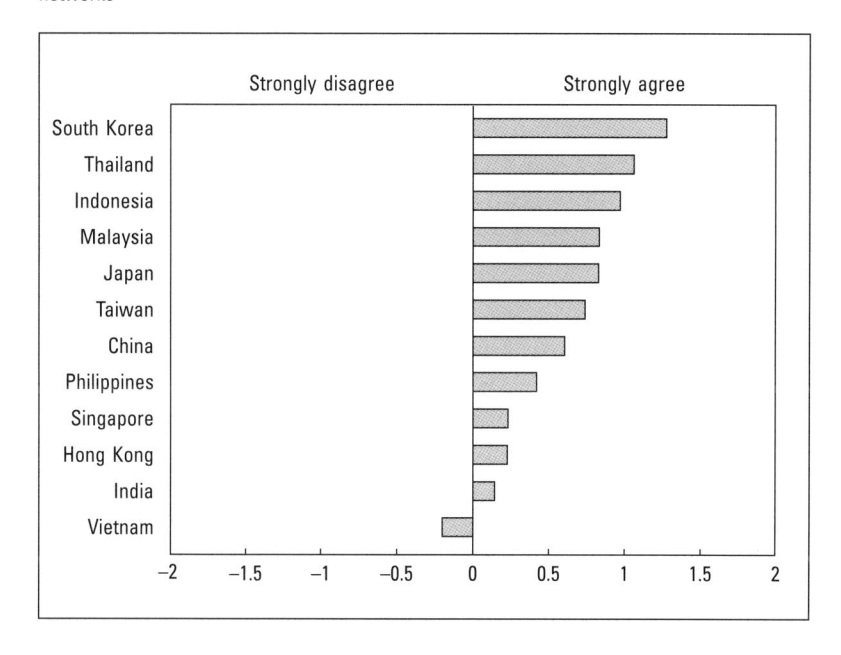

Bar chart showing responses (Strongly disagree to Strongly agree, scale −2 to 2):

- South Korea: ~1.3
- Thailand: ~1.05
- Indonesia: ~1.0
- Malaysia: ~0.85
- Japan: ~0.85
- Taiwan: ~0.75
- China: ~0.6
- Philippines: ~0.45
- Singapore: ~0.25
- Hong Kong: ~0.25
- India: ~0.15
- Vietnam: ~−0.2

FIGURE 2-15
When doing business it is often more important to know with whom one deals than to have technical expertise

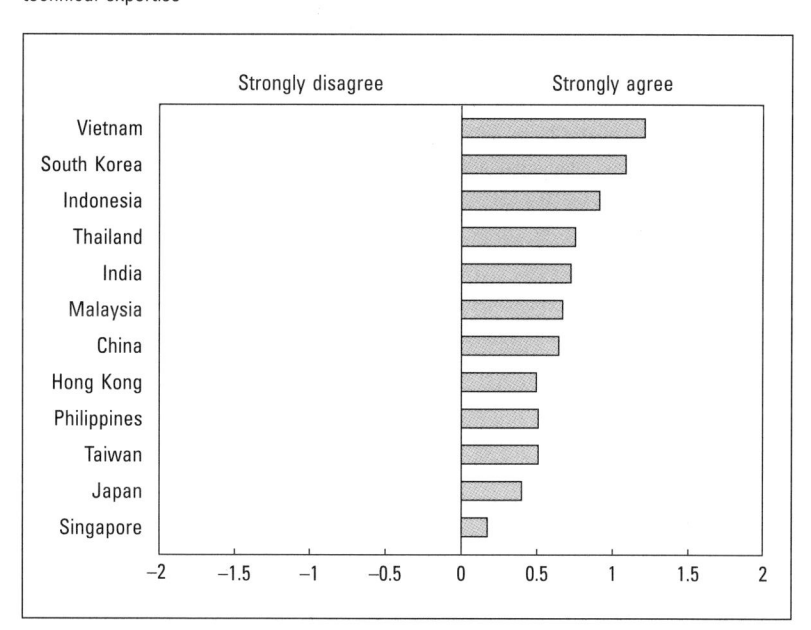

Bar chart showing responses (Strongly disagree to Strongly agree, scale −2 to 2):

- Vietnam: ~1.2
- South Korea: ~1.1
- Indonesia: ~0.95
- Thailand: ~0.8
- India: ~0.75
- Malaysia: ~0.7
- China: ~0.7
- Hong Kong: ~0.55
- Philippines: ~0.55
- Taiwan: ~0.5
- Japan: ~0.45
- Singapore: ~0.2

in the working environment—with employees, suppliers, partners, and others—take priority over rationally based argument (Figure 2-16). Business decisions that may seem incongruous to executives in Cologne, Lyon, or Minneapolis will make perfect business sense to the on-site manager in Asia. This is an important lesson for corporate headquarters to understand fully. All too often, token acknowledgment is immediately followed by uncomprehending impatience. The more Western-influenced countries of Asia, including Singapore, Hong Kong, and even India, however, are less prone to ignore the rational approach.

Evidence of marketplace rationality appears in other forms. In several countries, but most notably in Singapore and Japan, a good product is more important than having friends in the right places (Figure 2-17). Sophisticated consumers in a growing number of Asian countries increasingly select goods or services on their individual merit: a product which does not meet expectations will not last long in a competitive marketplace. In Indonesia, however, key sectors of the market remain in the hands of monopolies or quasi-monopolies. These rights, which are based on favoritism rather than sound business sense,

FIGURE 2-16

People prefer to work on the basis of personal relationships rather than on the basis of rational arguments

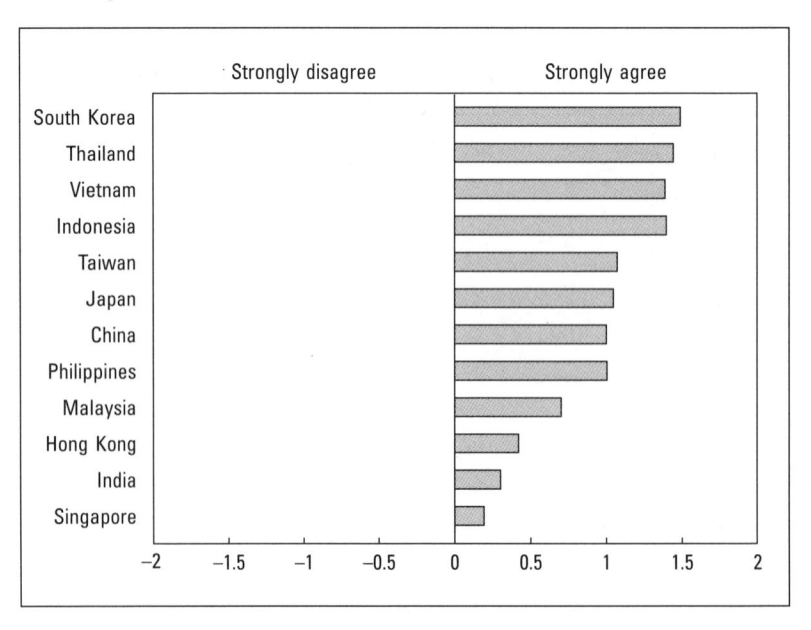

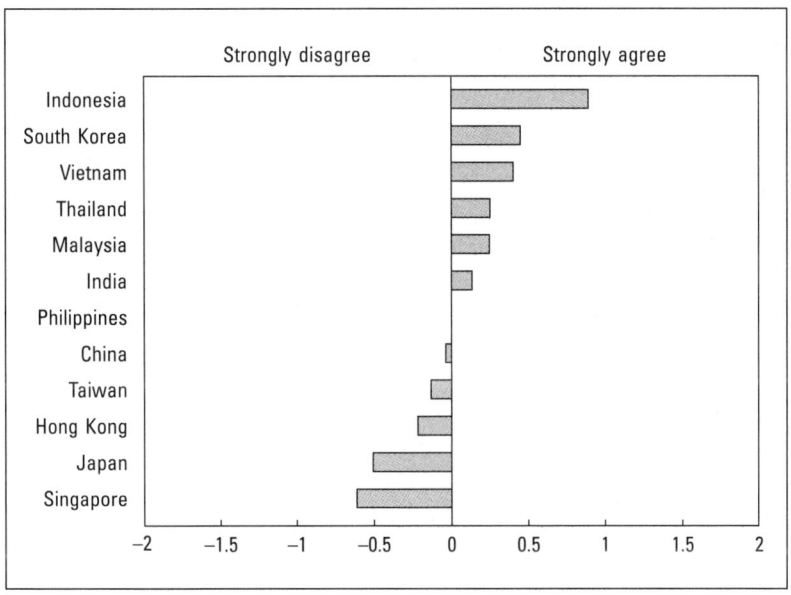

FIGURE 2-17
It is better to have a good friend than a good product

easily push good products to the sidelines by using tax and tariff systems to price them out of the market.

PARTNERSHIPS

Western executives frequently complain about the apparently unreliable legal environment in Asia (Figure 2-18). Large multinationals employ lawyers to examine contracts that are then regarded as sacrosanct. However, societies of several Asian countries, including Vietnam and China, have evolved from nonlegalistic foundations and lack experience of the Western legal or capitalist system. In Indonesia and Thailand a contract signifies to the local partner the beginning of a relationship, rather than the conclusion of a business deal. All points may therefore be subject to re-negotiation if the original basis for the agreement changes. This fundamental difference in attitude tends to be misinterpreted by some Westerners as a lack of good faith on the part of the local party.

Countries with long-standing Anglo-Saxon experience—Singapore and Hong Kong, but also India and Malaysia and even the Philippines—stand out as places where definitive legal contracts are

FIGURE 2-18
Legal or contractual agreements are not viewed as definitive

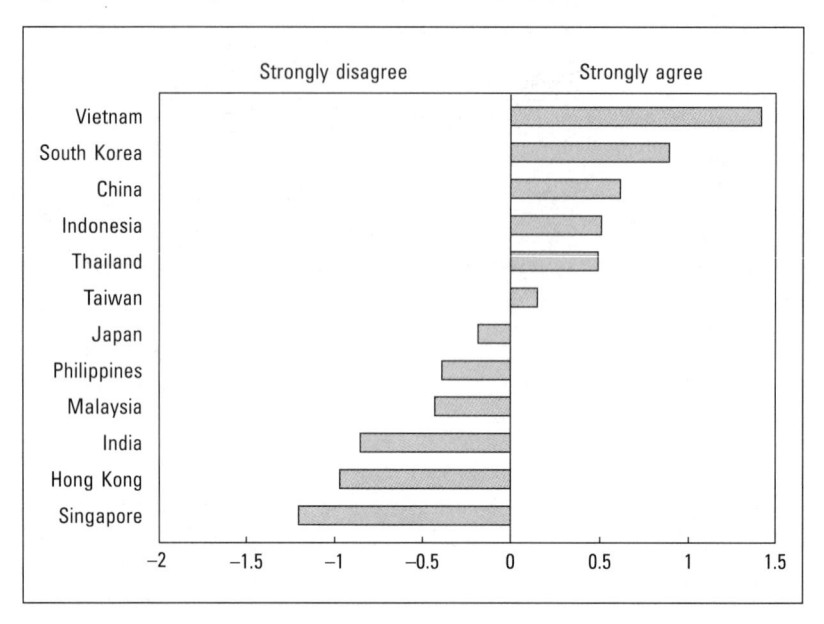

Country	Strongly disagree ← → Strongly agree
Vietnam	1.4
South Korea	0.9
China	0.6
Indonesia	0.5
Thailand	0.5
Taiwan	0.15
Japan	−0.2
Philippines	−0.4
Malaysia	−0.5
India	−0.8
Hong Kong	−0.95
Singapore	−1.1

increasingly the norm. Japan, too, is more likely these days to produce Western-style contracts for business deals involving Western counterparts. The fact remains that recourse to the legal system to resolve a dispute—even where the Western party has clearly been wronged—risks tainting the company which brings the lawsuit to the extent that, in some countries, it may be difficult to continue activity.

The idea that a contract simply represents the beginning of a relationship prevails throughout the region. Similarly firms must demonstrate to partners, whether they be employees, suppliers, or equity stakeholders, a long-term interest in a business venture (Figure 2-19). The venture is unlikely to be successful unless such a commitment is made, in whatever country it is based. A Western company which decides to withdraw from the Japanese market may lose its reputation entirely and find it very difficult to return at a later stage. Foreign firms in South Korea may be subjected to apparently irrational public attack for any misdemeanor that suggests less than full commitment.

In Vietnam, China, and India the authorities are highly suspicious of "carpetbag investors" and it is very easy for the tone of debate to become highly nationalistic. Some Western companies in India have

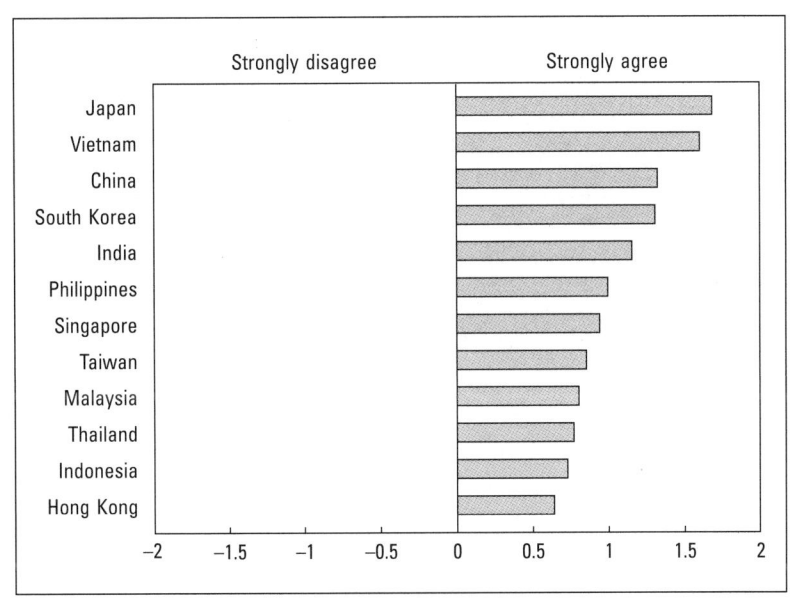

Figure 2-19
To succeed one has to demonstrate to partners a long-term interest in a business venture

Country	Value
Japan	~1.65
Vietnam	~1.55
China	~1.3
South Korea	~1.3
India	~1.15
Philippines	~1.0
Singapore	~0.9
Taiwan	~0.85
Malaysia	~0.75
Thailand	~0.75
Indonesia	~0.7
Hong Kong	~0.6

been strongly criticized by Indian politicians and businessmen for their perceived lack of good faith in setting up, in parallel to existing joint ventures, a wholly owned subsidiary through which most business development would take place. The implication is that such Western firms are betraying the relationship with the joint venture partner by seeking to keep all benefits to themselves.

The overall strength of agreement for the need throughout the region to demonstrate commitment suggests that country managers are well aware of this lesson. Whether corporate headquarters managers are as well aware of the market implications of retreat or withdrawal is less obvious.

The unspoken part of a business relationship (Figure 2-20) is always the most difficult for foreign managers to grasp, whether it be the reluctance of a supplier to admit a delivery deadline cannot be met, an employee's or local manager's unwillingness to express an opinion on a business plan, or a joint venture partner's silence on the exact nature of a business commitment or connection. In Western societies, and particularly in America, managers are used to frank, open, and often hard-hitting discussion with partners, but this approach can be destructive in Asia. A manager risks serious problems if he fails to

FIGURE 2-20
When dealing with business partners there are always some things which are not expressed but that one should understand

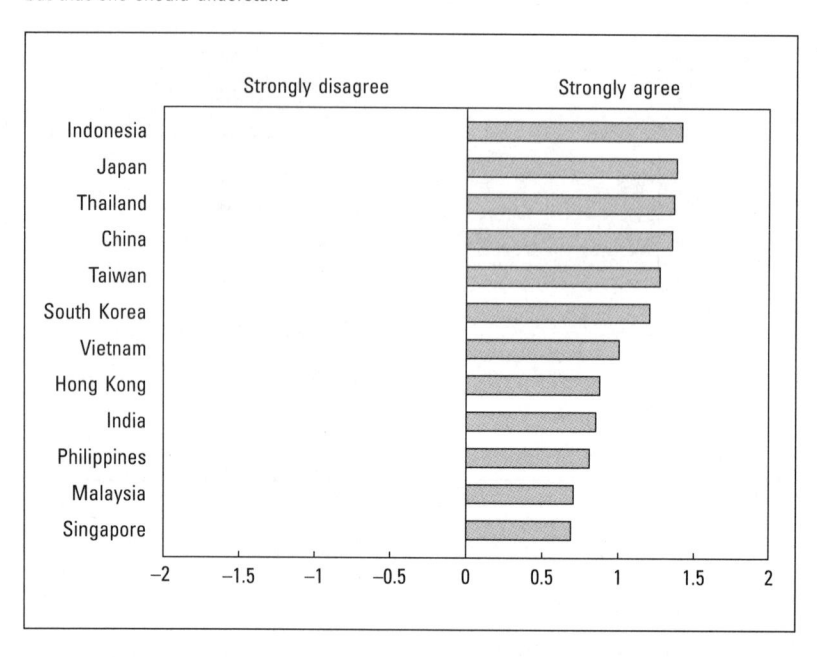

Country	Value
Indonesia	~1.5
Japan	~1.4
Thailand	~1.4
China	~1.4
Taiwan	~1.3
South Korea	~1.2
Vietnam	~1.0
Hong Kong	~0.9
India	~0.9
Philippines	~0.8
Malaysia	~0.7
Singapore	~0.7

(Scale: Strongly disagree −2 to Strongly agree +2)

interpret (either correctly or at all) the silences or smiles of counterparts. This does not mean there is a complete absence of frankness in Asia, rather that there is a time and place for it in each country and managers should be alert to implicit meanings of words and actions at all times.

CUSTOMERS

The quality versus price debate is not uniform across Asia (Figure 2-21). In Japan, quality is paramount: the packaging has to be perfect as well as the product inside. Japanese consumers readily accept that the price tag includes a service element, whether it be the ambience of the purchase location (e.g., an elegant department store) or an extensive after-sales service. In Hong Kong and Singapore and increasingly Taiwan, status-conscious consumers are more than happy to pay high prices for items that enhance their standing within the peer group. In China, on the other hand, price is perceived to be more important than quality, perhaps in reaction to a perceived invasion by foreign brands. In India, the notion of brand building and brand awareness is still in

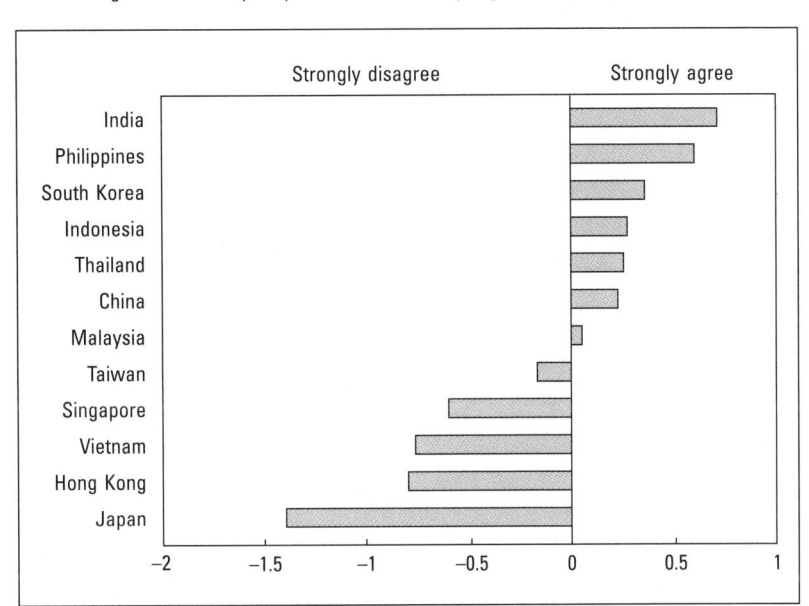

FIGURE 2-21
Customers go for the cheapest price with secondary regard for quality

its infancy and price is the determining factor. Nevertheless, whether customers are influenced by price or quality, there is throughout Asia a strong association between higher price and higher quality.

The concept of loyalty between customer and supplier (Figure 2-22) appears to be evolving in certain countries. In our 1992 survey, customers in all countries—but especially in Taiwan—were perceived to remain loyal to an established supplier even if the prices were high. In 1996 customers in Taiwan (and Malaysia also) appeared ready to switch allegiances if the price was right. China's greater opportunities of choice are also precipitating a readiness for change. In Japan, despite substantial changes to the consumer environment during five years of recession, the perception is that customers still highly value long-standing relationship built on trust and will continue to value them whatever short-term price advantage is offered. This does not necessarily mean the relationship is passive; indeed the customer may be even more demanding in other ways because the supplier's price is relatively high.

A Quality of Demand map (Figure 2-23) illustrates how various countries rate the innate quality of a product compared with other factors affecting purchasing decisions, in other words the importance of quality versus the importance of contacts. What emerges is that the

48 | Competing in Asia Pacific

FIGURE 2-22
Once a customer has developed a good relationship with a supplier he tends to be loyal to him even if the price is higher than other suppliers'

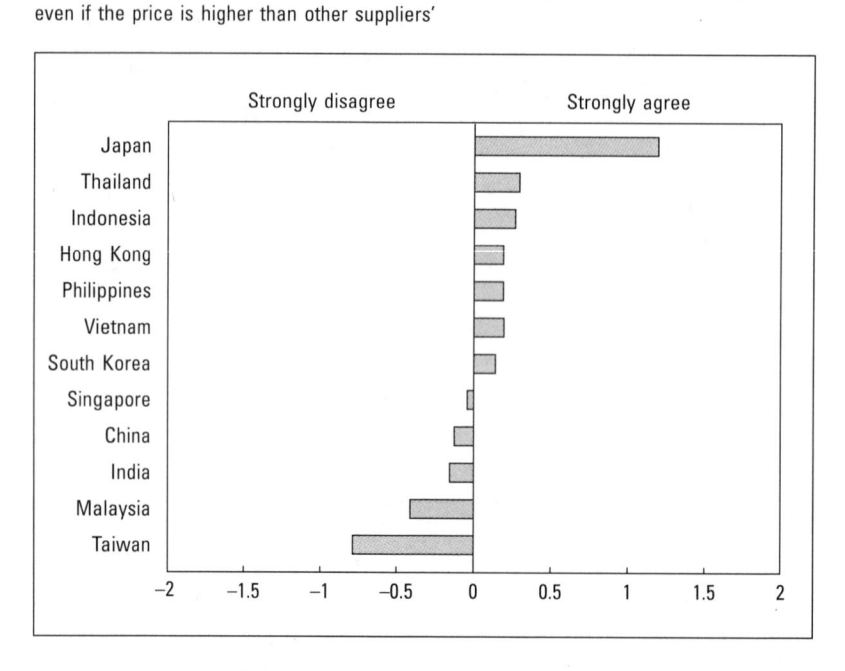

Country	Value
Japan	~1.2
Thailand	~0.3
Indonesia	~0.25
Hong Kong	~0.2
Philippines	~0.2
Vietnam	~0.2
South Korea	~0.1
Singapore	~0
China	~-0.1
India	~-0.2
Malaysia	~-0.5
Taiwan	~-0.8

FIGURE 2-23
Factors influencing demand

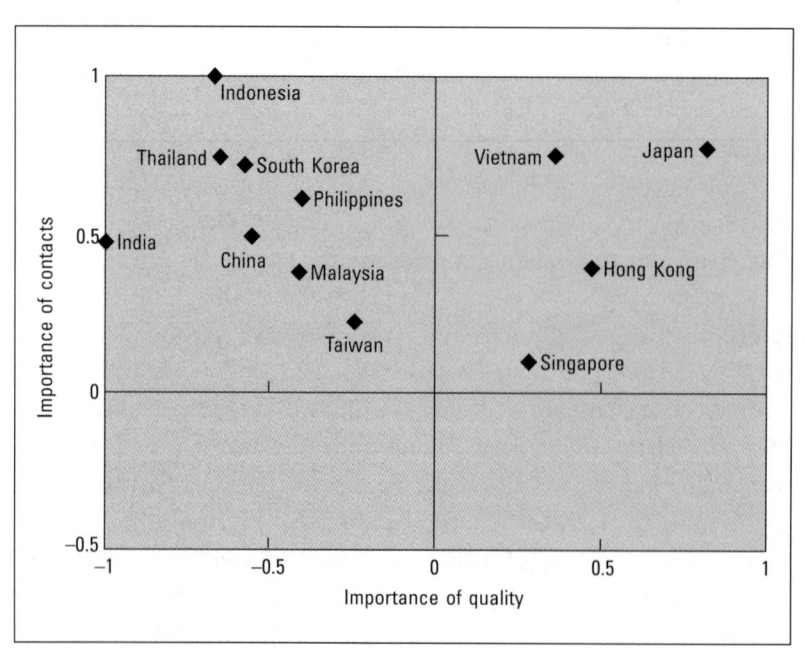

Scatter plot with axes "Importance of quality" (x-axis, -1 to 1) and "Importance of contacts" (y-axis, -0.5 to 1):
- Indonesia: (-0.6, 1.0)
- Thailand: (-0.6, 0.75)
- South Korea: (-0.5, 0.75)
- Vietnam: (0.3, 0.75)
- Japan: (0.8, 0.75)
- Philippines: (-0.4, 0.6)
- India: (-0.95, 0.5)
- China: (-0.5, 0.45)
- Malaysia: (-0.35, 0.4)
- Hong Kong: (0.5, 0.35)
- Taiwan: (-0.2, 0.2)
- Singapore: (0.3, 0.15)

importance of contacts cannot be underestimated anywhere in the region, but that attitudes to the importance of quality vary considerably.

In the sophisticated environment of Japan contacts and quality of product or service are of almost equal importance: it is not enough simply to have a good product because many other firms—domestic and foreign—have equally good offerings. What can make the difference is the ability of a firm to forge lasting relationships with a broad range of partners. While the presence of Hong Kong and Singapore in the same quadrant as Japan is to be expected, Vietnam's appearance is more surprising. The Vietnamese market has been open for such a short time it seems likely that the rating indicates pent-up purchasing desires rather than reality.

The next cluster of countries contains Taiwan and Malaysia, with China and the Philippines hovering on the edge. Taiwan is on the verge of sophistication, indeed this is already apparent in some sectors of the marketplace. Both China and the Philippines are less dependent on the quality of their contacts than they used to be, but India, which stands rather by itself, would seem to present major challenges for Western companies intending to take a quality-conscious approach to the market. The remaining group of countries—Thailand, South Korea, and Indonesia—all lay greater stress on the quality of contacts than on the quality of the product. In Indonesia the growing role of high-level political lobbying is particularly apparent.

Financial Issues

The role of government may extend into the financial arena through the tendency of the authorities to set the agenda for national development. In some countries the link between government and business is close, whether or not the state physically owns many business assets, and the emotional aspect of nationalism may be brought into play at strategic moments. The role of a business venture in promoting national development is strong in such countries (Figure 2-24). In Japan the story is slightly different: the concept—or expectation—of the shareholder has never been the same as in the Anglo-Saxon model of capitalism. In all other countries the "natural" interests of private business take precedence over the national role.

But what can we say about the financial attractiveness of one

Figure 2-24

In this country the role of business is more to contribute to national development than to transfer profit to shareholders

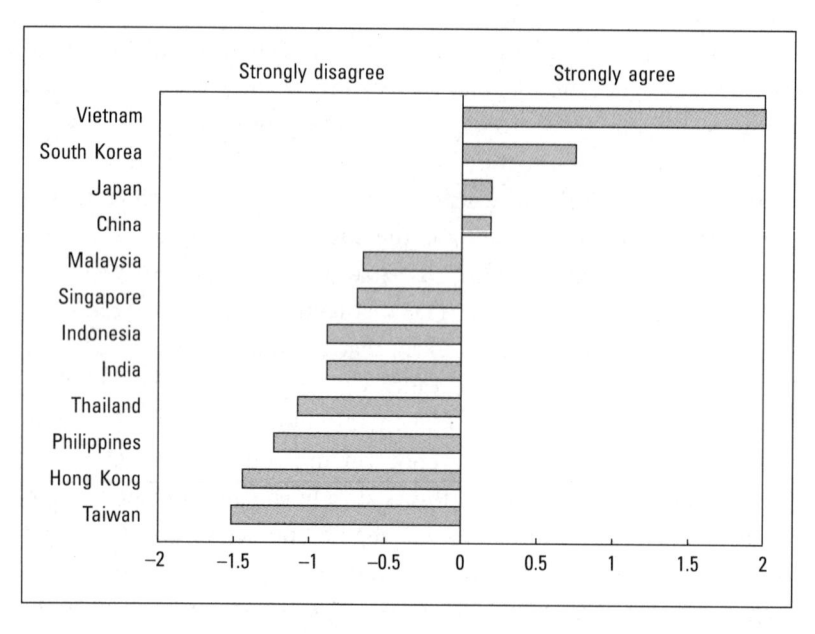

location over another? Overall, we can say on the basis of this survey that financial and business risks as well as return on investment (ROI) are generally perceived to be higher in Asia than in Europe (Figure 2-25). Only in Singapore and to a small degree in Hong Kong do executives feel that the risks are no greater than in Europe while ROI is higher. This is an interesting result, given the much faster growth rates in most Asian countries compared with Europe: one might expect that the opportunities for business development are so much more widespread in Asia that there is room for a company to make one or two mistakes. In a fast-growing economy where the overall pie is increasing, one firm's expansion need not take place at the expense of another firm; in Western Europe, on the other hand, where growth rates are generally small, a large increase in sales by one firm usually signals a balancing loss by another.

Conclusion

To summarize the findings of this survey we constructed a composite diagram of the perceptions expressed by our expatriate manager sample

FIGURE 2-25
Risk/return

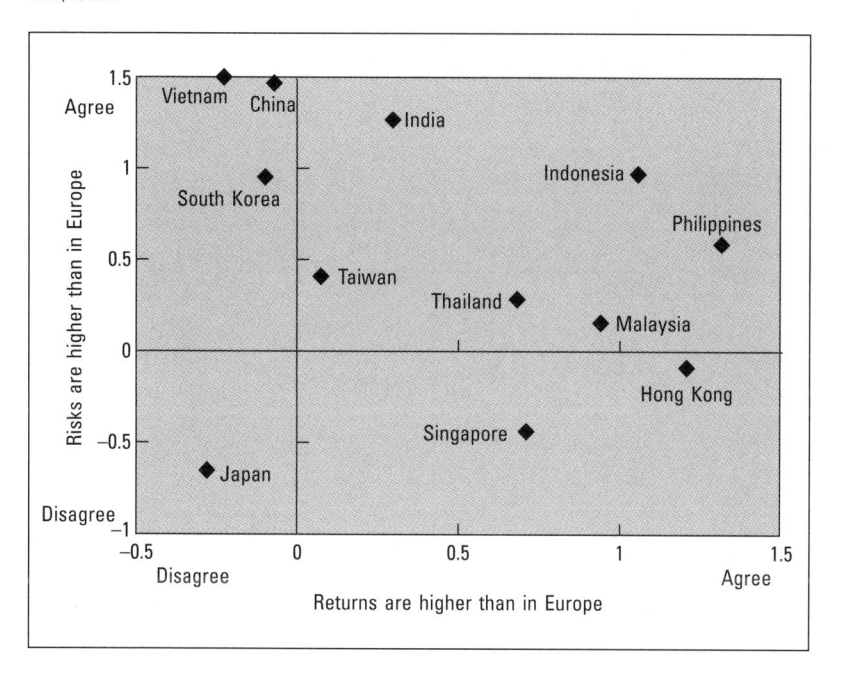

of each country in relation to the other countries in the Asia Pacific region (Figure 2-26).

Perceptions of the political, legal, and ethical context—which group questions concerning government influence, integrity, and the rule of law—are mapped against the competitive-context dimension—which includes such issues as the importance of networks, ambiguities in understanding business rules, and competitive practices.

It is immediately apparent that many countries in the Asia Pacific region remain fundamentally difficult places for Western firms to operate in. This is in spite of the many years of experience our sample managers have accumulated. Not only is the way of doing business (the competitive context) rather unfamiliar, but the political, legal, and ethical context is generally opaque.

Most Western firms are reasonably comfortable only in Hong Kong and Singapore, which at least offer the advantage of a clear political, legal, and ethical context.

However, six countries—Vietnam, Indonesia, South Korea, Thailand, China, and India—remain profoundly complex, puzzling environments where expatriate managers find few familiar points of

FIGURE 2-26
The Asia Pacific business context

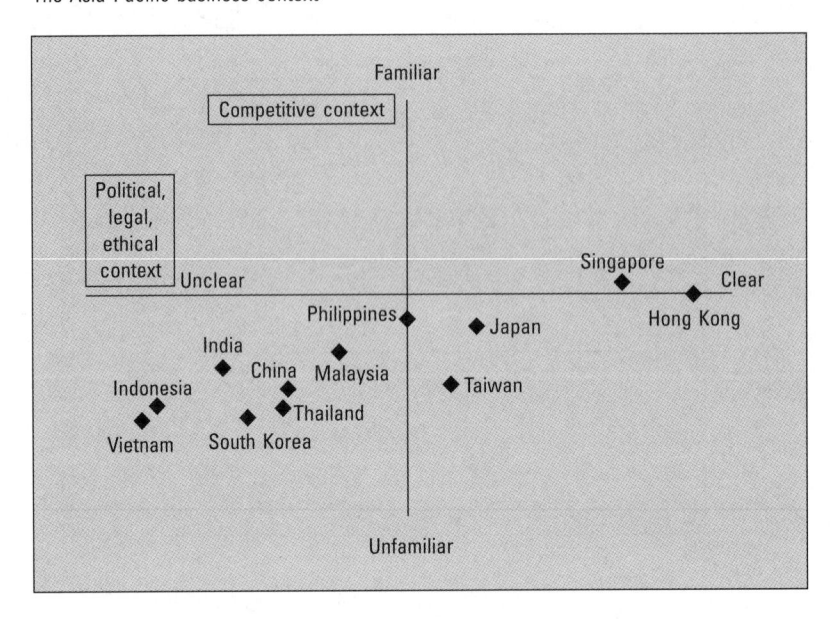

```
                        Familiar
            ┌─────────────────────┐
            │ Competitive context │
            └─────────────────────┘
  ┌──────────┐
  │ Political,│
  │ legal,    │
  │ ethical   │
  │ context   │                           Singapore
  └──────────┘ Unclear                       ◆              Clear
                            Philippines◆              Hong Kong
                                            ◆ Japan
                       India
                         ◆
                            China   Malaysia    ◆ Taiwan
              Indonesia   ◆        ◆
                  ◆          ◆ Thailand
                ◆         South Korea
              Vietnam

                        Unfamiliar
```

reference. In between lies what we might call the moderately accessible cluster of countries: Japan, Taiwan, the Philippines, and Malaysia. These four countries occupy a reasonably clear position on the political, legal, and ethical dimension, but challenge the notions of Western companies in the competitive context.

Comparing this outcome with our survey results in 1992, we can say that South Korea has been replaced in bottom position on the list of clear, familiar places to invest in the Asia Pacific region by Vietnam and Indonesia. Since Vietnam did not figure in the earlier survey—and indeed, the sample on which the current findings are based is perhaps too small to be representative—it is not obvious in which direction the situation is evolving. As far as Indonesia is concerned, however, there is a troubling deterioration in the political, legal, and ethical environment perceived by Western investors.

Thailand also scores rather poorly on this dimension compared with 1992, but both China and Japan have improved their positions: the former nevertheless remains in the "difficult" category; the latter is the most favorably positioned among the second-ranked countries. After several years of economic recession and a certain loss of confidence among Japanese companies in the superiority of their business practices, perhaps Western managers discern changes in the structure of the Japanese market that give them a competitive advantage not fully challenged by domestic firms.

Implications for Action

Companies who are engaged in developing or consolidating their presence in Asia Pacific should be aware of the salient features of the complex and varied business environments of the region.

The concrete consequences for companies, strategic planners, and expatriate managers are manifold, but three particular aspects have to be given priority.

First, when elaborating and evaluating strategies, global business managers and strategists should be flexible and adaptive in exercising their judgments on the business conditions and assumptions in the region. Strategic logic which works in the West may not apply in the same way in certain parts of Asia. The present survey gives some hints about the prominent characteristics which differ from American and European worlds. In their dialogue with front-line expatriate managers, global executives should "listen," and not "dictate."

Second, the qualification of expatriate managers sent to Asia should meet the demands of the Asian business environments. In addition to their professional and technical expertise, expatriate managers in Asia should exhibit social and political skills.

One such skill is the ability to build, develop, and maintain a network of personal contacts. Given the importance of relationship-based transactions in Asia, Western managers should refrain from adopting a legalistic and technical approach to their business dealings.

Another skill is political. Given widespread government intervention in business, Western managers should be able to understand the logic, the constraints, and the language of government officials in order to align their business strategies with the industrial policies of the individual countries.

Finally, cultural sensitivity constitutes a fundamental trait for managers if they are to communicate, lead, and negotiate with customers, partners, and employees. Subtle social codes cannot be decrypted without humility and respect for cultural heritage.

The third concrete implication relates to organizational systems and processes put in place to implement Asian strategies. Some companies resort to regional headquarters in order to lead and coordinate their development in the region (Lasserre, 1996). The data presented in this survey confirm the critical role that regional headquarters can play in collecting, analyzing, and consolidating competitive information across the region as well as fostering the visibility of local operations vis-à-vis the central corporate headquarters. A strong internal regional culture supported by intense networking among local subsidiaries is needed in order to take advantage of Asian business opportunities as well as overcoming the risks involved.

References

Lasserre, P. (1996). Regional headquarters: The spearhead for Asia Pacific markets. *Long Range Planning*, 29 (1): 30–37.

Lasserre, P. and J. Probert (1994). Competing on the Pacific Rim: High risks and high returns. *Long Range Planning*, 27 (2): 12–35.

THE ASIAN APOCALYPSE
Crisis Marketing for Consumers and Businesses

Swee Hoon Ang, Siew Meng Leong, and Philip Kotler

Analyses of consumers from various Asian countries indicate falling confidence and a tightening of belts during the recession. Strategies employed by consumers to tide them over the economic crisis include more comparative shopping; delaying purchases of expensive items; placing more emphasis on product durability and functionality; switching to lower-end and local brands; developing a product life-cycle cost perspective; relying more on informative and less on imagery-based advertisements; and buying more often at discount stores. Businesses face cash-flow challenges as banks and suppliers are less willing to provide favorable financial terms, whilst customers default more or buy less. Effective strategies that will help businesses during this period include expanding into crisis-resistant markets such as non-Asian and youth markets; introducing "fighter" lines; maintaining prices while augmenting existing products; developing adaptive positioning; using informative advertisements; and pruning marginal channels.

INTRODUCTION

Research on marketing during hard economic times suggests that consumers adapt their buying behavior in view of expected layoffs and rising interest rates (Kotler, 1980; Sharma, 1981). Fewer purchases are

---

Reprinted from *Long Range Planning*, Vol. 33, pp. 97–119. Copyright 2000, with permission from Elsevier Science.

made; purchases of selected products, especially luxuries, are postponed; price becomes a more critical consideration in decision making; and purchases are driven more by specific benefits sought. Psychologically and financially, crisis-hit consumers behave differently from those enjoying economic prosperity. Likewise, business strategies appropriate during good times may become ineffective when there is a downturn. Strategies that promote more purchases, conspicuous consumption, impulsive rather than deliberate decisions, and satisfying hedonism as opposed to necessities may not appeal to crisis-hit consumers. Instead, businesses need to reconsider their marketing strategies to capitalize on changes in consumer needs, values, and consumption patterns. The market targeted may need to be changed and the marketing mix adjusted to reflect values that are consistent with those of crisis-hit consumers. To do so, businesses must first understand how an economic crisis affects consumers.

This article examines the impact of the economic crisis on Asian consumers and businesses, and discusses the adjustments they have made in addressing their new economic reality. After a decade of flourishing economic activity, the Asian flu caught many, both businesses and consumers, off guard. Skeptics have raised concerns over whether Asia will be able to cope with this downturn. Therefore, it is managerially instructive to understand how Asian consumers and businesses have dealt with the crisis. In doing so, we can also assess how well businesses have adapted to the new values of the Asian consumer. Marketing strategies are suggested that provide lessons for businesses operating in periods of economic hardship—whether in Asia or elsewhere.

The background behind the genesis of the Asian crisis is described briefly. This is followed by the framework around which our discussion is organized. We then describe the effects of the crisis on consumer behavior in the region, as well as the resulting adjustments that Asian consumers have made. Next, we describe the impact of the crisis on businesses in the region. Finally, we discuss the marketing strategies employed by businesses in response to the crisis, and consider the adjustments made by regional consumers.

Background to the Asian Crisis

The Asian economic crisis began in July 1997 with the devaluation of the Thai baht, a day after Hong Kong became a special administration region in China. Since then, Asia's economies have undergone gut-wrenching changes, which have left their mark on almost every commercial, industrial, and even political activity in the region. Among the most affected are Asia's consumers and businesses. What Asian consumers eat, drink, and buy, how they spend their leisure time, and what they dream of have all taken an entirely different track. Carefree consumption has been replaced by the tightening of belts. Businesses once devoted to satisfying the unceasing needs of the burgeoning Asian middle classes have become preoccupied with finding ways to stimulate flagging consumer demand.

Several views have been advanced regarding what triggered the financial problems in Asia. These include the over-reliance on short-term capital to fund long-term projects; inadequate supervision of the banking and finance sector; and investment in nonproductive assets such as real estate. From a business perspective, some of the causes of the crisis may have been self-inflicted. Firstly, the abuse of *guanxi*, that nebulous web of connections linking influential political and commercial interests in the region, has led to charges of corruption, nepotism, and cronyism in countries such as Indonesia. Such less-than-transparent transactions may have inflated the cost of doing business in Asia. The greasing of the political machinery may well have led to higher prices charged to taxpayers by winning bidders of government contracts trying to recover their "investments." For example, Indonesia's state-owned oil company Pertamina recently called for a re-tendering of a liquefied natural gas plant project in Irian Jaya. The estimated $500 million contract was "improperly awarded" during the Suharto era to a consortium that included a company owned by Muhamad "Bob" Hasan, briefly a Minister of Trade and Industry toward the end of the former President's term of office.

A second business-related cause pertains to the unbridled and unsystematic expansion of Asian businesses into areas unrelated to their expertise. Whereas Western tenets were calling for corporate restructuring to focus on core competencies, East Asian businesses ventured into any and all areas that they perceived to be profitable. The core competence of Asian businesses appeared to be their ability to secure contracts via the *guanxi* mechanism, which precipitated an attitude of "it's who you know" rather than "it's what you know." As Western businesses discovered during their recession, such corporate diversification may yield short-term benefits in a benign economic environment. When times get tougher and leaner, systemic weaknesses are painfully exposed. The headlong plunge into real estate by businesses that originally focused on such diverse areas as textiles and public transportation is a classic illustration of this syndrome. Indeed, some 60 percent of all public-listed companies on the Hong Kong stock market are involved in some property-related business.

Thirdly, Asian businesses (other than the Japanese, and to a lesser extent the South Koreans) have never been strong at marketing, particularly in brand management. The largest and most profitable brands today are, with few exceptions, Western (especially American). In terms of brand equity, only Japanese brands such as Sony, Toyota, Honda, and National Panasonic appear atop global rankings. In a macro sense, the leadership of American brands mirrors the domination of the global marketplace by such U.S. businesses as Microsoft, GE, Intel, Coca-Cola, Gillette, and IBM. By the same token, the lack of well-known and internationally accepted Asian brands accentuates the relative weakness of the region on the world economic stage. Several reasons account for this deficiency:

- The tendency of Asian businesses to serve as low-cost contract manufacturers and OEMs for Western MNCs
- The traditional emphasis on trading and distribution in the region
- The role of Asian businesses as franchisees of Western franchisers
- State-owned or sponsored monopolies in certain sectors (such as telecommunications) that saw little need for marketing and branding
- The effects of a past socialist ideology which promoted equality rather than differentiation
- The perception of Asian names being a liability in certain product categories (such as fashion)
- Outright neglect and under-investment in maintaining and enhancing existing Asian brands

An Organizational Framework

The Asian economic crisis has affected both consumers and businesses in the region. Changes in the economic environment are in general likely to impact both consumers and businesses. In particular, prospects of greater unemployment, asset deflation, and slower growth combine to erode consumer confidence. This in turn adversely affects consumers' propensity to spend on products and services. Businesses are concerned with delays in collecting payments, pressure from customers and competitors to reduce prices, and reduced credit from banks. They respond by adjusting their targeting of markets, their product offering, positioning and pricing, and their promotion and distribution strategies. Marketing strategies that accommodate what consumers look for during such hard times are more likely to succeed than those that do not adequately address consumer concerns.

CONSUMERS AND THEIR REACTIONS

Asian consumers have been affected by the economic downturn both psychologically and financially. With layoffs arising from business closures and cost-cutting measures, people experience reduced job security. More than 45 percent of Japanese felt uneasy about their employment situation in late 1998, compared with 35 percent 14 months earlier (Hirose, 1998). Aside from the more obvious financial challenge of making ends meet, the psychological impact on Asian people cannot be over-emphasized, for several reasons. Firstly, Asians are used to the practice of lifetime employment, especially those employed in small- and medium-sized indigenous businesses, which tend to be more traditionally run. The idea of being made redundant from a job, which has all along been assumed to be held until retirement, is particularly difficult to accept. Whereas Western enterprises regularly downsize and de-layer, Asian businesses had previously tended to reallocate human resources rather than remove them.

Secondly, there is the issue of *mianzi* or face. Losing one's job is painful anywhere, but especially so in a hierarchical and collectivistic culture. In many Asian families, the husband is the sole (or main) breadwinner of the family. His loss of employment brings shame to himself since he is unable to fulfill his role expectations. Indeed, many husbands in Japan and South Korea have kept news of their redundancy from their spouse and children for extended periods of time, by adhering to their daily routine following their layoffs. In Indonesia, evidence exists that laid-off employees continued to socialize with their associates and friends in pubs to show that they are surviving the crisis, even though the amount spent on entertainment has been sharply curtailed. This phenomenon parallels that documented by Kotler (1980). Individuals during the early stages of an economic crisis will maintain their old spending patterns, refusing to take their loss of income seriously.

Thirdly, many Asians in developing countries such as Indonesia, Malaysia, and Thailand had only just joined the middle classes when the crisis struck. They had prospered under consecutive years of high economic growth and had begun to enjoy the fruits of their labors when, in a short and painful spell, the good life abruptly ended for them. Adjustments are all the more difficult under such circumstances than for those accustomed to a more basic lifestyle. Accordingly, middle-class Asians' faith in the future was severely shaken. Many now believe that the only certainty is that they are on their own (Wong, 1998).

Consequently, consumer confidence has been severely affected in the region (see Figure 3-1). As of mid-1998, the average confidence level is below the midpoint of 50 (Lee, 1998). Confidence in Japan was decimated with a score of 1 out of a maximum of 100, while Hong Kong registered only 13. Pessimism about Japan's future has also

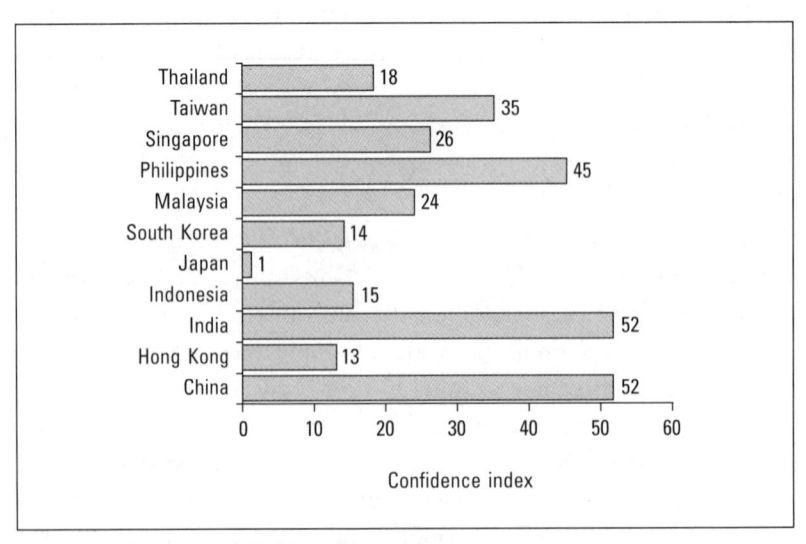

FIGURE 3-1
Asian consumer confidence index as of July 1998

Country	Confidence index
Thailand	18
Taiwan	35
Singapore	26
Philippines	45
Malaysia	24
South Korea	14
Japan	1
Indonesia	15
India	52
Hong Kong	13
China	52

Source: MasterCard Consumer Confidence Survey.

increased from 26 percent to 51 percent between 1989 and 1997 (Hirose, 1998).

We will now discuss the actual and potential reactions and adjustments of Asian consumers during the economic crisis. Our discussion can be divided and summarized as follows:

- **General reactions:**
  Reduced consumption and wastefulness
  More careful decision making
  More searching for information
- **Product adjustments:**
  Buying necessities rather than luxuries
  Switching to cheaper brands and generic products
  Buying local rather than foreign brands
  Buying products in smaller packages
- **Price adjustments:**
  Emphasizing product life-cycle costs—durability and value for money
  Emphasis on cheaper prices
- **Promotion adjustments:**
  More rational approach to promotions
  Reduced attraction to gifts
  Preference for informative rather than imagery-based advertisements
- **Shopping adjustments:**
  Increased window-shopping
  Preference for discount and neighborhood stores
  Fewer end-of-aisle impulse purchases

General Reactions

Reduced wastefulness

With the onset of financial hardship, Asian consumers have tended to be less wasteful, opting for a simpler lifestyle. Such voluntary simplicity mirrors the experience of American consumers during the 1970 recession in the U.S.A. Then, consumers embraced a "small is beautiful" attitude (Sharma, 1981; Shapiro, 1978). Now, in South Korea, 80 percent of consumers have reduced their spending on dining out, leisure activities, and buying clothing and accessories (Venkataraman, 1998b). Another 60 percent have reduced expenditure on beauty products, furniture, and appliances. Similarly, it has been reported that some 58 percent of Thai consumers have stopped buying fashion clothing, while 45 percent and 46 percent have stopped buying whisky and magazines, respectively (Ogilvy & Mather, 1998). Indonesian consumers indicated that they had reduced consumption of fast food (90.8 percent), imported fruits (85.2 percent), and beauty-care products (82.5 percent) (Kartajaya et al., 1998). In Singapore, over 73 percent of consumers indicated that they had become less wasteful in view of the economic downturn (Ang, 1998). These examples show that the economic slowdown has made consumers more frugal.

The consumption of most products has steadily declined as the crisis progresses. As shown in Figure 3-2, large decreases in consumption were observed for electrical goods such as washing machines and refrigerators, travel, clothing, and cosmetics. The drop in magnitude was generally less for essentials such as toiletries, food, and health-care products.

Decision making and information searching

Asian consumers now weigh the pros and cons of buying a product

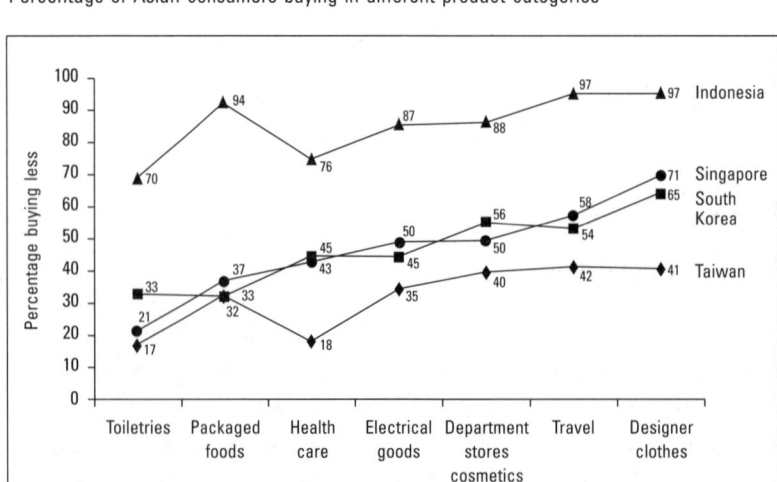

FIGURE 3-2
Percentage of Asian consumers buying in different product categories

Source: Taylor Nelson Sofres, Asia Pacific (1998).

more conscientiously. They will have more discussions with their friends or spouse before making a purchase, especially if it comes with a high price tag. Such involvement of important others in purchase decisions is not surprising given the collectivistic nature of Asians. In general, the views of important others in an Asian society are given considerably more weight than in non-Asian countries. The social influence of others on decision making has been enhanced during the economic crisis.

Furthermore, Asians are particular about saving face. While they desire to maintain their appearance and social solidarity, they also want to be more careful in how they spend their money. This dilemma between the need to save face and the need for belt-tightening prompts Asian consumers to consult more with friends and spouses before making purchasing decisions.

Such deliberate decision making leads to Asian consumers engaging in more comparative shopping. Information searches involving comparing prices, content, and product benefits across brands will be more intense during an economic crisis. In part, this arises from Asians' aversion to risk and greater avoidance of uncertainty. Together with the pressure for saving face, this leads Asians to minimize the possibility of making a poor purchasing decision by intensifying their search for information. This means that consumers become more educated about various brands. Indeed, some 93 percent of Indonesian consumers felt that with the economic crisis, they had become wiser in their shopping (Venkataraman, 1998a).

Product Adjustments

Necessities versus luxuries

The trend toward voluntary simplicity suggests that adjustments in product purchases by Asians will vary depending on whether necessities or luxuries are involved. Essentials such as cooking oil are less likely to see a drop in consumption. To some extent, personal-care products have also held up relatively well. By and large, people still have to eat, clean their teeth, and wash themselves. In contrast, consumption of luxuries such as fashion clothing and cosmetics has been more adversely affected by the crisis.

Given the close-knit family structure in the region, many products and services aimed at maintaining the welfare of Asian children are considered necessities. Some 83 percent of Indonesian parents would sacrifice their personal consumption (of cigarettes and soft drinks, for instance) to ensure that products deemed necessary for their children (such as food) can still be bought (Venkataraman, 1998a). Hence, products such as milk, fruit juice, and soap are less likely to experience large drops in sales as Asian parents tend to shelter their children from the harsh realities of the crisis. Another indication of the resilience of children's food products is the extent of brand loyalty for them. In Thailand, brand loyalty was found to be strongest for nutrition supplements (97 percent) and milk (89 percent)—both of which are child-related products (Ogilvy & Mather, 1998).

Aside from tangible products, leisure activities are also likely to see a decline. This includes vacation travel to countries whose currencies have appreciated relative to local currencies. Instead, travel to countries whose currencies have depreciated relatively, or vacationing within the home country, can be expected to rise. Eating out will also be reduced, with more consumers cooking at home.

As shown in Figure 3-2, the degree to which consumer expenditure is reduced varies by country, depending on the scale of the economic crisis. Indonesians appeared to be the worst off, while the Taiwanese were better insulated. Also, within each country, purchases of essentials such as toiletries were the least hit, although the effect on specific brands varies. Generally, consumers tend to move from a better-known to a lesser-known brand (e.g., from Colgate to Sparkleen). Thus, while overall purchases are held constant in some product categories, people buy lesser-known brands. Likewise, consumption of speciality products such as softeners may drop, but that of basic detergent is less affected. Similarly, sales in Asia of luxury cars such as Mercedes and BMW have been hit, while those of lower-end, smaller cars such as Hyundai have seen increases.

However, some luxury products appear to be more recession-proof than others. Ironically, gloom and doom has driven Asian consumers to seek solace in "vice" luxuries such as gambling, cigarettes, and beer—stress-relievers with escapist features.

Switching brands

The economic slowdown has seen consumer preferences shifting toward locally made products. Between 40 and 65 percent of Indonesian consumers have experimented with local brands, while over 80 percent of Thais spend less on imported products (ACNielsen, 1997). Figure 3-3 shows the percentages of various Asian consumers buying local products during the economic crisis.

While the increased demand for local brands is principally generated by their lower prices, a nationalistic sentiment is slowly growing in this region. Thailand's "Thai Buy Thai" program has stirred locals to do more for their country by buying Thai-made products. In Malaysia, a strong government campaign to buy local products has influenced 54 percent of Malaysian consumers, who now believe that local products are of the same quality as foreign-made products, with another 31 percent believing that local products are actually superior (Smurthwaite, 1998). In South Korea, patriotic smokers are switching from imported cigarettes such as Marlboro and Virginia Slims to local brands such as This and Get II. Some 69 percent of Koreans were found to disfavor foreign products. If a Korean company were to be acquired by a foreign company, 36 percent of previously loyal consumers would shift to "genuine" Korean products (Smurthwaite, 1998).

The economic crisis has also seen an increasing trend toward buying generic products. Middle-income Filipino consumers were reported to be buying fewer branded household and grocery items,

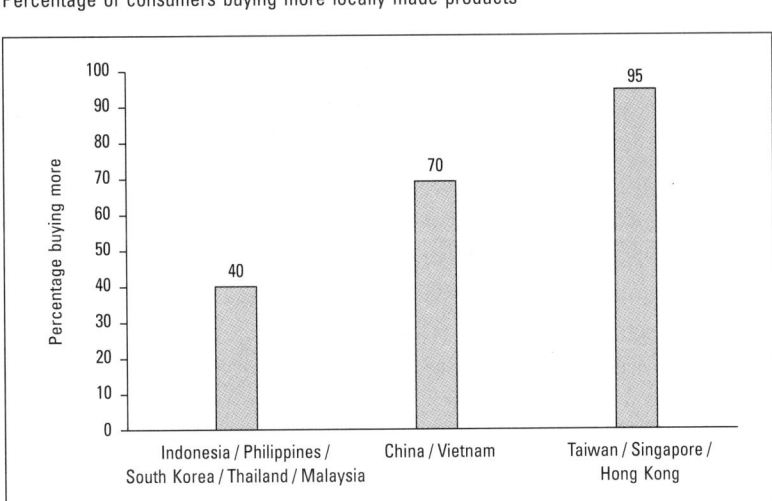

Figure 3-3
Percentage of consumers buying more locally made products

Region	Percentage buying more
Indonesia / Philippines / South Korea / Thailand / Malaysia	40
China / Vietnam	70
Taiwan / Singapore / Hong Kong	95

Source: Taylor Nelson Sofres, Asia Pacific (1998).

preferring generic (own-brand) products. However, the transition from branded to generic products has occurred in two steps, with consumers switching from premium brands to challenger brands first, and then to generic products as the economic crisis worsened.

Nonetheless, switching brands can be expected to be less prevalent for products with a high perceived risk. Products where the choice of the wrong brand can lead to disastrous outcomes are likely to be less affected. Brands with strong equity are also likely to be more resistant to shifts in consumer behavior. Indeed, such brands may provide a source of stability in an uncertain world. Consider personal finance: with many financial institutions in the region on the brink of bankruptcy, consumers have rushed to deposit their funds in better-known and stronger foreign banks. For example, in Malaysia and Indonesia, banks such as Citibank and Standard Chartered Bank have seen their local deposit base grow as funds traditionally placed in local institutions have been redirected to them. To a lesser extent, larger domestic banks have also benefited at the expense of smaller financial institutions. Asian consumers have recognized that the limited government and international funds for recapitalizing domestic banks would have to be prioritized, with the larger and more important local banks being bailed out first.

Package size

During the U.S. recession, American consumers turned toward buying in bulk for cost savings. This tendency has also surfaced during the Asian crisis. However, it only holds true for those Asian consumers who are less adversely affected. Smaller packages are appealing to those whose discretionary income is low. For such consumers, the outlay for each purchase is lower and thus more affordable, although the unit cost may be higher. Danone has reported that in Indonesia, sales of biscuits in smaller packages of 40 grams or less have increased. Psychologically, Asian consumers may feel that with smaller packages, they will be more frugal in their consumption; larger packages may offer a false sense of abundance and therefore result in wastage. Also, especially for products that are fragile or perishable, there may be more wastage in larger packages if the product is damaged or lost (e.g., a larger bag of rice stolen versus a smaller bag). Finally, smaller Asian homes may be less amenable to carrying large household inventories than U.S. residences.

Price Adjustments

The economic crisis will see the evolution of a more rational and savvy Asian consumer. More aggressive price bargaining and more frequent prepurchase price checking have already been seen (Ang, 1998). Yet, while Asian consumers appreciate low prices, product life-cycle costs—how long a product will last given the price paid and the maintenance costs incurred over its life—are equally if not more important. Value for money considerations are also expressed in terms of varied product usage. Multipurpose products will be less resistant to sales decline than products with limited and inflexible uses. For instance, an Indonesian lipstick manufacturer came up with the ingenious idea of a crisis lipstick—one that comes in two colors, one on each side of the stick. The product sold well because it offers dual use compared to a normal one-color lipstick.

The extent to which consumers emphasize durability and price depends on the degree of financial severity. In countries where the crisis is more severe (e.g., the IMF countries and Malaysia), consumers will tend to be more price conscious, while those in less severely hit countries (e.g., Singapore, Taiwan, and Hong Kong) can indulge their preferences for durability and value for money. For example, over 76 percent of Indonesian housewives indicated that they were switching to buying generic drugs because of the crisis (Kartajaya et al., 1998). Likewise, 23 percent of Indonesians would choose brands based on price, rather than quality, while 39 percent stated that the crisis had forced them to switch to lower-priced brands (Venkataraman, 1998a). In contrast, while over 83 percent of Singaporeans have become more careful with their money, over 68 percent indicated that product durability was still more important to them than price considerations alone (Ang, 1998).

Promotion Adjustments

The types of promotion favored by Asian consumers have also been affected by the crisis. Crisis-hit consumers rationally evaluate the benefits to be gained from buying during a promotion. The increased emphasis on durability and value for money suggests that the promotional message should include these qualities. Maintaining a higher price on products while including gifts is not necessarily successful. An overwhelming 92 percent of Indonesian consumers preferred to buy a product at a lower price without any gift than pay a higher price and receive an accompanied gift (Kartajaya et al., 1998).

The serious economic sentiment, the more intense information searches, and the more deliberate purchase decision-making call for advertising to be more informative. Some 62 percent of Singaporean consumers favored advertisements that explained brand benefits and gave them reasons to select a product over competitive offerings. By contrast, imagery-based advertisements were relied upon less. Some 59 percent of Singaporeans found such advertisements frivolous and wasteful (Ang, 1998). The advertised products were perceived not to offer any real benefits. Worse, brands using imagery-based advertisements were viewed as being unsympathetic toward the consumer's economic situation. Thus, not only may such advertisements harm product sales, but they may also lead to a company being perceived as socially inconsiderate. Since social responsibility is a key contributor to perceptions of corporate excellence in Asia (Kotler et al., 1999), this has potentially devastating long-term effects on identity management.

Shopping Adjustments

While Asian consumers are spending less during the economic crisis, they continue to window-shop for at least two reasons. Firstly, their more deliberate decision-making patterns encourage greater information-search behavior. This translates into more active window-shopping. Secondly, window-shopping is a relatively inexpensive pastime to indulge in during the crisis. Families may thus engage in window-shopping not only to keep up with market trends but also as a cheap form of leisure and recreation.

As with switching toward cheaper brands, Asian consumers have also traded down in terms of their selection of stores. Stores that offer lower prices for the same product are becoming more popular. These include hypermarkets, discount retailers, and neighborhood stores. Supermarkets have also benefited from the fact that Asian consumers are eating at home more. In contrast, downtown department stores have been hard hit by the crisis.

Consumers tend to be persuaded less by end-of-aisle displays meant for impulse purchases. However, they do continue paying attention to them while queuing to pay for their purchases.

Businesses and Their Marketing Strategies

Like consumers, businesses are not insulated from the economic crisis. Besides the impact on sales and profits, their marketing strategies are also affected. Competition becomes more intense as businesses fight for a shrinking market. Given the consumer adjustments discussed above, what marketing strategies can businesses in Asia adopt to perform effectively under the poor economic conditions in the region? The following list summarizes the marketing-mix strategies that businesses in Asia can consider to survive, upgrade, and expand during the economic crisis.

- **Marketing-mix strategies:**
  Withdraw from weak markets
  Fortify in markets where brand is strong
  Acquire weak competitors
  Consider non-Asian and youth markets
  Consider resale market for durable products

- **Product strategies:**
  Prune weak products
  Avoid introducing new products to fill gaps
  Introduce fighter or second-line brands
  Adopt adaptive positioning
  Concentrate on simple and durable products
  Augment products with warranties

- **Pricing strategies:**
  Improve quality while maintaining price
  Reduce price while maintaining quality
  Avoid reducing quality and price
  Consider product life-cycle pricing

- **Promotion strategies:**
  Maintain advertising budget
  Increase use of print media
  Provide assurances through rational appeal
  Use expert endorsements, traditionally respected figures, and satisfied-customer testimonials
  Avoid celebrity endorsements
  Adopt an advisory tone
  Capitalize on public relations

Use discounts and premiums, not contests and lucky draws
Introduce customer loyalty programs
Train sales force to anticipate questions and handle complaints
- **Distribution strategies:**
Location is still important
Sell in discount and wholesale centers
Prune marginal dealers
Consider alternative channels

Marketing-mix Strategies

During a downturn, a leaner and more efficient organizational mindset is needed. Businesses should withdraw from markets in which they are weak in order to fortify markets in which they are a leader or strong challenger. With scant resources, businesses must take stock and consolidate their activities.

Maintaining commitment in markets where the business is the leader or a close challenger is essential during a crisis. Those brands that can maintain or increase their sales volume are either likely to be the top brands (because of their strong equity) or cheaper generic brands. Brands with middling market share are the worst hit. For example, in Hong Kong's Tsuen Wan district, Carrefour has expanded its operations, while two local supermarkets (Nam Luen and Kwai Shing) have been forced to close. Therefore, market leaders should select the markets with the most potential and channel resources into expanding these markets. Strong market challengers should enhance their competitive advantage. Markets that are not growing and in which the business is weak should be divested. Resources from the divestment can be channeled to protect existing strong markets and to groom others into stronger positions.

An economic crisis also offers opportunities for acquisition. Devalued regional currencies make Asian businesses cheaper to acquire for foreign businesses. Further, during such times, businesses that have yet to enter Asia or which have entered Asia only lately can catch up with market pioneers through an acquisitions strategy. Aside from cash injections, foreign businesses may also provide much-needed human resource and technological capital for Asian companies. A host of acquisitions has taken place all over Asia, particularly in the real estate and telecommunications sectors. Morgan Stanley Asia estimates that there were $75 billion and $60 billion worth of such regional deals done in 1997 and 1998, respectively, mainly in Japan, South Korea, and Thailand. Once-reluctant Asian businesses are now more enthusiastic about being courted by foreign companies. For example, Societe Generale had failed to buy Asia Credit in Thailand, but managed to do so following the outbreak of the crisis.

Mergers and acquisitions can enhance a business' market position and drive out marginal competitors. However, buying market share does carry an added risk in Asia. In particular, cultural norms to do with saving face may be violated with aggressive bidding, which may lead to a nationalistic backlash when Asian economies eventually recover.

New market opportunities

The economic crisis has brought home the importance of a broader market base among Asian businesses. Those which relied on local and even regional markets found to their dismay that these were insufficient for long-term growth. In contrast, Asian businesses which had ventured into Europe and North America were better insulated from the crisis. For example, Singapore property developers such as Wing Tai, which focused solely on domestic and regional markets, reported huge losses as their real estate holdings were written down to reflect their lowered market values. However, others that had entered the European and U.S. real estate and hotel markets, like City Developments, fared much better as their earnings stream and asset appreciation in the West offset the poorer contributions from local and regional operations. Hence, the economic crisis has spurred Asian businesses to examine new markets worldwide. These include nontraditional markets where minimal business linkages had been established in the past. Thus, Giordano, the Hong Kong casual clothing chain, has opened new stores in South Africa, South America, and Australia.

In spite of the recession, there still exist new market opportunities within the region. Geographically, China and India have remained generally attractive markets during the crisis, given their positive economic growth. Demographically, the youth segment may also be targeted. Many Asian youths live at home with their parents, so although they do not earn much, their purchasing power is not so badly affected by the crisis. They are also less likely to have large bank loans. Thus, they are relatively resilient to the crisis. Evidence of this is suggested by the double-digit growth achieved by Pepsi in 1997 and 1998 (Ko, 1998). Designer coffee chains such as Starbucks and Coffee Bean & Tea Leaf—also targeted at the young—are flourishing in recession-hit Asia. Several Singaporean jewelry retailers are expanding by selling gold and diamond pieces priced below $300 that are targeted at the young.

Another market opportunity is the rural population. Although this market tends to buy cheaper, low-quality products, they have more brand loyalty than their urban cousins, who are more exposed to competitive advertising and promotion. In fact, Lever Brothers in Malaysia feels that there are some benefits to the economic crisis. As city workers are made redundant, they return to their rural home towns and bring along with them brands not available in the rural areas. These unemployed workers become mouthpieces for these brands and introduce them to the rural folk, who otherwise would not be exposed to them.

Nevertheless, the rural market is a heterogeneous one, even within one country. For example, while Indonesian farmers have been reported killing their livestock as they could not afford feed or fertilizer, the nation's nutmeg growers are prospering given the escalation of prices due to the rupiah devaluation and the increase in global demand for the spice. Thus, Banda Island has been a lucrative niche for such products as satellite dishes, pickup trucks, and motor boats (Wagstaff, 1998).

The recession will also see a strong resale market for durables. Asians have never been keen on buying second-hand products. However, chains of second-hand shops selling computers have sprung up in the region. The resale durables market has both a demand and a supply pool of customers. Expensive items have a high depreciation charge during their early years. Buying such items new may be considered wasteful by many consumers. Such consumers are more likely to buy expensive items from the resale market. Purchasing a used Mercedes enables the buyer to preserve face while saving money! At the same time, consumers who have bought new durable goods and want a change (e.g., upgrading from a 486 to a Pentium PC) seek a resale market to dispose of their products. The cash they get in the resale helps to offset the cost of buying another new product.

Product Strategies

Pruning existing products, developing new products

Businesses should prune weak product ranges and avoid unnecessary line extensions. A shorter product line is more manageable and allows scarce resources to be sufficiently and effectively devoted to brands that yield higher returns.

During a downturn, businesses should not introduce new products merely to fill gaps in their product line. Firstly, they are already financially stretched. Secondly, the crisis-hit consumer is more savvy and less likely to be attracted to any new product that comes by. Thirdly, competitors are also less likely to attack any gap in the product line as they are similarly strapped for cash. Instead, introductions of new products should focus on those that add significantly to the firm's bottom line. These tend to be products that are consistent with consumer values of frugality, durability, and functionality.

However, the economic crisis offers businesses which are financially strong the opportunity to plug holes in their product lines in order to block future competition. These new products would serve as fighter or second-line brands, protecting the flanks of the core brand from competition. Such fighter brands may also capitalize on existing brand equity if their product quality does not damage the core brand. Fighter brands are appealing because they assure consumers of quality at a lower price. Further, given Asians' tendency toward face-saving behavior, they provide the added benefit of good names at a lower price.

Managing existing brands

The economic crisis presents an opportunity for Asian businesses to strengthen existing brands (and perhaps develop new ones as well). Asian businesses should position their brands to appeal to Asian consumers, who are now more favorably predisposed toward domestic offerings, be it for financial or emotional reasons. Interestingly, the survival of the fittest Asian brands during this recession may signal an enduring strength sufficient to penetrate global markets in the future.

However, existing Asian brands will need to adjust to the new mood and habits of the consumer through adaptive positioning—

retaining the core benefits of their products while adapting them to suit the revised consumption environment. Brand's Essence of Chicken is an Asian health tonic known for providing mental and physical stimulation to children and expectant mothers. When the Asian crisis started, Brand's in Thailand adapted its positioning while maintaining its core benefit; it positioned itself as the tonic that helped employees tide over the crisis as they worked harder to keep their jobs. With adaptive positioning, Brand's core benefit of mental-physical stimulation is maintained but adapted to suit the crisis. In doing so, it has enlarged its market to include all adults.

Adaptive positioning requires recasting or reframing to suit consumer sentiments, as opposed to changing what the product stands for. Table 3-1 provides some classic illustrations of adaptive positioning by well-known businesses that Asian companies could perhaps emulate. Adaptive positioning signals that businesses are cognizant of the budget-conscious consumer and realize that ostentation and the flaunting of wealth is taboo during an economic crisis. Hence, instead of retaining the original positioning of luxury, they focus on austerity (e.g., leftover foods in Ziploc), economic wisdom (Volvo's financial safe haven), affordability (Michelin), and the ordinary (A-1 sauce for hamburgers).

Product augmentation

During such hard times, businesses should still keep their eyes on the future and invest in developing their long-term positioning. Businesses may also augment their product offerings with extended warranties or guarantees aimed at providing consumers with peace of mind and thus

TABLE 3-1
Adaptive positioning during an economic crisis

Brand	Product	Original positioning	Adaptive positioning
Michelin	Tires	"Expensive, but worth it"	"Surprisingly affordable"
Ziploc	Food bags	Airtight bags	Airtight food bags for leftovers
A-1	Steak sauce	For sirloin steaks	Also for hamburgers
Volvo	Car	Safety	"In a financial crash, keep your valuables in a safe place"

Source: Chadwick (1998).

persuading them that the product is worth purchasing. One such example is Hong Kong property developer Li Ka-shing's real estate development in Singapore. The recession brought about pessimism that the property market would fall further. Hence, buyers were deterred from committing to property purchases. To overcome such fears, Li augmented his real estate product by offering a guarantee of a 10 percent capital appreciation over five years.

Price Strategies

Raising quality, lowering prices

One strategy is to charge the same prices for higher-quality goods. Such a strategy of price maintenance induces consumers to remain loyal to the firm by adding value to the product offering. This assumes that the firm has high customer loyalty and is willing to lose poorer customers to competitors. Improvements in the product offering should be in terms of durability and functionality as these are the features important to consumers in a recession. In doing so, the firm's image of providing high-quality products is maintained, if not improved. Therefore, brand equity is not eroded. The firm, however, must be prepared for a smaller market share and lower profitability in the short term. But when the economy recovers, it will be easier for the firm to extend its product line to higher price brackets for higher profitability.

Another strategy is to charge a lower price for the same quality product. This strategy spells lower profit margins for the firm, but allows it to hold on to or expand its market share. It is appropriate if winning market share is a difficult task. In some industries, once market share is lost it is hard to recoup it because competitors work intensively to protect their own turf. However, businesses should bear in mind that once a price cut is implemented, it is very difficult to reverse it when times improve. Therefore, instead of offering a permanent price cut, businesses can offer promotional discounts. These are less likely to dilute brand equity compared to a price cut as they are temporary and meant only to thwart competition in the short term.

Lower prices, lower quality

A final option is to charge a lower price for a lower-quality product. This is somewhat similar to a market penetration strategy where a business targets the mass market. As the mass market is likely to grow if economic conditions worsen, there is market potential here. However, such a strategy may dilute brand equity in the long run. This may prove disastrous, especially when the upturn occurs, as consumers may continue to perceive the product as being of inferior quality even when subsequent product improvements are made by the business. Therefore, although market share and profit margin are maintained in the short run, long-term profitability is likely to be compromised.

Businesses resorting to aggressive price tactics should resist lowering their list prices because consumers may view them as permanent. Instead, rebates, lower-interest financing, free maintenance, loyalty programs, and longer product warranties can be offered as alternatives to a reduction in list price.

Promotional Strategies

Advertising

When a recession occurs, advertising budgets are one of the first things to be cut. Unfortunately, this has been shown by U.S. experience to be myopic (Rosberg, 1979). Businesses that did not cut their advertising budgets during a recession doubled their sales and increased their profits by 75 percent when the economy improved, while those that cut their budgets enjoyed sales and profits increases of less than 44 percent and 30 percent, respectively. Businesses in Asia should therefore view advertising not as a cost but as an investment. The rewards of advertising in a recession materialize when the economy improves.

The economic crisis provides a rare opportunity for businesses to leapfrog their competitors. When times are good, all businesses advertise intensively. Thus, advertising expenditure in the region grew in the years before the crisis. To rise above the advertising "clutter" and be noticed by consumers is extremely challenging during an economic boom. In contrast, competitors advertise less during a recession, leading to less clutter. Coupled with lower costs and better servicing from hard-pressed media owners and advertising agencies, it is easier and cheaper to gain a larger share of the advertising voice, and hence of consumer attention, during a recession.

More-involving media such as print become more relevant during an economic crunch. Consumers are likely to spend more of their time on and to pay more attention to these more-involving media, and so are more likely to digest the information communicated. The appropriateness of using such media during a recession rests on consumers being more deliberate in their decision making. Print advertisements offer consumers the opportunity to read about the product at their own pace and to deliberate on the benefits of the product offer. Television and radio commercials, because of their fleeting nature and reliance on other sensory cues besides words, tend not to satisfy the informative needs of crisis-hit consumers.

The extensive information searching conducted by Asian consumers also suggests that advertisers should find ways to make product information more accessible to consumers. For advertising, this means that understanding the media demographics or "mediagraphics" of the target audience is essential. Mediagraphics involves knowing what television programs consumers watch, what newspapers and magazines they read, and what radio programs they listen to, so that the relevant media are chosen to maximize the accessibility of product information.

The content of advertisements changes somewhat during an economic crisis. Since consumers cannot afford to experiment, they value advertisements with quality assurances and clear communication of benefits. Advertisements that discuss product benefits in a rational manner will be more attractive than those that rely on imagery. The endorsement of independent expert sources also reassures consumers. In Asia, where there are strong hierarchical delineations, expert sources are greatly respected for their opinions. Furthermore, as the risk of making a poor purchasing decision leads to greater discussions with the spouse and close friends prior to purchase, advertisements demonstrating the opinions of others are likely to strike a chord with crisis-hit Asian consumers. Similarly, the use of traditionally respected figures such as grandmothers (for cooking products) and mothers (for children's products) assures consumers that there will be social approval when buying the product. Advertisements that rely on testimonials of satisfied ordinary customers will gain popularity vis-à-vis celebrity endorsements. Besides costing less to produce these advertisements, consumers identify more with ordinary people during a crisis as they are similarly hit by the recession.

The tone of advertisements during a recession will tend to assume an advisory stance. The respected authoritative figure gives advice to consumers, while the satisfied customer recounts his favorable product experience. Product benefits are better communicated in the form of advice or product experience as they lend credence to the advertised claims. This lecture format differs from the psychological appeal and symbolic association formats more commonly observed in Asian advertisements (Zandpour et al., 1994), suggesting that a recession may bring about more reliance on rational appeal and the use of expert endorsements.

Public relations and publicity

Businesses should try to get publicity in the press. Newspaper articles are perceived to be credible because journalists are considered to be independent. During an economic crisis, when consumers are more skeptical of advertising, reliance on noncommercial sources such as newspaper and magazine write-ups increases. Besides being free publicity, these sources are perceived to be honest and objective. Moreover, their newsworthy characteristic enhances the perception that these sources are important.

Promotion

A larger proportion of the budget will be spent on promotion and public relations. Amway, for instance, introduced more promotions and offered better cash incentives to its distributors during the Asian crisis. Given the increased price consciousness, selected promotions such as coupons, premiums, and sales discounts are likely to find favor with Asian consumers. Such promotions offer immediate and concrete gains. These promotions therefore speak directly to consumers' pockets. Such promotional tools may not only persuade customers to switch to buying your brand, but may also expand the market by encouraging those who would otherwise not be purchasers of the product. An example of the sort of discounts given is the 5 percent waiver, equivalent to the nationwide sales tax, offered by major Japanese retail chains such as Ito-Yokado and Daiei. Many Japanese retailers feel that cutting the sales tax is the quickest way to boost consumption.

In contrast, promotions such as lucky draws and contests are unlikely to attract new buyers. They will generate purchases from consumers who have already decided to buy the product but who are not quite sure which brand to buy, but they do not encourage purchases from those who do not intend to buy the product. Lucky draws and contests also do not offer guaranteed returns, as not all customers are winners. Therefore, if purchases are necessary to enter the contest or lucky draw, tight consumer budgets are unlikely to encourage more consumption.

Customer loyalty programs will see more usage during an economic crisis. Airlines such as Singapore Airlines, which used to reward only first-class and business-class passengers, have moved toward offering frequent flyer programs to economy-class passengers as well. These loyalty programs help tie consumers to the brand. This is important, especially since brand switching tends to be heightened when pockets are tight.

Personal selling

As consumers are likely to ask salespeople for more information before they make a purchase, salespeople have to be trained to handle consumer questions and complaints. In particular, training should focus on anticipating the types of questions consumers will ask, handling complaints, and comparative product analyses. There may also be a need to empower salespeople to make some independent decisions to help close a sale. In such cases, clear guidelines of empowerment have to be drawn up. Avon's strategy during the Asian recession has been to increase customer sales representatives. Similarly, Amway plans to increase its number of representatives in Malaysia and Thailand. Hiring better-qualified salespeople (such as graduates) is more likely during such conditions. While many Asian graduates have generally not considered sales a worthwhile career, the recession has forced them to consider such lines as insurance selling.

In terms of compensation, Asians by far tend to shy away from a heavy reliance on commission, preferring instead to have a substantial fixed salary base. This stems in part from Asians' low tolerance for uncertainty. With the recession, however, businesses are more cognizant of costs. Therefore, there is increasing pressure to peg compensation to performance, with a larger percentage based on commission.

Distribution Strategies

Location is still the key to ensuring store patronage. Retailers may spruce up their store and window displays to attract the crisis-hit Asian consumer. Manufacturers may market their fighter lines to discount and wholesale stores favored by consumers during the recession. They may drop dealers who are unprofitable, and reallocate their scarce resources to those who show better promise and performance. Moreover, they may consider using alternative channels to reach their customers. Direct selling and marketing may be contemplated to reduce intermediary expenses.

CONCLUSION

It is not difficult for businesses to turn a profit when economic conditions are favorable. Corporate growth is more easily achieved when the entire market is growing. However, in a leaner environment, effective marketing planning and implementation becomes vital. There is simply much less margin for error. Certain marketing strategies applicable across various recession contexts prevail in Asia. These include the need to be more focused; to identify target segments more precisely; to cut nonessential costs via pruning marginal product lines and channels; to enhance productivity by leveraging on resource-saving tools such as public relations and publicity; and to understand and cater to a more value-conscious consumer by offering fighter lines, lower product life-cycle costs, and greater information to reduce perceived social and financial risks.

However, there are several aspects that are more important or peculiar to businesses operating under the economic crisis in Asia. Firstly, Asian businesses must venture beyond the region to tap nontraditional markets. They cannot afford to be satisfied with doing business in their own backyard in the same old way. Secondly, they must become more professional and disciplined in their approach to business and marketing. No longer is it appropriate for them to simply go where the profits are, no matter that the business may not fit their resources and competencies. Thirdly, they should exploit consumers' tendency to purchase more local offerings by developing and strengthening indigenous brands. The crisis affords the opportunity to place under severe scrutiny the branding expertise of Asian marketers as well as the brands they manage. Brands that survive this examination should prove fitter for the test of the global market.

The Asian recession will eventually end. Thus, businesses in Asia should adopt a longer-term view when making strategic marketing decisions. Indeed, the two Chinese words for "crisis" (*wei ji*) mean "danger" and "opportunity," respectively. When integrated, they refer to there being opportunity in danger. Clearly, those businesses in Asia which seek and exploit market opportunities during these turbulent times will benefit greatly when Asia recovers.

References

ACNielsen (1997). *Thailand / Indonesia*. December. Thailand and Indonesia.

Ang, S.H. (1998). *Marketing under Challenging Economic Conditions: Consumer and Business Perspectives*. Singapore: Marketing Institute of Singapore.

Chadwick, J. (1998). *Taking the Road Less Traveled: How to Increase Profits in Asia When Times Are Tough*. Singapore: Ogilvy & Mather.

Hirose, T. (1998). Changes in Japanese consumer attitudes according to Dentsu consumer confidence survey. In *Roundtable on the Asian Consumer: New Strategies for New Realities*, September 28–30, pp. 17–20.

Kartajaya, H., I.P.M. Wijayanto, and Yusohady (1998). Consumer behavior in the economic crisis and its implications for marketing strategy. *Kelola*, 18 (7): 104–36.

Ko, M. (1998). Market segmentation, market priorities: Asia's biggest challenge? In *Roundtable on the Asian Consumer: New Strategies for New Realities*, September 28–30, p. 59.

Kotler, P. (1980). *Marketing Management*. Englewood Cliffs, NJ: Prentice Hall.

Kotler, P., S.H. Ang, S.M. Leong, and C.T. Tan (1999). *Marketing Management: An Asian Perspective*, 2nd edition. Singapore: Prentice Hall.

Lee, L. (1998). Most consumers throughout Asia lose confidence. *Asian Wall Street Journal*, August 27: 4.

Ogilvy & Mather (1998). *Thailand Listening Post Study*. Thailand.

Rosberg, J.W. (1979). Is a recession on the way? It's no time to cut ad budgets. *Industrial Marketing*, 64 (April): 68–70.

Shapiro, S. (1978). Marketing in a conserver society. *Business Horizons*, April: 3–13.

Sharma, A. (1981). Coping with stagflation: Voluntary simplicity. *Journal of Marketing*, 45 (Summer): 120–34.

Smurthwaite, J. (1998). The economic crisis: The impact on consumer demand in Asia. In *Roundtable on the Asian Consumer: New Strategies for New Realities*, September 28–30, pp. 36–40.

Venkataraman, S. (1998a). *How Consumers Cope with Economic Crisis: Learning from Indonesia*. Indonesia: Research International Asia.

Venkataraman, S. (1998b). *How Consumers Cope with Economic Crisis: Learning from Korea*. Korea: Research International Asia.

Wagstaff, J. (1998). Indonesia's poverty: How bad is it? *Asian Wall Street Journal*, Asia Economic Survey 1998–1999, October 26: S13.

Wong, J. (1998). The big squeeze. *Asian Wall Street Journal*, Asia Economic Survey 1998–1999, October 26: S11.

Zandpour, F., V. Campos, J. Catalano, et al. (1994). Global reach and local touch: Achieving cultural fitness in TV advertising. *Journal of Advertising Research*, September–October: 35–63.

4

MARKETERS AND THE EXTERNAL ENVIRONMENT
The Indonesian Experience

Ike Janita Dewi

"Pay attention to the environment" is one of marketers' favorite slogans. Indeed, marketers should pay attention to and learn about forces that affect consumers' buying behavior. Consumers do not live in isolation and therefore are affected by their environment. Indonesia provides a unique situation where the economic crisis interacted with other factors to create a multifold crisis. The crisis and the ensuing reforms have produced significant changes in consumers' lives and created a new social, political, and economic atmosphere. This paper discusses how consumers' roles have been changed by these circumstances. It also examines the importance of incorporating macro factors in understanding consumer behavior and designing effective marketing strategies.

INTRODUCTION

In marketing, it is a mistake to assume that consumers live in isolation and are immune from the events happening around them. What people feel, experience, and think will affect their attitudes toward consumer products (Schiffman and Kanuk, 1997; Zajonc and Markus, 1982). Changes in their surroundings will directly or indirectly affect their lives and so influence their consumption patterns.

Ike Janita Dewi is a doctoral student at the Faculty of Business Administration, National University of Singapore.

Copyright © 2000 by Ike Janita Dewi.

Furthermore, macro factors such as currency exchange rates, inflation and interest rates, and national stability are part of the business environment. Marketing activities depend, to a large extent, on macro conditions. Other changes such as the deregulation of foreign investment and the media industries will also alter the competitiveness of companies (Aaker, 1995).

The revolutionary changes occurring in Indonesia have undoubtedly affected its people. The severe economic crisis—which cut the income per capita from US$1,000 to US$600—has a direct impact on consumers' purchasing power. Widespread retrenchments have resulted in consumer insecurity. Both the economic and political systems are undergoing sweeping reforms. Within the span of one year, Indonesians witnessed the downfall of the king-like former President Suharto, the short-lived Habibie government, and the rise of the "laissez-faire" President Abdurrahman Wahid (Gus Dur). They also face frequent riots in several parts of the country. Violence hogs the daily news. One of the provinces, East Timor, voted to become independent. And more turmoil is expected: several provinces have demanded autonomy or even independence, and the military are being investigated for human rights abuses.

These dramatic changes by no means can be overlooked by marketers. An obvious consequence of the crisis is consumers' decreased purchasing power, so companies must fight for their disposable incomes. Political and regulatory changes have also created a new sociopolitical and socioeconomic atmosphere, which affects consumer attitudes and behavior.

Marketers are fond of saying, "Pay attention to the changes in the environment." Indeed, marketers have to fully appreciate how broadly events and situations that seem unrelated to their products will affect their products and their ability to sell (Zyman, 1999). In this paper, the dramatic changes in macro conditions in Indonesia—both politically and economically—will be discussed. The macro- and micro-environments cannot be regarded as separate. Instead, they interact to influence consumers and businesses. Companies are facing a new competitive environment as the crisis has brought in international players. The political reform has also shown the importance of a civil society, which plays a significant role in societal progress. If consumers are playing active roles in and exposed to these developments, marketers must learn from these fast-occurring phenomena.

FIGHTING FOR DISPOSABLE INCOMES

The most apparent impact of the crisis is the fallen purchasing power. In just a few months, Indonesians' incomes were slashed by one-third. The inflation rate reached 80 percent and retrenchments were widespread. Companies then must fight for a share of consumers' dwindled disposable incomes. Because of the drastic rather than gradual drop in income level, consumers have tended to cling to their product portfolio of consumption, although they have much less purchasing power.

Consequently, affordability becomes the main theme in advertising messages. Leading brands have attempted to position themselves as economical. For instance, Nescafe's ad copy "can make 100 cups and … delicious," Ericsson T18s' "more complete and more affordable," Compaq's "Who said that high performance business computer has a price that hits you?" and Vitalac infant milk formula's "The first infant milk formula in its class with economical packaging" highlight their good-value deals.

In competing for disposable incomes, companies generally adopt two strategies: introduce a cheaper brand and/or make the existing products more affordable. From the consumers' perspective, with their lower purchasing power, they prefer less expensive products that can perform the same or almost the same functions as the original higher-priced items. For example, Unilever, the market leader in toiletries, has introduced a new, cheaper brand of detergent and made existing brands more affordable by introducing smaller packaging and holding special-price promotions.

The latter strategy of maintaining affordability by introducing either smaller packaging or special prices reflects the peculiar psychological state of Indonesian consumers when a drastic drop in both real and nominal incomes was experienced. The standard of living was relatively high before the crisis hit the economy. The GDP per capita was slightly above US$1,000. Such a level of income is often viewed as an indicator of a country taking off from its developing status. Unfortunately, the economic achievement did not have a steady ground at best and was an illusion at worst. In addition, the whole system, especially the political system, was discovered to be corrupt. These changes occurred suddenly, and since consumers have been enjoying a good economy, they are still in a sense of economic well-being. Therefore, during the crisis, Indonesians attempt to maintain the same product portfolio but with much less purchasing power. This translates into shifted but not altered demand for goods. Take the habit of spending leisure times at shopping malls as an example. During the economic crisis, consumers maintain the habit of shopping but have shifted to cheaper shopping malls; for instance, from Sogo to a local mall (*Tempo*, 1999). Therefore, demand for a product category remains strong but the individual product demand has shifted from the higher to the lower end in terms of prices.

The drop in value of the rupiah has also made imported products very expensive. Fast foods like KFC and McDonald's are no longer affordable. Consumers still like the products but have no purchasing power. This unfulfilled desire has created a market for similar but more affordable products. Thus, when imitations of international food chains emerged, providing the same kinds of menu at much lower prices, Indonesians welcome them. Local food chains imitating the international franchises—such as Yogya Chicken or Kwartet Chicken offering KFC-like fried chicken—have become a phenomenon in times of crisis (*KONTAN*, 1999a).

Capitalizing on Political Changes

The sudden and dramatic political turn of events has popularized political jargon, creating an opportunity for marketers to utilize political themes in product promotions (Ogilvy, 1963).

Analogies with events during the crisis have been used in ads to communicate product benefits. Tropicana Slim, for example, is a diet sugar offering the taste of sugar without its calories. Its ad wanted to convey the message that consuming too much sugar is fattening and not healthy. The ad targeted weight-conscious women. It showed a warning against sugar hoarding ("Serious warning to sugar hoard!"). The next scene showed an obese woman taking a lot of food and then turning into a sack of sugar. The analogy of an obese woman and a sack of sugar was drawn from the political issue of sugar speculation. The ad was aired at the start of the economic crisis. Prices were volatile and people were uncertain about the direction of the economy, which induced speculation on essential commodities such as sugar. The sugar speculation caused sugar shortage and widely affected people's lives. It quickly developed into a political issue when such conduct was regarded as a deliberate attempt to provoke social unrest. Sugar hoarding was charged as subversion against the legitimate government. Although there was no political agenda in the ad of Tropicana Slim, the use of a political issue to communicate product benefits resulted in high awareness of both the product and its benefits. The negative image of sugar speculation was transferred effectively to convey the negative effects of sugar consumption.

Another way is to adopt political "language" in promotions to generate affect and emotional responses toward a product. During the election campaigns, Komix (a cough syrup packaged in sachets) ran an ad with the headline, "Cough campaign? Just vote for 'Komix'!" And when Indonesians were preoccupied with discussions of a coalition government, its headline read, "Cough ... don't be coalesced ... just 'Komix' it!" These headlines pertained to consumers' political interests at that time, and thus were appealing and emotionally arousing. Further, the growing sympathy toward reform heroes was likely to transfer favorable responses toward the product.

The preceding examples illustrate the effectiveness of employing political themes in advertising in times of heightened political awareness. However, such ideas have not been heavily adopted by Indonesian marketers. An ad depicting a student demonstration can be very appealing to student consumers as it creates a sense of affinity between the product and the consumers. Also, instead of sponsoring conventional events such as sports tournaments, advertisers can sponsor "political" events, such as the People's Assembly meetings and student discussions on political issues.

The political reform has also brought about discussions on gender issues. The new first lady, Mrs. Sinta Nuriyah, is renowned for her concerns on these issues. There is a national commitment in dealing with this matter as indicated by the Indonesian President's standpoint on this issue and the empowerment of the Ministry of Women Empowerment. These developments will generate public awareness and change the attitudes of Indonesians toward gender issues. They will have implications on the stereotyping of women as sex symbols or housewives in ads. With changing attitudes toward gender equality, consumers will demand changes in the roles of women depicted in ads.

Further, a crisis gives companies the opportunity to present a positive image or impression to consumers. Activities showing community involvement and a socially responsible company make good public relations. In terms of brand-image building, an association between a company and the reform process can make distinctive and memorable stories. Such stories would personify the company—just like stories about the Body Shop's founder, Anita Roddick, who has strong views on social and political issues. This strategy was adopted by Indofood, the market leader in instant noodles. It introduced the "Indomie Care" package during the crisis, which was priced cheaper than normal. The word "care" conveyed Indomie's sympathy toward consumers' situation and personified Indomie's manufacturer as unselfish and understanding. Such a program launched in times of crisis would create a deep and lasting impression.

As important as the above strategies, marketers should also capitalize on the changed sociopolitical atmosphere and the underlying spirit of the transformation. The riots can create a sense of insecurity and uncertainty about the economy can induce conservatism. On the other hand, democracy encourages freedom of expression, and the newly elected President has introduced an atmosphere of informality. In addition, the federation and autonomy discourses have created a spirit of plurality.

Sergio Zyman (1999) argues that marketers should watch the world: "*Everything that happens to consumers and everything that consumers do should affect your marketing decisions. If you ignore a single bit of potentially valuable information about them, you are wasting money*" (p. 98; italics are original). For instance, the victory of Tony Blair's Labour Party in the U.K. taught Coca-Cola that the British public was tired of the status quo and was interested in anything new. The reaction to the death of Princess Diana conveyed the sense of loss of an icon of survival and hope. The information was utilized to re-explain Coke and adjust the mix of its ad messages. Two sets of Coke ads were created to send a balance of two basic messages. One set celebrated life and the other suggested comfort and dependability (Zyman, 1999: 98–101).

Similarly, the transformation in Indonesia indicates that people desire freedom—from fear and dictatorship. Indonesians had long been under the political tradition of the New Order, which had created, if not forced, the tradition that political scientists call *patron–client* and *benevolence–obedience* relationships. A single figure—the President—was projected as the protector and guardian of the people and who therefore demanded absolute loyalty (Alhumami, 1999). But the political reform has transformed the people, removed the taboos, facilitated freedom of expression, and changed the people's lives.

More importantly, the spirit of reform has become a public concern. Attitudes toward public issues may transfer to attitudes toward certain products. For example, attitudes toward colors, which affect consumers' feelings and in turn affect consumer attitudes toward products, are very much influenced by the politicizing of colors. Under the New Order government, red was always associated with communism—an outlawed ideology used to scare people—but now is the color of the winning party. The same happened to yellow, which is the color of Golkar, the former ruling party that kept Suharto in power for 32 years. Closely linked to Suharto and his New Order government, Golkar was condemned for its abuse of power and corruption. Since yellow is the "official" color of Golkar, Indonesians' negative feelings toward Golkar was transferred to yellow. These phenomena stem from the wide use of color by Indonesian political parties as a means of persuasion and power display. The political parties practice a "classical conditioning" strategy by exposing Indonesians as much as possible to their party's color. A sense of familiarity with the color is thought to translate to favorable attitudes toward the party. Because of the pairing of colors (or other signs) with political parties, a change in the political regime will result in changed meaning of colors (or other signs).

The underlying spirit of reform was captured by Indocafe-Coffeemix, the market leader in instant coffee mix, in communicating its product benefits. The ad encourages more coffee consumption—coffee can be enjoyed in the morning, afternoon, and nighttime, served either cold or hot. The ad copy conveys the spirit of freedom in drinking coffee, stating that "nobody wants to be limited by time in this era of freedom, above all for drinking coffee...." This message strategy will likely appeal to Indonesians, who are in euphoria over democracy.

Uncertainty has also created a thirst for information on the country's most recent developments. It has created the need for real-time news. A Web magazine *www.detik.com* fulfills the need and desire of the Indonesians by providing continuous updates of current events in Indonesia. It has grown fast, from 900,000 to 6,420,000 hits (or from 30,000 to 214,000 users) during the crisis (July 1998 to March 1999). Even though the news provided is similar to that of printed newspapers and magazines, the way it "communicates" it (i.e., on a real-time basis) differentiates it from competitors and has become its success factor. Hence, product communication strategies should match consumers' needs and desires.

Macro Factors Underlying Consumer Behavior

Macro indicators should be taken into account when studying consumer behavior. Factors such as interest rate expectation and political stability can affect consumer behavior. As an example, the car industry was the first to recover from the crisis. In 2000, demand for cars is expected to increase to 200,000 units (compared to 58,011 units in 1998 and 80,000 in 1999; precrisis demand was 300,000 units) (*KONTAN*, 1999c). However, other industries complained that consumers' purchasing power was still very low despite a negative inflation rate (*SWA*, 1999a).

Demand for cars is usually seasonal. When the festive season—Christmas, the New Year, and especially Idul Fitri or Aidilfitri, the Muslim New Year—approaches, cars are needed for visits to relatives and friends. Besides being a means of transport, a car is also a means to show off one's success.

However, this time the increased demand for cars was for a different reason. A high correlation exists between demand for cars and several macro factors such as interest rates, exchange rates, and political conditions (*KONTAN*, 1999b). Car sales doubled following the election of Abdurrahman Wahid and Megawati (as President and Vice President respectively), indicating the sensitivity of demand for cars to political stability (the election process was believed to be fair and the elected President and Vice President are well accepted). The phenomenon can be further explained by the falling interest rates. Cars have become an alternative to bank deposits as the annual interest rate has dropped sharply, from 60 percent in 1998 to 13 percent in 1999, so people are no longer motivated to invest at such low rates. This condition is worsened by the deteriorating image of banks. Therefore, cars are bought more for investment and speculation than for consumption purposes. The favorable political climate, low interest rates, and the unstable rupiah together have encouraged demand for cars.

It is thus misleading to conclude that increased demand is a sign of restored consumer purchasing power as other products have not experienced the same fortune. Interpreting consumer behavior without taking into account macro factors may lead to erroneous deductions.

On the other hand, reading the macro indicators could still lead to the wrong conclusion about purchasing behavior. Companies are puzzled as to why low and even negative inflation rates have not resulted in increased sales. The inflation figure in October 1999 was 0.06 percent and over the April–September 1999 period it was −3.85 percent (*SWA*, 1999a). Deflation means that prices have decreased generally, but it does not necessarily mean that consumers' purchasing power has strengthened. Goods may be cheaper but are still not affordable because incomes have not increased (Quanes and Thakur, 1997).

NEW PLAYERS IN THE MARKET: INTERNATIONAL FORCES AND A CIVIL SOCIETY . .

Following the political reform during the economic crisis, various aspects of business activities underwent major transformations. International forces such as the International Monetary Fund (IMF) cannot be ignored because they interact with and influence the political and economic reforms, altering and shaping a new competitive environment.

The deregulation process, established for the purpose of attracting foreign capital, has created a new arena. International players will and have entered the local markets and challenge existing companies. For instance, following the elimination of foreign investment in retail trade in January 1998, the door has been opened wide to foreign retailers. Big names such as Carrefour and Continent have entered the market. They compete with local retailers, such as Matahari, for the estimated total retail sales of US$20 billion (in 1998). They have also introduced the concept of hypermarket and established the culture of bulk shopping. Further deregulation and regulatory changes will take place as the new government strongly encourages foreign investment in almost all industries.

Further, the Letter of Intent signed between Indonesia and IMF regarding economic restructuring will play an important role in shaping the business environment. For instance, as a direct consequence of the banking restructuring program, many defaulting companies will be taken over by foreign investors. It is also important to observe the movements of the Indonesian Bank Restructuring Agency (IBRA), which manages 234 trillion rupiah (or approximately

US$32 billion) under its Asset Management Unit and has the authority to enforce sales of the assets of defaulting companies. Also, existing monopolies—such as food distribution, cloves, and plywood—will quickly dissolve, thus removing entry barriers and creating a new competitive environment.

More interestingly, the political reform has brought attention to the significant role played by a civil society. Such a development is based on the belief that it is the society itself that must struggle for the improvement of the society by serving as a movement to protect social rights (Korten, 1998). This development is marked by the resurgence of nongovernmental organizations (NGOs). Many new NGOs have been established to deal with various social and political issues from racism to environmental problems. These NGOs are credible and serve as public-opinion makers. For example, the Indonesian Consumer Foundation (YLKI), working in the area of consumer protection, has voiced out concerns over a number of promotions and ads. It has demanded the regulation of promotional programs targeting children, such as the free-milk-for-pupils promotion. The organization warned that such a promotion can make a child dependent on a certain brand of milk, which is not necessarily healthy (Cameron, 1999).

In addition, a lot of ads—from medicines to cosmetics—are deemed inappropriate because they give misleading and false claims. One of them is Unilever's Pepsodent, the leading brand of toothpaste, which claims to prevent cavities. Pepsodent's well-liked ad in Indonesia depicts a boy teasing his younger sister that her penchant for chocolates will prevent her from becoming an astronaut. Their mother then explains that the girl can eat chocolates and still become an astronaut as long as she brushes her teeth with Pepsodent, which prevents cavities. This claim is considered misleading since no toothpaste can prevent cavities.

Indonesians are protected from unethical ads by the Consumer Protection Act introduced on April 22, 1999. However, law enforcement is minimal, so YLKI continues to raise consumer awareness and use public pressure to weed out such inappropriate conducts. This trend of increased participation of the society will likely continue and intensify not just because it is a global trend but mostly because of a conducive domestic environment. The newly elected President himself has encouraged the people, rather than the government, to play a more active role in improving the society.

Marketers should therefore be aware of this development of NGOs playing a watchdog role in educating consumers.

Economic Recovery?

It is difficult to conclude whether Indonesia has passed the worst of the crisis and is in recovery. It depends on the indicators used in the assessment. Compared to its weakest point in 1998 when the exchange rate was 16,000 rupiah to US$1, it has stabilized at around 7,000/US$. Interest rates have dropped to 13 percent (from the peak at 70 percent). Inflation has been maintained at below 10 percent. Politically, a legitimate government has been elected. Using these factors as indicators, Indonesia can be said to have experienced the worst. However, huge problems in the restructuring of the banking and financial sector and threats of disintegration of the country by continuous ethnic and religious conflicts in several parts of the country can hinder recovery.

The recovery process is moving at different paces for different industries. In 1999, three sectors experienced negative growth: trade, hotel, and restaurant (–0.95 percent), transport and communication (–1.33 percent), and finance, rental, and related service firms (–8.58 percent). Positive growth was enjoyed by the electricity/gas/water, services (other than finance and rental), manufacturing, building, farming, and mining sectors (*Kompas*, 1999). In terms of household expenditure, the third quarter of 1999 recorded an increase of 6.42 percent (in real terms) over the previous year's third quarter, or 0.95 percent compared to the second quarter of 1999.

Indication of recovery is also reflected by the size of advertising budgets. Industrial and financial companies have assumed postcrisis position and are showing their optimism by increasing advertising spending. Overall, the national advertising budget is expected to rise further as more companies start advertising as a reflection of improved economic conditions and a positive outlook for the coming years (see Table 4-1). The growth in the advertising budget cannot be separated from government policies to encourage foreign investment. Increased spending is expected from new product categories: foreign products and foreign banks. Local banks have also increased their advertising expenditure mainly to restore their image damaged by the collapse of the Indonesian banking system.

TABLE 4-1
Advertising budget

Year	Total advertising budget in rupiah	in US$	TV advertising budget (% of total ad budget)
1995	3.33 trillion	475.71 million	49.1
1996	4.14 trillion	591.43 million	53.2
1997	5.09 trillion	727.14 million	52.6
1998	3.79 trillion	541.43 million	58.9
1999 (est.)	4.67 trillion	667.14 million	60.4
2000 (est.)	5.64 trillion	805.71 million	NA

Source: AC Nielsen Survey Research Indonesia, in *SWA* (1999b).

It is important to note that in terms of advertising media, television is preferred. A higher percentage of the advertising expenditure will be allocated to TV ads. Television and radio are the most popular information sources: eight out of ten people in major Indonesian cities watch television every day (*SWA*, 1999b). This explains the active role played by television in broadcasting news and events during the political turmoil and reform. Further, the political reform led to freedom of expression, which boosted the media industry. The government has granted more than 1,300 licenses for print publications (compared to the pre-reform 326 licenses) (*Tempo*, 2000) and five new licenses to private television channels (in addition to the existing four private TV channels). The relaxation of the media industry means greater promotional opportunities for marketers.

However, the recovery is still dependent on macro factors. Government deregulation is expected to open the domestic market to foreign products. As well, the recovery of the financial sector is very much dependent on the bank restructuring program. The government privatization program, whereby state-owned companies are sold to foreign entities, also will determine the economic prospect. Most of all, political conditions must be conducive for business activities.

In terms of implications for marketing strategies, these factors can change consumers' attitudes toward products as well as create opportunities. A vast flow of foreign investment can provoke nationalistic feelings, resulting in unfavorable attitudes toward foreign products. Political instability will create a sense of insecurity; therefore, durable products, such as cars, can be bundled with insurance against political disasters.

Economic recovery will create another set of threats and opportunities for marketers, thereby requiring different marketing strategies. Marketers will have to continue to monitor the macro developments of the country, especially when much uncertainty remains and unexpected changes can occur.

Conclusion

Indonesia's experience is unique in that the economic crisis sparked a chain of political events. The cause of the crisis is multifold and beyond marketers' control, but its impact on consumers has to be clearly understood. The crisis has definitely affected consumers' purchasing power. Beyond its obvious impact, it has created a new social, political, and economic climate, which influences how consumers evaluate and buy products. The changes also reflect how consumers feel and think about their environment. Attitudes toward various macro issues, such as political issues, would likely influence consumers' attitudes toward products. Marketers should use such information when developing their marketing strategies.

Marketing strategies should also reflect the psychological state of Indonesian consumers, who are still feeling a sense of prosperity. Therefore, the strategy of reducing packaging size to make a product more affordable could find willing consumers with lower purchasing power who want to maintain their product portfolio. However, the postcrisis period will require modification of such a strategy. As consumers regain their purchasing power, their demand may either remain or return to precrisis level.

Further, since marketing strategies must be sensitive to the environment, anticipating and understanding how the current situation will develop are crucial. This paper suggests that macro indicators such as exchange rates, interest and inflation rates, and the political climate often affect consumer behavior. Certain government policies and macro indicators, such as a commitment to maintain low inflation, have direct impact on consumer purchasing power. But the mechanism of such policies should be understood so as not to arrive at wrong conclusions. For instance, a low inflation rate can be the result of a monetary policy to reduce money supply and raise interest rates. The mechanism may affect consumers in unexpected ways.

The reforms have brought in international forces, which will shape a different competitive environment. Foreign companies with their huge resources will become new players in various industries. Competition is expected to intensify. Companies operating for years in Indonesia can expect to rely on their established relationships with customers and capitalize on their knowledge of Indonesian consumers' idiosyncrasies. However, foreign retailers, which have been operating for only a short time, have already taken out 20 percent of local retailers' market share (*SWA*, 1999c). Further, the strengthening civil society will alter the nature of the relationships between the government, business sector, and the people. Marketers need to consider these different factors.

In conclusion, Zyman's suggestion (1999) that marketers should fully appreciate and learn from all information is critical. Even seemingly unrelated information can tell us what consumers are thinking and feeling. As Kotler (1999) points out, the ever-changing environment offers countless opportunities for Indonesian companies as well as competitors'.

References

Aaker, David A. (1995). *Strategic Market Management*. New York: Wiley.

Alhumami, Amich (1999). Lompatan kuantum politik Indonesia. *Kompas*, December 16.

Cameron, Emma (1999). In Indonesia, ad regulations are created to be violated. *Jakarta Post*, December 26.

Kompas (1999). Kebijakan ekonomi masih tanpa arah. December 21.

KONTAN (1999a). Ayam Amerika di pinggir jalan: Bisnis ayam goreng, kecil modalnya gede untungnya. November 1.

KONTAN (1999b). Kereklah harga, mobil kuborong: Perilaku orang-orang berduit setelah suku bunga bank kurang menarik. November 1.

KONTAN (1999c). Pasar mobil ketika kijang dikejar kuda. November 28.

Korten, David (1998). *Globalizing Civil Society: Reclaiming Our Right to Power*. New York: Seven Stories Press.

Kotler, Philip (1999). *Kotler on Marketing: How to Create, Win, and Dominate Markets*. New York: Free Press.

Ogilvy, David (1963). *Confessions of an Advertising Man*. London: William Clowes.

Quanes, Abdessatar and Subhash Thakur (1997). *Macroeconomic Accounting and Analysis in Transition Economies*. Washington, DC: International Monetary Fund.

Schiffman, Leon G. and Leslie Lazar Kanuk (1997). *Consumer Behavior*, 6th edition. Upper Saddle River, NJ: Prentice Hall.
SWA (1999a). Harga turun, kok tak mampu beli? November 22.
SWA (1999b). Memilih berlaga di layar kaca. December 25.
SWA (1999c). Makin seru, perang harga di bisnis eceran. December 25.
Tempo (1999). Dari Sogo ke Manggadua. October 31.
Tempo (2000). Instrumen hukum pers di Indonesia. 2000 special edition, January.
Zajonc, Robert B. and Hazel Markus (1982). Affective and cognitive factors in preferences. *Journal of Consumer Research*, 9: 123–31.
Zyman, Sergio (1999). *The End of Marketing as We Know It*. New York: HarperBusiness.

⑤ ASIAN YOUTH AND IMPLICATIONS FOR MARKETING STRATEGIES
Changes and Differences in Consumption Attitudes and Lifestyle Values

Mariko Yasue and Gu Xiang Wen

This paper identifies changes in consumption attitudes and characterizes the lifestyle values of Asian youth, namely, people in their twenties, and their homogeneity and differences using survey results obtained in 1995 and 1997. Asian youth in large cities have become affluent in terms of possession of durables, as measured by the Mono-Mochi scale. Consumption attitudes of these young people have become increasingly cautious and mature, somewhat similar to young consumers in developed countries. Their values have also been shifting from the traditional group orientation to the Western individual orientation. However, the current harsh economic conditions in Asia and the influence of cultural differences should not be overlooked. Although Asian youth are generally progressing in the same direction, the extent of change varies by country.

....

Mariko Yasue is Senior Planner and Gu Xiang Wen is Planner of Marketing Resources Development Division, Dentsu Inc., Japan.

Copyright © ESOMAR® 1999. This paper was first presented at the 2nd ESOMAR Asia-Pacific Marketing Research Conference "Marketing in Asia: Meeting the New Challenges." Permission for using this material has been granted by ESOMAR® (European Society for Opinion and Marketing Research), Amsterdam, The Netherlands. For further information, please refer to the ESOMAR® Website: *www.esomar.nl*.

Introduction

Asian youth are marketing targets of a growing number of corporations in light of the massive size of the population. Population ratios of those under 30 years old in major Asian countries are 67 percent in Indonesia, 65 percent in Vietnam, 63 percent in Malaysia, 58 percent in China, 52 percent in Taiwan, and 46 percent in Singapore. It is extraordinary that on average close to 60 percent of the Asian population are in their twenties or teens. The difference is rather striking when comparing these figures against that in Japan where young people under 30 years old make up 40 percent of the total population and the older population has also become an important consumer segment. Asian youth are also unique in the sense that they are people of a new era who spent their adolescence in the 1980s when the Asian economy was growing rapidly and who react quickly to new ways of consumption and new lifestyles.

Dentsu Inc. has conducted two surveys of the actual conditions of consumption, desires and views about consumption, and lifestyles and values of Asian consumers since 1995. In the second-round survey conducted in 1997, 11 large cities in 7 countries in Asia were studied using a number of value scales and consumption consciousness scales so that a multinational comparison could be made easily with respect to lifestyles and attitudes toward consumption.

Attempts to apply marketing scales on values and consumption attitudes, which had already been employed in developed countries in Asia, and to quantitatively characterize youth in each country are unique to these studies and had never previously been attempted. This paper examines and characterizes the values and changes in the lifestyles of Asian youth, and compares their homogeneity and differences using survey results obtained in 1995 and 1997.

Specifications of Consumer Research

Analysis of this paper is based on the following large-scale surveys conducted in 1995 and 1997 with respondents between the ages of 15 and 54 years. This survey is called Dentsu's Global Compass consumer research, initiated by Dentsu Inc., an advertising agency in Japan.

The specifications of the surveys are basically the same in 1995 and 1997, but some new questionnaire items were added in 1997 to focus more closely on the lifestyle attitudes and values of consumers.

Consumer Research in 1995

- *Areas:* Beijing, Shanghai, Guangzhou, Chengdu, Ho Chi Minh City, Hanoi, Bangkok, Jakarta, Kuala Lumpur.
- *Respondents:* Individuals aged 18 to 54 years with monthly income in the upper 70 percentile.
- *Number of samples:* 500 for each city.
- *Survey method:* Face-to-face interview using a structured questionnaire.
- *Survey contents:* Possession of and future intention to purchase consumer durable goods, utilization of and intention to utilize services, sectors of life on which great importance is placed, words expressing important life values, how holidays are spent, active/steady consumption style scale, etc.
- *Survey timing:* October through November 1995.

Consumer Research in 1997

- *Areas:* Beijing, Shanghai, Guangzhou, Chengdu, Shenyang, Ho Chi Minh City, Hanoi, Bangkok, Jakarta, Kuala Lumpur, Seoul, Manila.
- *Respondents:* Individuals aged 15 to 54 years with monthly income in the upper 70 percentile.
- *Number of samples:* 600 for each city.
- *Survey method:* Face-to-face interview using a structured questionnaire.
- *Survey contents:* Same as in 1995 plus some marketing scales, such as materialism scale, rational vs. emotional scale, interpersonal influence susceptibility scale, achievement motivation scale, active/steady consumption style scale.
- *Survey timing:* October through December 1997.

In 1995 and 1997, 12 Asian cities and 11,700 samples in total were surveyed. Among these cities, this paper will examine the changes in consumption behavior and lifestyle values of people in their twenties (a total of 2,271 samples surveyed in both these years) in the following 8 cities: Beijing, Shanghai, Guangzhou, Ho Chi Minh City, Hanoi, Bangkok, Jakarta, Kuala Lumpur.

Trends of Asian Affluence Levels

Let us first discuss changes in affluence levels in Asian youth to give an overview of this segment of the consumer market.

Mono-Mochi Scale

Analyzing the data on the ownership of consumer durables, Dentsu created a new marketing scale capable of measuring households' affluence levels across the region. It is named Mono-Mochi scale, which translates literally in Japanese as "possession of goods."

To develop this scale, attention was paid to data regarding ownership of household durables because they reflect affluence in terms of "how many items you own" and are objective, factual data. First, 23 items were selected for the questionnaire that were available in all countries and whose usage was unaffected by macroeconomic variables such as economic development, weather conditions, and government regulations—in short, independent of the respondents' country of origin. Then, applying a multivariate analysis, it was found that there was a certain pattern in the purchase of durables across the entire Asian region, and Asian consumers followed this pattern as they increased their ownership of durables with a clear order of progression that was measurable and predictable. Based upon these findings, the scale succeeded in grouping households into six classes of affluence, from Group F to A, based on ownership of the 23 consumer durables.

The items included in each group are as follows:

Group F: Nearly nothing
Group E: Electric fans, radiocassette players, etc.
Group D: Refrigerators, washing machines, etc.
Group C: Cameras, telephones, etc.
Group B: VCRs, air conditioners, stereo sets, etc.
Group A: Cars, microwave ovens, personal computers, etc.

Groups F through A are in ascending order of ownership (Figure 5-1).

Wealthier consumers are generally found to own more of the items in the higher groups, or luxury goods. Thus, the groups of durable goods ownership were defined as scales for measuring people's affluence levels. According to the degree of ownership of the items in Groups A through E, the sample of consumers was divided into six levels, A

FIGURE 5-1
Ownership of durables: order of progression

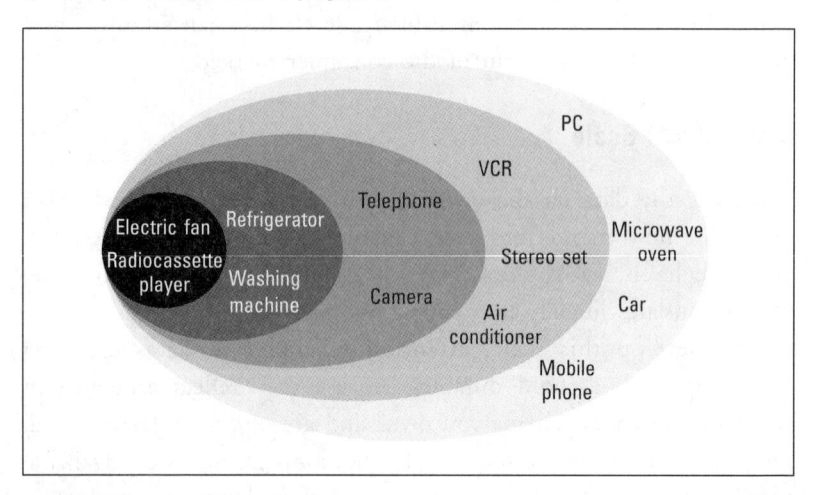

- Electric fan
- Radiocassette player
- Refrigerator
- Washing machine
- Telephone
- Camera
- VCR
- Stereo set
- Air conditioner
- PC
- Microwave oven
- Car
- Mobile phone

through F (see Figure 5-2). Starting from the most basic E group, each consumer was checked to see if they owned more than half of the items in that particular group. If the consumer owned more than half of the items, the procedure was repeated for the next group up. If the consumer was found to have fewer than half of the items, the analytical process stopped at that level. Using this hierarchical "yes or no" rule, all the consumers in the sample were categorized into Levels A through F. The levels so defined were referred to as the Mono-Mochi levels.

The major benefits of the scale are as follows:

- It describes the affluence level of households without dependence on the currency or socioeconomic situation specific to the countries.
- The scale is applicable with a high level of reliability throughout the entire Asian region without the need to consider macroenvironmental variables such as living standard, language, culture, geography, economic situation, and social and governmental structure.
- It works as an indicator of marketing feasibility of a specific product to a specific market because the particular ownership pattern is identical for every country. The scale can be utilized in predicting the progression and evolution of households from one purchasing class to the next.

FIGURE 5-2
Segmentation by ownership

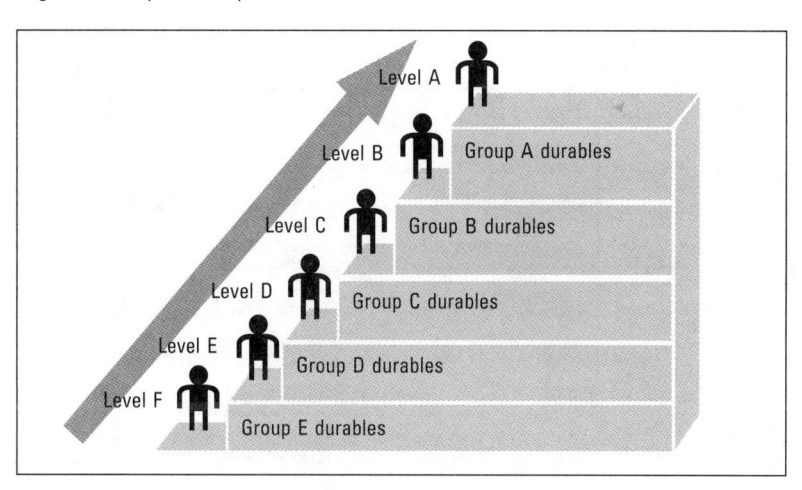

```
                  Level A  👤
              Level B  👤    Group A durables
          Level C  👤        Group B durables
       Level D  👤           Group C durables
     Level E  👤             Group D durables
   Level F  👤               Group E durables
```

Trends

Looking at the trends of distribution of the Mono-Mochi levels among Asian youths in 1995 and 1997, some drastic changes were observed in Asia.

Figure 5-3 shows the distribution of the six levels in major Asian cities in 1995. Youth in Bangkok led in affluence, followed by young people in the three cities in China, while youth in Jakarta were the poorest.

In 1997, the order of affluence has drastically changed: the three Chinese cities, particularly Shanghai, now lead the Asian cities in the level of wealth (see Figure 5-4). The degree of change in China can be regarded as being quite drastic and unheard of in other world markets, a reflection of Asian potential and dynamism.

In Bangkok, the Mono-Mochi C level has increased. As more young people fell into the C level, the difference in affluence in Bangkok has become smaller over the two years. This probably indicates that poorer young people benefited from the Thai economic boom from 1994 to early 1997 and now enjoy a better standard of living. On the other hand, the decrease of the B level may indicate that some richer young people were badly hit by the depreciation of the Thai currency in July 1997 and the recession that followed. Indonesia remains the poorest country and Jakarta lags far behind other major cities.

104 | Asian Youth and Implications for Marketing Strategies

FIGURE 5-3
Level distribution in Asian youth in 1995

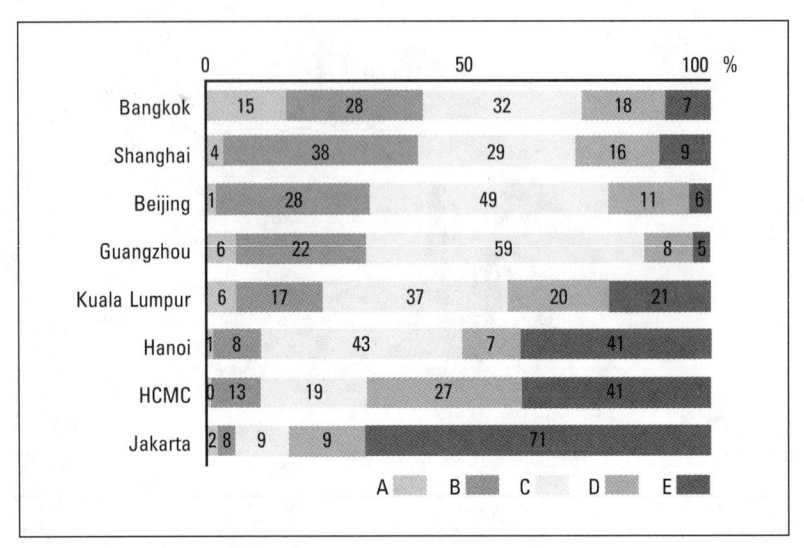

City	A	B	C	D	E
Bangkok	15	28	32	18	7
Shanghai	4	38	29	16	9
Beijing	1	28	49	11	6
Guangzhou	6	22	59	8	5
Kuala Lumpur	6	17	37	20	21
Hanoi	1	8	43	7	41
HCMC	0	13	19	27	41
Jakarta	2	8	9	9	71

N = 2,271 people in their twenties.

FIGURE 5-4
Level distribution in Asian youth in 1997

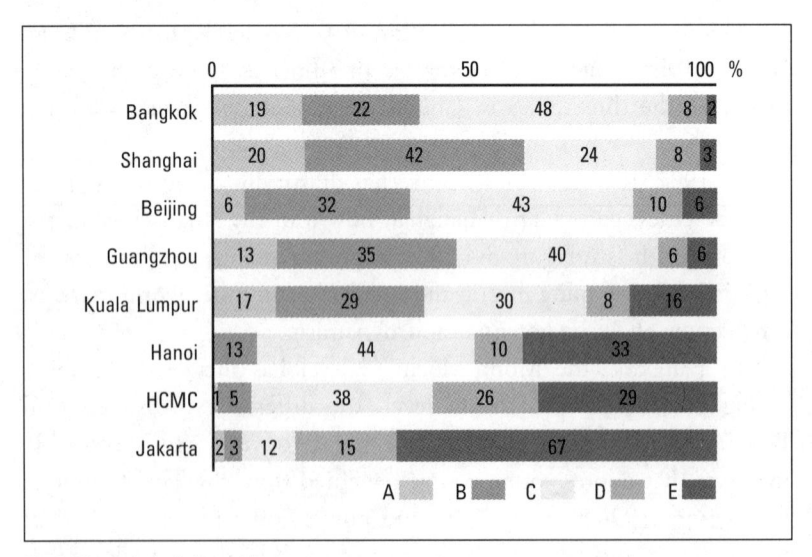

City	A	B	C	D	E
Bangkok	19	22	48	8	2
Shanghai	20	42	24	8	3
Beijing	6	32	43	10	6
Guangzhou	13	35	40	6	6
Kuala Lumpur	17	29	30	8	16
Hanoi	13	44	10	33	
HCMC	1	5	38	26	29
Jakarta	2	3	12	15	67

N = 2,271 people in their twenties.

Changes in Consumption Attitudes in Asian Youth

In order to look at the changes in consumption attitudes and behavior of people in their twenties, an "active/steady consumption style scale"[1] was used to compare between 1995 and 1997. The respondent was asked to rate five statements on a five-point scale.

Analyzing the resulting data of this scale, three major common trends among Asian youths were found. First, they are increasingly becoming price conscious. Two contrasting statements, "I buy quality goods even if they are beyond my budget" versus "I may accept lower quality to stay within my budget," were shown to respondents, who were asked to indicate preference using a five-point scale. Many of them were inclined to choose "lower quality to stay within my budget." (See also Figure 5-5.)

Secondly, the eagerness of Asian youth for branded products has weakened drastically, particularly in Bangkok. Even in Shanghai, which has not been hit by recession and where affluence levels have increased, branded products are not favored as before (see Figure 5-6).

Thirdly, interest in new things seems to have waned, as shown in Figure 5-7, which compares preference for the latest models of products and interest in new fashion trends among Asian youths between 1995 and 1997.

In the good old days of the Asian economic boom (from 1993 to early 1997), young people were fascinated with foreign brands or big brand names and were attracted by the latest goods and models. They placed much more importance on quality than price without much consideration for their budget. However, these very materialistic attitudes observed in 1995 have changed into more cautious and more mature attitudes. A number of reasons are considered to be behind this change. Experience of the Asian economic crisis and perhaps personal

---

[1] The active/steady consumption style scale was developed by Dentsu Inc. Dentsu has been conducting a Japanese Lifestyle Survey since 1976 to observe the trends of Japanese attitudes toward consumption and lifestyles. Resulting data accumulated from 1976 to 1989 were factor-analyzed and three major dimensions that group Japanese people's core lifestyle attitudes were found. "Active/steady consumption style" is one of them. A scale was devised based on this factor to measure chronological changes in consumption activeness and it has been used by Dentsu in its own consumer research conducted in Japan. Five contrasting statements are used and respondents are asked to indicate preference for each on a five-point scale. Calculating all the scores, an average figure is derived to indicate activeness in consumption. The higher their scores are, the more active consumers they are. Dentsu applied this scale in its consumer research to compare Asian consumers with Japanese.

Figure 5-5
Activeness of consumption in Asian youth: preference for "I buy quality goods even if they are beyond my budget"

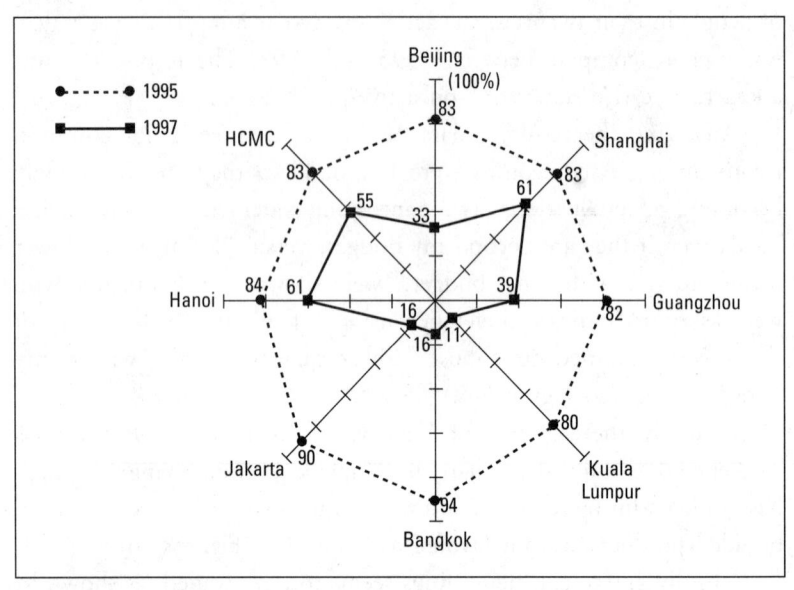

N = 2,271 people in their twenties.

Figure 5-6
Brand-oriented attitudes in Asian youth

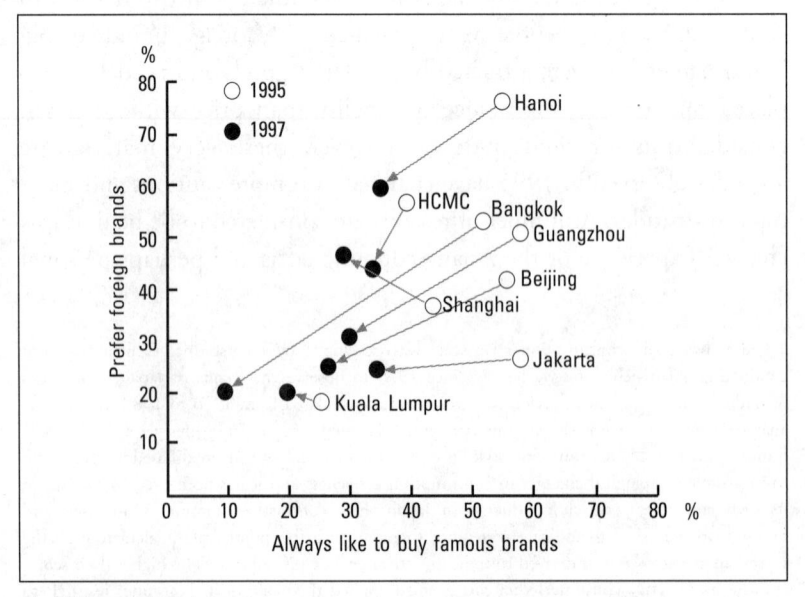

N = 2,271 people in their twenties.

FIGURE 5-7
Interest in new things

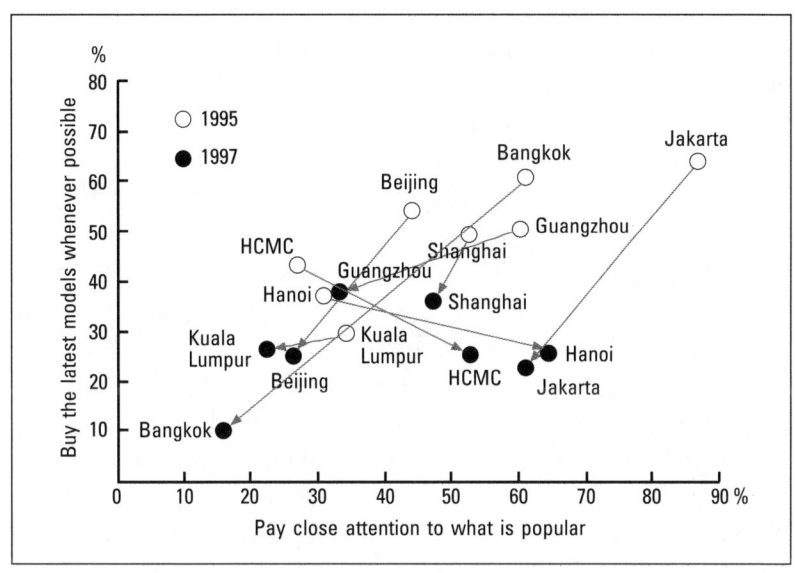

[Figure: scatter plot with x-axis "Pay close attention to what is popular" (0–90%) and y-axis "Buy the latest models whenever possible" (0–80%), comparing 1995 (open circles) and 1997 (filled circles) for Bangkok, Shanghai, Beijing, Guangzhou, Kuala Lumpur, Hanoi, HCMC, Jakarta.]

N = 2,271 people in their twenties.

setbacks should not be discounted. Also, because young people have attained a certain level of affluence, the heightened interest in or, rather, the frantic mood for consumption in 1995 may have cooled down in 1997. Moreover, a number of local products of good quality have been emerging in the market. Thus, young people may no longer feel the need to rush into the purchase of expensive products.

The average scores for active/steady consumption in each city and in different age groups in 1995 and 1997 are shown in Table 5-1.

TABLE 5-1
Average scores for active/steady consumption by generation and by city

		Bangkok	Shanghai	Beijing	Guangzhou	Kuala Lumpur	Hanoi	HCMC	Jakarta
20s	1995	11.2	10.2	11.3	12.6	10.0	12.2	11.8	11.1
	1997	8.5	11.9	10.8	11.0	10.5	13.1	11.4	10.5
30s	1995	10.6	12.7	10.3	11.5	9.6	12.0	11.2	10.8
	1997	7.8	11.1	10.0	9.8	10.2	12.3	11.1	10.4
40s	1995	10.2	9.2	9.2	10.0	9.8	11.1	11.1	10.5
	1997	7.9	9.9	8.5	9.3	10.2	12.7	11.2	9.8

CHANGES IN LIFESTYLE VALUES IN ASIAN YOUTH

Among young people, attitudes toward life and their ways of living seem to have matured steadily. In the survey, one question about lifestyle principles ("What are the values you feel are important in life?") consists of a choice of 16 words that describe important values in life. From the 16 conceptual words, respondents were asked to choose all those words that they considered important and tried to emulate in their life.

Between 1995 and 1997, young people's desire to enhance their own uniqueness, seek more social refinement, and live more creatively have increased greatly in many cities (see Figures 5-8 to 5-10).

In order to see the patterns of life values across major cities and generations, a factor-analysis was applied to the results. Two important factors emerged as major dimensions grouping people's core lifestyle values: traditional groupism (the first dimension, horizontal axis in Figure 5-11) and modern individualism (the second dimension, vertical axis). The former is considered to be a typical Asian value.

When the results were plotted, they clearly show differences between cities and between generations. People in their twenties have become more individualistic and are moving away from traditional groupism in nearly all the cities, although there are differences in degree and in patterns between the cities.

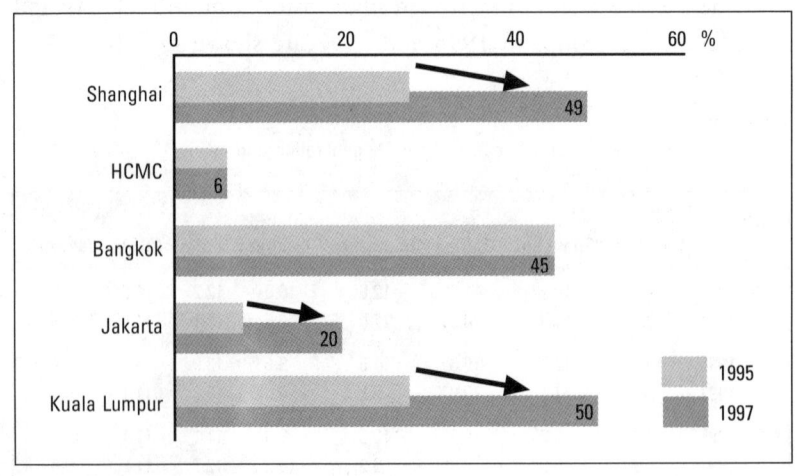

FIGURE 5-8
Life values of Asian youth: uniqueness and individualism

City	1997 value
Shanghai	49
HCMC	6
Bangkok	45
Jakarta	20
Kuala Lumpur	50

N = people in their twenties.

For instance, youth in Beijing, a politically important city, still value groupism while those in Shanghai and Guangzhou have become drastically individualistic. In the Chinese cities in particular, the generation gap is too wide to be easily reconciled, and this might lead to social unrest in the future.

FIGURE 5-9
Life values of Asian youth: social refinement

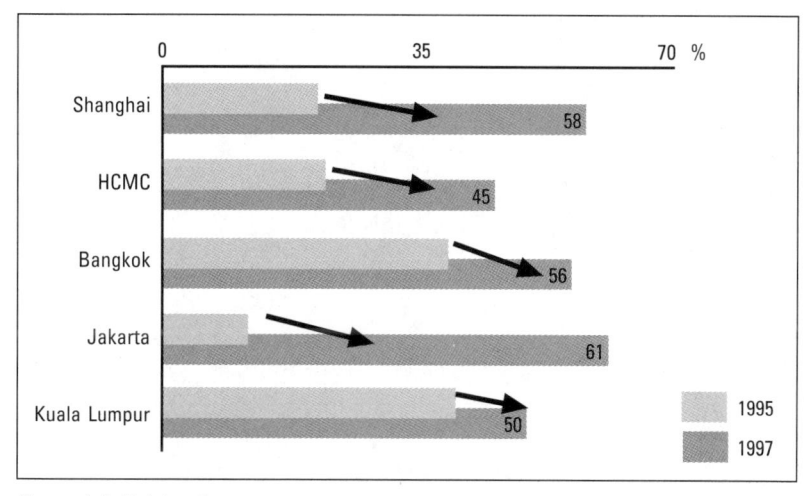

City	1995	1997
Shanghai		58
HCMC		45
Bangkok		56
Jakarta		61
Kuala Lumpur		50

N = people in their twenties.

FIGURE 5-10
Life values of Asian youth: creativity

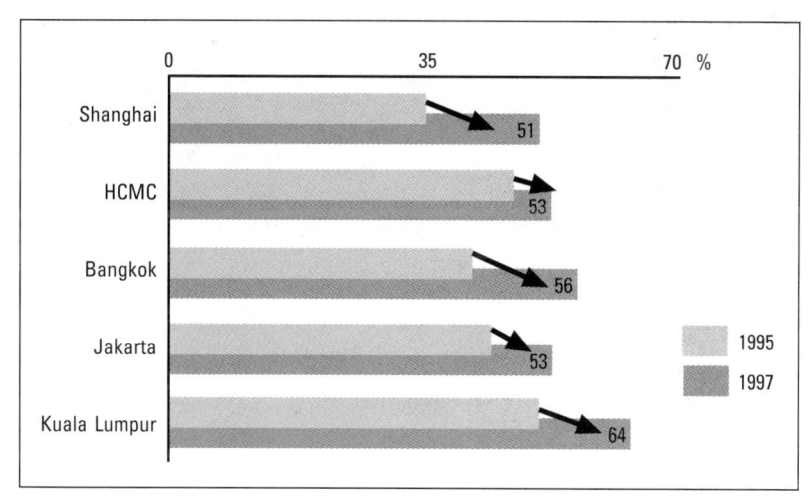

City	1995	1997
Shanghai		51
HCMC		53
Bangkok		56
Jakarta		53
Kuala Lumpur		64

N = people in their twenties.

FIGURE 5-11
Value map: modern individualism versus traditional groupism

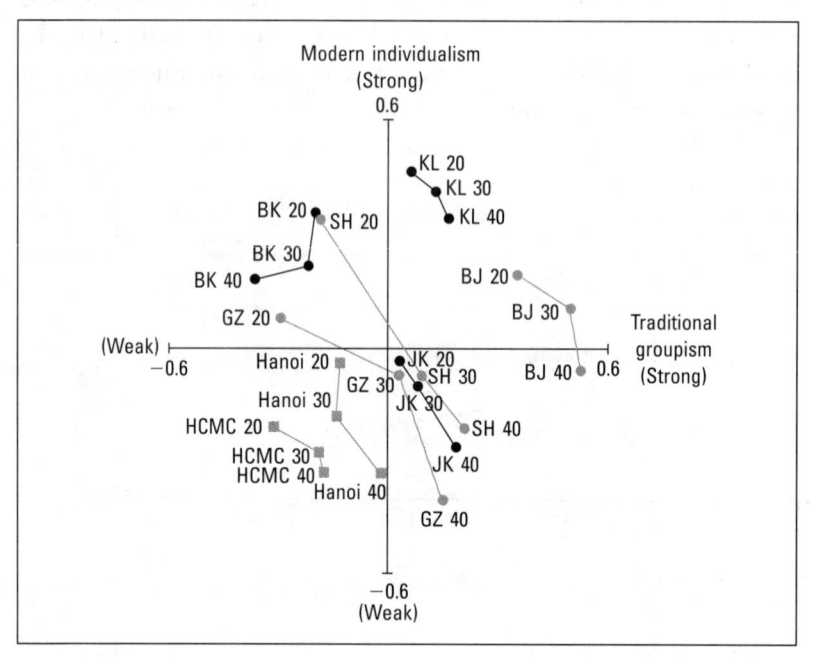

[Figure: Scatter plot with axes "Modern individualism (Strong) 0.6" (vertical, top) to "(Weak) -0.6" (vertical, bottom), and "(Weak) -0.6" (horizontal, left) to "Traditional groupism (Strong) 0.6" (horizontal, right). Data points plotted include: KL 20, KL 30, KL 40, BK 20, SH 20, BK 30, BK 40, BJ 20, BJ 30, GZ 20, Hanoi 20, JK 20, GZ 30, SH 30, BJ 40, Hanoi 30, JK 30, HCMC 20, SH 40, HCMC 30, HCMC 40, JK 40, Hanoi 40, GZ 40.]

N = all samples.

SHADES OF DIFFERENCES IN ASIAN YOUTH

From past studies of our consumer research, we found that there are some similarities among Asian youths in different countries in terms of lifestyle attitudes. Four characteristics were observed to be major trends common in young people in Asia:

- Strong materialistic desires
- Success-oriented
- Inclined to show off
- Sensitive and adaptive to global trends

The survey in 1997 then included a value scale to measure the trends and the differences between cities in the aforementioned Asian values. The value scale is made up of the following components to measure each of the four characteristics:

- Materialism scale
- Achievement motivation scale

- Peer influence scale
- Global influence scale

We will discuss the results of the achievement motivation scale in this paper. The scale was originally developed by Horino and Mori (1987) in Japan to measure the strength of motivation when people want to achieve something. They set two major dimensions in achievement motivation. One is "self-satisfaction," which is the pursuit of personally valuable objectives or fulfillment of one's desires, regardless of the opinions of others. The other is "competition," which places importance on success in society and on winning a better position over rivals.

Based on this scale, Dentsu's project team conducted a pre-test in other Asian countries and modified the scale to the Asian context. There are eight statements for the scale. Each gauges the respondent's agreement with the statement on a five-point scale. By giving scores to the respondent's answers and calculating them, three measurable dimensions emerged. The first is the degree of self-satisfaction, the second the degree of competition, and the third an overall degree of success orientation. It must be noted that the overall degree of success orientation is not a dimension developed by Horino and Mori. In our study, we refer to the total score as a measure of the pursuit of personal success, whether it is motivated by self-satisfaction or competition. The more a respondent is motivated by self-satisfaction or competition, the more he or she could be regarded as pursuing personal success.

Table 5-2 shows the average scores for "competition" in each city and age group, and Figure 5-12 shows that the degree of desire for success varies greatly between the countries. For instance, it is very strong in Beijing and Hanoi, but relatively weak in Bangkok.

Further analysis reveals the degrees of differences in the two dimensions (Figure 5-13). The desire for success by competition is very strong in China, while the need for self-satisfaction is higher in Vietnam. In contrast, the desire for overt success is relatively weak in Bangkok. One of the reasons may be that Thailand is less affected by foreign influence or political turmoil than countries such as China and Vietnam. Also, Buddhism does not encourage competition with others. Thai culture is well known for *mai pen rai*, meaning "never mind, let it be," which may have shaped the way of life and the unique values and traditions of Thailand.

Table 5-2
Achievement motivation scale: scores for "competition"

	Bangkok	Shanghai	Beijing	Guangzhou	Kuala Lumpur	Hanoi	HCMC	Jakarta
20s	16.9	20.1	19.7	19.3	19.3	18.7	17.5	18.1
30s	15.9	20.3	19.7	19.2	18.7	18.4	16.1	17.3
40s	15.3	19.8	19.4	18.9	18.6	17.6	16.7	17.2

Figure 5-12
Success orientation scale (total scores)

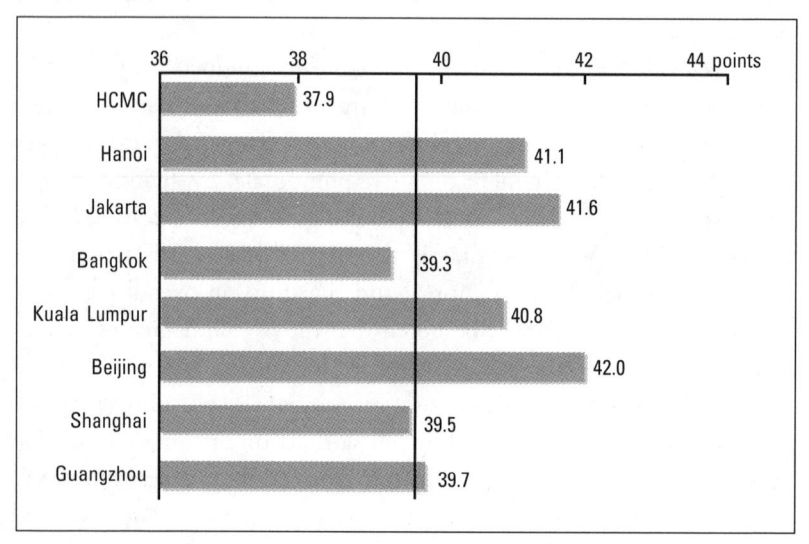

HCMC	37.9
Hanoi	41.1
Jakarta	41.6
Bangkok	39.3
Kuala Lumpur	40.8
Beijing	42.0
Shanghai	39.5
Guangzhou	39.7

N = 2,271 people in their twenties.

Concluding Remarks

From the analyses in this paper, Asian youth's consumption dynamics can be summarized as follows:

1. There is growing affluence despite some setbacks, notably a drastic increase in wealth in China. While there have been steady changes in Vietnam and Malaysia, both improvements and setbacks have occurred in Thailand.
2. The emerging sophistication in consumption attitudes among Asian youths can be perceived as a progression from the first stage of materialistic attitude. The financial crisis in Asia has accelerated the trend.

Figure 5-13
Direction of success orientation

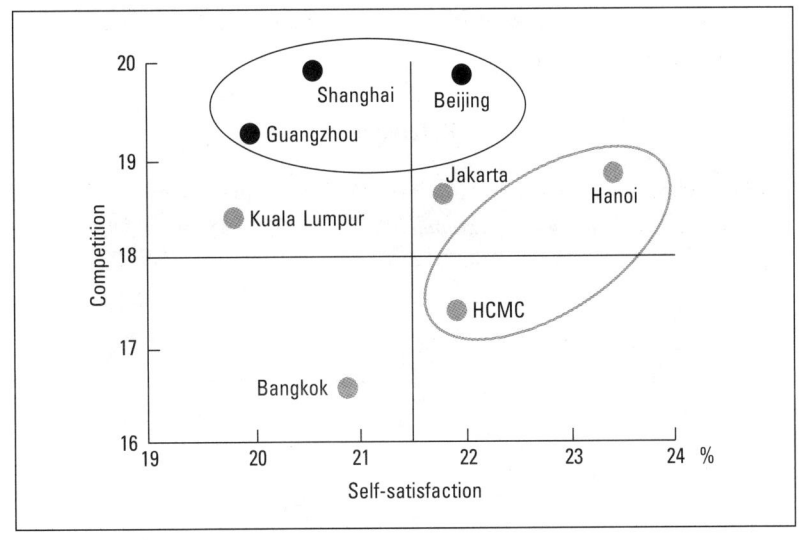

[Scatter plot with axes: Competition (y-axis, 16–20) vs. Self-satisfaction (x-axis, 19–24%). Data points: Shanghai (~20.5, 19.8), Beijing (~22, 19.8), Guangzhou (~20.5, 19.6), Jakarta (~22, 18.7), Hanoi (~23.5, 18.8), Kuala Lumpur (~20.5, 18.4), HCMC (~22, 17.5), Bangkok (~21, 16.5). Shanghai, Beijing, Guangzhou grouped in one ellipse; Jakarta, Hanoi, HCMC grouped in another.]

N = 2,271 people in their twenties.

3. There are growing modern, individualistic values and a move away from traditional groupism among Asian youths. This value shift was seen in 1995 as well and has not been affected by economic setbacks in 1997.
4. Overall, it can be said that young consumers have gained materialistic affluence and concomitant practicality and confidence in themselves in this short period. They are increasingly mature; in other words, becoming closer to young consumers in developed countries.
5. Asian youth are progressing in the same direction and share similar lifestyle values and traits, regardless of the country of residence. However, the degrees of similarities vary between countries.

For marketing people involved in Asia, the differences between areas and between generations has to be taken into account in marketing planning and execution. This paper suggests that a successful marketing strategy will not depend simply on how well we measure similarities or differences of a certain group. Nor should it encourage researchers to determine the markets as being "similar or different" based simply on "yes or no" answers in research findings. We would like to suggest a "degrees of differences" analysis using a particular set of similar values and traits. Subsequent implications may be extracted from such studies to formulate effective marketing planning and execution.

Reference

Horino, Midori and Kazuyo Mori (1987). Factor analysis of achievement motivation. *Study on Educational Psychology*, 35: 148–54.

ASIAN CULTURE AND THE GLOBAL CONSUMER

Hellmut Schütte

> *Asia is a crucially important market for international companies. But what sort of marketing strategy should be applied to it? Does conspicuous consumption of Western goods there indicate the presence of "global consumers," for whom Western strategies are appropriate? The answer is "no": despite globalization, regional culture remains the strongest influence on consumer behavior. Whereas Western consumers are motivated by a desire for individual expression, Asian consumers tend to seek status within a social group. This paper details the ways in which this difference manifests itself and argues that marketers who do not recognize its strength are guilty of wishful thinking.*

INTRODUCTION

In recent decades, Asia has been home to many of the world's most dynamic markets. The region contains about 50 percent of the world's population and, despite the recent economic crisis, represents a significant portion of the world's economy. For this reason, few international companies can afford to ignore Asia as a market of primary importance, despite the present crisis in parts of the region. Yet there is a surprising paucity of work that establishes a marketing theory specific to Asia. Most practitioners apply marketing concepts in

---

Hellmut Schütte is Affiliate Professor of International Management at INSEAD. He has spent and continues to spend half of his life in Asia, both as an executive and as an academic.

Copyright © 2000 by Hellmut Schütte.

the region developed from a distinctly Western (and primarily U.S.) perspective.

The underlying assumption is that consumers around the world are driven by similar needs and desires, and that consumer behavior is universal. This thinking is very much in line with the trend toward global markets and global competition. However, as consumer behavior is strongly influenced by culture and Asian culture is distinctly different from Western culture, one may doubt whether many global consumers can be found in Asia. Cultural bonds run deep and different tastes, habits, and customs prevent consumers from universally preferring the same product attributes, advertising messages, packaging, and presentation.

The advent of the global product, one has to remember, is not the result of consumers' preferences for products available worldwide. Global products are being *pushed* upon consumers as companies try to capture savings through standardization, rather than *pulled* by them.

The immense popularity of Western luxury goods among high-income earners and teenagers in Asia is therefore not proof that they have joined the global bandwagon. They may try the same goods but for different reasons. Brand-name goods such as a Louis Vuitton bag may be bought more for "face" reasons and the importance of the regard of others than from an individual preference for the product. Remy Martin cognac and Lafitte red wine may not be consumed because consumers really prefer it over local liquor or beer but because of peer pressure.

Strong market positions can therefore be built on foundations different from those in the West and requiring different marketing activities. In other words, an approach especially geared toward an Asian culture may be less efficient in terms of standardization and globalization but more efficient in terms of creating value for the consumers and, thus, in earning higher returns.

ASIAN CULTURE

Culture has a profound impact on how individuals perceive who they are, what they are allowed to do, and what their role is as a member of society. These perceptions are often so thoroughly internalized that they are difficult to express explicitly, but they are revealed through behavior such as consumption. This is one means through which individuals express who they perceive themselves to be and who they aspire to be.

Although Asia is culturally more heterogeneous than, for example, Europe, the emphasis on social harmony is an overriding and unifying belief across all societies. Asian societies are fundamentally collectivist, meaning that the rights of the individual are subordinated to those of the group. This is considered necessary in order not to disturb social harmony. Such thinking, grounded in Confucianism, Buddhism, and Islam, contrasts sharply with Western individualism. The difference is profound and has major implications for consumer behavior. While Asians tend to identify themselves in terms of their social frame or relationships, Westerners define themselves in terms of personal attributes or achievements.

Of course, all societies were traditionally more collectivist than individualist due to the interdependence characteristic of agrarian communities. Individualism has come to be considered a natural component of a "modern" society. However, Asian cultures are now challenging this assumption. Japan, a "modern," first-world nation by any standard, is still strongly collectivist. South Korea, Hong Kong, Singapore, and Taiwan, too, are all thoroughly modern societies that continue to have firmly entrenched collectivist orientations.

Collectivism in Asia expresses itself in a number of ways, some of which are described below.

Belongingness

Much emphasis is placed on belonging to a group, which implies an individual's identification with a collective goal. There is strong concern about acceptance by peers, anxiety about exclusion, and a near compulsion to be always among the in-group. Thus, individual desires are secondary to those of the group, since belonging is the ultimate satisfaction. This strong sense of belongingness is an anchor for self-identity, which in turn demands the individual's loyalty to the group.

Reciprocity

The rules concerning reciprocity and the ways in which it is conceived tend to be far more formalized and binding than in the West. They reflect the importance placed upon relationships and social ties in a collectivist culture and acknowledge the embeddedness of individuals in groups. Gift-giving is seen as the most immediate and tangible means of cultivating *guanxi* (in Chinese cultures), or fulfilling *on* or discharging *giri* (in Japan). Whether or how well a person observes the intricate etiquette of gift-giving is essential to assessing that person's social character.

Self-esteem

Cultural differences also appear in self-appraisal of one's expertise or lack thereof and self-esteem can be correspondingly high or low. Education in the U.S., in particular, tries to instill in students a sense of high self-esteem in order to motivate them to achievement and self-confidence. Children are encouraged to be assertive and self-assured. Asian children, on the other hand, are taught the values of modesty and self-effacement, which are considered conducive to cultivation of the mind. This is not to say that Asians lack self-respect, rather that they do not assume they automatically deserve to regard themselves with esteem in comparison with others.

Group Conformity

Stronger pressure is placed upon the individual in Asia to conform to group norms than in individualist societies. The desire to be different, an essential element in Western culture and consumer behavior, exists in Asia too. However, it implies being different as a member of a group in comparison with other groups, while complying with the norms of the individual's group. An Asian consumer who deviates from the group norm may be treated as an outsider who does not know how to adjust to the group.

Status

Within the context of typically highly hierarchical Asian societies, individuals are always conscious of their place in a group, institution, or society as a whole and of the proper behavior, dress, and speech corresponding to status. They are also extremely aware of the need to maintain their own dignity, or face, and that of others.

Careful attention is given to purchasing products whose price, brand, and packaging match one's social standing. In terms of personal appearance, the color, material, and style of clothing should match an individual's status, which is defined by age, gender, occupation, and so on. In Japan, for example, a married woman's kimono is much more subdued in color than a single woman's.

Product Diffusion

In most Asian cultures uncertainty is strongly avoided, resulting in consumer behavior exhibiting high brand-name consciousness, brand loyalty, greater insistence on quality, and the active use of reference groups and opinion leaders. Shopping tends to be done in groups and new products are more slowly accepted. While consumers worldwide are concerned about monetary, functional, physical, psychological, and social risks, Asians tend to be more sensitive to social risk than Westerners.

In traditional Western diffusion theory, consumers are categorized in relation to others by their speed in adopting a new product. The five categories often cited are innovators, early adopters, early majority, late majority, and laggards. These categories are generally depicted as a symmetrical, bell-shaped distribution curve (see Figure 6-1). Very few Asian consumers, however, are prepared to take the social risk of being innovators by trying a new product first. The discomfort of being left behind, however, induces them to follow suit if they think that others have tried it. Trials by early buyers thus soften the perceived risk for followers, who are then inclined to "jump aboard" hastily.

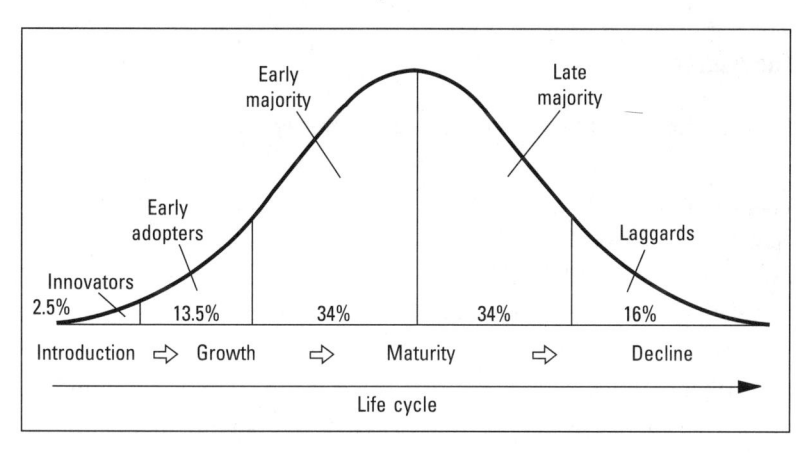

Figure 6-1
Diffusion of innovation: the Western concept

This suggests that the percentage of both innovators and laggards is much lower among Asian consumers, resulting in a steeper distribution curve (see Figure 6-2). The curve will also no longer be symmetrical, as it is thought to be in the West: the left tail will be longer, reflecting hesitancy to try the new product, and the right tail will drop off sharply, as consumers are ready to switch brand once the standards of their reference group change. Referral is thus a very powerful way of expanding product trials by the first wave of consumers.

FIGURE 6-2
Diffusion of innovation in an Asian context

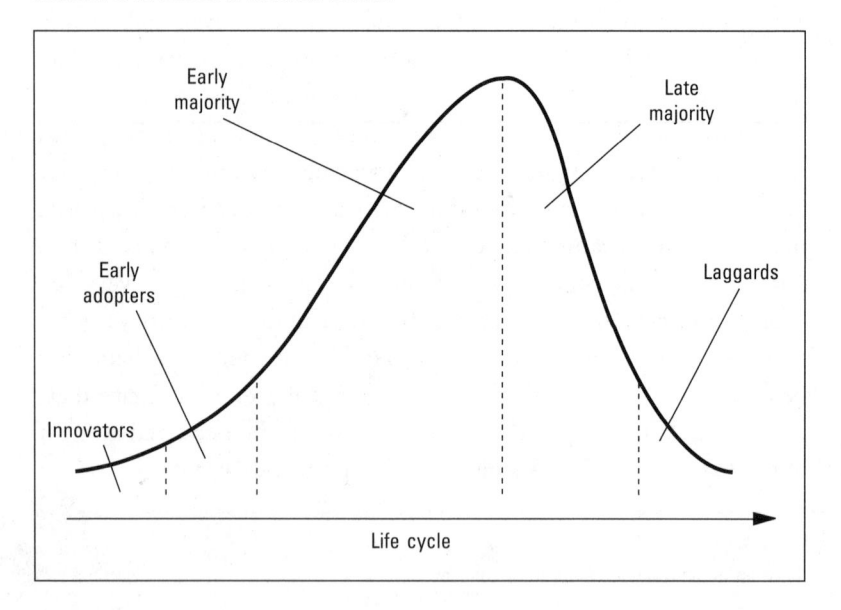

Faddism

Instilled from childhood, reinforced by the educational system, and solidified by peer pressure, the desire to conform is the engine behind faddism in Asia. Once risk-aversion is overcome, the speed of diffusion is dramatic, particularly in Japan, where product life cycles can be extremely short. Faddism in Japan is facilitated by a homogeneous population and an efficient, widespread, and centralized mass media. Everyone seems to be reading, watching, talking about, or doing the same thing at any one time. Faddism covers not only the rapid diffusion of material culture or gadgetry such as the world-famous *tamagotchi* (an electronic pet), but it also includes modes of behavior, including vocabulary. New words, typically a mix of Japanese and English, seem to be born overnight and spoken by everyone the next day.

Conspicuous Consumption

The importance of gaining social recognition turns Asians into probably the most image-conscious consumers in the world. The importance of status makes it imperative to project the "right" image, which usually means up-market and prestigious. The social acceptability of conspicuous consumption in Asia corresponds with the high regard for hierarchy. Differences in hierarchical level and power are expected to be visible. Conspicuous consumption, therefore, corresponds directly with status propriety. Status-conscious Asians will not hesitate to spend freely on premium brands such as BMW, Mercedes-Benz, and the best Scotch whisky and French cognac. Mercedes-Benz's highest market share worldwide is in Asian markets. The French luxury group LVMH sells more than 50 percent of its wares to Asian consumers.

Times have changed with the economic troubles in Japan since the beginning of the 1990s and in many other parts of Asia since autumn 1997. It should not be presumed, however, that brands have lost their luster for the Asian consumer. The need for recognition is deep seated. Experience in Japan has proved, and reports from Southeast Asia indicate, that demand for luxury products is not disappearing, although it is becoming far more selective.

MOTIVATION AND NEEDS

Comparing some of the distinctive features of Asian culture with those in cultures of the West, we are better able to understand the motives behind consumption decisions. The two most important questions to answer are

- *what* are the needs consumers are seeking to meet?
- *why* do they choose to meet them in the way they do?

Years ago the psychologist Abraham Maslow proposed his five-tiered "hierarchy of needs," a means of understanding motivation that has gained general acceptance. Each level of the hierarchy specifies a certain type of need, ranked in order of importance from lower- to higher-level needs: from physiological needs to safety, belonging, prestige, and, ultimately, self-actualization (see Figure 6-3).

This hierarchy, although originally proposed as a means of understanding personal growth, is also an appropriate way of explaining the needs and motivations of consumers. The lowest level at which an individual experiences an as yet unsatisfied need serves to motivate the individual's behavior. Upon satisfaction of that need, a still higher need will emerge, again motivating the consumer to fulfill it. As no need is ever completely satisfied, dissatisfaction continuously creates new demands.

Maslow's hierarchy seems particularly suited to Western culture, especially with regard to his description of self-actualization as the highest category of need. In the case of the Asian consumer, however, we must question the definition of and even the very existence of such needs. As Asians, like everyone else, must first be fed and then protected in order to survive, changes are not required as far as physical needs are concerned. However, it is debatable whether self-actualization as a personally directed need actually exists for the Asian consumer. Rather, it may be a socially directed need reflecting a desire to enhance one's image and position through contributions to society.

Among the collectivist cultures of Asia, the idea that personal needs are the highest level of need would be neither readily accepted nor positively regarded by others. Indeed, the emphasis on achieving

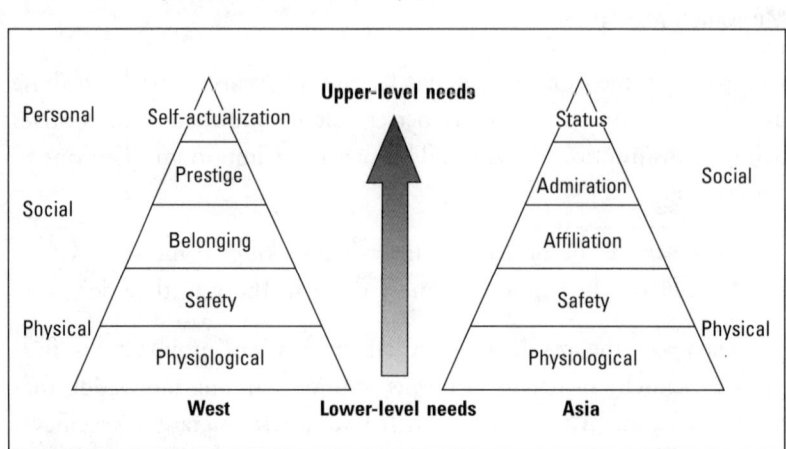

FIGURE 6-3
Maslow's hierarchy of needs and the Asian equivalent

West	Asia
Personal: Self-actualization	Status
Social: Prestige	Admiration (Social)
Belonging	Affiliation
Physical: Safety	Safety
Physiological	Physiological (Physical)

Upper-level needs ↑ Lower-level needs

independence, autonomy, and freedom characteristic of Western cultures is strikingly absent from Asian cultures. In the Asian context, the highest level of satisfaction is not derived from actions directed at the self but from the reactions of others to the individual. Therefore, a more accurate hierarchy of needs in the Asian context is one that eliminates the personally directed self-actualization need and instead emphasizes the intricacies and importance of social needs. The social needs of belonging and prestige can in fact be broken down into three levels: affiliation, admiration, and status.

Affiliation is the acceptance of an individual as a member of a group. In the family this acceptance is automatic, but in most other groups certain qualifications must be met in order to join. In terms of consumer behavior, the affiliation need will encourage conformity with group norms.

Once affiliation has been attained, the individual will desire the **admiration** of those in the group. This is a higher-level need and requires effort, as admiration must typically be earned through acts that demand the respect of others.

Next the individual will want the **status** arising from the esteem of society at large. Fulfillment of this need requires the regard of outsiders, whereas fulfillment of the admiration need occurs on a more intimate level. The status level most closely resembles the Western need for prestige and manifests itself in conspicuous consumption.

Modernization or Westernization?

At present, talk of a "global consumer culture" in which people are united by common devotion to certain brands, movie stars, and musical celebrities is generally understood to mean the global presence of Western culture. Western companies marketing products in Asia may be tempted to believe that, given time, consumers in Asia will become more like Western consumers. Therefore, if we were to wait long enough, marketing strategies developed in the West would be perfectly appropriate to the Asian consumer. This may be a fallacy or wishful thinking on the part of marketing gurus.

What Asian countries are experiencing is not "Westernization" or even "globalization" but "modernization." Modernization may be interpreted as Westernization because it is a social change initiated by the West. True Westernization, however, would assume that non-

Western countries will become like the West. This cannot be the case because Asia prior to modernization had its own deeply rooted cultures, which continue strongly to influence people's upbringing and behavior. As Asians themselves would argue, a century of modernization cannot erase millennia of cultural development.

The high level of consumption of Western goods is typically used as an argument for the loss of Asian culture in favor of Westernization. That consumption is so visible, however, is testimony to the fact that it is not the norm but the exception. Even with the fame of McDonald's and Domino's pizza in Asia, 98 percent of all restaurants in Asia serve indigenous food. In Indonesia, the advent of *teh botol* (bottled tea) has been to the detriment of sales of Coke and Pepsi, and consumption of *kretek* clove cigarettes has not declined in the least despite the success of the Marlboro man. There may not be so many "global consumers" in Asia after all.

THE EFFECTS OF LANGUAGE ON MARKETING
A Comparison of the Use of Chinese and English Idioms in Print Advertisements

Elison A.C. Lim

The prevalence of both Chinese and English idioms in advertising suggests that idioms have the ability to improve communication effectiveness. Despite differences in the two languages, this paper shows that Chinese and English idioms can be categorized using the same idiom characteristics: type of meaning, decomposability, and familiarity. Among other points raised, this paper argues that while Chinese and English idioms may have both literal and figurative meanings, Chinese idioms are more easily understood than English idioms even when consumers are less familiar with the idioms. Further, it suggests that Chinese idioms generally elicit more imagery than English idioms. Based on the similarities and differences in the characteristics of idioms in the two languages, and the differences in their abilities to elicit imagery, some guidelines on the appropriate use of Chinese and English idioms in advertising are advanced.

INTRODUCTION

Spoken by more people than any other language, Chinese is used by more than twice the number of people compared to the English language. In fact, the Chinese language is used not only in China, but

---

Elison A.C. Lim is a doctoral student at the Faculty of Business Administration, National University of Singapore.

Copyright © 2000 by Elison A.C. Lim.

also in Taiwan, Thailand, Hong Kong, Malaysia, Singapore, and Vietnam. Although the Chinese language is not as universally accepted as English, it is gaining popularity as Chinese-speaking countries like China open their doors to foreign investors. It is thus not surprising that the study of the Chinese language has attracted much research in recent years (Perfetti and Zhang, 1991; Zhang and Simon, 1985), and especially so when studied against the English language (Huang and Hanley, 1994; Tavassoli, 1999; Yu et al., 1985).

Yang (1988) observed that Chinese print ads often use a smooth flow of words and poetic phrasing. Further, the use of idioms in Chinese print ads is not uncommon. For instance, Singapore Press Holdings used the idiom 一触即发 *yi chu ji fa* (which literally means "to erupt at the touch of the finger") to promote the ability of its mini-ads to make a large impact. Even in English ads, the use of idioms is an emerging trend. For example, Singapore Telecom used the idiom "paint the town red" in its ad headlines for its anniversary celebrations. In a world where consumers are increasingly skeptical about the motives of advertisers, the use of idioms in an ad makes the ad stand out from the conventional clutter, thus achieving the initial step of capturing consumers' attention and encouraging them to read on. The effectiveness of the ad is therefore increased.

Despite the increasing popularity of idioms in ad language, there are no existing guidelines that advertisers can follow to ensure that the use of idioms enhances, rather than jeopardizes, ad effectiveness. It is therefore the objective of this paper to generate such guidelines, which advertisers can follow when selecting idioms for use in ads. This paper first reviews published literature on two languages, Chinese and English. By cross-examining the Chinese and English languages, it provides an understanding of the different processing styles required to comprehend information written in each language. Next it compares Chinese and English idioms using three idiom characteristics—type of meaning, decomposability, and familiarity—and in their ability to evoke imagery. Finally, this paper concludes with a discussion of advertising implications concerning the use of Chinese and English idioms in ads.

Processing Chinese and English Words: A Comparison

The English language follows an alphabetic writing system with four structural levels (i.e., letter, word, phrase, and sentence) while the Chinese language follows a logographic writing system with at least five structural levels (i.e., radical, character, word, phrase, and sentence) (Zhang and Simon, 1985). In its written form, Chinese seems to be a more complicated language given that 7,000 characters are employed in general use while English words are formed out of merely 26 letters. The most fundamental unit used in written Chinese is the character, or 汉字 *hanzi*. Most of these characters have meaning when used alone, but others only make sense when used in combination with other characters.

In terms of processing, Chinese words have consistently achieved the visual superiority effect, which means that words are better learnt when they are presented visually rather than auditorily (Fang, 1982; Turnage and McGinnies, 1973). On the other hand, studies using English words have yielded ambiguous findings concerning modality effects (Conway and Gathercole, 1987; Engle and Mobley, 1976; Penny, 1989).

Several explanations based on script differences between logographic and alphabetic systems have been proposed for the observed consistency in a visual superiority effect for Chinese words. In an extensive study undertaken by Liu and colleagues (1992), four explanations for the occurrence of the visual superiority effect were reviewed. First, the direct-image hypothesis suggests that because logographs leave image traces of the object they represent while alphabetic words do not, Chinese words map onto their corresponding meaning more directly than English words, resulting in a visual superiority effect. The Chinese character 马 *ma* (horse) is often cited as an example for the direct-image hypothesis because the logograph itself resembles the body of a horse.

An alternative perspective, the discriminability hypothesis, argues that the visual traces left by Chinese logographs as a result of their more unique and distinctive shapes (compared to alphabetic words) explain the occurrence of the visual superiority effect. For instance, the Chinese characters for "file" and "life" are 夹 *jia* and 命 *ming* respectively. While the two English words are visually similar in that both consist of the letters "e," "i," "f," and "l," the Chinese characters have entirely different shapes.

Third, the graphic-feature hypothesis attributes the occurrence of the visual superiority effect to the similarity between Chinese characters within a category. Characters with the same radical often belong to the same category with similar meanings. For instance, 汁 *zhi* (juice), 河 *he* (river), 浪 *lang* (wave), and 汤 *tang* (soup) are all liquids.

Lastly, the long-term priming interpretation asserts that the extent to which words can be recalled depends on the availability of the visual and auditory traces. Under this perspective, there are two types of frequency: visual frequency (e.g., how often words are seen in print) and auditory frequency (e.g., how often words are used in speech). Thus, this view suggests that some words have higher visual frequencies while others have higher auditory frequencies, and the visual superiority effect is observed only for words with high visual frequencies.

Idioms

Since idioms make up "a form of language peculiar to a language, person, or group of people" (*The Concise Oxford Dictionary*, 1995), it is reasonable to assume that some differences between Chinese and English idioms exist. Chinese idioms, or 成语 *chengyu*, consist of four characters, and their meaning is often rooted in history or historical literature. Although English idioms are also short phrases, they do not have a fixed length. English idioms can have as few as three words (e.g., by and large) or as many as six words (e.g., put the cat among the pigeons).

Idiom Characteristics: Type of Meaning, Decomposability, and Familiarity

A review of published psycholinguistic research on idioms (which typically used English idioms as the experimental stimuli) reveals that idioms have some distinct characteristics. First, idioms may possess a literal meaning in addition to its figurative meaning (Popiel and McRae, 1988), with both meanings being apparent to consumers to different degrees. Second, the figurative meaning of some idioms may be inferred from the meanings of their constituent words (Gibbs, 1980). This view, that some idioms are decomposable, is a rather contemporary perspective that opposes the traditional research viewpoint that the figurative meaning of idioms cannot be interpreted from their constituent words alone. The third characteristic, consumers' familiarity with an idiom, represents the degree to which consumers know the meaning of the idiom. Schweigert (1986) identified three categories of idiom: familiar, less familiar, and unfamiliar. In this paper, familiar idioms refer to those that consumers recognize as idioms and whose meaning is known to them. Less familiar idioms are those that consumers recognize as idioms but whose meaning is unknown to them. Lastly, unfamiliar idioms are those that consumers do not recognize as idioms and whose meaning is unknown to them.

Comparison of Chinese and English idioms

Table 7-1 provides some examples of idiom in both languages with different idiom characteristics, and shows that the three idiom characteristics (i.e., type of meaning, decomposability, and familiarity) can be used to describe both Chinese and English idioms. Next, we examine each idiom characteristic separately to see the differences between Chinese and English idioms.

Type of meaning. The first idiom characteristic describes idioms using the type of meaning embedded in idioms. Idioms may have literal and/or figurative meanings. An idiom's literal meaning is the meaning obtained by merely considering the meanings of its individual words. On the other hand, the figurative, or overall, meaning of an idiom may not be obtainable from the meanings of the words alone, but has historical origins that are forgotten. For instance, the English idiom "kick the bucket" has a literal meaning of "to strike the pail with one's foot" but a figurative meaning of "to die."

Both Chinese and English idioms may have only figurative meaning, or both literal and figurative meanings. However, since most Chinese characters have unique meaning on their own, figurative idioms (e.g., 张三李四 *zhang san li si*, which means "any person picked at random") whose characters do not mean anything independently are rarer in the Chinese language than in English. Another interesting phenomenon is that while English idioms do not have literal-only meaning, Chinese idioms with literal-only meaning exist (e.g., 忍无可忍 *ren wu ke ren*). In addition, while Chinese idioms

TABLE 7-1

Examples of Chinese and English idioms bearing different idiom characteristics

Idiom characteristic		Chinese idiom	English idiom
Type of meaning	Literal only	忍无可忍 ren wu ke ren (to exceed one's threshold of forbearance)	NA
	Figurative only	张三李四 zhang san li si (any person picked at random)	By and large (generally speaking)
	Literal and figurative	隔岸观火 ge an guan huo (to watch on while someone is in trouble without offering assistance)	Carry the torch for (to be filled with unreturned love)
Decomposability	Decomposable	温故知新 wen gu zhi xin (to understand the present by reviewing the past)	Miss the boat (to lose an opportunity)
	Less decomposable	张冠李戴 zhang guan li dai (to attribute doings to the wrong person)	Shrinking violet (a very shy person)
	Nondecomposable	NA	Kick the bucket (to die)
Familiarity	Familiar	人山人海 ren shan ren hai (very crowded; packed with people)	Pain in the neck (a troublesome person or thing; a nuisance)
	Less familiar	明珠暗投 ming zhu an tou (a talented person whose potential goes unnoticed or unappreciated)	Upset the applecart (to cause trouble, especially by spoiling someone's plans)
	Unfamiliar	太阿倒持 tai'e dao chi (to come under threat after giving someone one's own authority and power)	Sang-froid (staying calm in a difficult or dangerous situation)

(e.g., 隔岸观火 *ge an guan huo*[1]) with both literal and figurative meanings are hardly used for their literal meaning as nonidiomatic phrases, English idioms with both meanings (e.g., carry the torch for[2]) make sense when used literally, as in the sentence, "During the blackout, I asked John to *carry the torch for* me while I searched for candles." This is perhaps due to the existence of a defined structure for Chinese idioms, which clearly distinguishes them from other nonidiom phrases.

Decomposability. Chinese and English idioms can also be classified into categories depending on their decomposability (see Table 7-1 for examples). Idioms whose component words or characters help one to understand their figurative meaning are termed *decomposable*. For instance, the characters in the Chinese idiom 温故知新 *wen gu zhi xin* mean "to revise or review," "of old," "to know," and "new," respectively. Taken together, the words in the idiom contribute toward the idiom's figurative meaning "to understand the present by reviewing the past." Similarly, the words "miss" and "boat" in the English idiom "miss the boat," which literally means "fail to catch" and "a small vessel propelled on water by engine, oars, or sails" respectively, help one decipher its figurative meaning "to lose an opportunity."

On the other hand, nondecomposable idioms are made up of words or characters that do not help the understanding of their figurative meaning. Such idioms are more common in the English language than in the Chinese language. Nondecomposable English idioms typically have historical origins for the figurative meaning that have been forgotten. For instance, English idioms like "kick the bucket," which has a figurative meaning of "to die" originating from a traditional method of killing pigs, are nondecomposable in nature. Chinese idioms, on the other hand, are seldom nondecomposable; instead, they vary along a decomposability scale ranging from less to more decomposable. For instance, the figurative meaning of the Chinese idiom 张冠李戴 *zhang guan li dai* (i.e., "to attribute doings to the wrong person") cannot be directly inferred from the individual words, but one can guess that two persons must be involved since

---

[1] Literally means "to watch the fire burn from across the shore" but has a figurative meaning of "to watch on while someone is in trouble without offering assistance."

[2] Literally means "to hold a hand-held lamp" but has a figurative meaning of "to be filled with unreturned love."

zhang and *li* represent surnames. In addition, *guan* means "a crown or hat" and *dai*, "to wear." Taken together, it can be inferred from the Chinese characters that something has been passed from one person to another.

Less decomposable idioms lie somewhere in between decomposable and nondecomposable idioms, with their words contributing somewhat to the overall meaning of the idioms (e.g., "shrinking violet" and *zhang guan li dai*).

Familiarity. Familiarity with idioms depends on a number of factors like consumers' native language and education level. For instance, people whose native language is English will be more familiar with English idioms while Chinese people will be more familiar with Chinese idioms.

Both Chinese and English idioms vary on a familiarity continuum, ranging from familiar to less familiar and unfamiliar. These three categories were defined in an earlier section. Examples of idioms with different degrees of familiarity are shown in Table 7-1.

Mental Imagery and the Imagery Potential of Idioms

Mental imagery resembles somewhat the actual experience of perceiving the objects or events, and can occur with or without direct external stimuli (Finke, 1989). The elicitation of mental imagery usually involves the generation of visual images, but sometimes other senses like hearing and smell may be used as well.

Marketing research has demonstrated the mediating role of mental imagery in enhancing ad processing (Babin and Burns, 1997; Childers and Houston, 1984). In addition to using pictures as the stimuli for evoking mental imagery, words may also be used (Paivio, 1965). Words have been shown to evoke imagery to varying degrees (Paivio et al., 1968). Specifically, concrete words are rated high, and abstract words low, in their ability to arouse imagery.

Idioms have been shown to evoke imagery portraying either the literal or figurative meaning (Cacciari and Glucksberg, 1995; Gibbs and O'Brien, 1990). Since concrete words elicit more imagery than abstract words, idioms whose constituent words make sense on their own should elicit more imagery. In the Chinese language, each character in an idiom carries a unique meaning. For instance, every character in the idiom 破釜沉舟 *po fu chen zhou* has a meaning on its own (*po* means "break"; *fu*, "cooking pot"; *chen*, "sink"; and *zhou*, "ship"). On the other hand, not all words used in English idioms have unique meaning. For example, the words "by" and "and" in "by and large" have no meaning on their own. Therefore, the characters in Chinese idioms seem to be both more concrete and meaningful compared to the words in English idioms. Following the research findings of Paivio et al. (1968), Chinese idioms should therefore elicit more imagery than English idioms.

Conclusion and Implications for Marketers

The objective of this paper is to compare Chinese and English idioms and, in so doing, provide marketers with some useful guidelines for ad design. A summary of the similarities and differences between Chinese and English idioms based on three idiom characteristics (i.e., type of meaning, decomposability, and familiarity) is provided in Table 7-2.

There are several implications for marketers arising from the discussion presented in this paper. First, the fact that both Chinese and English idioms may be described by the three characteristics suggests that there are idiom categories with varying suitability for use under

Table 7-2
Similarities and differences between Chinese and English idioms

Idiom characteristic	Chinese idioms vs. English idioms
Type of meaning	• Both Chinese and English idioms may have both literal and figurative meanings. • There are no literal-only English idioms, but Chinese idioms with only literal meaning exist. • There are fewer figurative-only Chinese idioms compared to English idioms.
Decomposability	• Chinese idioms are generally more decomposable than English idioms. • While English idioms can be used literally as nonidiomatic phrases (e.g., "kick the bucket" and "cook his goose"), Chinese idioms are not commonly used as nonidiomatic phrases.
Familiarity	• For both Chinese and English idioms, idiom familiarity depends on consumers' native language. • Both Chinese and English idioms can be classified as familiar, less familiar, and unfamiliar.
Mental imagery	• Chinese idioms elicit more imagery than English idioms.

different conditions. Different categories of idiom should in turn have varying impacts on ad effectiveness, and the selection of idioms for use in both Chinese and English ads alike should follow certain guidelines, and not be ad hoc in nature.

Next, since idioms vary in the extent to which they possess the three idiom characteristics, several guidelines for the selection of both Chinese and English idioms to enhance ad effectiveness can be drawn from this paper. Since Chinese idioms are generally decomposable, they can be used in Chinese ads even if consumers are not familiar with them. Advertisers therefore do not have to worry about consumers' familiarity with Chinese idioms when using them in Chinese ads, since consumers will likely be able to figure out their meaning from an analysis of the characters making up the idioms. Thus, an idiom should be selected based on the extent to which its figurative meaning conveys the messages that advertisers wish to communicate to the consumers.

On the other hand, English idioms may evoke ambiguity when consumers are unfamiliar with the idioms used because many idioms make sense when used literally (e.g., "cook his goose," "kick the bucket," and "upset the applecart"). Consumers' familiarity with English idioms is therefore an important factor when choosing appropriate idioms to use in English ads, since consumers will take on the literal meaning of idioms if they are unfamiliar with, and do not recognize, the idioms used. If less familiar idioms were to be used, advertisers must ensure that they are decomposable, or that they are accompanied by cues to help consumers guess their figurative meaning (e.g., by inserting suggestive pictures). This strategy is a double-edged sword in that consumers' success at guessing the meaning of less familiar idioms is somewhat beyond the control of advertisers since it depends on other factors (e.g., education), but their guessing the meaning also creates a sense of accomplishment, which is likely to translate into liking for the ad. It therefore appears that for English ads, the safest approach is to use familiar idioms. The choice of English idioms that are appropriate for use in ads is therefore narrower than that of Chinese idioms.

In terms of imagery-eliciting potential, Chinese and English idioms vary in their ability to evoke imagery, but it has been suggested that Chinese idioms possess a higher ability to evoke imagery than English idioms. Advertisers operating in a Chinese-speaking market should therefore consider using Chinese idioms in ads, especially if mental imagery is likely to enhance consumers' evaluation of the advertised product. For instance, tour agencies that often portray scenic views of advertised holiday packages can instead use appropriate idioms to elicit mental pictures of beautiful mountains and rivers. The elicitation of mental imagery may be more involving and evoke more feelings even though it requires the same amount of mental resources as perceptual tasks (Unnava et al., 1996).

References

Babin, Laurie A. and Alvin C. Burns (1997). Effects of print ad pictures and copy containing instructions to imagine on mental imagery that mediates attitudes. *Journal of Advertising*, 26 (3): 33–44.

Cacciari, Cristina and Sam Glucksberg (1995). Imagining idiomatic expressions: Literal or figurative meanings? In Martin Everaert, Erik-Jan van der Linden, André Schenk, and Rob Schreuder (eds.), *Idioms: Structural and Psychological Perspectives*, pp. 43–56. Hillsdale, NJ: Erlbaum.

Childers, Terry L. and Michael J. Houston (1984). Conditions for a picture-superiority effect on consumer memory. *Journal of Consumer Research*, 11 (September): 643–54.

The Concise Oxford Dictionary (1995), 9th edition. New York: Oxford University Press.

Conway, M.A. and S.E. Gathercole (1987). Modality and long-term memory. *Journal of Memory and Language*, 26: 341–61.

Engle, R.W. and L.A. Mobley (1976). The modality effect: What happens in long-term memory? *Journal of Verbal Learning and Verbal Behavior*, 15: 519–28.

Fang, S.P. (1982). Interaction between mode of presentation and serial position in serial recall of Chinese characters and words. In H.S.R. Kao and C.M. Cheng (eds.), *Psychological Studies of the Chinese Language*, pp. 227–43. Taipei: Wen-Ho.

Finke, Ronald A. (1989). *Principles of Mental Imagery*. Cambridge, MA: MIT Press.

Gibbs, Raymond W. (1980). Spilling the beans on understanding and memory for idioms in conversation. *Memory and Cognition*, 8: 149–56.

Gibbs, Raymond W. and Jennifer E. O'Brien (1990). Idioms and mental imagery: The metaphorical motivation for idiomatic meaning. *Cognition*, 36: 35–68.

Huang, H.S. and Richard Hanley (1994). Phonological awareness and visual skills in learning to read Chinese and English. *Cognition*, 54: 73–98.

Liu, In-mao, Ying Zhu, and Jei-tun Wu (1992). The long-term modality effect: In search of differences in processing logographs and alphabetic words. *Cognition*, 43: 31–66.

Paivio, Allan (1965). Mental imagery in associative learning and memory. *Psychological Review*, 76 (3): 241–63.

Paivio, Allan, John C. Yuille, and Stephen A. Madigan (1968). Concreteness, imagery, and meaningfulness values for 925 nouns. *Journal of Experimental Psychology*, 76 (1), Part 2: 1–25.

Penny, C.G. (1989). Modality effects in delayed recall and recognition: Visual is better than auditory. *Quarterly Journal of Experimental Psychology*, 41A: 455–70.

Perfetti, Charles A. and Sulan Zhang (1991). Phonological processes in reading Chinese characters. *Journal of Experimental Psychology*, 17 (4): 633–43.

Popiel, Stephen J. and Ken McRae (1988). The figurative and literal senses of idioms, or all idioms are not used equally. *Journal of Psycholinguistic Research*, 17 (6): 475–87.

Schweigert, Wendy A. (1986). The comprehension of familiar and less familiar idioms. *Journal of Psycholinguistic Research*, 15: 33–45.

Tavassoli, Nader T. (1999). Temporal and associative memory in Chinese and English. *Journal of Consumer Research*, 26: 170–81.

Turnage, T.W. and E. McGinnies (1973). A cross-cultural comparison of the effects of presentation mode and meaningfulness in short-term recall. *American Journal of Psychology*, 86: 369–81.

Unnava, H. Rao, Sanjeev Argarwal, and Curtis P. Haugtvedt (1996). Interactive effects of presentation modality and message-generated imagery on recall of advertising information. *Journal of Consumer Research*, 23 (June): 81–88.

Yang, Charles (1988). Advertising effectiveness across cultures: A comparison of American, Japanese, and Chinese ad appeals. Presentation at Lianhe Zaobao Desaru Weekend, November.

Yu, Bolin, Wutian Zhang, Qicheng Jing, et al. (1985). STM capacity for Chinese and English language materials. *Memory and Cognition*, 13 (3): 202–7.

Zhang, Guojun and Herbert A. Simon (1985). STM capacity for Chinese words and idioms: Chunking and acoustical loop hypotheses. *Memory and Cognition*, 13 (3): 193–201.

THE POWER OF MONEY
A Cross-cultural Analysis of Business-related Beliefs

Swee Hoon Ang

> *This study compared beliefs in money, business ethics and social responsibility, and guanxi; and Machiavellian personality among youths in two Asian economies—Hong Kong and Singapore—and two Western economies—Canada and Hawaii. It found interesting variations across economies. The factors that influence how much one believes in the power of money also varied.*

INTRODUCTION

It has been said that money makes the world go round. The famous Swedish pop group, Abba, has carved the importance of money in their song by the same name; in the movie *Wall Street*, the Gordon Gekko tycoon character eulogizes that "greed is . . . good"; and in numerous bestsellers, much has been written on how to make more money.

However, there has been little research on whether an individual's belief in money and the factors influencing such a belief are universal. Insights can be gained from understanding whether certain groups of individuals differ in their belief of whether money works wonders. Those that believe more in the power of money will have different

---

This research was funded by the National University of Singapore. The researcher would like to thank Kathy Gallagher, Don Hong, Teri Ursacki, and Nancy Wong for collecting the data.

Reprinted from *Journal of World Business*, Vol. 35, No. 1, pp. 43–60. Copyright 2000, with permission from Elsevier Science.

expectations in life and different views about what success means compared to those who hold less strong a belief. Of relevance to business are issues such as compensation packages and negotiation strategies. Insights can also be gained into the motivation for having more money by studying the factors influencing whether an individual believes in the power of money.

Therefore, the objectives of this study are twofold. First, it compares individuals' belief in the wonders of money across four economies, two East Asian, one Anglo-Saxon Western, and one Western with Asian heritage. Hong Kong and Singapore, predominantly Chinese in population, represent East Asian cultures. Canada represents the Anglo-Saxon Western culture, whereas the U.S. state of Hawaii is a Western economy with mixed East Asian heritage. The latter is therefore not representative of the rest of the U.S.

As a second objective, this study investigates possible factors influencing whether an individual believes that money works wonders. The factors studied are belief in business ethics and social responsibility, belief in *guanxi*, and Machiavellianism. Belief in ethics and social responsibility pertains to the belief in the role businesses should play in a society to ensure that practices conducted are fair and with integrity. Belief in *guanxi* or networking concerns the extent to which individuals place importance on connections and relationships in business. Machiavellianism refers to the personality trait of making use of others for one's success.

These factors are studied for at least two reasons. First, they are business related and since business success is often equated with profits, and hence money, they are intuitively appealing to study. Second, although these beliefs tend to be studied in one culture, they may be applicable in others as well. For instance, belief in *guanxi* has been touted to be an Asian value (Alston, 1989). However, this does not restrict *guanxi* to the East. The "old boys' club" and relationship building, notions familiar in the West, share some characteristics to *guanxi*. Belief in ethics and Machiavellianism have been studied extensively in the Western literature, but these concepts are also of significance to the East. For instance, Hong Kong people have been found to have a high level of Machiavellianism (Ralston et al., 1993). Further, because Confucianism is prevalent in many East Asian countries, its emphasis on ethics may influence business practices. Paradoxically, de George (1997) observed that in Asia, business ethics is not a popular notion. Therefore, it would be interesting to see how beliefs in ethics vary and influence belief in the power of money.

BELIEF THAT MONEY WORKS WONDERS

The belief that money works wonders is related to the concept of materialism. Specifically, such a belief concerns possession-defined success (e.g., owning things to indicate success) and acquisition as a pursuit of happiness (e.g., feeling happy about owning things).

Among youths in Mainland China, some 64 percent believed that money works wonders (China Association for Promoting Democracy, 1997). Further south, Hong Kong people have often been viewed as having a penchant to become millionaires. According to Waters (1995), Hong Kong people have an ambition likened to the "gold digger in the old American West, getting rich quick, and spending it" (p. 150). They display a high passion for money, with making money the most important goal in life. In Singapore, a 1996 values and lifestyle survey among 1,600 Singaporeans found that they have a strong drive for financial advancement (Kau et al., 1998). More than two out of five (46 percent) Singaporeans believe that money can solve most problems. This belief tends to be more prevalent among better educated Singaporeans, and among the Chinese and Indians.

Kao (1993) explained Chinese people's penchant for money. In his observation of Chinese people's sense of insecurity, he highlighted nine "life-raft" values originating in part from historical economic disasters and diaspora that the Chinese have experienced. Of these, three are financially related—thriftiness, a need for a high and sometimes irrational level of savings, and a possession of tangible goods such as real estate and gold bars—portraying Chinese people's concern over money.

As a summary, a Gallup opinion poll found that a priority among Chinese is to "work hard and get rich" (cf. *World Competitiveness Yearbook*, 1998). In contrast, Europeans and Americans value self-achievement more than wealth. Therefore, based on the above discussion, we expect Hong Kong people and Singaporeans to have a stronger belief that money works wonders compared to Canadians and Hawaiians.

BELIEF IN ETHICS AND SOCIAL RESPONSIBILITY

Research on belief in ethics and social responsibility among Asians is somewhat scant. Mehta and Kau (1984) found that Singaporeans are less ethical than Americans in nine of ten situations. Unlike Americans, Singaporeans do not consider padding expense accounts as unethical. In another study, Kau et al. (1998) found that almost 30 percent of Singaporeans did not agree that honesty pays.

In Hong Kong, managers have been observed to be less ethical than their expatriate counterparts from the U.S. and Britain, but similar to those from China and Macau (McDonald and Kan, 1997). They are more agreeable to using deception for gaining competitor information, protecting dishonest employees, practicing deceptive advertising and labeling, having deceptive pricing, manipulating expenses, and engaging in insider trading. This observation is supported by Nyaw and Ng (1994) who found that Hong Kong managers are more tolerant of unethical behavior toward customers and suppliers than Canadian managers. At a corporate level, deception of various forms has been observed among East Asians (Tung, 1994). For instance, the Japanese speak with soft-spoken voices so that their American counterparts underestimate their tenacity. In the process of gathering market intelligence, some East Asian firms spread erroneous information to contaminate and frustrate competitors' strategies.

As a summary, the 1998 Corruption Perceptions Index (Transparency International, 1998) provides a comparative ranking of how 85 countries fare on corruption. Canada ranks 6th, Singapore 7th, Hong Kong 16th, and the U.S. 17th. In general, although Asian countries have a higher degree of corruption, Singapore and Hong Kong are relatively "clean" countries.

Tung (1994) provided reasons for the practice of and tolerance for deception among East Asians. Unlike Westerners who are influenced by Judeo-Christian values that deception is immoral, East Asians consider deception as amoral and acceptable if it results in a greater good such as the well-being of the state, the clan, the extended family, the company, or the self. Therefore, practices that are considered unethical to the West may not be considered so in the East.

Additionally, such practices must be viewed in light of the collectivistic nature of the Chinese culture. Triandis et al. (1986) found that Hong Kong people are more collectivistic than Americans. Collectivistic societies believe that the group is the basic unit of analysis, where there is a higher level of homogeneity within the in-group than with out-groups. Therefore an in- and out-group phenomenon exists in which protection for each other pertains to only in-group members. Unethical practices such as sharing competitive information are adopted to benefit the in-group at the expense of the out-group.

In contrast, Americans and Canadians have been found to be more ethical than their Asian counterparts. American businesses have a high degree of institutionalized ethics such as business ethics ratings, corporate ombudspersons, and special tax and regulatory breaks for socially responsible behavior. The *World Competitiveness Yearbook* (1998) by the Institute of Management Development has also shown that social responsibility is low in Hong Kong at 5.42, with Canada and the U.S. scoring 6.63 and 6.06, respectively. Thus, based on the above discussion, we expect Asian Chinese, especially those in Hong Kong, to hold a weaker belief in ethics and social responsibility compared to individuals from the West.

Belief in *Guanxi*

First originated from Chinese feudalism, *guanxi* or connections pertains to the special relationships between parties characterized by reciprocal obligations and personal interactions for the purposes of smoothening negotiations, establishing significant business relationships, and obtaining scarce resources (Alston, 1989).

Guanxi has several characteristics. The reciprocity or *bao* underlying such relationships requires individuals to make an effort to repay favors. The belief is that if individuals do not repay the favors of others, their relationship will become difficult and social harmony will be hard to sustain. Herein lie the differences between the Chinese and the West regarding reciprocity. Western societies tend to emphasize short-term, symmetrical reciprocation while the Chinese recognize that they are "in it for the long run" and hence emphasize the extension of the relationship into the future (Yum, 1991). The Chinese mentality of duality in which *guanxi* reciprocities can be put away in times of abundance to be later "cashed in" in times of need suggests a long-term perspective (Yeung and Tung, 1996). In a sense, *guanxi* is a social capital. Further, when a Chinese reciprocates, he or she repays with a higher value than the favor given (Yeung and Tung, 1996). However, in Western social transactions, such unequal reciprocity may not exist; or even if it does, the repayment is of a smaller value than the favor.

Another characteristic of *guanxi* is *renqing*. *Renqing* refers to the resource that an individual can present to another as a gift in the course of social interaction or assistance during difficult times (Gabrenya and Hwang, 1996). This stems from the Confucian tenet to right the wrongs of the world where those in a privileged position must assist the disadvantaged (Yeung and Tung, 1996). *Renqing* also connotes the social norms by which one has to abide to get along with others. This involves keeping contact with business associates by greetings, visits, and gift exchanges.

Such gift-giving and reciprocity are used to establish *guanxi* so that one is accepted as a member of an in-group. This opens opportunities and assistance in hard times from other members. For example, when Avon initially failed to convince the Chinese government of the workability of direct marketing, it obtained the assistance of the head of a local bank, well known for his *guanxi* with the Chinese government (*renqing*). He successfully introduced Avon to the Bureau of Light Industry (establish *guanxi*). In return, he became a partner in Avon with a 5 percent equity (reciprocity).

Comparative research shows that Chinese tend to place more emphasis on building relationships than their American counterparts (Brunner and Taoka, 1977). Several reasons account for this. *Guanxi* is practiced when resources are scarce and competition is intense. It offers access to such resources for a competitive edge. Before and after the Chinese cultural revolution (1966–76), *guanxi* was practiced in rural communities to obtain raw materials for factories; and extra fertilizer, bricks, and nails for the communities so that they can perform better than others. Similarly, *guanxi* practices such as gift-giving and invitations to wedding banquets prevailed despite communist rule to ensure that an individual is assigned lighter and easier work or receive better work evaluations. In modern China, enhanced consumer desire resulted in the scarcity of products, especially foreign-made ones. Therefore, consumers resort to *guanxi* to acquire goods that are not readily available in state stores.

Guanxi is also practiced because more intense competition demands that competitive edge be sought on all grounds including relationships. It is practiced to ensure that doors will open for future opportunities. Charoen Pokphand, a Thai conglomerate with extensive business in China, practices *guanxi* by employing "power brokers" who have strong ties with the government. Their job is to be among the first to learn of new government regulations, smooth the path for new projects, and iron out differences when disputes arise. Another example is the overseas Chinese who practice *guanxi* in part because the in- versus out-group membership is more pronounced. An overseas Chinese experiences external insecurity and overcomes it by fostering *guanxi* with other Chinese to assist in business operations.

Scarce resources and intensive competition are characteristics more pertinent to Hong Kong and Singapore than Hawaii or Canada. In terms of scarcity, Hong Kong and Singapore are island states where there are no natural resources except personnel. With small markets, competition to survive is intense and the attainment of scarce resources becomes pivotal to business success. Thus, the role of *guanxi* becomes more critical. In terms of competitiveness, Singapore and Hong Kong rank as the second and seventh most open economies, respectively, despite the economic crisis (*World Competitiveness Yearbook*, 1999). They were ranked second and third in 1998 (*World Competitiveness Yearbook*, 1998). Therefore, given the Chinese origin of Hong Kong and Singapore, and the scarce resources and intense competition in these economies, we expect Asian Chinese to believe more in *guanxi* than their counterparts in the West.

Machiavellianism

Machiavellianism refers to the personality trait of immorality in which others are manipulated to accomplish one's goals. Named after the shrewd Renaissance statesman, a Machiavellian is dispassionate and devoid of sentiments. McMurry (1973), in his thesis on the Machiavellian and the ambitious executive, suggested that Machiavellians are interested in gaining and keeping power. One route to power is monetary. Thus, Machiavellian executives would position themselves where they approve all budgets, as the power to cut off financial support is effective in coping with recalcitrant employees, while providing such monetary support promotes gratitude to and cooperation with oneself. In a cross-cultural study of office politics, Ralston et al. (1994) observed that compared to their American counterparts, Hong Kong professionals were more likely to engage in information control and strong-arm coercion tactics for power. Similarly, Hong Kong managers were found to score significantly higher on Machiavellianism than U.S. managers (Ralston et al., 1993).

The need for information control for self-interest is sometimes extended to the sharing of such information among in-group members so that all will benefit relative to out-group members. This may be the case in collectivistic countries such as Hong Kong and Singapore. In such instances, Machiavellianism is practiced for the interest of a larger unit—the in-group. Although information is shared, self-interest is still preserved as such information control is tight within the in-group, and thus also benefits self, relative to out-group members.

Another characteristic of a Machiavellian is the need for achievement (Christie and Geis, 1970). This drives individuals to run their own businesses as it gives them the opportunity to be their own boss, the power to make decisions, and the strive for excellence. To this end, some indication of the level of Machiavellianism across cultures is furnished in the entrepreneurial scores by the *World Competitiveness Yearbook* (1998). It showed that Hong Kong ranks second on entrepreneurship with a score of 7.39, whereas the U.S. has a rating of 6.63, Singapore 6.12, and Canada 6.11. Therefore, we expect Hong Kong people to be more Machiavellian compared to individuals from the other economies.

THE MODEL

Based on the above review, we expect belief in the wonders of money to be positively influenced by belief in *guanxi* and Machiavellianism, and negatively influenced by belief in ethics and social responsibility (see Figure 8-1). *Guanxi* is practiced for several reasons including a sense of righteousness to help the disadvantaged and role obligation toward in-group members. Such noble motivations help to open doors, obtain scarce resources, and facilitate business dealings for others. These result in opportunities for success for the beneficiary, where such success is usually financially related (e.g., more business contacts and expanded business means a higher top line). Additionally, although the motivations underlying *guanxi* are noble, the execution of a successful *guanxi* requires financial resources in most instances. Relationships are cultivated with gift exchanges and frequent socializing. Even if the favors are nonmonetary (e.g., introducing a beneficiary to a supplier), the benefactor is usually in a financially sound position to be able to offer such assistance. Based on the financial benefits of a *guanxi* to the beneficiary, the resources invested to cultivate *guanxi* by the beneficiary

Figure 8-1
The model

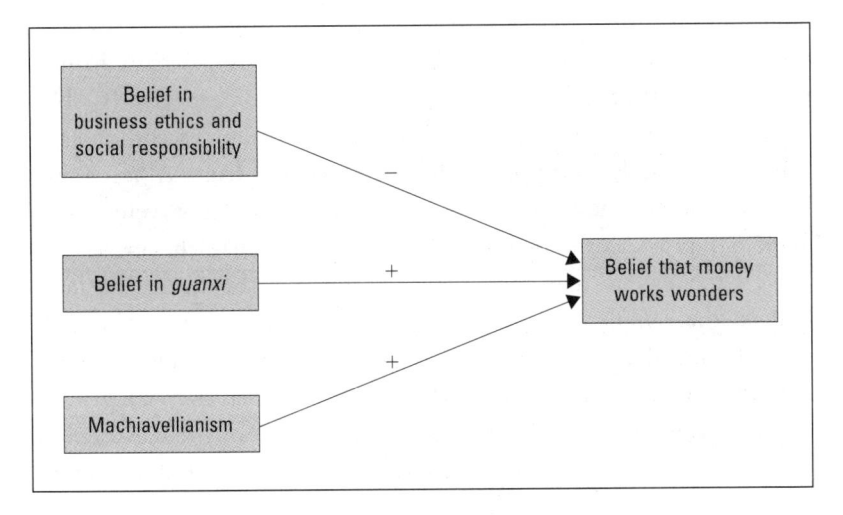

```
┌─────────────────────────────────────────────────────────┐
│  ┌──────────────────┐                                    │
│  │    Belief in     │                                    │
│  │ business ethics  │──────┐                             │
│  │ and social       │       ─                            │
│  │ responsibility   │        ╲                           │
│  └──────────────────┘         ╲                          │
│                                ╲    ┌──────────────────┐ │
│  ┌──────────────────┐    +      ╲   │  Belief that     │ │
│  │ Belief in guanxi │────────────▶│  money works     │ │
│  └──────────────────┘            ╱  │  wonders         │ │
│                                 ╱   └──────────────────┘ │
│                           +    ╱                         │
│  ┌──────────────────┐         ╱                          │
│  │ Machiavellianism │────────┘                           │
│  └──────────────────┘                                    │
└─────────────────────────────────────────────────────────┘
```

and benefactor, and the usually superior financial background of the benefactor, it suggests that money plays a key role and can do wonders. Thus, a positive relationship is hypothesized where individuals who believe strongly in *guanxi* will also believe that money works wonders.

Similarly, a Machiavellian individual who wants power is likely to believe more in the wonders of money. Glover (1992) observed that the Machiavellian streak of being power-hungry and money-loving are related. Individuals preoccupied with wealth tend to be selfish and pursue individual as opposed to community goals. As alluded to earlier, Machiavellianism is often associated with entrepreneurship. Entrepreneurs are motivated by material and financial outcomes. Therefore, an individual high in Machiavellianism is also likely to believe more that money works wonders.

In contrast, an ethical and socially responsible individual is likely to believe in doing deeds for the good of the community and frown on the abuse of money. Greater materialism results in a loss of a sense of community, which in turn makes individuals more selfish and less altruistic. Also, when one becomes too focused with materialism, one may bend ethical rules to gain these possessions (Muncy and Eastman, 1998). Thus, a negative relationship is hypothesized between ethical belief and belief that money works wonders.

The Survey

Some 393 youths, aged 18 to 21 years old, studying business at universities were surveyed. There were 80 and 113 Chinese respondents from Hong Kong and Singapore, respectively. The Hawaiian sample had 101 respondents of East Asian descent, and the Canadian sample comprised 99 Anglo-Saxons from Alberta and Newfoundland. Some 42.7 percent of the respondents were males. Table 8-1 provides the demographic breakdown for each sample.

To the extent that these youths represent the future business leaders, the sample is reflective of the values they carry when they embark on their business careers. Further, these values are also reflective of the community in which they live.

The paper-and-pencil self-administered questionnaire consisted of 13 items on beliefs in business ethics and social responsibility taken

Table 8-1
Demographic profile of respondents (in percentages)

Characteristics	Hong Kong	Singapore	Hawaii	Canada
Gender				
Male	44.3	31.3	50.5	46.5
Female	55.7	68.8	49.5	55.7
Ethnicity				
Caucasian	–	–	–	100
Chinese	100	100	28.3	–
Filipino	–	–	4	–
Indian	–	–	1	–
Japanese	–	–	20.2	–
Korean	–	–	4	–
Mixed Asian ethnicity	–	–	42.4	–
Where they grew up				
West[a]	–	–	20.4	100
Hawaii	–	–	58.2	–
Asia[b]	100	100	21.4	–
Business major				
Accounting/finance	67.2	33.6	22.4	11.9
Marketing	9.4	23.9	51	58.4
Policy/strategy	3.1	6.2	16.3	13.9
General	–	27.4	–	–
Others[c]	20.3	8.8	3	15.8

[a] Western countries included Canada, France, Germany, and the U.S.
[b] Asian countries included China, Hong Kong, India, Japan, Korea, Macau, and Taiwan.
[c] Majors in Human Resource Management and Operations Management.

from Singhapakdi et al. (1996). Respondents were also asked how much they agree that money works wonders. Based on the literature, nine items were developed to measure belief in *guanxi* (see Appendix). Machiavellian inclination was measured using Christie and Geis' (1970) 20-item Mach IV scale. Finally, respondents' gender, ethnicity, country where they were brought up, and major field of study were recorded.

The Results

Respondents' beliefs and their Machiavellian personality scores are presented in Table 8-2. Comparisons were made across the four samples. Tests were also conducted to determine the influence of beliefs in ethics and *guanxi*, and Machiavellianism on one's belief that money works wonders.

The results show the following:

- Belief in the wonders of money was most strongly held by Canadian youths ($x = 7.00$), followed by Hawaiians ($x = 6.57$), Singaporeans ($x = 6.21$), and lastly Hong Kong youths ($x = 5.96$). Test showed that Hong Kong people and Singaporeans held significantly less of this belief than Canadians. No other differences were observed.
- In terms of belief in ethics and social responsibility, respondents from all countries differed significantly from one

Table 8-2
Beliefs and Machiavellianism

Variables	Hong Kong	Singapore	Hawaii	Canada
Belief that money works wonders	5.96 [a]	6.21 [a]	6.57 [a,b]	7.00 [b]
Belief in ethics and social responsibility	5.51 [a]	6.39 [b]	6.75 [c]	7.11 [d]
Belief in *guanxi*	7.27 [a]	7.50 [a]	7.40 [a]	7.79 [b]
Machiavellianism	5.04 [a]	4.80 [b]	4.30 [c]	4.45 [c]

Mean scores are based on a nine-point scale; 9 = agree.

Row-wise, pairs of mean scores with different letters indicate significant difference at $p < 0.05$; e.g.:
- For "Belief that money works wonders," the scores from Hong Kong and Singapore differ significantly from the score from Canada as they have different superscripted letters. The score from Hawaii does not differ significantly from Hong Kong, Singapore, and Canada as there are common superscripted letters.
- For "Belief in ethics and social responsibility," all scores are significantly different from one another as the superscripted letters are different.

another. Hong Kong people held the least belief in ethics ($x = 5.51$), followed by Singaporeans ($x = 6.39$), and Hawaiians ($x = 6.75$). The most ethical and socially responsible were the Canadians at 7.11.
- Belief in *guanxi* was most prominently held by Canadians ($x = 7.79$). This belief was significantly higher than that observed among Hong Kong people, Singaporeans, and Hawaiians.
- Hong Kong people were the most Machiavellian ($x = 5.04$). This score was significantly higher than those observed for the other countries. The least Machiavellian were the Hawaiians and Canadians ($x = 4.30$ and 4.45, respectively).
- The more an individual believed in *guanxi* and the more Machiavellian he or she was, the more he or she believed that money works wonders. Men believed more than women that money works wonders.
- Among Hong Kong people, their belief in money was influenced by belief in ethics, Machiavellianism, and gender. The more they believed in ethics, the less they believed in what money can do. However, the more Machiavellian they were, the more they believed in money. Gender also influenced belief in the wonders of money, with women believing this more so than men ($x = 6.05$ vs. 5.80, respectively).
- Among Singaporeans, the more they believed in *guanxi* and the more Machiavellian they were, they more they believed in the power of money.
- Among Hawaiians, gender was the only significant predictor. Hawaiian men believed more in the power of money than their female counterparts ($x = 7.52$ vs. 6.47, respectively).
- Among Canadians, belief in *guanxi* was the only significant predictor, where the more one believed in *guanxi*, the more one believed in the power of money.

Discussion

The results showed that Canadians believe money can do wonders more so than Hong Kong people and Singaporeans. Hawaiians' belief hovered between those of Canadians and Asians, but not significantly different from any of these groups. The findings appear to suggest a negative relationship between belief in money and cost of living. The higher the cost of living (as in Hong Kong and Singapore), the lower is the belief that money works wonders. It is possible that Hong Kong people and Singaporeans perceive that for money to work wonders, it has to be of a substantial magnitude especially given the high cost of living. Property and car prices, for instance, are exorbitant in these economies, and therefore money does not stretch very far. To work wonders, money has to be of a substantial amount. Generally, these come from old wealth—inheritance from generations past. By comparison, hard-earned money through salary does not go far compared to those accumulated over the generations. For instance, the social elite in Hong Kong and Singapore tends to come from old wealth families. Hong Kong tycoon, Richard Li, comes from old wealth because his father, Ka Shing Li, has accumulated this over the generation. Canada, in contrast, with a highly developed social welfare system, has a relatively lower cost of living than the other three economies studied. Such lower cost of living may have influenced Canadians into believing that money can buy more things compared to individuals in Hawaii, Hong Kong, or Singapore. Thus, belief in the power of money is highest among the Canadians. Hawaii, with cost of living higher than in Canada but lower than in Hong Kong and Singapore, shows moderate belief in the power of money.

The findings also suggest that in a welfare society, belief in money is the highest compared to nonwelfare societies. This may stem from the security that such welfarism provides. In Canada, where social welfarism exists, there is a safety net during unemployment. Social welfare benefits help toward daily expenses during unemployment. Therefore, money earned during gainful employment can be spent without undue concern regarding how one can tide over should unemployment occur. Such peace of mind regarding monetary concerns offered by social welfarism may have influenced belief that money works wonders. In Hawaii where there are also social welfare benefits but not to the extent practiced in Canada, belief that money works wonders is moderate. In contrast, in Hong Kong and Singapore where welfarism is not practiced, individuals have to fend for themselves at all times. During unemployment, and without social security benefits, money may not go very far. Money saved during employment has to be channeled for such possible hard times. This may have influenced less belief in the power of money.

An alternative explanation is that with the onset of the Asian economic crisis in late 1997, Hong Kong people and Singaporeans may have some firsthand experience that material wealth can be eroded quickly (e.g., sharp falls in the equity market), which can devastate market confidence. Another explanation is that Asians may provide more socially desirable responses than their Western counterparts. The Confucian philosophy calls for modesty. Therefore, although Asians may strongly believe in wealth accumulation, they do not indicate so in an explicit manner so that they do not appear to be aggressive. This explanation is consistent with Tung's (1994) assessment of how the Chinese would pretend so that others do not know their true self. It is also congruent with the notion of face or *mianzi*. To state outright that one believes in wealth accumulation may be somewhat embarrassing and potentially makes one lose face.

In terms of belief in *guanxi*, Canadians were found to believe in it more than Hong Kong people and Singaporeans. Again, Hawaiians' belief was between those of Canadians and the East Asian respondents. The findings do not imply that *guanxi* is viewed unfavorably by East Asians. Rather, they are more familiar with the concept of *guanxi* and know its benefits and limitations. Therefore, their belief in *guanxi* is more realistic compared to possibly a more glamorized view of what *guanxi* is by Canadians. As novices with respect to the intricacies of *guanxi*, Canadians may have been exposed to the ideals of *guanxi* and hence put more faith in this practice. Some evidence that East Asians know better of what *guanxi* can and cannot do is furnished by the Asian economic turmoil. A substantial proportion of bank loans was given without security but based on personal relationships. This resulted in poor loan portfolios and an array of nonperforming investments among Asian bankers and businesses. As Hong Kong people and Singaporeans are closer to and harder hit by the Asian crisis, they may be more cognizant that *guanxi* can be abused, leading to imprudent practices. Hence, they have a less idealistic view of *guanxi*. Given that Hawaiians with Asian descent were surveyed, they may still have a more realistic notion of *guanxi* than Anglo-Saxon Canadians. Further, Hawaii's geographic proximity to Asia may also partially explain why Hawaiians' belief borders between the Canadians' and East Asians' responses. They have more interaction with and information about Asia that may have moderated their response.

Of the four variables investigated in the present study, belief in *guanxi* showed the least difference between respondents from the Asian and Western economies. One possibility is that the differences between *guanxi* and the Western notion of networking were not sufficiently teased apart in this research. The literature espouses that *guanxi* has a longer-term and reciprocal orientation than Western networking. Future research may improve the scale by highlighting the six similarities/differences identified by Yeung and Tung (1996) between *guanxi* and networking. These are role obligation versus self-interest, self-loss versus self-gain, long term versus short term, relationship between the strong and the weak, personal versus institutional authority, and shame versus guilt. Such research not only has methodological implications but managerial ones as well. Managers, especially those involved in Asia Pacific businesses, will be interested in knowing how to play the organizational game in dealings with their business associates in Asia vis-à-vis the West.

The present study found that Asian youths display more Machiavellian personality than their Hawaiian or Canadian counterparts. That Hong Kong youths are the most Machiavellian followed by Singaporeans suggests that perhaps the competitive business orientation of these economies encourage such a personality. In both economies, natural resources are scarce, land is limited, and population dense. Competition is therefore intense not only in business but also in personal lives. As early as preschool, children compete to enter the better kindergartens and elementary schools. Private tuition is necessary to ensure that they do well every year. Competition continues after graduation to ensure that career potential is realized. Therefore, the intense competition in these two export-dependent economies may have cultivated a more Machiavellian spirit among its people to strive for achievement.

Hong Kong people and Singaporeans have the least belief in business ethics and social responsibility, whereas Canadians are the most ethical and responsible-minded. Hawaiians' belief is moderate between the Canadians and the East Asians. The findings are not surprising as anecdotal evidence of unethical business practices and lack of civic-mindedness in Asia abound. As noted by Tung (1994), this is partly because East Asians are not influenced by Judeo-Christian values and do not view deception as immoral. Alternatively, they may be accustomed to such practices and do not view them unfavorably. The lack of Judeo-Christian influence may also account for Hawaiians' moderate belief in ethics and social responsibility. As Hawaii has a fairly large Japanese and Korean community where Judaism and Christianity are not the predominant religions, and given that the respondents are of Asian descent, the influence of Judeo-Christian values is likely to be moderate. In contrast, for Canada, the influence of Judeo-Christian values results in the business community being more steeped in integrity and human rights. Further, the value system operating in the Western social network focuses on honesty and helping the community. This explains why Canadians scored the highest in belief in ethics and social responsibility among the economies surveyed.

The findings also yielded interesting insights on the personal characteristics that determine whether an individual is obsessed with money. The differences observed across countries suggest that what makes an individual believe that money works wonders is unlikely to be universal. In Hong Kong, Machiavellianism and belief in ethics play pivotal roles in determining one's belief in money. In Singapore, the key influential factors are one's belief in *guanxi* and Machiavellianism; whereas none of these variables are significant predictors in Hawaii. In Canada, belief in *guanxi* influences belief in money. Collectively, the findings suggest that in Asia, belief in money is strongly tied to Machiavellianism and to some extent *guanxi*. However, in the West, belief that money works wonders takes its root elsewhere and is less likely to be business related. Perhaps, in such countries, individuals believe in money when these are associated with a personal crisis (e.g., money is needed to save someone's life or to tide over hardships) or the society (e.g., money is needed to save the environment or victims of natural disasters).

Interestingly, Hawaiians' responses are between those given by Canadians and their East Asian counterparts for three of the four variables. They share with Anglo-Saxon Canadians concerning belief in money and Machiavellianism, but with Chinese in East Asia regarding *guanxi*. However, in terms of ethics, they are more ethical than their East Asian counterparts. Also, unlike East Asians, a different set of variables affected their belief that money works wonders. Given that Hawaiians with East Asian heritage were surveyed, the results suggest that they have been acculturalized into the value system of the adopted country, that is, the U.S. This is consistent with Kelley et al.'s (1987) finding that Japanese-Hawaiians and Chinese-Hawaiians are more similar to Caucasian-Hawaiians than Japanese and Chinese in work attitude that may be affected by culture. The convergence hypothesis that individuals adapt to the values of their adopted culture appears to be evident. Future research may study how fast acculturalization or convergence takes place. This will be interesting to international marketers who are considering entering markets which appear to be similar ethnically to their home country. It also has implications for marketers interested in knowing how acculturalization affects various product acceptance.

Because the Hawaiian sample is non-Caucasian, the respondents are not representative of the rest of the U.S. The results should therefore be interpreted with this in mind. Future research employing a cross-section of the U.S. population can be conducted to examine whether similar observations are found. Similarly, future studies can use working adults as respondents to see if the findings replicate those observed in this student sample. It is possible that the hypotheses not supported here may be supported with a working adult sample.

Gender was also observed to influence belief in the power of money. In general, men believe more in what money can do than women. This is consistent with previous research that showed more men than women believe that money can buy happiness (*Adweek*, 1995). However, Hong Kong women believe more in the power of money than Hong Kong men. Perhaps Hong Kong women see money as a means to obtaining things and experiences that they can enjoy now, whereas Hong Kong men see money as investment for their business. The example of *tai tai*s (rich wives) who spend time shopping in brand-name boutiques, playing mahjong, and having high teas while their businessman husbands work may suggest that the former sees money as providing a means to enjoy life. Therefore, these differing perspectives of money as a means to enjoyment now and as an investment for the future may account for why Hong Kong women believe more in the power of money than their male counterparts.

For the overall sample, beliefs in *guanxi* and Machiavellianism were found to similarly influence belief that money works wonders. Yet, *guanxi* and Machiavellianism appear to offer conflicting values. On the one hand, *guanxi* implies trust among members in a relationship—"deliver what you have promised" and "don't cheat" (Yeung and Tung, 1996); whereas Machiavellianism suggests manipulation. Managerially, this implies that a successful business relationship needs to balance between these two elements. There must be trust and reciprocity among business partners, where one understands that by delivering one's promise, one serves to meet the objective of the other party, who in turn can be trusted to deliver his promise to meet one's objective. Managers therefore should learn that to trust and reciprocate do not necessarily imply that one's goals are compromised.

Managerially, the findings are insightful because they demonstrate that an individual's belief in money varies from culture to culture. This has implications on employee review and compensation packages, marketing, and business negotiations. For instance, in employee review and compensation, the stronger predictor relationship between Machiavellianism and belief that money works wonders in Asia suggests that Asian employees may engage in Machiavellian acts such as office politics to ensure that they are rewarded and climb the corporate ladder ahead of their colleagues.

Interestingly, such Machiavellian behavior may have been inadvertently encouraged via the nature of the performance review process adopted in Asia. When evaluating sales-force performance, qualitative measures such as knowledge of firm, products, and markets; personal appearance; and motivation are used in addition to sales-to-quota ratio in Asia (Kotler et al., 1999). These qualitative measures lend themselves to Machiavellian manipulation. Perception of whether an employee is knowledgeable or dresses well can be influenced by office politics. Therefore, management must be more wary of such Machiavellian acts by less credible employees that may undermine more deserving performers. To this end, more quantitative measures such as number of customers gained and lost, expense-to-sales ratio, and number of sales calls per week should be included in the performance review. In particular, given the practice of *guanxi* in this region, such objective criteria as calls made, expenses incurred, and customers gained or lost are indicators of how effective *guanxi* is toward bottom-line performance. Effective *guanxi* will have a low expense-to-sales ratio. The amount of expenses incurred may be high, but the returns in sales and new customers gained should more than offset the cost. On the other hand, if expenses incurred are high and yet the increase in sales is minimal, then either the Asian salesperson does not know how to effectively establish *guanxi* or is abusing it at the firm's expense.

The influence of Machiavellianism on Asians' belief in money also has implications on the structure of the compensation package. Traditionally, Asians favor a high portion of fixed salary and a small variable commission portion (Kotler et al., 1999). For more Machiavellian Asians, however, a larger variable component will serve to motivate them toward goal achievement and satisfy their competitive spirit as they will be duly rewarded. A fixed salary may not reward the Machiavellian who delivers the bottom line. In Malaysia, employees of property developer Sunrise earn about 40 percent of their annual salary through ordinary wages. The remaining 60 percent is paid out as discretionary bonuses based on performance. An additional 30 percent can be earned for "above the call of duty" performance.

The type of compensation package is also affected. As more Machiavellian Asians tend to believe that money can work wonders, bonuses in the form of cash should be the most popular. Incentives such as travel awards and training are not as popular in boosting morale and increasing productivity because of the expense and time incurred by the employee to be away from the office. For a Machiavellian individual with his or her eyes set on money, such incentives inhibit job performance and increase personal expenses.

The finding also has implications for marketing in Asia. In consumer promotions, offering rewards or prizes tied to personal material enrichment may be more attractive to Asians than, say, tying such rewards to nonpersonal entities such as donation to a charity. For instance, to encourage credit card usage, a loyalty program with personal rewards may be more attractive than an affinity program in which a small percentage of expenses is donated to a given cause. In Asia, Citibank, Hongkong and Shanghai Banking Corporation, and several other banks have loyalty programs with rewards such as gifts and travel. Affinity programs tied to charitable causes are less popular.

The findings also affect business negotiations in Asia. Knowing that belief in money is grounded on advancement of personal well-being has implications on the facilitating tools needed to ensure speedy and smooth negotiations. The literature on gift-giving is a case in point. Giving gifts to facilitate business negotiations requires certain etiquette, such as choosing the appropriate gifts. When negotiating with an Asian party, one should therefore be mindful of gifts that are centered on furthering the recipient's personal goals.

For business dealings with Hong Kong, managers should take note that Hong Kong people who endorse ethics will not consider money as fundamentally important. Foreign executives should be mindful that monetary bribes may not go down well with all their Hong Kong counterparts. This suggests that the ability to size up a person's ethical values early is important in determining how the negotiations should be conducted.

That Singaporeans associate belief in *guanxi* with belief in what money can do implies that in such relationships, face or *mianzi* in the form of display of ostentation is of paramount importance. Managerially, it suggests that in business dealings, the establishment of relationships requires a splurging of wealth. For instance, numerous lavish banquets may be served to business partners. Such display of ostentation is to impress upon the foreign business partner their credibility as well as a way of enhancing face. Foreign business executives should therefore do likewise when returning the favor of the dinner by throwing a similar gesture of lavishness.

Among Canadians, belief in *guanxi* was also found to influence belief in what money can do. It is possible that the advantages of networking and knowing the right people influence perception that money works wonders. Further, Canadians believe strongly in money. Therefore, in matters involving financial success such as closing a business deal, relationship cultivation is crucial. Among Canadians, business relationship needs to be cultivated and is perceived to go hand in hand with monetary rewards.

Appendix
Guanxi measure*

---

1. In business, it is important to maintain a good network of relationships.
2. Doing business involves knowing the right people.
3. Developing the right contacts helps in the smooth running of a business.
4. One must always build and maintain social relationships with others in case their services are needed in the future.
5. Being in the "inside" circle helps in obtaining preferential treatments.
6. Returning favor for favor is part of doing business.

7. Gift-giving is an important feature when we want business to succeed.
8. Maintaining a good relationship is the best way to enhance business.
9. Frequent cooperation reduces problems in business relationships.

* Measured on a nine-point disagree (1)/agree (9) scale.

References

Adweek (1995). Can money buy happiness? 36 (3): 16.

Alston, J.P. (1989). Wa, guanxi, and inhwa: Managerial principles in Japan, China, and Korea. *Business Horizons*, March–April: 26–31.

Brunner, J.A. and G.M. Taoka (1977). Marketing and negotiating in the People's Republic of China: Perceptions of American businessmen who attended the 1975 Canton trade fair. *Journal of International Business Studies*, 8 (2): 69–82.

China Association for Promoting Democracy (1997). Self-interest comes first for Guangzhou youths. *Straits Times* (Singapore), March 20: 20.

Christie, R. and F.L. Geis (1970). *Studies in Machiavellianism.* New York: Academic Press.

de George, R.T. (1997). Ethics, corruption, and doing business in Asia. *Asia Pacific Journal of Economics and Business*, 1 (1): 39–52.

Gabrenya, W.K., Jr. and K.K. Hwang (1996). Chinese social interaction: Harmony and hierarchy on the good earth. In M.H. Bond (ed.), *The Handbook of Chinese Psychology*, pp. 309–21. Hong Kong: Oxford University Press.

Glover, H.D. (1992). Organizational change and development: The consequences of misuse. *Leadership and Organization Development Journal*, 13 (1): 9–16.

Kao, J. (1993). The Worldwide Web of Chinese Business. *Harvard Business Review*, March–April: 24–36.

Kau, A.K., S.J. Tan, and J. Wirtz (1998). *Seven Faces of Singaporeans: Their Values, Aspirations and Lifestyles.* Singapore: Prentice Hall.

Kelley, L., A. Whatley, and R. Worthley (1987). Assessing the effects of culture on managerial attitudes: A three-culture test. *Journal of International Business Studies*, 18 (2): 17–31.

Kotler, P., S.H. Ang, S.M. Leong, and C.T. Tan (1999). *Marketing Management: An Asian Perspective*, 2nd edition. Singapore: Prentice Hall.

McDonald, G.M. and P.C. Kan (1997). Ethical perceptions of expatriate and local managers in Hong Kong. *Journal of Business Ethics*, 16: 1605–23.

McMurry, R.N. (1973). Power and the ambitious executive. *Harvard Business Review*, 51 (November/December): 140–45.

Mehta, S.C. and A.K. Kau (1984). Marketing executives' perceptions of unethical practices: An empirical investigation of Singapore managers. *Singapore Management Review*, 6 (2): 25–35.

Muncy, J.A. and J.K. Eastman (1998). Materialism and consumer ethics: An exploratory study. *Journal of Business Ethics*, 17: 137–45.

Nyaw, M.K. and I. Ng (1994). A comparative analysis of ethical beliefs: A four country study. *Journal of Business Ethics*, 13: 543–55.

Ralston, D.A., D.J. Gustafson, F.M. Cheung, and R.H. Terpstra (1993). Differences in managerial values: A study of U.S., Hong Kong, and PRC managers. *Journal of International Business Studies*, 4: 249–75.

Ralston, D.A., R.A. Giacalone, and R.H. Terpstra (1994). Ethical perceptions of organizational politics: A comparative evaluation of American and Hong Kong managers. *Journal of Business Ethics*, 13: 989–99.

Singhapakdi, A., S.J. Vitell, K.C. Rallapalli, and K.L. Kraft (1996). The perceived role of ethics and social responsibility: A scale development. *Journal of Business Ethics*, 15 (11): 1131–40.

Transparency International (1998). 1998 Corruption Perceptions Index.

Triandis, H.C., R. Botempo, H. Betancourt, M. Bond, et al. (1986). The measurement of the ethic aspects of individualism and collectivism across cultures. *Australian Journal of Psychology*, 38 (3): 257–67.

Tung, R.L. (1994). Strategic management thought in East Asia. *Organizational Dynamics*, 22 (Spring): 55–65.

Waters, D. (1995). *Faces of Hong Kong*. Singapore: Prentice Hall.

World Competitiveness Yearbook (1998). Lausanne, Switzerland: Institute for Management Development.

World Competitiveness Yearbook (1999). Singapore is 2nd most competitive economy. *Straits Times* (Singapore), April 21: 42.

Yeung, I.Y.M. and R.L. Tung (1996). Achieving business success in Confucian societies: The importance of guanxi (connections). *Organizational Dynamics*, 25 (Autumn): 54–65.

Yum, J.O. (1991). The impact of Confucianism on interpersonal relationships and communication patterns in East Asia. In L.A. Samovar and R.E. Porter (eds.), *Intercultural Communication: A Reader*, 6th edition, pp. 66–78. Belmont, CA: Wadsworth.

CULTURE, CUSTOMERS, AND CONTEMPORARY COMMUNISM
Vietnamese Marketing Management under *Doi Moi*

Rohit Deshpandé and John U. Farley

Effective implementation of Doi Moi in the centrally planned Vietnamese economy requires an understanding of successful Vietnamese companies. We find that financially successful firms in a sample of 128 major Vietnamese companies share the "High Performance Model" characteristics of their successful counterparts elsewhere, that is, innovativeness, customer orientation, and positive work climate in entrepreneurial and competitive corporate cultures. The degree of these characteristics differs from those in other countries, apparently due to special characteristics of the Vietnamese national culture, but the pattern is unmistakable. Only minor differences exist in Vietnam between public and private firms and between the North and South. We conclude that despite contextual differences in political, economic, and social systems, the most successful Vietnamese companies use an organizational approach similar to that of successful companies in highly industrialized economies in other parts of the world.

....
Rohit Deshpandé is Professor of Business Administration at Harvard Business School, and Executive Director at the Marketing Science Institute, Cambridge, MA. John U. Farley is C.V. Starr Distinguished Research Fellow at Dartmouth College, Hanover, NH, and Henkel Professor of Industrial Marketing of the China–Europe International Business School, Shanghai.

The authors are indebted for support of this project by the Center for Developing Economies of the Wharton School at the University of Pennsylvania, Joseph Massey and the Center for China and East Asia of the Amos Tuck School, the Tuck Vietnam Project, and the Division of Research, Harvard Business School.

Reproduced with permission from *Asian Journal of Marketing*, 1998/99.

INTRODUCTION

> "Socialism is whatever brings happiness to the people."
> General No Nguyen Gap, 1995

> "We are not afraid of capitalist enterprises, but of not being able to supervise and control them."
> Party Leader Do Muoi, 1996

> "Ideal people are universal and not clannish."
> Confucius, Analects 2:14, 500 B.C.

The transformation of planned economies into more market-oriented economies depends largely on government policy, but it also depends heavily on the success of firms—old and new—in responding to the new economic environment. This includes challenges to creating a market-oriented focus in firms in both the private and public sectors.

The study reported in this paper explores in a sample of Vietnamese firms a type of "success" model involving market orientation, innovativeness, and externally oriented corporate cultures that we call the "High Performance Model." This model, developed and tested in industrial nations of Asia, North America, and Europe (Deshpandé et al., 1993, 1997), is examined in the specific context of values held by senior Vietnamese managers as well as in comparison to results profiling successful firms elsewhere.

VIETNAM UNDER *DOI MOI*

Doi Moi—variously translated as renovation, change, and newness—dominates the discussion of business in Vietnam. Under *Doi Moi* and related economic policies oriented toward a market economy, indications are that the country of 75 million stands poised to enjoy an extended period of economic growth like that experienced by many of its neighbors (Hiebert, 1996). For example, GDP of US$200 measured in terms of official exchange rates compares poorly with US$460 in China and US$2,000 in neighboring Thailand; but in terms of purchasing power parity, Vietnam stands at US$1,200—lower than US$2,500 in China and US$5,500 in Thailand, but with very considerable purchasing power for modern goods and services (*The Economist*, 1995).

The situation is, of course, somewhat unclear. The 1986 social reform program (*Doi Moi*) has opened up possibilities for foreign investment, particularly through joint ventures; but the progress has been irregular and perhaps half of the joint ventures come to nothing (Kohut, 1996). New advertising billboards are posted even as others are torn down or painted over, reflecting the June 1996 policy of caution and economic orthodoxy. Some experts estimate that to meet the goal of 15 percent annual growth of the industrial sector, Vietnam will need US$15 million to $20 million in capital over the next decade to sustain economic growth—a clear contrast to the US$2 million so far disbursed. Taiwan and South Korea are, so far, the major investors; postrecognition U.S. commitments of US$700 million are focused on the offshore oil sector (Karnow, 1996).

In many discussions of market developments concerning Vietnam, there is an obvious lack of knowledge about the management of Vietnamese firms. These include 6,400 state enterprises (down from 12,000 in 1986, but with the share of GDP increased to 46 percent from 32 percent) and also cooperatives, which have historically exerted huge influence on social economic advances. "Equitation" (privatization) has been slow as has been development of equity markets. Hence, in our study, we focus on the management of Vietnamese firms, and not on the political or economic factors shaping the environment in which they are managed. We are, of course, well aware of the close interplay of political and economic reforms in Vietnam.

Conceptual Background and Hypotheses

As Vietnam enters the Asian economic growth scene, understanding the behavior of its business firms is important to understanding Vietnamese both as customers and competitors. We use a framework of analysis that was first applied in Japan (Deshpandé et al., 1993). In this framework, firms that perform the best have the following characteristics:

- An *organizational culture* with an external orientation—to markets and to sources of new ideas
- A *customer orientation* that puts customers first
- *Innovativeness*, especially with really new products and services
- *Positive work climate*

We refer to this pattern as a "High Performance Model" and, given the lack of prior theoretical and empirical documentation of such factors in Vietnam, the conceptual framework and hypotheses that follow assume that the same pattern will apply to the best-performing Vietnamese firms as their counterparts in other countries.

The Marketing Science Institute, a leading nonprofit U.S.-based think-tank, has recently stated as among its highest research priority areas topics including innovation, global marketing, management organization and processes, and market orientation (*Marketing Science Institute*, 1996). We do not mean to imply that there are no other factors affecting business success, but Capon et al. (1996), who considered a much broader set of factors, showed that the relationship between organizational factors (such as culture and climate) and business performance has not been studied adequately, relative to, for example, strategic and environmental factors. Hence, this study is timely both in its conceptual scope and its focus on an empirically under-studied economy.

Organizational Culture

Organizational culture has been defined as the pattern of shared values and beliefs that help individuals understand organizational functioning and thus provide them with the norms for behavior in the organization. Based on a framework proposed by Smircich (1983), five alternative theoretical paradigms emerge for studying corporate culture, each with unique implications. One such paradigm, organizational cognition, has been developed relatively more than the others in terms of formal conceptual framework, specification of variables, and operationalization of measures and is therefore the one used in the current study.

The seminal work of Quinn and his colleagues (Quinn, 1988; Quinn and McGrath, 1985) proposed a "competing values" model of organizational effectiveness. This model, which was first described in an award-winning paper by Quinn and Rohrbaugh (1983), is based on an empirical analysis of the values individuals hold regarding organizational performance. Using a list of organizational effectiveness criteria developed by Campbell (1977), Quinn and Rohrbaugh found that clusters of values reproduced the dimensions developed by Jung (1923) to describe psychological archetypes. As Cameron and Freeman (1991) note: "Because cultures are defined by the values, assumptions, and interpretations of organization members, and because a common set of dimensions organizes these factors on both psychological and organizational levels, a model of culture types can be derived."

Figure 9-1 shows the two key dimensions defining culture types. These key dimensions represent a merging of two major theoretical traditions from the organizational behavior literature, the systems-structural perspective (Zey-Ferrell, 1981; Van deVen, 1976) and the transaction cost perspective, which is grounded also in economics (Williamson, 1975). As noted in Figure 9-1, one axis describes the continuum from *organic* to *mechanistic* processes, that is, whether the organizational emphasis is more on flexibility, spontaneity, and individuality, or on control, stability, and order. The other axis describes the relative organizational emphasis on *internal maintenance* (i.e., smoothing activities, integration) or on *external positioning* (i.e., competition, environmental differentiation). The four resulting culture types are labeled consensual, bureaucratic, entrepreneurial, and competitive. These labels are consistent with much theorizing on alternative organizational forms and the use of similar terms by scholars including Williamson (1975), Ouchi (1980), and Mintzberg (1979). They are also consistent with the descriptors used in previous studies of changes in cultures over organizational life cycles, a study of effective leadership types in organizations (Quinn, 1988), and the organizational frameworks proposed by Bennis (1973) and Mitroff (1983).

Figure 9-1
Dominant organizational cultural characteristics

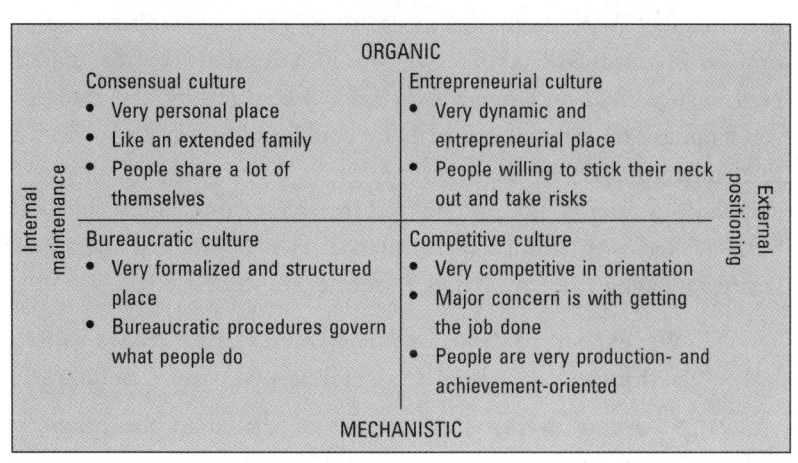

	ORGANIC	
Internal maintenance	Consensual culture • Very personal place • Like an extended family • People share a lot of themselves	Entrepreneurial culture • Very dynamic and entrepreneurial place • People willing to stick their neck out and take risks
	Bureaucratic culture • Very formalized and structured place • Bureaucratic procedures govern what people do	Competitive culture • Very competitive in orientation • Major concern is with getting the job done • People are very production- and achievement-oriented	External positioning
	MECHANISTIC	

Sources: Adapted from Cameron and Freeman (1991) and Quinn (1988).

The lower right quadrant, called a competitive culture, emphasizes competitiveness and goal achievement (Cameron and Freeman, 1991). Transactions are governed by market mechanisms (Ouchi, 1980). The key measure or organizational effectiveness is productivity achieved through these market mechanisms. This culture type is in direct contrast to the set of values expressed in a consensual culture (hence the terminology of a "competing values" approach). In the latter (also called a clan), the emphasis is on cohesiveness, participation, and teamwork. The commitment of organizational members is ensured through participation, and organizational cohesiveness and personal satisfaction are rated more highly than financial and market share objectives.

The upper right quadrant, called an entrepreneurial culture, emphasizes values of entrepreneurship, creativity, and adaptability. Flexibility and tolerance are important beliefs and effectiveness is defined in terms of finding new markets and new directions for growth. Once again, the competing set of values is found in the bureaucratic culture, which stresses order, rules, and regulations. Transactions are under the control of surveillance, evaluation, and direction. Business effectiveness is defined by consistency and achievement of clearly stated goals.

The four classifications of culture developed above imply varying degrees of business performance in a competitive marketplace. The *competitive culture*, characterized by its emphasis on competitive advantage and market superiority, might be expected to result in the best business performance. At the other extreme, we would expect a *bureaucratic culture* to contribute to relatively unsatisfactory business performance. Also, given the focus in an *entrepreneurial culture* on innovation and risk-taking, we would anticipate better market performance than in a *consensual culture* where loyalty and tradition and emphasis on internal maintenance could lead to a lack of attention to changing market needs. In a more general sense, the organizational emphasis on external positioning over internal maintenance is likely to be associated with stronger performance. Hence, our first hypothesis (again following from the High Performance Model) is

H1: We expect to find in Vietnamese firms that business performance is related to organizational culture as follows:

- Above average performance is related to the extent of competitive culture and entrepreneurial culture.

- Below average performance is related to the extent of consensual culture and bureaucratic culture.

Organizational Climate

Organizational climate has a long-established history in organization research and in popular books on the performance of firms. A useful definition of organizational climate is a relatively enduring quality of the internal environment of an organization that (1) is experienced by its members, (2) influences their behavior, and (3) can be described in terms of a particular set of characteristics (or attributes) of the organization. One insightful definition describes culture as "why things happen the way they do" versus organizational climate, "what happens around here." The particular type of climate we study here is one that encourages management processes stressing communication, participation and decentralization, an atmosphere of friendliness and trust, and reward of performance. We refer to this as a positive climate. Hence, our second hypothesis is

H2: In Vietnamese firms, we expect the more positive the organizational climate, the higher the business performance.

Customer Orientation

Customer orientation is a taken-for-granted fundamental principle in marketing practice. Kohli and Jaworski (1990) point out that discussion of customer orientation (or the term they use, market orientation) has come within the context of implementation of the marketing concept, and Narver and Slater (1990) have taken a conceptually similar approach to the measurement of market orientation. Deshpandé et al. (1993) develop a similar scale for testing in Japan. Deshpandé and Farley (1998) show that these three different approaches to measuring customer/market orientation produce quite similar substantive results, and that in fact the three scales are highly correlated. The concept of customer orientation is at the heart of the management philosophy of the marketing concept (Drucker, 1954; Levitt, 1960; Webster, 1988) and is presumed to contribute to long-term profitability. Yet, as noted, this relationship has received relatively little empirical study or verification outside of the U.S. context.

We define customer orientation as *the set of beliefs that puts the customer's interest first, while not excluding those of all other stockholders such as owners, managers, and employees in order to develop a long-term profitable enterprise.* Our third hypothesis is

> *H3*: In Vietnamese firms, customer orientation should be positively related to business performance.

Organizational Innovativeness

In an often-cited passage, Peter Drucker wrote: "There is only one valid definition of business purpose: to create a customer.... It is the customer who determines what the business is.... Because it is its purpose to create a customer, any business enterprise has two—and only these two—basic functions: marketing and innovation" (1954: 37). Despite increased interest in conceptualizing and measuring the marketing concept, little attention has been devoted recently to Drucker's second "basic function": innovation. Economists have noted the importance of organizations being innovative (Mansfield et al., 1977) and scholars have increasingly linked innovativeness to organizational performance (Capon et al., 1992), suggesting that a firm needs to be innovative "to gain a competitive edge in order to survive and grow" (Grønhaug and Kaufmann, 1988: 3). Hence, our final hypothesis is

> *H4*: The more innovative Vietnamese firms will perform better.

Covariates: Type of Vietnamese Firm and Regional Location

In addition to these factors, there are key characteristics of Vietnam and Vietnamese industries that we consider. There are three principal types of Vietnamese firm in our sample: government firms, cooperatives, and the newer, private firms. While few firms are really distant from the public sector in terms of important elements of decision making and capital supply, we make comparisons to see if private firms appear to be different in terms of important factors like innovation and entrepreneurship. We also examine the impact of the industry type of the firm on performance.

Geography may also play a role. While the capital of imperial Vietnam was centrally located in Hue, the recent colonial history of Vietnam has involved geographic and cultural partitioning, which might have a residual effect on the factors under study here. The fact that government corporations tend to be headquartered in Hanoi may also make geographic location important.

Data Collection

Face-to-face interviews were conducted with a representative sample of 100 senior executives of 100 Vietnamese companies, half headquartered in the Hanoi area and half in the area of Ho Chi Minh City. The sample universe was a near-census of firms taken from a collection of firm directories from government and private sources maintained by a major international market research firm. The sample used in this study was randomly drawn from that universe. To these were added 28 members of a senior management executive program, whose responses showed no significant statistical differences from those of the original sample on any of the individual characteristics of the managers or on the organizational factors describing their organizations. Interviews were conducted by personnel from a major market research firm. All respondents were guaranteed anonymity for themselves and their companies, and were promised a report of the results, as an incentive to participate in the study.

The questionnaire items for organizational culture and climate, customer orientation, innovativeness, and performance used in all countries in appropriately translated form are shown in Appendix 9-A. The respective scales are also shown in Appendix 9-A. Confirmatory factor analysis of each scale found unidimensionality, reflected by one eigenvalue greater than one. It should be noted that reliabilities of the scale measurements in Vietnam, while directionally correct, were weaker than in Japan. (A detailed discussion of reliability is in Appendix 9-B and Table 9-B1.)

The Vietnamese Managers Themselves

The individuals in the sample represent the very same senior managers who will oversee any transformation of the Vietnamese economy. Like Vietnamese history, they are steeped in traditions with a heavy Confucian overtone, and there is considerable homogeneity among sample members. Table 9-1, which shows the measures of these values, is divided into two parts.

- **What is important?** These Vietnamese managers especially value perseverance and having a sense of shame, but face and tradition are also important, all measuring over 5.5 on a 7-point scale (Table 9-1, part A). There are no differences over the type of firm or geographic area on assessment of what is important.

- **Confucian values.** The Vietnamese sample values family and group norms (the means of all six items in part B of Table 9-1 are above 5.0 on a 7-point Likert scale). On three of these measures, we see systematic differences within Vietnam, as managers of private firms in Vietnam average lower on family interactions, compromising needs with those of the family, and conformity to group norms.

- **Regional differences.** Some two-thirds of the Vietnamese

TABLE 9-1
Values of Vietnamese managers

A. What is important?

Perseverance	6.59
Having a sense of shame	6.12
Protecting face	5.95
Respect for tradition	5.68

1 = very unimportant, 7 = very important.

No significant differences in what is important over firm type, i.e., government vs. co-ops vs. private; or region, i.e., North vs. South.

B. Personal values

I have strong affection for my family	6.69
I interact frequently with family members (Government firms 6.44; co-ops 5.52; private 5.00)	5.65*
I often compromise my own needs with my family needs (Government firms and co-ops 5.70; private 4.68)	5.37*
I gave up personal wishes and desires to conform with social norms (Government firms and co-ops 5.70; private 4.48) (North 5.52; South 4.81)	5.22*
My parents have greatly influenced my way of thinking and behaving	5.21
I behave according to what others expect of me	5.17

1 = strongly disagree, 7 = strongly agree.

* Significant differences over type of firm and/or region, based on two-way analysis of variance. No interactions between firm type and region are significant.

managers reported that they identify with their region as opposed to a third with Vietnam as a whole and a handful with Asia. The identification is relatively strong, averaging 6.1 on a 7-point scale. Northerners are more likely to identify with region, and they also identify more strongly (6.4) than Southerners (5.8).

We conclude that Vietnamese managers believe in perseverance, protecting face, and tradition. They also believe in Confucian values. These norms are held strongly regardless of the region from which managers came, and despite the fact that strong regional identification persists.

Vietnamese Organizational Culture

The overall pattern of organizational culture

In terms of general pattern, Vietnamese firms are highly bureaucratic in culture and have a much lower level of competitive culture (Table 9-2). This may be related to the centralized planning and control of the economy. They are also relatively low on consensual and entrepreneurial cultures.

Mean score values of organizational culture scales for a representative sample of Japanese firms (Deshpandé et al., 1993) are also shown in Table 9-2 to provide comparison. Japanese firms are highly consensual (Ouchi, 1980), but also show a greater degree of competitive culture and less bureaucratic and entrepreneurial cultures compared with Vietnamese firms.

TABLE 9-2
Mean score values of organizational culture types in Vietnam and Japan

	Vietnam	Japan	Culture type significantly different (α = 0.05) between countries?
Consensual	97.2	117.0	Yes
Entrepreneurial	99.4	78.9	Yes
Bureaucratic	113.9	100.9	Yes
Competitive	89.4	106.1	Yes
Significantly different (α = 0.05) over culture types?	Yes	Yes	

Differences over industry, firm type, and geographic area

We find no differences in organizational cultures, customer orientation, organizational climate, or innovativeness between industries, so the results are Vietnamese- and not industry-specific. The industries included here are financial and other services, consumer durables and nondurables, and industrial equipment, components, and supplies.

There are some differences in our measures for the Vietnamese sample between different types of firm and between geographic areas (Table 9-3). We should not over-interpret the differences, as there is more homogeneity than difference (only 6 of 16 are significantly different in Table 9-3) and also since the four significant North–South differences are small in magnitude. The results are summarized as follows:

- There is no significant difference over firm types in innovativeness or in entrepreneurial organizational culture, which fundamentally provides favorable conditions for innovation. This is somewhat surprising in that we might have expected higher values on both in the private firms.

TABLE 9-3

Differences between Vietnamese firms in mean values of organizational culture, customer orientation, organizational climate, and innovativeness by type of firm and geographic area

	Overall mean	Firm type Government	Firm type Co-op	Firm type Private	Area North	Area South	F-ratio in 2-way ANOVA (p-level)
Organizational culture							
Consensual	97.2	−5.8	−3.8	13.5	NS	NS	0.00*
Entrepreneurial	99.4	NS	NS	NS	NS	NS	0.84
Bureaucratic	113.9	NS	NS	NS	+5.2	−5.2	0.01*
Competitive	89.4	+6.3	+1.5	−11.6	−2.7	+2.7	0.03**
Customer orientation	31.2	NS	NS	NS	+1.5	−1.5	0.01*
Organizational climate	27.8	NS	NS	NS	+1.4	−1.4	0.00*
Innovativeness	21.1	NS	NS	NS	NS	NS	0.14
Performance	12.0	NS	NS	NS	NS	NS	0.58

NS: Individual two-way ANOVA coefficient not significant.
* Both firm type and area individually are significant, but interaction is not significant.
** Only individual effect with significant ANOVA coefficients is significant.

- While Southern firms are slightly more competitive, this is not due to the private sector firms, which in fact are more consensual.
- Northern firms see themselves slightly more bureaucratic and slightly less competitive. However, these are offset by their being slightly more customer-oriented and have slightly more positive organizational climate.

These patterns raise questions as to whether foreign firms should seek out a particular type of firms or firms in a particular geographic area to form partnerships. By the same token, government firms may ultimately constitute formidable competitors, both for the Vietnam market and for foreign markets, where they now make a significant portion of their sales.

How Organizational Culture and Climate, Innovativeness, and Customer Orientation Relate to Performance in Vietnam and Elsewhere

Perhaps the most important issue for this research is how organizational culture and climate, customer orientation, and innovativeness—all to some extent controllable by management—relate to performance. We have shown elsewhere (Deshpandé et al., 1997) that such relationships exist in five major countries in the industrialized world, including Japan. As noted earlier, we call this pattern the "High Performance Model."

A multivariate analysis of covariance (Table 9-4), with location and firm type (Table 9-3) as covariates, was used to establish overall significance of the differences between the top performers and the others on the eight organizational variables included in our hypotheses. We then examined the differences in the eight individual items to establish whether their signs are also consistent with the hypotheses. The results are summarized as follows:

- As a set, the eight organizational variables are significantly different between the top performers and the other firms based on a multivariate test. The four organizational culture variables are also significantly different. The type of firm and location are not significantly different.

Table 9-4
Statistical analysis of better-performing Vietnamese firms

Results of MANCOVA tests of general hypotheses concerning organizational variables

Hypothesis	Statistically significant at $\alpha = 0.05$
Top quarter of firms differ from others in terms of all organizational variables as a set	Yes
Top quarter of firms differ from others in terms of organizational culture measures	Yes
Top quarter of firms differ from others in terms of geographic area or industry type	No

Profiles of top quarter of Vietnamese firms in terms of performance

	Mean Top performers	Mean Other firms	Sign of mean difference (Top performers – Others) Hypothesized	Sign of mean difference (Top performers – Others) Actual	Individual variable statistically significant at $\alpha = 0.05$?
Organizational culture					
Consensual	94.8	98.0	–	–	No
Entrepreneurial	110.7	95.8	+	+	Yes
Bureaucratic	101.8	117.8	–	–	Yes
Competitive	92.6	88.4	+	+	No
Innovativeness	10.3	8.5	+	+	Yes
Customer orientation	36.2	34.8	+	+	Yes
Organizational climate	28.9	27.4	+	+	Yes
Performance	16.5	10.8	+	+	Yes

- All eight signs of the differences conform with those hypothesized, the differences being significant based on a sign test at $\alpha = 0.05$; and six of the eight differences are individually significant, based on individual t-tests with the degrees of freedom adjusted to reflect simultaneity.
- The individual hypotheses are confirmed:

    H1: Mean scores on competitive and entrepreneurial cultures are higher for the top performers and mean scores on consensual and bureaucratic cultures are lower. As a group, the organizational culture scores of the top performers are significantly different from those of the other firms (using MANCOVA as shown in Table 9-4).

H2: The top performers have a significantly higher score on the scale measuring positive organizational climate.

H3: The top performers have a significantly higher score on the customer orientation scale.

H4: The top performers have a significantly higher score on innovativeness.

- Demographics are not good predictors of good performance:
  - As reported above, the type of firm and geographic location of firm have no significant effect on performance.
  - The type of industry has no significant effect on performance, as measured by analysis of variance using an eight-category classification including financial and other services, consumer durables and nondurables, and producer durables, nondurables, and supplies.
  - There are no significant differences in *t*-tests comparing the values of the managers of the top quarter of performers versus the others (Table 9-1).
  - The top performers do not have a higher share of sales abroad, which reinforces findings in other studies (see Capon et al., 1996).

Discussion

Rapid economic development plus reforms permitting a more market-oriented economic structure characterize the contemporary Vietnamese business environment. Vietnamese organizations—public sector and private—are participating in this new environment through both their own ventures and joint ventures with foreign firms. This paper examines how a representative sample of 128 Vietnamese companies in a variety of industries are managing and performing in this new environment. Since this is, we believe, the very first empirical study linking organizational factors to Vietnamese firm performance, we must consider our measurements as needing replication and our results as being preliminary. With these caveats noted, we can summarize the major conclusions from our study.

First, Vietnamese managers are heavily steeped in Confucian values, which influence both their personal and managerial lives. We find that Vietnamese firms' cultures in general are bureaucratic and not highly competitive. However, like firms in some industrial countries and some industrializing countries as well, the *best-performing* Vietnamese firms are innovative and customer-oriented, and have cultures that are externally oriented toward markets and innovation. More specifically, these relatively successful Vietnamese firms share more "High Performance Model" characteristics of innovativeness, entrepreneurial and competitive organizational cultures, positive organizational climate, and a high degree of customer orientation.

Within Vietnam, we find only minor differences between the three types of firm (government, cooperative, and private) in our sample. For example, we find no significant differences in performance, innovativeness, and customer orientation between the three types of firm. In addition, we find all three types of firm about the same in terms of bureaucratic and entrepreneurial cultures. The one exception is somewhat surprising—that private firms tend to be more consensual and less competitively oriented than the other two types of firm. This may be in part due to the fact that government firms report significantly more international business than do the other types of firm.

Despite relatively strong personal identification of the managers with geographic region, we find few regional differences, with the exception that Northern firms consider themselves slightly more bureaucratic. This pattern of similarity in all likelihood reflects the unification of Vietnam since 1975.

The relative similarities of all types of firm and the regions may imply that prospects for both collaboration with and competition from a broad variety of Vietnamese firms are comparable. However, the relatively high degree of bureaucratization and relatively low degree of competitive organizational culture may imply a fairly long and difficult path for general management practices of Vietnamese firms of all kinds to become truly compatible with a market economy.

Appendix 9-A
Measures: operationalizations

Customer Orientation

The statements below describe norms that operate in businesses. Please indicate your extent of agreement about how well the statements describe the actual norms in your business.

1	2	3	4	5
Strongly disagree	Disagree	Neither agree nor disagree	Agree	Strongly agree

Instruction: Answer in the context of your specific product/market or service/market business.

1. We have routine or regular measures of customer service.
2. Our product and service development is based on good market and customer information.
3. We know our competitors well.
4. We have a good sense of how our customers value our products and services.
5. We are more customer-focused than our competitors.
6. We compete primarily based on product or service differentiation.
7. The customer's interest should always come first, ahead of the owner's.
8. Our products/services are the best in the business.
9. I believe this business exists primarily to serve customers.

These same customer orientation items above were used in other countries with customers and with the first-person pronoun replaced by "the supplier," which was identified at the beginning of the interview.

Organizational Culture

These questions relate to what your operation is like. Each of these items contains four descriptions of organizations. Please distribute 100 points among the four descriptions depending on how *similar* each description is to your business. None of the descriptions is any better than any other; they are just different. *For each question, please use all 100 points.* You may divide the points in any way you wish. *Most businesses will be some mixture of these described.*

1. Kind of organization (Please distribute 100 points)

_____ points for A
(A) My organization is a very personal place. It is like an extended family. People seem to share a lot of themselves.

_____ points for B
(B) My organization is a very dynamic and entrepreneurial place. People are willing to stick their neck out and take risks.

_____ points for C
(C) My organization is a very formal and structured place. Established procedures generally govern what people do.

_____ points for D
(D) My organization is very production-oriented. A major concern is with getting the job done, without much personal involvement.

2. Leadership (Please distribute 100 points)

_____ points for A
(A) The head of my organization is generally considered to be a mentor, sage, or a father or mother figure.

_____ points for B
(B) The head of my organization is generally considered to be an entrepreneur, an innovator, or a risk taker.

_____ points for C
(C) The head of my organization is generally considered to be a coordinator, an organizer, or an administrator.

_____ points for D
(D) The head of my organization is generally considered to be a producer, a technician, or a hard-driver.

3. What holds the organization together (Please distribute 100 points)

_____ points for A
(A) The glue that holds my organization together is loyalty and tradition. Commitment to this firm runs high.

_____ points for B
(B) The glue that holds my organization together is a commitment to innovation and development. There is an emphasis on being first.

_____ points for C
(C) The glue that holds my organization together is formal rules and policies. Maintaining a smooth-running institution is important here.

_____ points for D
(D) The glue that holds my organization together is the emphasis on tasks and goal accomplishment. A production orientation is commonly shared.

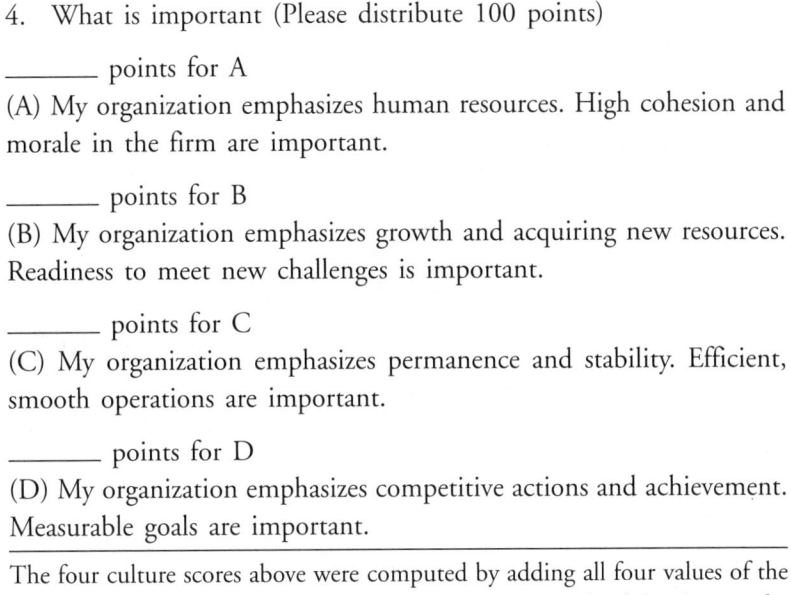

4. What is important (Please distribute 100 points)

_____ points for A
(A) My organization emphasizes human resources. High cohesion and morale in the firm are important.

_____ points for B
(B) My organization emphasizes growth and acquiring new resources. Readiness to meet new challenges is important.

_____ points for C
(C) My organization emphasizes permanence and stability. Efficient, smooth operations are important.

_____ points for D
(D) My organization emphasizes competitive actions and achievement. Measurable goals are important.

The four culture scores above were computed by adding all four values of the A items for consensual, of the B items for entrepreneurial, of the C items for bureaucratic, and of the D items for competitive cultures. The results shown in Table 9-2 can therefore equal more or less than 100, which would be the result only if respondents distributed points equally on each question. The scale was adapted from Cameron and Freeman (1991) and Quinn (1988).

Innovativeness

In a new product and service introduction, how often is your company

	Always				Never
• first to market with new products and services	1	2	3	4	5
• later entrant in established but still growing markets*	1	2	3	4	5
• entrant in mature, stable markets*	1	2	3	4	5
• at the cutting edge of technological innovation	1	2	3	4	5

*Reverse-scored in forming the scale.

The innovativeness scale above was constructed from the items used by Capon et al. (1988) to describe organizational innovativeness.

Organizational Climate

We are also interested in your opinions about your organization's decision-making style. We would like to know whether you agree or disagree with the following statements:

1	2	3	4	5
Strongly disagree	Disagree	Neither agree nor disagree	Agree	Strongly agree

1. In our organization, there is excellent communication between line managers and staff.
2. People trust each other in this organization.
3. Decision making in our organization is participative.
4. A friendly atmosphere prevails among people in our organization.
5. In our organization, people feel they are their own bosses in most matters.

The organizational climate scale above was derived by factor analysis from a 54-item scale reported in Capon et al. (1988).

Performance

Relative to our businesses' largest competitor, we are

	1	2	3	4	5
(a)	Much less profitable	Less profitable	About equally profitable	More profitable	Much more profitable
(b)*	Much larger	Larger	About the same size	Smaller	Much smaller
(c)*	Have a much larger market share	Have a larger market share	About the same market share	Have a smaller market share	Have a much smaller market share
(d)	Growing much more slowly	Growing more slowly	Growing at about the same rate	Growing faster	Growing much faster

*Reverse-scored in construction of the scale.

The performance scale above was based on work from the PIMS program reported by Buzzell and Gale (1987).

APPENDIX 9-B
Scale reliabilities

The fundamental conceptual material on which this study is based was primarily developed with the industrial world in mind. The first application involved scales developed in the U.S. and applied in Japan—again both industrial countries. In the initial applications, pairs (dyads) of managers were used in all samples to allow analysis of inter-rater reliabilities within firms as well as conventional intra-scale reliabilities across firms measured in terms of Cronbach α's. A very high degree of reliability was found in Japan (Table 9-B1), where the conventional threshold of 0.6 (out of 1.0) was met in all but one scale. As the research program moved beyond the highly industrialized economies, the question of whether the measurement methods were adequate became important. It should be noted that the results reported in this paper should be considered preliminary because of the relatively low levels of scale reliabilities in Vietnam.

TABLE 9-B1
Scale reliabilities for Vietnam and Japan measured by Cronbach α

	Vietnam	Japan
Organizational culture		
Consensual	0.35	0.82
Entrepreneurial	0.31	0.66
Bureaucratic	0.43	0.42
Competitive	0.74	0.71
Customer orientation	0.67	0.69
Organizational climate	0.61	0.69
Innovativeness	0.56	0.85
Performance	0.70	0.71

References

Bennis, Warren G. (1973). *The Leaning Ivory Tower*. San Francisco: Jossey-Bass.

Buzzell, Robert D. and Bradley T. Gale (1987). *The PIMS Principles: Linking Strategy to Performance*. New York: Free Press.

Cameron, Kim S. and Sara J. Freeman (1991). Cultural congruence, strength, and type: Relationships to effectiveness. In Richard W. Woodman and William A. Pasmore (eds.), *Research in Organizational Change and Development*, Vol. 5. Greenwich, CT: JAI Press.

Campbell, J.P. (1977). On the nature of organizational effectiveness. In Paul S. Goodman and Johannes M. Pennings (eds.), *New Perspectives on Organizational Effectiveness*. San Francisco: Jossey-Bass.

Capon, Noel, John U. Farley, and James M. Hulbert (1988). *Corporate Strategic Planning*. New York: Columbia University Press.

Capon, Noel, John U. Farley, James M. Hulbert, and Donald R. Lehmann (1992). Profiles of product innovators among large U.S. manufacturers. *Management Science*, 38 (February): 157–69.

Capon, Noel, John U. Farley, and Scott Hoenig (1996). *Toward an Integrative Explanation of Corporate Financial Performance*. New York: Kluwer.

Deshpandé, R. and J.U. Farley (1998). Measuring market orientation: Generalization and synthesis. *Journal of Market Focused Management*, 2: 213–32.

Deshpandé, R., J.U. Farley, and F.E. Webster, Jr. (1993). Corporate culture, customer orientation, and innovativeness in Japanese firms: A quadrad analysis. *Journal of Marketing*, 57 (January): 22–27.

Deshpandé, R., J.U. Farley, and F.E. Webster, Jr. (1997). Factors affecting organizational performance: A five-country comparison. Marketing Science Institute Working Paper, Report No. 97-108, Cambridge, MA.

Drucker, Peter F. (1954). *The Practice of Management*. New York: Harper and Row.

The Economist (1995). A survey of Vietnam. July 8.

Grønhaug, Kjell and Geir Kaufmann (1988). *Innovation: A Cross-disciplinary Perspective*. Oslo: Norwegian University Press.

Hiebert, Murray (1996). *Chasing the Tigers: A Portrait of the New Vietnam*. New York: Kodansha.

Jung, Carl G. (1923). *Psychological Types*. London: Routledge and Kegan Paul.

Karnow, Stanley (1996). Vietnam now. *Smithsonian*, January: 32–42.

Kohli, A.K. and B.J. Jaworski (1990). Market orientation: The construct, research propositions, and managerial implications. *Journal of Marketing*, 54 (April): 1–18.

Kohut, John (1996). Doi Moi: Now for the hard part. *Asia, Inc.*, May: 29–35.

Levitt, Theodore (1960). Marketing myopia. *Harvard Business Review*, 38 (May–June): 45–56.

Mansfield, Edwin, et al. (1977). *The Production and Application of New Industrial Technology*. New York: W.W. Norton.

Marketing Science Institute (1996). Research priorities: A guide to MSI research programs and procedures, 1996–1998. Cambridge, MA.

Mintzberg, Henry (1979). *The Structuring of Organizations*. Englewood Cliffs, NJ: Prentice Hall.

Mitroff, Ian I. (1983). *Stakeholders of the Organizational Mind.* San Francisco: Jossey-Bass.

Narver, John C. and Stanley F. Slater (1990). The effect of a market orientation on business profitability. *Journal of Marketing Research,* 54 (October): 20–35.

Ouchi, William G. (1980). Markets, bureaucracies, and clans. *Administrative Science Quarterly,* 25 (March): 129–41.

Quinn, Robert E. (1988). *Beyond Rational Management.* San Francisco: Jossey-Bass.

Quinn, Robert E. and Michael R. McGrath (1985). Transformation of organizational cultures: A competing values perspective. In Peter J. Frost et al. (eds.), *Organizational Culture.* Beverly Hills, CA: Sage.

Quinn, Robert E. and J. Rohrbaugh (1983). A spatial model of effectiveness criteria: Toward a competing values approach to organizational analysis. *Management Science,* 29 (3): 363–77.

Smircich, Linda (1983). Concepts of culture and organizational analysis. *Administrative Science Quarterly,* 28 (September): 339–58.

Van deVen, Andrew (1976). On the nature, formation, and maintenance of relations among organizations. *Academy of Management Review,* 1 (October): 24–36.

Webster, Frederick E., Jr. (1988). The rediscovery of the marketing concept. *Business Horizons,* 31 (May–June): 29–39.

Williamson, Oliver E. (1975). *Markets and Hierarchies: Analysis and Antitrust Implications.* New York: Free Press.

Zey-Ferrell, M. (1981). Criticisms of the dominant perspective on organization. *Sociological Quarterly,* 22 (Spring): 181–205.

STRATEGIC ALLIANCES IN CHINA
Negotiating the Barriers

Ajit S. Nair and Edwin R. Stafford

Capitalism in China has been evolving rapidly in the form of joint ventures and strategic alliances joining Chinese and Western organizations. Many Westerners developing alliances in China, however, have been frustrated by complexities in the negotiation process, including how to manage cultural differences, overcome language barriers, handle copyrights, and work through China's complex bureaucracy. In-depth interviews with 29 Western executives experienced with Sino-Western alliances describe some of these challenges and offer some strategies for success.

INTRODUCTION

Recent events have continued to ignite the West's anxieties about China. The death of economic reformer Deng Xiaoping, persecution of dissidents, labor abuses, military threats to Taiwanese elections, and trade disputes with the U.S. have dominated recent world news

---

Ajit S. Nair is manager for operations at Aces International, Inc., in San Jose, California, U.S.A. Dr. Edwin R. Stafford is Assistant Professor of Marketing at the College of Business, Utah State University, U.S.A., and was named the 1997 "College of Business Professor of the Year."

The authors thank Richard Brecher (U.S.–China Business Council), Cory Yeates (SIETEC International), and Martin Lin (Rockwell International) for their valuable comments on earlier drafts of this article. The authors also thank Wendy Littlejohn for transcribing the many hours of interview recordings.

Reprinted from *Long Range Planning*, Vol. 31, No. 1, pp. 139–46. Copyright 1998, with permission from Elsevier Science.

headlines (*Business Week*, 1997). With Hong Kong's reversion to China, both American and European political leaders are concerned with China's emerging role in the world's geopolitical stage. Because China's Open Door Policy has continued to attract Western technology and capital in most industries, it is hoped that expanded economic ties with the West may foster a freer society and create a China more willing to play by "all the rules" of world trade and relations (*The Economist*, 1996; Woodward and Liu, 1993). Western firms eyeing China's vast labor force, natural resources, and market potential view joint ventures and strategic alliances as the most logical entrance strategies into China. The ways to go about negotiating such partnerships, however, are less obvious. China's social, economic, and political dilemmas, as well as its unique culture, create an enigmatic climate for Westerners to navigate.

China is the world's oldest and most pervasive bureaucracy, only now emerging from feudalistic Communism. The teachings of Confucius have had a profound influence. Family devotion is paramount. Obedience and respect for authority is almost sacred, and carefully prescribed codes of conduct affect virtually every aspect of Chinese behavior and life. Trusting relationships are fundamental; the Chinese believe that one should build the relationship first and if successful, business will follow (Ambler, 1995). The Chinese consider "change" potentially disruptive to "balance and harmony," making nonaction better than action (Kenna and Lacy, 1994). This can make negotiations long and arduous. This article focuses on the common obstacles Westerners face when negotiating alliances in China and makes recommendations based upon interviews with 29 Western executives involved in Sino-Western joint ventures and strategic alliances (see Box 10-1 for methodology details). Interview quotes recount our informants' insights, experiences, and recommendations for Chinese negotiations.

Establishing an Alliance in China

Although frequently changing laws and varying practices across localities make it difficult to present a detailed "road map," some broad stages can be expected in the approval process for equity joint ventures. Compared to other forms of alliance possibilities in China (licensing, supplier–distributor arrangements, etc.), joint ventures can be the most

Box 10-1
Methodology

> Interviews with 29 executives from firms based in the U.S., Hong Kong, the People's Republic of China, Germany, and Canada were conducted both in person and by telephone. Respondents were identified with the assistance of the U.S.–China Business Council and were contacted regarding their interest in the study. To encourage candor, respondents were assured complete anonymity in terms of their names and companies. Firms were from the aircraft manufacturing, automobile, computer, telecommunications, chemical, and pharmaceutical industries; more than half represented the Fortune 500. Both large and mid-sized firms were included to broaden the findings. The recorded open-ended interviews focused on executives' perceptions and experiences with negotiating partnerships in China, factors that inhibited or facilitated negotiations and key recommendations. Interview transcripts were content analyzed by the authors to identify emerging themes and practical issues. Findings were then reviewed by three of the interviewed executives to verify the validity and usefulness of the information.

elaborate, and at present the Chinese government grants the best trading privileges to Western firms in joint ventures with Chinese companies. Five expected phases for set-up include (1) partner selection and alliance proposal approval; (2) preliminary feasibility study approval; (3) joint feasibility study approval; (4) signing of the cooperative agreement; and (5) final contract approval and registration (Lee and Ness, 1986). The process can take years going through layers of local and state planning commissions and authorities. Success at one stage does not guarantee success at another. Specific challenges in this process and ways to manage them are described next (see summary in Box 10-2).

NEGOTIATING WITH THE CHINESE

Building Trust

Trust is *essential* for working with the Chinese. While trust has been touted as central to all interorganizational collaborations (Madhok, 1995; Morgan and Hunt, 1994; Stafford, 1994), the Chinese feel that trust *cannot* be removed from business and is all the more important in long-term partnerships. By contrast, Westerners (particularly

Box 10-2
Summary of negotiation challenges and recommendations

- **Building trust**: Trust is a prerequisite to Chinese business exchanges.
- **Identifying decision makers**: Reliance on authority is pervasive in China. Westerners need to identify decision makers and recognize that these decision makers may not be present during negotiations.
- **Overcoming language barriers**: Westerners should employ multiple interpreters who understand Chinese culture and business.
- **Managing business culture differences**: Westerners should always show respect and not treat China like a third world nation that needs to be "instructed" on Western ways. Westerners should avoid excessive "flash" and arrogance.
- **Negotiating resource contributions**: The Chinese tend to undervalue their Western partner's contributions. Westerners should be diplomatic and advise their Chinese counterparts about the economic value of proposed partnership contributions.
- **Negotiating control of alliance**: Because the Chinese are fearful of being cheated, diplomacy and openness concerning alliance policies are critical.
- **Bargaining on exports**: Typically, the Chinese prefer to export products whereas Westerners wish to serve domestic Chinese markets. Westerners should ask for export waivers.
- **Handling legal/copyright issues**: Western firms should advise their Chinese partners that copyright compliance serves their long-term interests for exporting. Promises of introducing new technology to the venture can also encourage compliance.
- **Getting closure on issues**: Negotiation meetings should open with a recap of past settled issues and agreements to inhibit Chinese negotiators from bringing back those issues for discussion.
- **Handling professional negotiators**: While professional negotiators may facilitate the negotiation process, they may not hold the best interests for the long-term good of the alliance. Westerners should strive to focus the negotiations on "win-win" cooperation.
- **Using consultants effectively**: Westerners should use seasoned consultants who have time and dedication.
- **Cultivating team work**: Because personal relationships are so important, team continuity over the life of the negotiation process should be maintained on both sides.
- **Exercising patience and flexibility**: The average negotiation period for the companies of this study was 18 months. Westerners need to be committed for the long haul.

Americans) can separate business exchanges from personal relationships and are more willing to engage in alliances even before personal trust has emerged (Anderson and Narus, 1990; Spekman et al., 1996). Trusting relationships must *precede* any Chinese business transaction. "An alliance with the Chinese should be like a good marriage," noted one executive. Another lamented, "Americans are only good at courting and not in marriage," and this can create frictions. Once the Chinese know a Western company and experience a positive working history with it, trust can be formed. One executive added:

> *"If they feel they can trust you, you can pretty much write your own check. If they do not feel they can trust you, you will have a difficult time doing more than just buying and selling."*

Another explained:

> *"Once they have the feeling that you're no longer working in their best interest, they'll withdraw. They'll become hard and put up a lot of barriers."*

The Chinese are very concerned about being exploited by foreigners, and Western executives should develop personal relationships with their negotiation counterparts from the start (Martinsons and Tseng, 1995). Friendships can be achieved through socializing over golf or dinner. Simple gestures, such as giving your Chinese counterparts a ride home after a hard day of bargaining, can also build bonds. In China, however, friendship also implies *obligation*. The Chinese will expect concessions, and returned favors will be weighed carefully (Kenna and Lacy, 1994). One company we interviewed treated their Chinese colleagues to a trip to Disneyland, and some managers suggested that it is good to perform such favors to put the Chinese into your debt. Carefully crafted relationships in the negotiation room set the partnership on the right footing.

Identifying Decision Makers

In general, senior Western managers have "more ammunition" to decide issues compared to their Chinese counterparts. Chinese negotiators basically gather information from their Western colleagues, report this to top Chinese officials and come back with new questions and counter-offers. These ranking officials seldom participate in the actual negotiations. Decision making works its way up the Chinese bureaucracy, taking a lot of time. The implication then is that negotiators should find out if there are Chinese nationals with decision-making authority present at negotiations. When entering a room, the highest ranking Chinese person will lead the group. Knowing the position of this person will help Westerners assess how much can be accomplished. More recently, because of growing empowerment among middle levels of the Chinese hierarchy, Westerners seem to deal more and more with Chinese negotiators who have some authority. Western negotiators should utilize social get-togethers as a means of learning the position and power of Chinese negotiators. One respondent observed, however, that respect and reliance on authority is very pervasive and:

> "Issues that could be resolved at lower levels [of management] tend to get bumped up to higher levels because folks are very reluctant to think critically and resolve issues themselves as they go along."

Beyond negotiations, this can place excessive burdens on senior managers when the partnership is up and running.

Overcoming Language Barriers

The official dialect in China is *putonghua* (standard Chinese), but the Cantonese dialect is spoken in some parts of South China as well. *Outside interpreters* are used by many Western companies. One informant cautioned, however, "I don't think you can really rely on translators." One should not assume a translator has fully understood what a negotiating party has said. Another vice president added that an interpreter has "the ability to totally change the gist of what is being said and the feel for what is happening." Many outside interpreters, Western or Chinese, may not have business backgrounds and subtle nuances of business meaning can get lost. "Many misunderstandings in negotiations come from inaccurate translations," explained one manager. Some respondents noted time as an important element in negotiations, and the interpretation process can double the time required for setting up a partnership. One advised, however, that "most negotiators would value the extra time provided by interpretation. It allows one time to think and prepare a response." Another added, "Language should be translated by a person who not only knows the language, but also the culture to get a correct interpretation." Negotiators need to develop a mechanism to check the nuances of communications. One way is by having *multiple interpreters*; while one is in the process of translating, another can monitor progress, verify interpreted meanings and observe body language. Considering what is at stake, interpreters are not a point one should neglect or attempt to cut corners. "The best translators are in-house," explained one executive, "they know your business, your terminology, how you conduct business, and your objectives." Some informants recommended that one should try to have as many Chinese-speaking individuals as possible on the Western side. Many companies are having *expatriates learn Chinese*. This practice has helped in day-to-day operations once the alliance is up and running.

Managing Business Culture Differences

Understanding China's business culture is especially important. The greater the sensitivity, the easier it is to manage disparities.

Reward systems and compensation

A reward system, an important tool in Western business used to encourage productivity, is relatively new to the Chinese. Training and education abroad are considered "very desirable" by the Chinese and can be used as motivation tools. Another major difference is that Westerners are economically driven, whereas the Chinese are more socially driven. "There is no concept of competition," said a respondent. The Chinese believe that everything must be in harmony for the world to balance and that competition leads to disharmony (Kenna and Lacy, 1994). Most Chinese are accustomed to working in state-owned companies and having lifetime employment with extensive benefits like social welfare, retirement, schooling, and housing even though their salaries may be low. Providing all these benefits can make Chinese labor more expensive than commonly perceived.

Western expatriate compensation may be another contention point with the Chinese. The Chinese perceive expatriates as being expensive and do not want joint venture funds to be used to pay for foreign executives. A respondent explained:

> "We had to limit our expatriates to just three or four as the Chinese

> *would get upset. I have heard of joint venture companies that were actually using foreign people in marketing and management functions, but they couldn't be included as part of the joint venture costs. They had to be paid from the regional headquarters' [of the Western company] budget as opposed to being part of the local budget."*

Westerners should negotiate up front about expatriates, their salaries, and the time period they are expected to be in China.

Government approvals

A business agreement will need approvals by many different departments of local, state, and central government. A frustrated negotiator observed:

> *"There is not only the central government that really plays a 'go' or 'no go' decision, but there are a provincial government and a municipal government. There are all forms of government that are involved [with approvals] and largely these are state-owned enterprises ... I'm not talking about 'one stop' agencies."*

Another added:

> *"Everybody [in the Chinese government] has his own idea on how he can squeeze the best deal out of the foreign company ... they come back and say the government won't approve this, so you'd better make this concession."*

Spirit of cooperation

Westerners tend to be very concerned with legally binding agreements, demanding all documents to be detailed with spelled-out contingencies. The Chinese, however, may attach little importance to any signed document.

> *"The whole issue of relationships versus legal structure is a major difference ... parties from the U.S.A. in particular want neatly tied legal documents, but the Chinese don't really do business that way. They depend more on a network of relationships and trust built over time."*

The Chinese weigh the integrity of their personal ties and trust over a binding contract. Therefore, "getting across the 'understanding' is what is really important," and Western negotiators should strive to obtain Chinese commitment to the "spirit" of an agreement. While commercial law is emerging in China, largely to meet Western expectations, personal ties and trust continue to drive business. In Beijing, McDonald's was evicted from a building after two years, despite a 20-year contract, because it let its personal relationships with Chinese authorities wane (Ambler, 1995). The building's new tenant had strong "connections," called *guanxi*.

Guanxi

Another surprise for Western executives is the practice of granting favors. The Chinese call this *guanxi*, which literally means "personal connections." *Guanxi* is not unique to China; business in Japan, Korea, and India is permeated by similar thinking (Ambler, 1995). In Western terms, it is similar to the concept of "networking." However, in the virtual absence of commercial law in China before opening to the West, the trusting relationships and bonds embedded in *guanxi* assured honorable, long-term exchanges. This is why building trusting relationships with the Chinese is so important. The Chinese like to think of *guanxi* as friendship leading to business as opposed to business leading to friendship (Ambler, 1995). Receiving and returning favors with personal connections in government is common in China and is frequently an accepted way for getting approvals. *Guanxi* can make Westerners uncomfortable, however, as *guanxi* may take on a form that may be perceived improper. "You have to maintain your integrity," noted a respondent, "but that slows things down because they keep testing you." Granting favors stems from China's authoritarian and bureaucratic society structure; *guanxi* facilitates working through the system.

Etiquette of politeness and respect

Westerners tend to strive for upfront honesty with a well-paced negotiation process. Many of our interviewed executives expressed frustration that the Chinese "sometimes never tell the whole truth." This does not mean they lie, but the Chinese can be evasive and discussions can go on and on. This may spring partly from Chinese protocol, which calls for politeness and respect. Being polite is of more value than being forthright and the Chinese tend to avoid saying "no." Euphemisms are used to spare listeners' feelings; expressions of anger are unacceptable. Telling others what is believed they want to hear is considered part of Chinese hospitality (Kenna and Lacy, 1994; Martinsons and Tseng, 1995). "Face saving" is also important. The Chinese feel it is important to never put someone in the position of having to admit a mistake or failure. Criticism and ridicule are improper because the need for revenge is common when someone loses face (Kenna and Lacy, 1994). Negotiators should not flagrantly disagree with the Chinese as this could be considered rude. Chinese do not separate business from personal relationships and Westerners must be diplomatic with disagreements.

Humble modesty

"The Hong Kong Chinese and Taiwanese are certainly not put off by flash, fancy dressing and expensive pens," commented a respondent, "but Mainland Chinese don't have much money so a flashy image might put some of them off." Another executive cautioned, "Americans are very appearance-oriented and they judge a person, their ability, their position, and their success by the trappings around them." Such a perception is a mistake in China.

> "One of the people we do business with in China looks as if he's slept in his clothes and he has a very humble demeanor. The first time our partners met him, he insisted on carrying their bags and doing subservient things ... This man, however, controls 10,000 people and 30 factories that do over a billion dollars a year!"

Making false assumptions based on appearances and inadvertently mistreating a modestly dressed Chinese business or government official can ruin the prospects of a trusting relationship. In China, Westerners need to temper their "image mindset."

In summing up his perceptions of Chinese culture, one European manager declared, "I think too much importance is placed on this cultural differences stuff. The Chinese respect power, intelligence, and hard work, just like we Germans do." Thus, Western negotiators should be sensitive to cultural differences, but not to the point of inhibiting effective bargaining. The Chinese are not ignorant of cultural disparities and pressures from diverging traditions and values are inevitable.

Negotiating Resource Contributions

In most joint ventures, the Chinese partner will contribute the land, offices, and manufacturing facilities while the Western partner will contribute the machinery, equipment, technical skills, and capital. A common problem is that the Chinese tend to overvalue their contributions. An executive remarked, "They base their valuation of their assets on their own knowledge of what they have been able to produce in the past in a very closed, protected market." Contributions of the Western company, especially technology, are usually undervalued by the Chinese. Thus, Western managers must try to advise the Chinese about the economic values of proposed partnership contributions. Further, they must avoid having the Chinese partner perceive the cooperative contributions as unfair.

Negotiating Control of the Alliance

Western companies seem to prefer majority control of the partnership via majority ownership or seats on the board of directors. At present, however, Chinese law requires that a Chinese national be the chairperson of a joint venture. Partnership control is more easily given to Western firms if the alliance is in an area highly valued by the Chinese, such as electronics, communications, energy, transportation, and export-oriented products. These industries bring foreign capital and advanced technology to China. Having more control in an alliance will help Western firms implement Western business policies, control corruption, and select aspects of Chinese business policies that may be beneficial to the partnership. Clearly, a carefully blended culture is needed in a successful Sino-Western alliance. A respondent noted, "In China, people tend to think more technical or scientific rather than commercial." However, another added that the Chinese are used to "taking short-cuts" to get things done, which may hurt a Western company's quality control. Thus, Westerners will want to preserve Chinese respect for science, but develop values of economic rewards and quality among Chinese personnel. A Hong Kong businessman explained, "Our controlling shares are not aimed at the distribution of profits, but at the use of our management methods." Another remarked, "We demand that our corporate culture prevail rather than theirs because we know ours works!" Therefore, Westerners want control of the partnership largely to prevent traditional Chinese business practices from hampering alliance operations and not necessarily to exploit the Chinese economically. The Chinese may not fully understand this, however, and when making demands about partnership operations, Western negotiators must be diplomatic and sensitive to Chinese perceptions of mistreatment. One executive observed, however:

> *"Even if you have majority ownership and control, the reality is, if the other partner doesn't agree with what you do, he can say 'no.' Majority control does not mean total control. It is not a black and white issue."*

Therefore, alliance management actually depends more on the trusting relations of the managers from both sides. Western managers should demonstrate credibility and trustworthiness and take on the role of "advisors" to educate their Chinese counterparts about recommended policies.

Bargaining on Exports

Bargaining on exports can sometimes spark problems. This is because exports are seen by the Chinese as a way to fan joint venture growth. Generating foreign exchange is important to the Chinese government. Most Western firms, however, seek a share of China's growing internal markets and want alliance products to be sold domestically. Without a significant export commitment for alliance products, it is difficult to obtain approval from various administrative agencies. A solution sought by many Western companies is to have as much flexibility as government officials will allow and act accordingly. The Western company may ask for an export waiver for a few years and then promise to export a certain percentage of the products manufactured. This way, the joint venture can establish a position in the Chinese market and export later.

Handling Legal/Copyright Issues

Copyright laws and their importance are relatively new to the Chinese and, in recent years, have become sensitive issues, particularly among U.S. firms. Despite recent efforts by the Chinese to curb counterfeiting and brand piracy, such problems are likely to persist in the future. Contracts should incorporate copyright protections so that Western brands and technologies are reasonably safeguarded. To protect intellectual and copyrighted property, Clifford Shultz and Bill Saporito (1996) recommend a host of strategies, including the following:

1. *Doing nothing*, if cost/benefit analysis indicates that litigation and enforcement costs outweigh market losses; sometimes taking action might offend an otherwise congenial Chinese partner or local markets that might view the Western firm as unfairly heavy-handed.
2. *Advertising to end users* that the "real" product is superior to pirated products, thus devaluing the status of pirated brands.
3. *Using high-tech labeling*, such as special inks and dyes, holograms, and electronic signatures.
4. *Creating a moving target* by continually improving product performance, bettering the price/value offering, or redesigning packaging and labeling (Shultz and Saporito, 1996; Rabino and Enayati, 1995).

While no strategy is foolproof, perhaps the best long-term strategy for keeping your Chinese partner from pirating your technology is *educating* him that compliance to copyright agreements serves his long-term self-interest for exporting to world markets that honor such protections. Also, promises of introducing new technology to the alliance as it is developed can be used as an added incentive to honor copyright agreements (Martinsons and Tseng, 1995).

Getting Closure on Issues

Many executives said that the Chinese tend to bring back issues which have already been settled. One executive said:

> "It seemed every couple of months we rewrote the chapters [of our agreement]. Later we told them, we couldn't accept this as we had already agreed to all these issues some time back. We did not want to re-negotiate all this, which was a totally new concept for them. We told them, 'If you want to continue negotiation with us, let us know by 9:00 A.M. tomorrow morning, or we will find a way to terminate our negotiations.'"

Western managers should be aware that Chinese negotiators may resort to such tactics to test the will of Westerners. Before the start of negotiations each day, a summary of all important points that have been discussed earlier and agreed upon should be recapped. Western negotiators need not be afraid to hold firm. It can earn Chinese respect.

Handling Professional Negotiators

The Chinese often hire outside professional negotiators who are good at bargaining, but not necessarily good at designing "win in" cooperative relationships. A respondent noted:

> *"These professional negotiators are focused basically on the concept of negotiations rather than what is best for the partnership itself. They are always looking at proposals and counter-proposals, and they always try to change the structure of the agreement for what they perceive to be better ... Their training is primarily on the negotiation process and not on the actual project itself."*

The benefit of professional negotiators, however, is that they know how to negotiate and the process can become much simpler and take less time. Western managers should be responsive to Chinese professional negotiators and "go the extra mile" to lay out all the facts and explain various models and assumptions used to calculate proposed benefits and burdens of each partner. Nonetheless, Westerners must bear in mind that they "are laying the groundwork for an ongoing relationship with people they may never see again." The strategy of Western negotiators should be to refocus the professional Chinese negotiators on developing a balanced partnership that creates benefits to both prospective partners.

Using Consultants Effectively

Consultants who can help develop Sino-Western alliances are easily accessible in Hong Kong, Mainland China, and in the West. These consultants can play a vital role in forming the alliance. For companies new to China,

> *"A good consultant can let you know what's going on, what's normal and not, and how to get around some of the obstacles ... You can waste a lot of time if you don't know what you are doing."*

Managers should try to use seasoned consultants who have solid track records, referred by reliable business connections. Moreover, "you have to make sure that they [consultants] have enough resources to be dedicated to your business because they'll have other clients."

Cultivating Team Work

Westerners usually work well in teams. By contrast, the Chinese may not like to take initiative when working in groups and they tend to work less effectively in teams. Western managers should learn to use their negotiating teams for leverage when dealing with the Chinese. Moreover, it is also critical to have continuity in the team. This is to assure that "you don't have to go through the learning curve with new players," noted one respondent. With new players, trust and rapport, so crucial to the Chinese, would need to be re-established as well. Therefore, when assembling a negotiation team, strategic planners will want to select team players committed to see the negotiations to the end. The Chinese negotiating team should be encouraged to maintain continuity as well.

Exercising Patience and Flexibility

Western managers try to accomplish tasks with tight deadlines. To them, time is money. As members of a culture that looks back across 5,000 years of recorded history, however, the Chinese usually do not feel such urgency. Meeting deadlines is not always possible, and this frustrates many Western managers. Some of our respondents said negotiations for a joint venture can take more than three years, with 18 months a typical time frame (given stable conditions). Western managers not used to so many delays can grow impatient. The Chinese realize this. "They use this as a good leverage," observed a respondent. One vice president said his company deals with delays in this manner: "We continue to put pressure on them through faxes, phone calls, and visits on a regular basis." Western negotiators need to be patient but persistent.

Working toward Long-term Success

China is emerging as an economic giant. However, "few markets are as underdeveloped and as large as China," explained one aircraft engine manufacturing executive, "China requires a very long-term strategy." The country continues to be plagued with problems caused by a fast transition to capitalism within a centrally controlled society cut off for so long from commercial, technological, and political developments occurring beyond its borders. China's raw resources, abundant labor, and growing markets, however, present opportunities for Western firms. One respondent summed up his interview by saying:

> *"I think if there is any single key to doing business in China, it is to respect the Chinese as a people ... Don't assume any attitude of superiority. They feel like it is a historical anomaly that the West has some technological superiority over their very ancient civilization ... if you aren't genuinely respectful and appreciative of them, they will be very wary of forming any business alliance."*

References

Ambler, T. (1995). Reflections in China: Re-orienting images of marketing. *Marketing Management*, 4 (Summer): 23–30.

Anderson, J.C. and J.A. Narus (1990). A model of distributor firms and manufacturer firm working partnerships. *Journal of Marketing*, 54 (January): 42–58.

Business Week (1997). China after Deng. March 3: 30–33.

The Economist (1996). Keep knocking, keep opening. 34.

Kenna, P. and S. Lacy (1994). *Business China.* Lincolnwood, IL: Passport Books.

Lee, S. and A. Ness (1986). Investment approval. *China Business Review*, May–June: 14–18.

Madhok, A. (1995). Revisiting multinational firms' tolerance for joint ventures: A trust-based approach. *Journal of International Business Studies*, 26 (1): 117–37.

Martinsons, M.G. and C. Tseng (1995). Successful joint ventures in the heart of the dragon. *Long Range Planning*, 28 (October): 45–58.

Morgan, R.M. and S.D. Hunt (1994). The commitment–trust theory of relationship marketing. *Journal of Marketing*, 58 (July): 20–38.

Rabino, S. and E. Enayati (1995). Intellectual property: The double-edged sword. *Long Range Planning*, 28 (October): 22–31.

Shultz, C.J. II, and B. Saporito (1996). Protecting intellectual property: Strategies and recommendations to deter counterfeiting and brand piracy in global markets. *Columbia Journal of World Business*, 31 (Spring): 18–28.

Spekman, R.E., L.A. Isabella, T.C. MacAvoy, and T. Forbes, III (1996). Creating strategic alliances which endure. *Long Range Planning*, 29 (June): 346–57.

Stafford, E.R. (1994). Using co-operative strategies to make alliances work. *Long Range Planning*, 27 (June): 65–75.

Woodward, D.G. and B.C.F. Liu (1993). Investing in China: Guidelines for success. *Long Range Planning*, 26 (March): 83–89.

EAST VS. WEST

Strategic Marketing Management Meets the Asian Networks

George T. Haley and Chin Tiong Tan

Strategic management in Asia is different. Decision making differs from that taught in Western, and even Asian, schools of business. In the last decade, the influence of Japanese management systems on Western management practice has become evident. Though the Japanese economy is the world's second largest, and Japan's population substantial, neither compares with the combined economies and combined populations of non-Japanese Asia. The influence of the most aggressive elements of the non-Japanese Asian business communities, the overseas Chinese and overseas Indian networks, cannot help to be felt on Western management practice. This paper explains why this difference in decision-making styles exists, analyzes the implications of the Asian decision-making style for managing in Asia, and discusses its implications for the future of strategic marketing management practice.

INTRODUCTION

Strategic decision making in Asia is different (Haley and Tan, 1996; Hofstede, 1994). One of the major differences in Asian decision

---

George T. Haley is Associate Professor at the School of Business, University of New Haven, West Haven, Connecticut, U.S.A. Chin Tiong Tan is Professor and Provost of Singapore Management University, Singapore.

Reproduced with permission from *Journal of Business and Industrial Marketing*, Vol. 14, No. 2, 1999, pp. 91–101. © MCB University Press.

making stems from the base of information available to, and desired by, Asian decision makers: this base often differs significantly from the base of information used by traditional Western executives and strategic theorists (Haley and Tan, 1996).

Various explanations have been posited to explain differences that emerge between Asian and Western strategic decision making. Haley and Tan (1996) suggested competitive advantage as a possible explanation. Hofstede (1994) argued that the reason for differences in decision-making styles was ethnic and cultural; alternatively, Haley and Stumpf (1989) found differences in decision making traceable to personality type. Later, Haley (1997) found evidence that there may be significant personality-type differences between the managerial cadres of different nationalities, thereby giving support to Hofstede's arguments. The truth probably is a combination of all the different explanations. Haley and Tan's (1996) argument that the amount of data available to decision makers about local markets can be described as an informational void relative to the amount available on industrialized economies, however, is unquestioned. This has led to a unique strategic-management style for many major Asian firms.

The Asian Business Environment

By looking at Table 11-1, we can see why South and Southeast Asia, the region in which these firms carry out the bulk of their operations, is so important. When comparing the 14 nations that make up the region to the U.S., although the land area and gross domestic product are smaller than those of the U.S., their population is almost 650 percent that of the U.S. Additionally, their economies, with some few exceptions, are growing faster than the economies of virtually all Western (we include Japan, Asia's developed economy) economies, even during the present difficult economic period. Significantly, South and Southeast Asia are not only made up of 14 basic sets of environments (business, economic, regulatory, political, etc.), but 13 of the nations are influenced by both their own native and colonial cultures. India alone has 17 different languages and dozens of dialects.

Three major clusters of large businesses exist in Asia: government-linked corporations (GLCs), either wholly or partly government controlled; family businesses (many controlled by Indians or overseas Chinese); and MNCs. Historically, in Asia, business prospered without

TABLE 11-1
A comparison of South and Southeast Asia with the U.S.

	Population*	GDP** ($ billions)	Area (sq. miles)
Bangladesh	128,094,948	122.0[b]	57,295
Brunei	292,266	2.5[a]	2,226
Burma	45,103,809	41.0[b]	261,228
Cambodia	10,561,373	6.0[b]	70,238
India	936,545,814	1,700.0[c]	1,222,243
Indonesia	203,583,886	571.0[b]	741,052
Laos	4,837,237	4.1[b]	91,429
Malaysia	19,723,587	141.0[b]	127,584
Pakistan	131,541,920	239.0[b]	339,697
Philippines	75,265,584	171.0[b]	115,860
Singapore	2,890,468	42.4[b]	247
Sri Lanka	18,342,660	53.5[b]	25,332
Thailand	60,271,300	323.0[b]	198,115
Vietnam	74,393,324	72.0[b]	127,246
Total	**1,711,448,176**	**3,538.5**	**3,309,624**
U.S.	263,814,032	6,380.0[b]	3,679,192
Comparison (%)	648.7	55.4	90.0

* U.S. Census Bureau (1995).
** International Monetary Fund, purchasing power equivalents unless otherwise noted.
[a] 1991 figure; [b] 1993 figure; [c] 1994 estimate.

local business and market information—they have not desired it and have adapted their strategies to their environment.

GLCs usually began as suppliers of products/services in protected domestic markets. For GLCs, strategic planning followed national plans for economic growth and development; market information was never a critical success factor. Hence, information was not a top priority. MNCs first entered Asia over two centuries ago; however, the manufacturing-based MNCs, which were the first to have a significant economic impact in Asia, entered primarily after World War II. They did not seek more local market information because they seldom served local markets, but were investments aimed at rationalizing the MNCs' production costs for products intended for their traditional markets in Japan and the West (Haley and Tan, 1996).

The overseas Chinese networks (OCNs) probably constitute the single, most dominant private business grouping in Asia outside of China, Japan, and South Asia. In virtually every East and Southeast Asian country, the degree of the OCNs' participation in the economy far outstrips their numbers in the population. Today, they have used their networks to extend their reach dramatically, and, increasingly, they are facing fierce competition from MNCs and the growing overseas Indian networks (OINs). Many OCNs started as merchants and traders. They moved into property-related businesses, and then into any businesses deemed profitable. The OCNs were generally characterized by an entrepreneurial, intuitive, and fast decision-making style and paternalistic management. This was initially due to low levels of education, especially business education, among the OCN founders.

The OINs and Indian family businesses, in general, make decisions in a similar way largely due to the highly regulated and protected competitive environment. Senior managers' educational levels are frequently higher than the norm for these countries.

Among these groups, decisions to invest, to grow, and to compete are made mainly on the basis of business sense, experience, and their individual propensity to take risks. With truly difficult decisions, when additional information is necessary, the groups usually depend on their network of friends and government officials for the information. Trust and loyalty are central concerns. Desired data are often subjective views or beliefs that raise the businessmen's confidence in their decisions.

This somewhat holistic, intuitive decision-making style is well suited to information-scarce environments or environments where market-survey data seem suspect; it also serves to exclude new entrants without the established communities' experience and network. For instance, many Asian banks have historically served particular networks, not geographic areas; these community bases persist today. Consequently, individuals applying for business loans from Indonesian banks often find that the information included in their applications has been transferred to the banks' related company in the same business as the applicants', and that the related company has even implemented the submitted business plans when entering the applicants' projected markets (East Asia Analytical Unit, 1995)! Many attribute the rapid growth of many OCN businesses in Southeast Asia to their speed of decision making (Chu and MacMurray, 1993); this speed and domination of information makes it possible to seize major business opportunities and constitutes a major competitive advantage for them.

The important characteristics that distinguish successful local companies operating in South and Southeast Asia are as follows:

1. The companies appear highly diversified; often they undertake unrelated diversification, contravening mainstream theoretical notions of business.
2. The companies have good relationships with the often enormous public sectors in these countries.
3. The companies have very strong family and informal networks.

As indicated earlier, foreign MNCs entered the region later. Manufacturing-based MNCs (M-MNCs) were not the first foreign firms, but they were the first to have great economic effect. In Southeast Asia, M-MNCs were key to the region's export-led economic growth: when M-MNCs began rationalizing manufacturing policies worldwide, they found Southeast Asia's tax incentives, investment benefits, and cheap labor attractive, and transferred some manufacturing operations to the region. Alternatively, at a much later date, MNCs in India found the very large middle class, the very large number of highly trained and qualified people, and the wide use of the English language and legal system highly attractive. Yet, by some measures, the Indian infrastructure lags behind even China. The public sector continues to throw an imposing shadow over the economy, and the zeal for economic reform does not seem uniform.

MNCs' managers seldom found decisions to relocate to South and Southeast Asia difficult; in many instances, the host governments compiled and offered the MNCs information relevant to such decisions. In Southeast Asia, the MNCs' Asian operations did not serve local markets, but rather sought production-cost advantages in worldwide operations. Products were manufactured for export markets. Hence, the informational void was unimportant. Their decisions to relocate manufacturing operations were decisions made to maximize operational efficiency rather than to serve local markets; decisions regarding the latter require much greater knowledge of local environments. In South Asia, MNCs did concentrate on domestic markets, but with a long-term focus, striving to build alliances with local firms and public goodwill. Business, however, does not come easy and costs loom high. For example, as one American MNC's CEO confided, "the Indians did not invent bureaucracy, but they have elevated it to an art form."

The informational black hole in Asia exists because of historical business practice and because of participants' goals. As decision makers have not desired more objective information, the region is an informational void for those who do.

Cultural Effects on Asian Decision Making

Nakamura (1992), in considering strategic decision making in East Asia, argued that strategic decision-making processes in these countries were following the same line of development that strategic decision making did in Japan. There are certain similarities in the manner in which the Japanese economy and the economies of the East Asian nations he considered have evolved, but there are also significant economic and cultural differences which would indicate that Nakamura's arguments are faulty.

Economic similarity exists because most Asian economies, like Japan's, are managed economies that have grown primarily through exports. The differences lie in the source and direction of exports. The primary source of exports for Japan has always been Japanese companies, and their exports, until only recently, have been dominated by exports to North America and Europe. The primary source of exports from non-Japanese Asian nations to Western nations has usually been MNCs. Local firms have concentrated on local markets, the markets which are now considered so important to Western MNCs. Rather than building size and managerial expertise in competition with Western companies, companies from other Asian nations have built their size and managerial expertise within the informational void. For this reason, the economic similarities between Japan and its Asian neighbors are less significant than they might be.

There are also significant cultural differences that have resulted in very different economic environments. If you consider Japanese firms, especially the large ones, one thing which impresses is the age of the firms. Most of Japan's major firms began as family firms which were built through growth and evolved into the modern Japanese *keiretsu* conglomerates. The Japanese Daoist culture and way of life incorporates an economic philosophy of growth which includes primogeniture. The Confucian culture and way of life also includes an economic element; however, Confucian economics is a subsistence economic philosophy in which the peasant is exalted and the merchant reviled and persecuted. By ancient Chinese custom, the merchant is prohibited from wearing silk and riding, and he must go everywhere on foot. It is no accident that there have been innumerable waves of overseas Chinese over the centuries. Every wave corresponds to a period of persecution against the merchant classes. Confucian custom also emphasizes large families and bans primogeniture; hence, there is an ancient Chinese saying which goes, "No fortune survives the third generation." Chinese firms are relatively young; most of the major OCNs of today are only in their first or second generation. The Confucian ban on primogeniture has been breaking down in more economically developed Chinese societies such as Hong Kong and Singapore, as exemplified by Li Ka Shen's transferring control of the bulk of his business holdings to his eldest son. Hence, one can expect many of the present OCN companies to grow and develop beyond the third generation into true multinationals. Other differences lie in the relationship between the individual and society. In Indian culture, for example, there is no relationship between patriotism and filial piety. In Japan, a saying goes, "To be a good patriot is to be a good son"; the equivalent saying in China is, "One cannot be both a good patriot and a good son." A subtle, but significant, difference which leads us into the area of loyalty. In Japan, loyalty is very strong and functionally based; for example, filial loyalty is owed to the breadwinner, not the actual father. In both Chinese and Indian cultures, filial loyalty is owed to the father, regardless of who the breadwinner is, and loyalty is very personalized. Among the Indians, loyalty is very strong. Loyalty among the Chinese, however, though personalized, is not very strong. Loyalty to a friend, master, or employee is to the individual, and does not survive the death of that individual. Hence, the father's friend is not necessarily the son's. Ethical duty in Confucianism is limited to five relationships:

1. Sovereign–minister
2. Father–son
3. Husband–wife
4. Elder brother–younger brother
5. Friends

If a relationship does not fall within one of the above relationships, there is no ethical duty or loyalty owed except to maintain social harmony. Thus, without ties of family or friendship, duties owed in a commercial relationship under Confucian ethical standards are not manifested in the same legalistic perceptions and patterns of behavior as in many Western business cultures. In the Indian cultures, commercial relationships are aided by ties of family or friendship, but in commercial relationships contractual duties are viewed as ethically binding in much the same legalistic way as they are in Western cultures. Among the Japanese, contractual duties are viewed as binding, but the ties that will help cement commercial relationships are not familial or ties of friendship, but ties of personal and corporate mutual self-interest. Due to the above-mentioned cultural differences, among others, there is substantial doubt that even with the passage of time and economic evolution, the South and Southeast Asian business networks' decision making will ever simply follow in the steps of the Japanese. It is much more likely that the businesses of South and Southeast Asia will go their own unique routes, and make their own unique contributions to management theory and practice.

A significant difference which exists between the overseas Chinese and the overseas Indian operating in South and Southeast Asia lies in the educational levels of the founders. The founders of the OCNs were generally highly intelligent individuals, but poorly educated. The overseas Indian firms were generally founded by people who were both very intelligent and well educated. Hence, while both groups operate well in their region's informational void, the overseas Indians tend to be better prepared to operate in the Western strategic mode using all the data and strategic marketing management techniques developed by strategic theorists. Thus, the OINs have tended to operate like Western firms when they have the available data, and like the OCNs when they do not. An example which indicates the importance of this difference is that few Singaporean firms have been profitable in their U.S. operations; Indian firms, however, have regularly been highly successful. Increasingly, the younger generation of OCN leadership has the same educational characteristics as the leadership of the OIN firms.

The result of culture, education, and environment has resulted in a strategic planning process that is very different from that of the West. Strategic planning in South and Southeast Asia has developed into a process which is ad hoc and reactive, highly personalized, idiosyncratic to the leader, and which uses relatively limited environmental scanning. Though Western theorists and managers would tend to name these characteristics as poor management, they have lauded many firms which are managed in just this way. Singapore Airlines is regularly named as the best-run airline in the world, yet it is run very much in accord with the principles and practice of Asian management, and with an emphasis on good and efficient service and a heavy investment in the best, proven technology.

Ghosh and Chan (1994) studied strategic planning behavior among firms in Singapore and Malaysia and came to the same conclusions. They found planning activities to be ad hoc and reactive. The only market-related factor of any importance was the "CEO's personal knowledge of market," which was the fourth most important factor in contributing to success in planning. While a CEO's experience is important in any situation, how many failures must occur before the CEO gains that experience and how can a firm expand beyond its local market? The experience of the OCNs and OINs indicates that there are other ways of learning a relatively similar market which may help avoid the great bulk of these failures.

Characteristics of Asian Management

When sequential information and hard data contribute little to the relevance or consequence of a decision, and in fact are simply nonexistent, Western managers must study Asia's holistic/intuitive decision making to be effective in Asia if they are going to be able to compete with the major local firms on their home turf. Little is known of Asia's holistic/intuitive decision making. Drawing on their observations and study of Asian executives, Haley and Tan (1996) and Haley and Haley (1997) posited that the following characteristics are common to experience-based holistic/intuitive decision making:

1. Hands-on experience
2. Transfer of knowledge
3. Qualitative information
4. Holistic information processing
5. Action-driven decision making

Hands-on Experience

To make decisions quickly, without detailed analyses of hard data, managers must be hands-on line managers who know the firm's work routines and processes, and know the product, market, business environment, and industry firsthand. Without sufficient exposure to the workings of the trade, managers will have difficulty putting things in perspective quickly enough to make timely decisions. Consequently, many senior Asian businessmen remain active in all aspects of their businesses. This level of involvement is necessary to make the right decisions without data support. Wada (1992) gives an example of a Hong Kong businessman responding within 15 minutes to an offer by Li Ka Shen, Chairman of Hutchinson/Cheung Kong, to enter into a major joint venture. The businessman's confidence in Li's judgment and word, and his in-depth knowledge of the business and markets under consideration, allowed him to make such a rapid decision.

Transfer of Knowledge

Managers often have difficulty making decisions within new environmental contexts. However, Asian companies often diversify into totally different, noncore businesses. This runs contrary to given business wisdom of staying within one's core business. For executives to succeed in industries where they have no prior experience, they must be able to generalize from past experience, and to apply those generalizations in the new context. The ability to use knowledge to tackle new problems in different situations involves conceptualization skills different from analytical skills. Successful Asian executives are more able to see the big picture, and to sense intuitively winners from losers. Chu and MacMurray (1993) believe that conglomerate diversification in Asia must change; yet, many businessmen in the region feel that it is a major reason for their firms' enviable growth rates.

Qualitative Information

Many Asian executives appear to take unnecessary risks by not doing sufficient research or analysis before acting; this is misleading. The executives often process myriad bits of information and consider several alternatives in depth before they act. They differ from Western executives in that their analysis may be, almost entirely, internal. Though their decision making may be highly articulated, Asian executives may not present the results in a written analytical form.

Asian executives almost always use external sources of information in making strategic decisions. Experience indicates that executives actively seek out critical information that will impact their decisions. However, Asian executives are less likely to seek published data. They use qualitative, even subjective, information supplied by friends, business associates, government officials, and others whose judgment and character they trust. They prefer to personally visit localities to check on information rather than to rely on secondary data. Their local contacts can often supply up-to-date, accurate unpublished information superior to available published or traditional primary research alternatives.

Network building goes beyond linking oneself to senior government officials or great industrialists. Asian businessmen, while criticized for not building their firm's internal base of managerial talent, often invest heavily in promising individuals they feel will be valuable future contacts without seeking immediate favors. For example, long ago, Liem Sioe Liong of the Salim Group met an army lieutenant he thought showed promise. Over the years, he offered this officer his support in his military and political career. The young lieutenant later became President Suharto of Indonesia and remains Liem's close friend.

Holistic Information Processing

Conventional analytical problem solving stresses sequential, systematic, and step-by-step approaches to decision making. This works best when managers can obtain needed data. In an informational void situation, it is likely to be unworkable. In the experience-based intuitive model, managers take a general approach to problems, define parameters intuitively, and explore solutions holistically. Such an approach resembles Asian thinking and learning processes. It is an alternative mode of decision making that frequently works well, especially in those markets where it has evolved.

Action-driven Decision Making

Speed constitutes a key characteristic of decision making in Asian business. Executives often make key decisions without consulting anyone. The preference is for action. Many stories exist of well-known Asian executives deciding on important matters in minutes and implementing the results almost immediately. This speed reflects the executives' empowerment and accountability. Executives often have great latitude in deciding matters. Long debates and committee meetings rarely occur.

The Asian decision-making model reflects authoritative management. However, when one person has both responsibility and authority, a little authoritativeness can get work done faster. This was Kazuo Wada's conclusion, and the main reason why he moved Yaohan's headquarters from Japan to Hong Kong, and the international headquarters for all operations outside of Hong Kong and China, to Singapore; the domestic Japanese operations remained the only ones still with headquarters in Japan.

IMPLICATIONS FOR MNCs

Determine which markets are to be served. One aspect of doing business in Asia is the lack of information tied to the abundance of opportunities. While information is lacking, it does exist. Dredge it up, collate and analyze it, seek out both hard and subjective data, the most up-to-date and historical data. Treat your research as an investment that will produce substantial returns and remember that those returns come both in the form of earning future profits and avoiding future losses. Use the data to prioritize your potential product/markets and to identify the major players and influences in them. Determine which of those players would be legitimate, beneficial partners to work with, and which should be avoided at all cost. A firm should use this information to move into a product market on its own, or to help it make a decision rapidly if a desirable partner approaches the firm with an opportunity. One aspect of the overseas Chinese and Indian firms is that they can make decisions blazingly fast—it is one of their key competitive advantages in competition with MNCs. Unlike Japanese firms, which sometimes seem to move glacially, the Asian network firms move quickly and expect rapid decisions from their potential partners; if an MNC follows standard operating procedures, it is likely to lose a good opportunity. To move rapidly, however, they cannot wait until they perceive a potential opportunity to research a market, they must have the knowledge substantially on hand and, as Slywotsky and Shapiro (1993) say, "leverage to beat the odds."

The firm must develop a flexible corporate culture which can react to dealing with different managerial cultures in different parts of the world, promote cultural sensitivity, and seek out home/host similarities. The best way to manage Asian operations is with Asians. As fast decisions are critical, managers must have close links in each country to speed decision making and have ready access to the highest levels of corporate management. Using more locals with strong local connections and building trust-based relationships are some of the ways to establish stronger links to local information. When this is not possible, however, since MNCs are large, highly complex organizations, somewhere in the MNC's management group, there is usually someone whose background is likely to have better prepared them to deal with the Asian environment than is the norm for the firm's managers. Phillips selected a highly trusted and historically successful Mexican executive from its Latin American operations to their regional headquarters in Singapore on the premise that the Latin American environment, with its high uncertainty, poor information base, and highly personal, autocratic style of management, would better prepare an executive for Asia than would working in their European headquarters; in this instance at least, they were right.

It is very hard to develop the kind of familiarity with a firm's markets and operations necessary to react rapidly in a highly fluid, uncertain situation without actual line management experience. Experience-based training and manning Asian operations with line managers rather than people who have come up in staff functions are generally highly desirable. Line managers are better able to understand their senior counterparts at most Asian firms as they will have had many of the same operational experiences. People who have come up in staff functions, without any line experience, have based decisions on analysis of figures and reports which may not formally exist in the Asian firms with which they will be dealing and will have great difficulty in judging the legitimacy of some claims without experience in dealing with similar operational situations. This kind of experience will also help executives build local information links more rapidly as the senior Asian managers with whom they will interact will be better able to relate to the line manager as an equal than they will to the staff member.

Finally, managers should learn to recognize the evolution of Asian relationships. Unlike many other networks around the world, an individual's acceptance within an overseas Chinese network is flexible, and can vary as a result of events on which the individual has no influence; acceptance does not depend solely on the individual's actions, but also on others that affect situation(s) in which the individual interacts with the network. Western executives do not have total freedom to undertake some behaviors that may help cement their position with an overseas Chinese network. (This has nothing to do with bribery, but with freedom to act independently and to involve their families in business relationships as completely as the OCNs often do.) Given this situation, it is imperative that Western executives learn to recognize the cues given by the Chinese to indicate what the state of a relationship between two people is at any one time.

IMPLICATIONS FOR THE MARKETING FUNCTION

The implications of being drawn into competing with the networks on their home turf for the practice of the marketing function in Asian markets are significant, and cannot help but spill over into the practice of marketing in the MNCs' home markets. The implications in terms of marketing's traditional four P's are as follows.

Product

Product management in Asia is severely affected by the widespread lack of respect for intellectual property rights. This problem is often attributed to there being no rule of law—the Indian government openly uses this argument in urging MNCs to invest in India rather than in other parts of Asia. The truth is both better and worse. In Confucian Asia, to respect the property rights of those with which you have no relationship depends on associating those rights with social harmony. Where there is no historical precedence for the particular property rights in question, as in the case of intellectual property rights, this becomes highly problematical. The government must shift people's way of thinking through strict enforcement of intellectual property rights in a situation where not only the property rights pirate, but the lower- and middle-level legal authorities feel that the property rights pirate is being unjustly persecuted. Intellectual property rights have never existed under Confucian custom and tradition. Thus, it is very easy, when confronted with intellectual property rights piracy, for local legal authorities to look the other way given even a minimal incentive to do so regardless of the most severe pressure from central governments. Though it is highly desirable to move production of products as close to major markets as possible, it is imperative for a firm to consider the differences that can exist between the legal statutes of a nation and what can be considered the "natural law," or the ethical perceptions, of a nation. The latter are very powerful and difficult for mere legal statutes to overturn. So far, besides India, the major Asian economies most successful in protecting intellectual property rights are Singapore and Thailand, with Malaysia making an increasingly successful effort.

Place

Many of the limitations of distributing goods through any developing nation's infrastructure apply to South and Southeast Asia. The networks create the same kind of situation in the region as the major commercial families do in Latin America due to their early and continuing dominance of most significant distributors, wholesale and retail, in the region. Only last year, Kmart was forced to withdraw from Singapore after a costly attempt to break into the cut-throat, minimal margin environment of the mass market in a major Asian retailing center. The overseas Chinese have several advantages when it comes to distribution within their home markets which Western retailers should not ignore. Kmart's strength has always been a good selection of moderate-quality goods at a low price. When it tried to break into Asia, it ran into local retailers which could match their prices through the ability to accept even lower margins than Kmart at the same time that they matched or bettered Kmart quality; also, the Confucian loyalty relationship of friendship created a situation in which threatened local retailers would receive the support of most, if not all, of their long-term suppliers.

Promotion and Pricing

Promotion practices are affected by the Asian cultures just as they are affected by all cultures. Firms must seek to ensure they do not offend local custom and mores, and that they remain within the law. To one extent or the other, most Asian cultures are linguistically sensitive: public signboards in foreign languages are illegal in many Asian countries. Enforcement is usually lax; however, there are periodic crackdowns (recent ones occurred in Indonesia and Vietnam). Much more problematical for Western firms are the difficulties incurred in India, where some regions, such as the state of Tamil Nadu, contain linguistically sensitive populations which resent the incursion of the national Indian language, Hindi.

Pricing is often difficult for Western firms because of the additional costs associated with international business operations, but also because the networks are able to accept very low margins due to the family control of most network firms. They are also frequently able to subsidize predatory pricing practices due to the conglomerate diversification which most of the large networks have adopted, and due also to the fact that predatory pricing is not recognized as a crime in most Asian nations. When it is, the networks usually are able to deflect legal action through their government contacts.

In sum, the invasion of Asian markets by Western MNCs is occurring because of the wealth and immense potential of these markets. Their increasing international importance will cause Asian strategic planning to follow Japanese planning concepts in one way, and in so doing cause Nakamura to be correct in an unintended manner. As the Japanese MNCs introduced to the West many standards of Japanese strategic planning, such as just-in-time inventory systems and quality circles, so too will the overseas Chinese and Indian networks. The importance of non-Japanese markets, the growing participation of Western MNCs in Asian markets, and the increasing size and participation of Asian firms in Western markets will introduce many of the best Asian strategic marketing processes and concepts to Western firms and strategic theory.

References

Chu, T.C. and T. MacMurray (1993). The road ahead for Asia's leading conglomerates. *McKinsey Quarterly*, 3: 117–26.

East Asia Analytical Unit (1995). *Overseas Chinese Business Networks*. Canberra: AGPS Press, Department of Foreign Affairs and Trade, Australia.

Ghosh, B.C. and C.-O. Chan (1994). A study of strategic planning behavior among emergent businesses in Singapore and Malaysia. *International Journal of Management*, 11 (2): 697–706.

Haley, G.T. and U.C.V. Haley (1997). Making strategic business decisions in South and Southeast Asia. In *Conference Proceedings of the First*

International Conference on Operations and Quantitative Management, Jaipur, India, Vol. 2, pp. 597–604.

Haley, G.T. and C.T. Tan (1996). The black hole of Southeast Asia: Strategic decision-making in an informational void. *Management Decision*, 34 (9): 37–48.

Haley, U.C.V. (1997). The Myers-Briggs type indicator and decision-making styles: Identifying and managing cognitive trails in strategic decision making. In C. Fitzgerald and L. Kirby (eds.), *Developing Leaders, Research and Applications, Psychological Type and Leadership Development*, pp. 187–223. Palo Alto, CA: Consulting Psychologists Press.

Haley, U.C.V. and S.A. Stumpf (1989). Cognitive trails in strategic decision-making: Linking theories of personalities and cognitions. *Journal of Management Studies*, 26 (5): 477–97.

Hofstede, G. (1994). Cultural constraints in management theories. In D.E. Hussey (ed.), *International Review of Strategic Management*, Vol. 5, pp. 27–47. West Sussex: Wiley.

Nakamura, G.I. (1992). Development of strategic management in the Asia Pacific region. In D.E. Hussey (ed.), *International Review of Strategic Management*, Vol. 3, pp. 3–18. West Sussex: Wiley.

Slywotsky, A.J. and B.P. Shapiro (1993). Leveraging to beat the odds: The new marketing mind-set. *Harvard Business Review*, September/October: 97–107.

U.S. Census Bureau (1995). *World Population Profile*. Washington, DC.

Wada, K. (1992). *Yaohan's Global Strategy: The 21st Century Is the Era of Asia*. Hong Kong: Capital Communications Corporation.

BUSINESS-TO-BUSINESS MARKETING IN ASIA PACIFIC
The Telecommunications Competitiveness of Regional Economies

Siew Meng Leong

This paper describes the rationale and development of an index to assess the telecommunications competitiveness of economies in Asia Pacific. The Index comprises four components deemed important by large multinationals seeking to locate their telecommunications hubs in the region: service quality, pricing, choice, and regulation. Findings based on three annual surveys of end users for each dimension as well as the overall competitiveness of regional economies are then summarized and their implications discussed. The paper concludes with some directions for future research for this strategically important aspect of business-to-business marketing in Asia Pacific.

INTRODUCTION

The trend toward globalization has increased the role of telecommunications in the marketplace. Businesses with international operations select specific locations around the world as their telecommunications hubs to coordinate their activities in this important area. Similarly, telecommunications service providers and policy makers need to benchmark their performance relative to their competitors'. Asia Pacific is no exception, where countries like Australia, Japan, Hong Kong, and Singapore position themselves as regional telecommunications hubs.

Copyright © 2000 by Siew Meng Leong.

Clearly, attracting global businesses to locate their regional telecommunications hub in a particular country provides numerous economic and strategic benefits. Aside from the direct, tangible returns generated from increased telecommunications traffic, the telecommunications-location decision may affect the siting of the regional headquarters of large multinational corporations. As the multiplier effects of such a decision are enormous (e.g., employment provision, residential and commercial property rental, and financial services to name a few spinoffs), regional economies are competing aggressively to woo the custom of large multinationals in this strategically important business-to-business market.

Various indices assessing national telecommunications competitiveness have been developed to inform multinationals, service providers, and public policy makers in their decision-making processes. Typically, these are constructed as a component of competitiveness evaluation of countries around the world. Leading examples are the *Global Competitiveness Report* and the *World Competitiveness Yearbook*. Both reports cover about 50 countries worldwide. To assess telecommunications competitiveness, they employ such measures as the cost of a three-minute telephone call to the U.S., number of fixed telephone lines per capita (fixed line teledensity), number of mobile telephone subscriptions per capita (mobile teledensity), number of Internet hosts per capita (Internet density), telecommunications investment per capita, and business executives' satisfaction with telecommunications infrastructure.

These indices of telecommunications competitiveness are not without flaws. For example, Canada and Mexico will easily prevail over Asian countries for the cheapest three-minute call to the U.S. The use of fixed line teledensities and Internet densities as measures for the whole country may also be problematic. The densities for rural areas are not particularly relevant for a multinational thinking of establishing headquarters in the capital city. Given that most Asian nations have a large rural community, the bias against these economies becomes even more evident.

In contrast, *Data Communications*, a widely read trade journal, assesses the service quality of international telecommunications service providers. It conducts an annual survey to rate the quality of four telecommunications services (leased circuits, ISDN, packet switching, and frame relay). However, the survey does not consider the pricing of these telecommunications services nor the attributes of specific countries that may be pertinent for multinational corporations. It is also restricted to the evaluation of the publication's readership, rather than large multinationals which constitute the target market of interest in this context.

THE ASIA PACIFIC TELECOMMUNICATIONS INDEX

Given the shortcomings of existing measures to meet the requirements for the region, the Centre for Telemedia Strategy at the National University of Singapore developed an Asia Pacific Telecommunications Index. The Index provides a comprehensive measure of the relative competitiveness of regional locations as hubs for international telecommunications services. Four dimensions are employed to assess the telecommunications performance of each economy. These are service, pricing, choice, and regulation. The dimensions were established based on published studies and personal interviews with selected regional telecommunications managers from companies in the financial, transportation, and manufacturing sectors. From an initial coverage of 10 economies in its inaugural edition in 1998, the Index now assesses the competitiveness of 13 countries in the region: Australia, China, Hong Kong, India, Indonesia, Japan, South Korea, Malaysia, New Zealand, the Philippines, Singapore, Taiwan, and Thailand. Hence, the relative competitiveness of these economies can be ascertained for each of the four dimensions as well as on an overall basis.

In particular, four subindices (one each for service, pricing, choice, and regulation) and an overall index were developed based on the responses to a systematic survey of relevant end users. To obtain an objective and representative sample of respondents, the CD-ROMs provided by *WorldScope* and *Moody's Global Company Data* were sourced. The largest companies were selected from these databases, which furnished these companies' financial information as well as information on senior executives to whom the questionnaire could be directed. Over 100 responses from large multinationals were solicited for each of the three years the study was conducted. In the latest (2000) edition, for example, some 129 businesses with average assets and revenues of US$50.3 billion and $17.1 billion, respectively, participated. Most, as expected, were incorporated in the advanced economies of North America, Europe, and Japan.

The construction of each of the four telecommunications subindices and the overall index will now be discussed, followed by a summary of the findings of the various surveys over the years (Centre for Telemedia Strategy, 1998, 1999, 2000). Because of updating and refinement of the research methodology employed and changes to the economies covered, rankings, rather than actual index scores, are furnished for more meaningful comparative analyses.

Service Quality

Two aspects of service quality were relevant to the construction of the telecommunications index: technical service quality and account servicing. To assess technical service quality, the major telecommunications services were identified first. In 1998, these included international direct dial (IDD), leased circuits, frame relay, ISDN, packet switching, and telex. Telex and packet switching were dropped in 1999 while ISDN was excluded in 2000 as these services declined in importance. Account servicing included billing and customer service.

To measure the service quality competitiveness, respondents rated the extent to which the dominant service provider in each economy performed for each telecommunications service and for account servicing on seven-point scales anchored at poor to excellent quality. The technical service scores were then weighted by their importance to respondents and combined to yield a standardized rating. This was then averaged with a standardized rating from the converted raw scores on account servicing to yield the service quality subindex for each economy. The 1998 to 2000 rankings for the five best performing economies (ordered by their 2000 scores) are shown in Table 12-1. The dominant service provider of each economy is indicated in parentheses.

As Table 12-1 suggests, the most competitive economies based on service quality have been Japan and Singapore over the three years of the Index. Overall, the ranking of the top five economies exhibited some reshuffling among the third to fifth positions involving Hong Kong, Australia, and New Zealand. It thus appears that these economies, which are among the more advanced of the region, have maintained their superiority over the others during the period studied.

TABLE 12-1
Service quality rankings, 1998–2000

Economy	1998	1999	2000
Japan (KDD)	1	1	1
Singapore (SingTel)	2	2	2
Hong Kong (C&W HKT)	3	4	3
New Zealand (NZ Tel)	–*	5	4
Australia (Telstra)	4	3	5

* New Zealand was not covered in the 1998 Index.

Pricing

The second factor in the Index is price. For each economy, the list prices of the dominant service provider for the typical quantities of each of the telecommunications services from the main financial center to London and New York were converted to U.S. dollars using an average of the exchange rates prevailing over the relevant period. Survey respondents were then asked the average discount they received from the dominant service provider for each service to obtain the discounted price in U.S. dollars. The simple average of the discounted prices for each service across the economies was then standardized by the highest average discounted price among the service providers. These were then converted into index scores, weighted by the importance of the respective telecommunications services. Table 12-2 presents the 1998 to 2000 rankings of the five leading economies (ordered by their 2000 scores). The dominant service provider of each economy is again furnished in parentheses.

As Table 12-2 suggests, the picture for pricing over the three years of the Index shows substantial movement in rankings. Specifically, Australia and Japan improved on their 2000 rankings by moving up

TABLE 12-2
Pricing rankings, 1998–2000

Economy	1998	1999	2000
Australia (Telstra)	4	4	1
Singapore (SingTel)	1	1	2
Hong Kong (C&W HKT)	5	3	3
South Korea (Korea Tel)	2	7	4
Japan (KDD)	8	8	5

three places to first and fifth respectively over their 1998 and 1999 positions. Likewise, South Korea's performance fluctuated from a high of second in 1998 to a low of seventh in 1999, before settling in fourth position in 2000. Its competitiveness may have been affected by movements in the dollar–won exchange rate. Interestingly, this is the only subindex which figures South Korea among the leading regional economies. Hong Kong started off fifth in 1998 and moved up to third in 1999 and 2000. Only Singapore seemed relatively stable in price competitiveness, being placed in first or second over the three years covered.

Choice

The third component of the Index is choice. While both service quality and pricing focus on the dominant service provider's competitiveness in each economy, end users can mitigate poor service and/or high prices by buying from alternative local and global providers.

Choice was assessed as the average of two measures using data from the end-user survey. The first is the average of the expenditure incurred with local and global competitors to the dominant service provider in each economy. The other, introduced in 2000, reflected end users' evaluation of the degree of choice in the respective economies measured on seven-point scales anchored at not liberal and extremely liberal. Average ratings of respondents were then standardized and combined with the expenditure scores to yield the choice subindex. Table 12-3 displays the rankings of the leading performers over 1998 to 2000, ordered by their 2000 scores.

As Table 12-3 indicates, there are also substantial changes in the choice competitiveness rankings over time. Only 2000 leader, New

TABLE 12-3
Choice rankings, 1998–2000

Economy	1998	1999	2000
New Zealand	–*	2	1
Australia	3	4	2
Japan	1	5	3
Philippines	5	6	4
Hong Kong	7	7	4

* New Zealand was not covered in the 1998 Index.

Zealand, remained relatively stable, being second in 1999, the year in which coverage of the country in the Index began. Australia, runner-up in 2000, was also placed consistently in the top five, being third in 1998 and joint fourth in 1999. However, Japan fluctuated between tops in 1998, fifth in 1999, and third in 2000. Hong Kong demonstrated improvement, moving up from seventh in 1998 and 1999 to joint fourth in 2000. Notably, the Philippines performed well on the choice component, being placed fifth, sixth, and joint fourth respectively in 1998, 1999, and 2000. It was a leading performer only on this dimension of the Index.

Regulation

The fourth and final dimension of the Index is regulation. Ideally, an economy would be most competitive if its telecommunications rules are clear and fairly enforced and its regulators are responsive to user requirements. In 1998 and 1999, respondents rated on two seven-point scales the transparency of regulation and the regulating agency's responsiveness for each economy. The scores were standardized across respondents to compute the regulation subindex. Due to space constraints, both items were combined in the 2000 survey, and data from the single item converted into index scores. Table 12-4 contains the 1998 to 2000 rankings of the leading economies ordered by their 2000 scores.

As Table 12-4 shows, the five leading economies' rankings over time on the responsiveness dimension were fairly stable. Mirroring the service quality rankings, the more advanced regional economies of Australia, Japan, Hong Kong, Singapore, and New Zealand consistently outperformed the rest. Within this cluster, however, some

TABLE 12-4
Regulation rankings, 1998–2000

Economy	1998	1999	2000
Australia	2	2	1
New Zealand	–*	4	2
Japan	4	3	3
Hong Kong	1	1	4
Singapore	3	5	5

* New Zealand was not covered in the 1998 Index.

movements can be observed. In particular, Hong Kong slipped from first in 1998 and 1999 to fourth in 2000, while Singapore fell from third in 1998 to fifth in 1999 and 2000. In contrast, Australia, runner-up in 1998 and 1999, went one better in 2000, while Japan moved up from fourth in 1998 to third in both 1999 and 2000.

Overall Competitiveness

To determine the overall telecommunications competitiveness of regional economies, their respective scores on the four subindices were weighted by the importance respondents held for each dimension. For all three years, service was perceived to be the most important dimension, followed by pricing, regulation, and choice. Table 12-5 lists the five leading economies in terms of overall competitiveness, ranked by their 2000 scores.

As Table 12-5 implies, the five leading economies outperformed the rest of the region in terms of overall telecommunications competitiveness. This is not surprising as it reflects the findings obtained for service quality, the most important dimension of the Index, and regulation. Within this leading cluster, however, some movements may be discerned. Specifically, Australia improved on its second placing in 1998 and 1999 to become the leader in 2000. Hong Kong also improved consistently over time, being fourth in 1998, third in 1999, and joint second in 2000. Similarly, New Zealand, not covered in 1998, moved up from sixth in 1999 to fifth in 2000. The rankings of Japan and Singapore fluctuated over the years. Japan was tops in 1998, slipped to fourth in 1999, but recovered to be joint second in 2000. In contrast, Singapore rose from third in 1998 to emerge leader in 1999, only to fall back to fourth in 2000.

TABLE 12-5
Overall rankings, 1998–2000

Economy	1998	1999	2000
Australia	2	2	1
Japan	1	4	2
Hong Kong	4	3	2
Singapore	3	1	4
New Zealand	–*	6	5

* New Zealand was not covered in the 1998 Index.

DISCUSSION

Several key insights may be observed from the Index findings over the years. First, the most competitive economies were consistently found to be Australia, Japan, Hong Kong, New Zealand, and Singapore. These economies dominated the top five rankings both overall and on each of the telecommunications subindices. The only exceptions to this leading cluster were South Korea and the Philippines. Even so, these economies only excelled selectively, being in the top bracket for the pricing and choice subindices respectively.

That this generally reflected the overall state of economic development in the region may be one implication drawn from the rankings. Yet, it could be argued that the state of telecommunications competitiveness may also contribute to the overall level of economic development in a nation. However, such inferences should be qualified in light of the finding that other developed Asian Tiger economies, notably Taiwan and (except for pricing) South Korea, were conspicuously missing from the top five lists. Further, these lines of argument suggest that the rapid development of China and India as global economic powerhouses should find future expression in their upward movement into the top echelons of telecommunications competitiveness in the region. To the extent that these developments may not materialize, other forces may be operative in shaping both economic and telecommunications development in the region.

Second, while the five leading economies clearly outperformed the rest in the region, their telecommunications competitiveness rankings, when compared to each other, varied across time and dimensions. Consider Japan's and Singapore's performances as an illustration. Both economies appeared to offer superior service quality over the three years of the Index's existence. However, with regard to pricing, Singapore was ranked in the top two over the years, while Japan did not figure in the top five until 2000. On choice, Japan's ranking fluctuated across all three years within the top five, while Singapore was unplaced throughout mainly because it did not permit alternative providers to SingTel until recently. In terms of regulation, Japan improved from fourth to third over the years, while Singapore slipped from third to fifth. These movements were reflected in the overall rankings, where both economies exhibited variations over time as a result of their competitiveness fluctuating on the individual dimensions. Japan thus led initially in 1998, slipped to fourth in 1999, and recovered to second in 2000, while Singapore began in third position in 1998, moved up to lead in 1999, but fell to fourth in 2000.

These results imply a highly dynamic landscape in the telecommunications market in the region. Large multinationals appear to be sensitive to developments in this strategic aspect of business, particularly in the pricing and choice dimensions which witnessed the largest fluctuations in rankings. The ranking changes further suggest that service providers and regulators must be on their toes regarding technological, marketing, and policy moves in the region. The pace of change in the regional telecommunications market is expected to accelerate rather than slow down in future. Coincidentally, Hong Kong and Singapore have completely opened their markets shortly after the Index was released in late January 2000. These policy measures would be felt across the region and should be captured in future editions of the Index.

Third, Australia emerged as the most consistent overall performer among regional economies in telecommunications competitiveness. It was second in the first two years, but climbed to first place in the latest edition of the Index. Its rankings came despite its being placed less well among the top five in terms of service quality, the most important dimension of the Index, over the years. However, as the overall scores were a weighted composite of all four dimensions, Australia's service quality drawback was more than offset by consistently better performances on the other subindices of pricing, choice, and regulation.

However, the extent of this compensatory effect may decline over time as regional economies become more competitive. To remain on top in future will likely require an economy being well placed in each of the four dimensions of the Index. Excelling on one dimension as South Korea did on pricing and the Philippines on choice is inadequate. This implies that economies must work on their weaknesses while maintaining their advantages in their areas of strengths. For Australia, for example, this translates to Telstra's improving on its technical and account service quality performance in future.

Indeed, it is anticipated that Singapore's (and to a lesser extent, Hong Kong's) choice performance will see substantial improvement. Similarly, both these economies' regulation rankings should also be raised with the more liberal policies being enacted recently. Such deregulation may have beneficial spillover effects on the two economies' competitiveness on the remaining dimensions of service and pricing. By liberalizing their markets, dominant service providers may be pressured to improve their service and cut their prices in the wake of increased competition from local and global telecommunications providers. Hence, shortly after their regulators' market-opening moves, SingTel and Cable & Wireless HKT announced merger plans. Had the merger materialized and brought about scale and cost economies, the service and pricing competitiveness of these dominant service providers would have been enhanced.

Broadly, the findings suggest that wooing the custom of large multinationals to locate their telecommunications hubs in a particular economy demands attention from several constituencies. These include dominant service providers, local and global alternatives, and public policy makers. Perhaps most vitally, enlightened regulators should enact and implement market-friendly policies that ensure a level playing field for all competitors in the marketplace.

Conclusion

Research on the Asia Pacific Telecommunications Index is an ongoing effort to monitor the performances of regional economies in this vital sphere of business-to-business marketing. Over the three years of its existence, the Index has witnessed several changes to its methodology and scope of coverage. Such changes were made to better reflect developments in the competitive marketplace. For example, more countries were included while some telecommunications services were excluded over time.

Future research should continue to see refinements made to the Index. Clearly, technological developments would also imply that new services be included in future for the service and pricing subindices. However, such inclusion would only occur should the new technologies become more widely adopted by the large multinationals who form the target segment of interest in this study. Similarly, the replacement of existing services in the Index would also take place when these are considered less important to end users.

It would be instructive for future research to be expanded to derive more fine-grained insights on the regulation of telecommunications services in the region. For example, specific questions may be asked of respondents on the nature of policies that could be considered by regulators to enhance the competitiveness of the marketplace. However, this must be balanced by length considerations as respondents in the survey place a premium on time. A lengthy questionnaire may produce adverse effects on response rate, which will undermine the representativeness of the sample.

Finally, as alluded to earlier, market-liberalization measures may result in dominant service providers in the region merging their operations. As the Index's service and pricing dimensions measure those of the dominant service provider in each regional economy, changes may be necessary to reflect such events.

In conclusion, the changing competitive landscape of telecommunications in the region clearly implies a continuing need for a comprehensive updating of developments in the marketplace. The Asia Pacific Telecommunications Index would thus remain a relevant and valuable source of information and insights for large multinationals, service providers, and regulators both within and outside the region.

References

Centre for Telemedia Strategy (1998, 1999, 2000). *Asia Pacific Telecommunications Report*. Singapore: National University of Singapore.

⑬

ASSESSING NATIONAL COMPETITIVE SUPERIORITY
An Importance–Performance Matrix Approach

Siew Meng Leong and Chin Tiong Tan

A well-established strategic marketing technique assesses Singapore's strengths and weaknesses in attracting foreign investments.

INTRODUCTION

It is well accepted that effective strategy is founded on continuous and diagnostic monitoring of one's competitive position. Evidence revealing the skills and resources affording the greatest leverage on future cost and differentiation advantages is particularly critical. Businesses that succeed are those which develop distinctive competencies and manage for lowest delivered cost or differentiation through superior customer value (Day and Wensley, 1988).

Increasingly, the same dictum appears applicable on a more macro level. Competition for capital and human resources has intensified between nations with the globalization of markets and business operations. Both capitalist and socialist governments are now turning toward some form of international strategic marketing planning (Nielsen, 1983) in an effort to solve problems of high unemployment, sluggish growth, and low foreign exchange earnings (Weigand, 1985).

Germane to this process is a thorough and balanced assessment of the reasons for the competitive position of a country in attracting

---

Reproduced with permission from *Marketing Intelligence and Planning*, Vol. 10, No. 1, 1992, pp. 42–48. © MCB University Press.

foreign investments. Ideally, such assessments of national competitive superiority should be both competitor-centered and customer-focused. The former necessitates a comparison of the relative skills, resources, and cost position of the country with target competitors. The latter requires such an evaluation to be conducted with key consumers rather than be based on internal, managerial sources. It is therefore consistent with the marketing concept which seeks to satisfy the needs and wants of target customers more effectively and efficiently than the competition. Gathering insights from the marketplace thus provides a more intimate understanding of customer needs and wants.

One technique which permits such simultaneous assessment is the Importance–Performance Matrix approach (Martilla and James, 1977). This method uses customer judgments of the importance of various attributes and the relative performance of a company on the attributes in assessing comparative advantage. It has a long history of successful use by consumer goods companies and has recently been adapted to equally good effect by industrial and service-oriented firms (Root, 1986). Du Pont, for example, has found that the overall ratings of competitive standing correlate well with market share.

The Importance–Performance Matrix approach appears ideally suited to assessing national competitive superiority in attracting foreign investments. By obtaining customer evaluations of relative country performance based on customer judgments of attribute importance, insights may be gathered regarding (1) the particular consideration set of nations used in relative performance evaluation; and (2) the strengths and weaknesses of a particular country on the attributes studied. Diagnostic information regarding the priority and extent of resource allocation in rectifying weaknesses may also be obtained.

This article thus employs the Importance–Performance Matrix approach in assessing the competitive standing of one nation— Singapore—with its key foreign investors. Singapore is a particularly appropriate context for this application because it relies heavily on foreign investments in achieving its economic mission of evolving into a "global city with a total business orientation" (Economic Development Board, 1987/88).

The remainder of this article is organized as follows. The next section discusses in greater detail the rationale and nature of the Importance–Performance Matrix approach. This is followed by a description of the research method used in data collection and analysis.

The results of the study are then presented. Finally, implications of the research findings are discussed.

The Importance–Performance Matrix

The fundamental assumption of the Importance–Performance Matrix is that not all attributes contribute equally to corporate success. To the extent that an enterprise performs well in attributes considered important to consumers, its likelihood of success is enhanced. On the other hand, poor performance on important attributes may have detrimental consequences for the firm.

Essentially, a four-cell matrix is obtained via a dichotomization of two dimensions of the approach. Attributes are divided into those of low or moderate importance versus those of high importance to the firm. Similarly, an enterprise's performance on these attributes can also be divided into excellent versus adequate or poor levels. Based on the locations of attributes in the matrix, enhanced understanding of the enterprise's strengths and weaknesses can be obtained. Remedial action can be undertaken to correct the weaknesses of the enterprise.

In extending this framework to analyze a nation's strategic position, the resultant matrix may have the following dimensions: (1) the target country's competitiveness on attributes used by investors; and (2) the importance of the attributes. Both may be dichotomized into high and moderate levels, thus yielding the matrix depicted in Figure 13-1.

Figure 13-1 illustrates the implications based on a particular attribute's location on the matrix. Specially, four categories of attributes may be delineated and actions implemented based thereon. Where a country is highly competitive on a highly important attribute, the strategy is one of maintenance—of keeping up the good work. In contrast, where a country is only moderately competitive on an important attribute, it needs to invest and improve on that attribute. High competitiveness on moderately important attributes provides a competitive edge but may be a sign of over-investment. Finally, moderate competitiveness on moderately important attributes suggests keeping a watching brief—improvements need to be made but are of a lower priority.

The Importance–Performance Matrix is sufficiently flexible to be generalized. Thus the cost competitiveness of a country in respect of

FIGURE 13-1
Importance–Performance Matrix

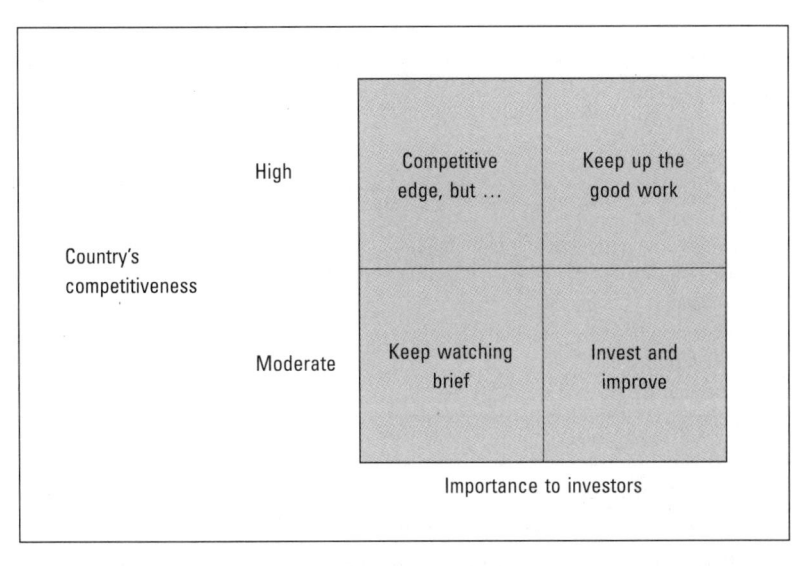

		Importance to investors	
Country's competitiveness	High	Competitive edge, but ...	Keep up the good work
	Moderate	Keep watching brief	Invest and improve

various factor inputs may be analyzed relative to the importance of the various factor inputs. In all cases, the approach requires the identification of key customers (investors), and seeking their inputs in respect of the importance of various attributes (or factor inputs), and the target country's performance (or cost competitiveness) on those attributes.

METHOD

Respondents

Respondents were international companies based in Singapore of world-class standing. The Singapore Economic Development Board (EDB) identified 50 such companies out of which 37 (74 percent) participated. Table 13-1 provides the background data for the survey respondents.

Attributes

It is essential to generate a representative and preferably exhaustive list of attributes for respondents to evaluate to ensure an adequate operationalization of the Importance–Performance Matrix approach. To this end, a pre-test was used to elicit the relevant attributes for inclusion in the survey. The pre-test was conducted at the Global

TABLE 13-1
General data on respondents

	Percentage
Sector	
Manufacturing	83
Services	17
Country	
U.S.	33
Europe	28
Japan/Asia	39
Global sales	
More than US$10b	13
US$1b to US$10b	50
Less than US$1b	37

Strategies Conference, a three-day seminar at which senior-level executives from major corporations from around the world participated.

Based on the open-ended responses of 211 of the executives, and with input from the EDB's Planning Division, a list of 28 attributes was employed in the survey. These fell into five major categories: (1) physical infrastructure (five attributes, e.g., seaport); (2) industrial infrastructure (three attributes, e.g., training centers); (3) services (five attributes, e.g., financial services); (4) quality of human resource skills (five attributes, e.g., technical); and (5) living environment (ten attributes, e.g., health-care facilities).

Measurement

Respondents evaluated the importance of each attribute on five-point scales with end-points of 5 = very important and 1 = not important. Respondents then named the country they were next most likely to consider for the location of new activities besides Singapore. They evaluated Singapore's performance on the same attributes on five-point scale (5 = Singapore is much better and 1 = Singapore is much worse) vis-à-vis the competing nation mentioned.

Respondents then furnished their impressions of the importance of various factor inputs in production. The inputs selected were a subset of ten of the attributes previously elicited. Five-point rating scales (5 = very important and 1 = not important) were employed for this purpose. They then evaluated Singapore's cost competitiveness relative to the next alternative investment option using five-point scales (5 = Singapore is much better and 1 = Singapore is much worse).

Finally, respondents provided background data and responded to some open-ended questions regarding general suggestions for improvement and plans for upgrading.

Results

Major Competitors

Companies generally consider a subset of available alternatives in choosing between locations for future investments. The evoked set of Singapore's key customers is depicted in Table 13-2.

Clearly, most (50 percent) international key customers consider Malaysia to be the alternative location for investments. No other country received more than 10 percent of such mentions. ASEAN countries received 60 percent of mentions in total, while the developed countries and newly industrialized economies (NIEs) received 30 percent. Singapore thus faces dynamic competition from other countries in terms of business location, from developed countries to newly industrialized countries to even the more advanced developing countries like Malaysia. The latter, for example, are developing the capability to produce some of the products manufactured by the more established industries in Singapore.

TABLE 13-2
Next most likely country of investment

Country	Percentage of mentions
Developed countries and NIEs	
U.K.	10
Hong Kong	10
Australia	5
South Korea	5
ASEAN countries	
Malaysia	50
Thailand	5
Philippines	5
Other countries	
People's Republic of China	5
India	5
Total	**100**

Importance–Performance Matrix Analysis

Following identification of its major competitors, it is now appropriate to conduct an analysis of Singapore's competitiveness, using the Importance–Performance Matrix. Table 13-3 documents the mean ratings of the importance of the attributes selected for study and how well Singapore performs on them relative to her closest competitors.

Examination of Singapore's performance scores reveal her strong competitiveness on all the attributes studied. In no case did an average performance rating fall below the scale midpoint. Thus Singapore was perceived to be generally more competitive than her closest rivals on all the attributes studied. However, added insights may be obtained using the Importance–Performance Matrix. To obtain this, the two sets of scores in Table 13-3 were dichotomized, using median splits into highly and moderately important attributes and high and moderate levels of competitive superiority of Singapore. This produced Figure 13-2.

Figure 13-2 clearly indicates that Singapore must keep up the good work on its hardware support. The airport, seaport, telecommunications, health-care facilities, public utilities, and road transport network were important attributes in the eyes of key customers, where Singapore enjoyed a distinct advantage vis-à-vis competitors. Physical safety and financial services were seen in the same way.

Singapore also performed well on the attributes of government skills-training centers, training centers, government technical/R&D centers, pollution level, professional support services, and information network.

However, these attributes were considered somewhat less important to key customers. While Singapore's competitive superiority in these attributes needs to be preserved, care must be taken not to over-invest in these attributes nor to over-emphasize them in promotional programs targeted at investors.

Singapore needs to improve performance in five critical areas—schooling facilities, supporting industries, and executive/managerial, professional, and technical human resource quality. These are attributes which are highly important to investors but on which Singapore does not enjoy a clear-cut competitive advantage over her nearest rivals. Significantly, three of these five attributes concerned her "liveware"—her human resources.

TABLE 13-3
Infrastructural and environment ratings

	Mean ratings	
Item	Importance	Competitiveness
Technical human resources	4.89	3.88
Telecommunications	4.86	4.51
Executive/managerial human resources	4.67	3.96
Professional human resources	4.62	3.96
Airport	4.59	4.62
Public utilities	4.54	4.44
Physical safety	4.50	4.55
School facilities	4.45	4.18
Health-care facilities	4.43	4.48
Seaport	4.37	4.84
Financial services	4.37	4.30
Supporting industries	4.22	3.96
Road transport network	4.08	4.55
Information network	4.08	4.30
Industrial land/factories	4.02	3.69
Clerical/support human resources	3.97	3.76
Training centers	3.94	4.40
Government skills-training centers	3.94	4.41
Pollution level	3.94	4.25
Direct (shopfloor) human resources	3.80	3.41
Professional support services	3.78	4.23
Publication/freedom of press	3.73	3.11
Religious freedom	3.55	3.85
Recreational amenities	3.43	3.55
Entertainment facilities	3.43	3.48
Censorship policies	3.33	3.26
Shopping amenities	3.27	4.22
Government technical centers	3.22	4.40

Attention also needs to be directed toward enhancing Singapore's competitiveness in shopping amenities, religious freedom, clerical/support and direct (shopfloor) human resource quality, industrial land/factories, recreational amenities, entertainment amenities, censorship policies, and publication/freedom of press. However, these attributes merit less immediate and/or less extensive attention—given that they are considered moderately important to investors.

Cost Competitiveness

Table 13-4 contains the mean importance and competitiveness ratings

236 | Assessing National Competitive Superiority

FIGURE 13-2
Importance–Quality Competitiveness Matrix: infrastructure and environment (with respect to next most likely country of investment)

		Moderate Importance	High Importance
Competitiveness of Singapore	High	Government skills training centers Government technical/R&D centers Pollution level Professional support services Information network Training centers	Seaport Airport Physical safety Road transport network Telecommunications Health-care facilities Public utilities Financial services
	Moderate	Shopping amenities Religious freedom Clerical/support human resources Industrial land/factories Recreational amenities Entertainment amenities Direct (shopfloor) human resources Censorship policies Publication/freedom of press	School facilities Executive/managerial human resources Professional human resources Supporting industries Technical human resources

Importance to investors

TABLE 13-4
Factor pricing ratings

	Mean ratings	
Item	**Pricing importance**	**Price competitiveness**
Telecommunications	4.48	4.14
Skilled labor costs	4.49	2.85
Public utilities	4.45	3.76
Financial services	4.32	3.50
Overall labor costs	4.28	2.30
Land costs	4.13	2.34
Office/factory rental	4.13	3.50
Unskilled labor costs	4.08	1.73
Infrastructural costs	3.89	3.48
Semi-skilled labor costs	3.83	2.29

of ten attributes by investors that will be used in assessing Singapore's cost superiority relative to her closest rivals. These scores were used to construct Figure 13-3, which illustrates a Factor Price Importance–Competitiveness Matrix of Singapore vis-à-vis her competitors. Scale midpoints of three were used as cut-off points to categorize factors into moderately/very important/competitive.

Figure 13-3 suggests that Singapore should maintain her highly competitive offerings of four key cost factors—telecommunications, public utilities, financial services, and office/factory rental. These were highly important price factors on which Singapore enjoyed a much superior competitive pricing advantage. Singapore's infrastructural costs were also competitive, although these were of moderate price importance to investors.

However, Singapore must concentrate efforts on enhancing price competitiveness on such highly important pricing considerations as skilled, overall, and unskilled labor costs, as well as land costs. On these factor prices, Singapore was less competitive than her nearest rivals (all mean scores of price competitiveness were less than the scale midpoint). Some attention toward enhancing price competitiveness on semi-skilled labor costs also warrants consideration, albeit of a less crucial nature, given its moderate importance to investors.

FIGURE 13-3
Factor Price Importance–Competitiveness Matrix

Price competitiveness	Moderate	High
High	Infrastructure costs	Telecommunications Public utilities Financial costs Office/factory rental
Moderate	Semi-skilled labor costs	Skilled labor costs Land costs Overall labor costs Unskilled labor costs

Factor price importance

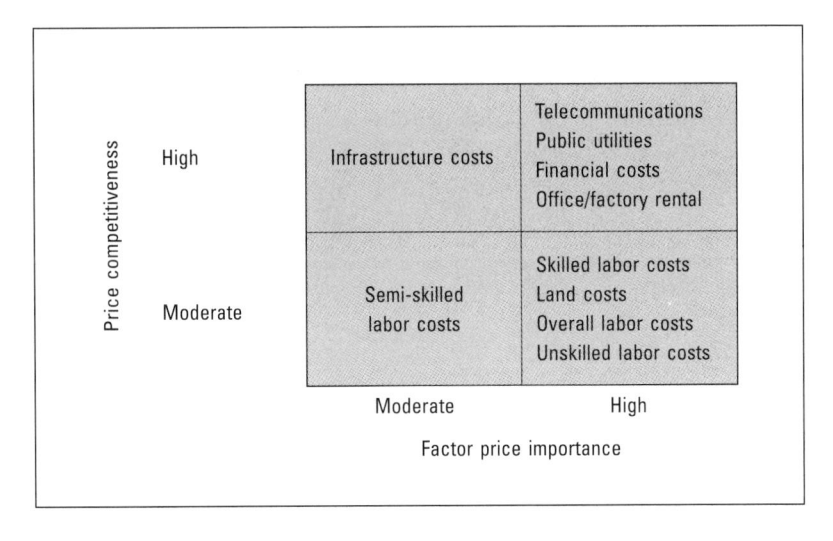

Discussion

The relationship between marketing and economic development has long been recognized. Early research sought to determine this relationship via the comparative analysis of the marketing systems of different nations (Cundiff, 1965; Douglas, 1971; Goldman, 1972; Hilger, 1978; Moyer, 1964). More recently, various macromarketing approaches have been employed toward optimizing national economic development (Cundiff, 1982; Darian, 1985; Dominguez and Vanmarcke, 1987; Hosley and Wee, 1988).

This article continues the latter line of inquiry by drawing the parallel between the formulation of corporate marketing strategy and national economic policy (see Figure 13-4). Both must be predicated on an intimate understanding of the strategic position of the company (country) and its products (infrastructural and environmental attributes) in the marketplace. The success or failure of a business or nation may well hinge on how well it competes against other businesses or nations, as well as on the ability to capitalize on its strengths and rectify its weaknesses. Clearly, such an understanding is most valuable if the views of its customers or investors are sought and competitive considerations incorporated.

The Importance–Performance Matrix approach is a simple, sound, and flexible method that national economic planners may consider employing. It forces planners to focus on the views of investors

FIGURE 13-4
Parallels between corporate strategic formulation and national economic planning

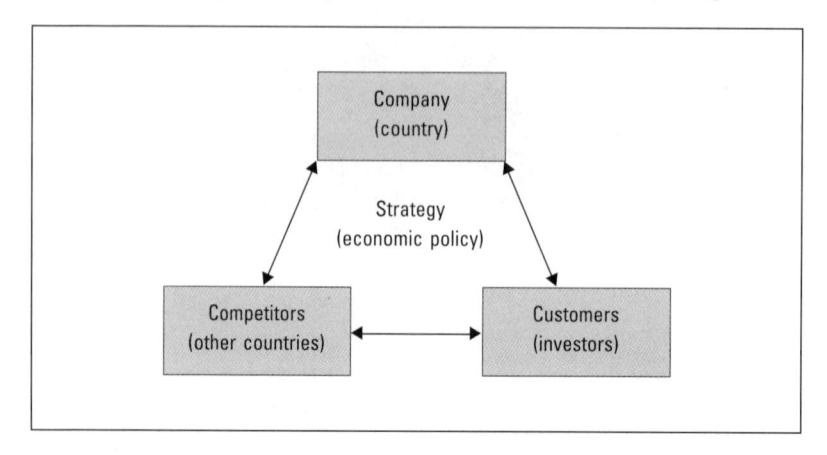

regarding the importance of various attributes and the country's performance on these attributes relative to its closest competitors. This counteracts the tendency of economic planners to presume to know what the most important attributes are and how well or poorly the country fares on them. Astute judgments from economic planners are, however, required in implementing the approach. The dichotomization of attributes into high versus moderate importance and performance is one area which calls for considerable attention. In the illustration presented, median splits were used in obtaining the Importance–Quality Competitiveness Matrix, while scale midpoints were employed to construct the Factor Price Importance–Competitiveness Matrix. The choice of one approach over the other was a function of the range of scores obtained. In the former case, all mean scores exceeded the scale midpoint. Using scale midpoints would thus provide little, if any, diagnostic insights regarding which attributes merit attention in resource allocation decisions.

The Importance–Performance Matrix approach requires advanced, precise, and detailed specification of the attributes to be studied. Such specificity comes at a cost, as the attributes selected may be highly correlated, but the diagnostic insights obtained are certainly superior (Day and Wensley, 1988). Use of the approach also reduces the temptation of economic planners to develop every aspect of a country's resources simultaneously and with equal attention. It directs a rational and systematic review of which attributes require higher priorities for resource allocation at different stages of the country's development.

In the case of Singapore, human resources appear to be the principal strategic area for improvement quality and cost competitiveness. The future success of Singapore is very dependent on its ability to provide access to an adequate supply of human resources at all levels and elevate their skills to world-class standing. Moreover, Singapore's focus must be to attract companies which intensively utilize those factors on which Singapore enjoys a clear-cut cost and quality competitive advantage—telecommunications, public utilities, and financial services. Typically, these include higher value-added industries and service firms which may benefit from Singapore's superior infrastructure and excellent total business capability.

In addition, it is imperative that Singapore does not allow factor costs to become out of line with those of her competitors. Increments in costs can be justified only by commensurate, if not greater, increases in value offered to customers vis-à-vis Singapore's competitors. Such value enhancements may take the form of improvement in productivity, quality, time savings, worker's attitude, and work ethic.

Finally, the Importance–Performance Matrix approach suggests that an entity's competitiveness is measured with respect to a particular consideration set. In Singapore's case, investors viewed Malaysia as the major alternative location for their investments. If Singapore is unable to overcome land and labor shortages (e.g., through reclamation projects and more relaxed immigration policies, respectively), it makes strategic sense (1) to avoid attracting low-labor-cost manufacturing and companies with extensive land requirements; and (2) to develop linkages or networking arrangements with her neighbor. The latter is analogous to corporations forming strategic alliances (Kotler, 1986) with each other. Singapore may, in fact, be positioned as a conduit through which international investors may channel, oversee, and monitor their investments in the Asia Pacific region.

Conclusion

The Importance–Performance Matrix approach has been introduced and applied to analysis of a nation's competitive superiority in attracting foreign investments. Obtaining the views of key customers and acting on them will enhance national competitiveness and lead to a more market-driven philosophy in economic planning. The application presented is illustrative. Future research may consider a wider array of countries and attributes. Direct comparisons with specific nations (e.g., Malaysia in the case of Singapore) may be envisaged. Other key attributes (e.g., nature of regulatory framework, existence of incentives or subsidies, trade bloc membership, market size, geographic location, and costs of using various infrastructural facilities such as seaports) may likewise be included for more comprehensive analyses. Longitudinal studies may also be useful to track investor changes in preferences and perceptions. Additional insights may also be garnered through segmentation of investors by industry and country of origin to more finely tuned plans targeted at particular sets of investors.

To conclude, Porter (1990) has argued that nations succeed in particular industries because their home environment is the most dynamic and challenging. This stimulates them to upgrade and widen their competitive advantage over time. By attracting globally oriented, successful corporations, countries like Singapore may provide an environment that catalyzes domestic entrepreneurship. Such a development may be facilitated by technology transfer, the nurturing of local supporting industries, and increased domestic competition. Investor firms, on the other hand, may also be challenged to improve and upgrade, based on insights and assistance from host nations which themselves possess competitive advantage as suppliers (Porter, 1990). Clearly, a mutually beneficial relationship can be fostered between host nations and foreign investor firms.

References

Cundiff, E.W. (1965). Concepts in comparative retailing. *Journal of Marketing*, 29 (January): 59–63.

Cundiff, E.W. (1982). A macromarketing approach to economic development. *Journal of Macromarketing*, 2 (Spring): 14–19.

Darian, J.C. (1985). Marketing and economic development: A case study from classical India. *Journal of Macromarketing*, 5 (Spring): 14–26.

Day, G.S. and R. Wensley (1988). Assessing advantage: A framework for diagnosing competitive superiority. *Journal of Marketing*, 52 (April): 1–20.

Dominguez, L.V. and C. Vanmarcke (1987). Market structure and marketing behavior in LDCs: The case of Venezuela. *Journal of Macromarketing*, 7 (Fall): 4–16.

Douglas, S.P. (1971). Patterns and parallels of marketing structures in several countries. *MSU Business Topics*, 19 (Spring): 38–48.

Economic Development Board (1987/88). *Annual Report*. Singapore.

Goldman, A. (1972). Outreach of consumers and the modernization of urban food retailing in developing countries. *Journal of Marketing*, 38 (October): 8–16.

Hilger, M.T. (1978). Theories of the relationship between marketing and economic development: Public policy implications. In P.D. White and C.C. Slater (eds.), *Macromarketing: Distributive Processes from a Societal Perspective: An Elaboration of Issues*. Boulder, CO: Graduate School of Business Administration, University of Colorado.

Hosley, S. and C.H. Wee (1988). Marketing and economic development: Focusing on the less developed countries. *Journal of Macromarketing*, 8 (Spring): 43–53.

Kotler, P. (1986). Megamarketing. *Harvard Business Review*, 64 (March–April): 117–24.

Martilla, J.A. and J.C. James (1977). Importance–performance analysis. *Journal of Marketing*, 51 (January): 77–79.

Moyer, R. (1964). The structure of markets in developing economies. *MSU Business Topics*, 12 (Fall): 43–60.

Nielsen, R.P. (1983). Should a country move toward international strategic market planning? *California Management Review*, 25 (January): 34–44.

Porter, M.E. (1990). *The Competitive Advantage of Nations*. New York: Free Press.

Root, H.P. (1986). Industrial market intelligence systems: A source of competitive advantage. Paper presented at the Business-to-Business Marketing Conference, American Marketing Association, New Orleans, April.

Weigand, R.E. (1985). Searching for investments: The race is on; the runners should be wary. *Business Horizons*, 28 (March/April): 46–52.

MANAGING BRANDS FOR THE LONG RUN
Brand Reinforcement and Revitalization Strategies

Kevin Lane Keller

Effective brand management requires taking a long-term view of marketing decisions. A long-term perspective of brand management recognizes that any changes in the supporting marketing program for a brand may, by changing consumer knowledge, affect the success of future marketing programs. Additionally, a long-term view necessitates proactive strategies designed to maintain and enhance customer-based brand equity over time in the face of external changes in the marketing environment and internal changes in a firm's marketing goals and programs. This article discusses strategies for reinforcing and revitalizing brands.

INTRODUCTION

One of the challenges in managing brands is the many changes that occur in the marketing environment. The marketing environment evolves and changes, often in very significant ways. Shifts in consumer behavior, competitive strategies, government regulations, and other aspects of the marketing environment can profoundly affect the fortunes of a brand. Besides these external forces, the firm itself may engage in a variety of activities and changes in strategic focus or direction that may necessitate adjustments in the way that its brands are being marketed. Consequently, effective brand management

---

Copyright © 1999 by The Regents of the University of California. Reprinted from the *California Management Review*, Vol. 41, No. 3. By permission of The Regents.

requires proactive strategies designed to at least maintain—if not actually enhance—brand equity in the face of these different forces.

The customer-based brand equity framework, developed by the author,[1] defines customer-based brand equity as the differential effect that consumer knowledge about a brand has on the customer's response to marketing activity. Positive customer-based brand equity results when consumers respond more favorably to a product, price, or communication when the brand is identified than when it is not. According to this framework, consumer brand knowledge can be characterized in terms of brand awareness and brand image dimensions. Sources of brand equity occur when consumers are aware of the brand and hold strong, favorable, and unique brand associations. There are a number of ways to create those knowledge structures in the minds of consumers. Broadly, they involve choosing brand elements, developing supporting marketing programs, and creating secondary associations.

One direct implication of this view of brand equity is that effective brand management requires taking a long-term view of marketing decisions. Any action that a firm takes as part of its marketing program has the potential to change consumer knowledge about the brand in terms of some aspect of brand awareness or brand image. These changes in consumer brand knowledge will also have an indirect effect on the success of *future* marketing activities. Thus, from the perspective of customer-based brand equity, it is important when making marketing decisions to consider how the changes in brand awareness and image that could result from those decisions may help or hurt *subsequent* marketing decisions. For example, the frequent use of sales promotions involving temporary price decreases may create or strengthen a "discount" association to the brand, with potentially adverse implications on customer loyalty and responses to future price changes or non-price-oriented marketing communication efforts.

Managing brand equity, however, requires more than taking a long-term perspective. Brand equity must be actively managed over time by reinforcing the brand meaning and, if necessary, by revitalizing the brand.

---

[1] This paper is based in part on material from Chapter 13 of Kevin Lane Keller, *Strategic Brand Management* (Upper Saddle River, NJ: Prentice Hall, 1998).

Reinforcing Brands

How should brand equity be reinforced over time? How can marketers make sure that consumers have the desired knowledge structures such that their brands continue to have the necessary sources of brand equity? In a general sense, brand equity is reinforced by marketing actions that consistently convey the meaning of the brand to consumers—in terms of brand awareness and brand image—as follows:

- *What products does the brand represent; what benefits does it supply; and what needs does it satisfy?* For example, Nutri-Grain has expanded from cereals into granola bars and other products, cementing its reputation as "makers of healthy breakfast and snack foods."
- *How does the brand make those products superior?* What strong, favorable, and unique brand associations exist in the minds of consumers? For example, through product development and the successful introductions of brand extensions, Black and Decker is now seen as offering "innovative designs" in its small appliance products.

Both of these issues—brand meaning in terms of products, benefits, and needs as well as brand meaning in terms of product differentiation—depend on the firm's general approach to product development, branding strategies, and other strategic concerns.

Maintaining Brand Consistency

Without question, the most important consideration in reinforcing brands is the consistency of the marketing support that the brand receives—both in terms of the amount and nature of marketing support. Brand consistency is critical to maintaining the strength and favorability of brand associations. Brands that receive inadequate support, in terms of such things as shrinking research and development or marketing communication budgets, run the risk of becoming technologically disadvantaged or even obsolete.

Market leaders and failures

From the perspective of maintaining consumer loyalty, inadequate marketing support is especially dangerous when combined with price increases. Once the comfortable leader in its market, Tampax lost market share to brands from Playtex and Johnson & Johnson when its prices were raised while its ad spending was simultaneously cut. To recover lost ground, management was eventually forced to quickly introduce a $20 million ad campaign for the brand that promoted "Trust is Tampax Tampons" (Bird, 1993).

In terms of qualitative aspects of positioning, a cursory examination of the brands that have maintained market leadership for the last 50 or 100 years or so is a testament to the advantages of staying consistent. Brands like Budweiser, Coca-Cola, Hershey, and others have been remarkably consistent in their strategies once they achieved a preeminent market leadership position. Philip Morris has single-mindedly focused its marketing communications for their Marlboro cigarette brand on a Western cowboy image. Since the mid-1970s, Marlboro has been America's No. 1 cigarette brand. The romantic images of the rugged cowboy have since been taken worldwide and even successfully transferred to billboards and print ads when Marlboro's cigarette commercials were banned from television and radio (Alsop, 1989a).

Perhaps an even more compelling demonstration of the benefits of consistency is to consider the fortunes of those brands that have been inconsistent in their marketing program—for example, by constantly repositioning or changing ad agencies. Since its highly successful mid-1970s "Have It Your Way" campaign that touted the uniqueness and quality of their hamburgers, Burger King suffered through 20 years of false starts and wrong turns in brand support. The disastrous $40 million Herb campaign in 1985—featuring a nerd-like character who was supposed to be the only person in America never to have tasted a Whopper—was pulled after only three months. While watching its market share of the total fast food market drop, Burger King went through a number of company presidents, marketing directors, and ad agencies. Eventually, Burger King advertising returned to perhaps their strongest and most favorable brand association—the popular Whopper hamburger—in a new campaign themed "Get Your Burger's Worth," which brought a corresponding return to good fortunes.

Consistency and change

Consistency does *not* mean, however, that marketers should avoid making any changes in the marketing program. On the contrary, the opposite can be quite true—being consistent in managing brand equity may require numerous tactical shifts and changes in order to maintain the proper strategic thrust and direction of the brand. There are many ways that brand awareness and brand image can be created, maintained, or improved through carefully designed marketing programs. The tactics that may be most effective for a particular brand at any one time can certainly vary from those that may be most effective for the brand at another time. As a consequence, prices may move up or down, product features may be added or dropped, ad campaigns may employ different creative strategies and slogans, and different brand extensions may be introduced or withdrawn over time in order to create the *same* desired knowledge structures in consumers' minds.

Nevertheless, despite these different types of changes in marketing programs, the strategic positioning of many leading brands has remained remarkably consistent over time. A contributing factor to the success of these brands is that despite these tactical changes, certain key elements of the marketing program are always retained and continuity has been preserved in brand meaning over time.

For example, many brands have kept a key creative element in their marketing communication programs over the years and, as a result, have effectively created some "advertising equity." Recognizing the latent value of their past advertising, new ad campaigns have seen the return of such advertising icons as Colonel Sanders for Kentucky Fried Chicken, Charlie the Tuna for Star-Kist tuna, American Tourister's luggage-thumping gorilla, the percolating Maxwell House coffeepot, and the sing-song Oscar Mayer wiener jingles.

From an awareness standpoint, such efforts obviously make sense. It is important to determine whether these old advertising elements have enduring meaning with older consumers and, at the same time, can be made to seem relevant to younger consumers. More generally, the entire marketing program should be examined to determine which elements are making a strong contribution to brand equity and therefore must be protected.

Protecting Sources of Brand Equity

Consistency should therefore be viewed in terms of strategic direction and not necessarily the particular tactics employed by the supporting marketing program for the brand at any one point in time. Unless there is some change with either consumers, competition, or the company that somehow makes the strategic positioning of the brand less powerful—for example, changes that somehow make key brand associations for the brand less desirable or deliverable—there is likely to be little need to deviate from a successful positioning. Although brands should always look for potentially powerful new sources of brand equity, a top priority under those circumstances is to preserve and defend those sources of brand equity that already exist.

For example, a few years back, Procter & Gamble made a minor change in the formulation of their Cascade automatic dishwashing detergent, primarily for cost-savings reasons. As a result, the product was not quite as effective as it had previously been under certain, albeit somewhat atypical, water conditions. After discovering the fact, one of their chief competitors, Lever Brothers, began running comparative ads for their Sunlight brand featuring side-by-side glasses that claimed "Sunlight Fights Spots Better Than Cascade." Since the consumer benefit of "virtually spotless" is a key brand association and source of brand equity for Cascade, P&G reacted swiftly. They immediately returned Cascade back to its original formula and contacted Lever Brothers to inform them of the change, forcing them to stop running the new Sunlight ads as a result. As this episode clearly demonstrates, Procter & Gamble fiercely defends the equity of their brands, perhaps explaining why so many of P&G's brands have had such longevity.

As another example, consider the public relations problems encountered by Intel Corp. with the "floating decimal" problem in their Pentium microprocessors in December 1994. Although the flaw in the chip resulted in miscalculation problems in only extremely unusual and rare instances, Intel was probably at fault—as company executives now admit—for not identifying the problem and proposing remedies to consumers more quickly. Once the problem became public, Intel endured an agonizing six-week period where the company was the focus of media scrutiny and criticism for their reluctance to publicize the problem and their failure to offer replacement chips. Two key sources of brand equity for Intel microprocessors like the

Pentium—emphasized throughout their marketing program—are "power" and "safety." Although consumers primarily think of safety in terms of upgradability, the perceptions of financial risk or other problems that might result from a potentially flawed chip certainly should have created a sense of urgency within Intel to protect one of their prize sources of brand equity. Eventually, Intel capitulated and offered a replacement chip. Perhaps not surprisingly, only a very small percentage of consumers—an estimated 1 to 3 percent—actually requested a replacement chip, suggesting that it was Intel's stubbornness to act and not the defect per se that rankled so many consumers.

Ideally, key sources of brand equity would be of enduring value. If so, these brand associations should be guarded and nurtured carefully. Unfortunately, their value can easily be overlooked as marketers attempt to expand the meaning of their brand and add new product-related or non-product-related brand associations.

Fortifying vs. Leveraging

There are a number of different ways to raise brand awareness and create strong, favorable, and unique brand associations in consumer memory to build customer-based brand equity. In managing brand equity, it is important to recognize tradeoffs between those marketing activities that attempt to fortify and further contribute to brand equity versus those marketing activities that attempt to leverage or capitalize on existing brand equity to reap some financial benefit.

The advantage of creating a brand with a high level of awareness and a positive brand image is that many benefits may result to the firm in terms of cost savings and revenue opportunities. Marketing programs can be designed that primarily attempt to capitalize on or perhaps even maximize these benefits—for example, by reducing advertising expenses, seeking increasingly higher price premiums, or introducing numerous brand extensions. The more there is an attempt to realize or capture brand equity benefits, however, the more likely it is that the brand and its sources of equity may become neglected and perhaps diminished in the process. In other words, marketing actions that attempt to leverage the equity of a brand in different ways may come at the expense of other activities that may help to fortify the brand by maintaining or enhancing its awareness and image.

At some point, failure to fortify the brand will diminish brand awareness and weaken brand image. *Without these sources of brand equity, the brand itself may not continue to yield as valuable benefits.* Just as a failure to properly maintain a car eventually affects its performance, neglecting a brand can catch up with marketers. For example, as Coors Brewing devoted increasing attention in its marketing on growing the equity of less established brands (Coors Light beer) and introducing new products (Zima clear malt beverage), ad support for the flagship Coors beer slipped from a peak of about $43 million in 1985 to a meager $4 million by 1993. Perhaps not surprisingly, sales of Coors beer dropped in half from 1989 to 1993. In launching a new ad campaign to prop up sales, Coors returned to its iconoclastic, independent Western image. Marketers at Coors now admit they did not give the brand the attention it deserves, "We've not marketed Coors as aggressively as we should have in the past 10 to 15 years" (Charlier, 1994).

Fine-tuning the Supporting Marketing Program

Although the specific tactics and supporting marketing program for the brand are more likely to change than the basic positioning and strategic direction for the brand, brand tactics also should only be changed when there is evidence that they are no longer making the desired contributions to maintaining or strengthening brand equity. Dove soap has been advertised in a remarkably consistent fashion over the years, even across geographical boundaries. Dove is positioned as a beauty bar with one-quarter cleansing cream that "creams skin while it washes." Dove advertising has consistently been positioned to consumers on a performance basis with the slogan "Dove Doesn't Dry Your Skin." For years, advertising has always been trial-oriented, using consumer testimonials to vouch for the quality of the product ("Take the 7-Day Dove Test").

Reinforcing brand meaning may depend on the nature of brand associations involved. Several specific considerations play a particularly important role in reinforcing brand meaning in terms of product-related and non-product-related associations.

Product-related associations

For brands whose core associations are primarily product-related attributes and/or functional benefits, innovation in product design, manufacturing, and merchandising is especially critical to maintaining or enhancing brand equity. After Timex saw brands like Casio and Swatch gain significant market share by emphasizing digital technology and fashion, respectively, in their watches, they made a number of innovative marketing changes. Within a short period of time, Timex introduced Indiglo glow-in-the-dark technology, showcased popular new models such as the Ironman in mass media advertising, and launched new Timex stores to showcase their products. Timex also bought the Guess and Monet watch brands to distribute through upscale department stores and expand their brand portfolio. These innovations in product design and merchandising have significantly revived the brand's fortunes (Roush, 1993).

Failure to innovate can have dire consequences. Schwinn Bicycle once owned the kids bike market with famous models such as the Phantom (a 1950s workhorse with balloon tires) and the Varsity (a ten-speed stalwart of the 1970s). Unfortunately, its market share, which peaked at 25 percent in the 1960s, slipped to single digits by the early 1990s. The problem? In part, Schwinn was slow to adjust to changing consumer tastes and take aggressive new rivals seriously. While other companies won over biking enthusiasts with lighter, sleeker models in the early 1980s, Schwinn continued to crank out its durable, but bulky, standbys. As one custom bicycle dealer observed, "Schwinn never spent the money on research and development or planned for the long-term, like so many American companies. Except for their name, they really have nothing to sell" (O'Brien, 1992).

Thus, product innovations are critical for performance-based brands whose sources of brand equity primarily rest in product-related associations. In some cases, product advances may involve brand extensions based on a new or improved product ingredient or feature, for example, Sony televisions with special Trinitron color tubes, Oreo Double Stuff cookies with extra filling, and Ziploc Gripper Zipper storage bags (Farquhar et al., 1992). In fact, in many categories, a strong family sub-brand has emerged from product innovations associated with brand extensions, for instance, Wilson Hammer wide-body tennis racquets. In other cases, product innovations may center on existing brands. For example, General Mills "Big G" cereal division strives to improve at least a third of its nearly two dozen brand lines each year, recently reformulating Cheerios and Wheaties (Gibson, 1994).

At the same time, it is important not to change products too much, especially if the brand meaning to consumers is wrapped up in the product design or makeup. In a classic marketing story, Coca-Cola encountered strong consumer resistance when they changed their cola formula to "New Coke" in 1985. Thus, in making product changes to a brand, it is important that loyal consumers feel that a reformulated product is a *better* product not a *different* product. The timing of the announcement and introduction of a product improvement is also important: if the brand improvement is announced too soon, consumers may cease to buy existing products; if the brand improvement is announced too late, competitors may have already taken advantage of the market opportunity with their own introductions.

Non-product-related associations

For brands whose core associations are primarily non-product-related attributes and symbolic or experiential benefits, relevance in user and usage imagery is critical. Because of their intangible nature, non-product-related associations may be potentially easier to change, for example, through a major new advertising campaign that communicates a different type of user or usage situation. Nevertheless, ill-conceived or too-frequent repositionings can blur the image of a brand and confuse or perhaps even alienate consumers. Pepsi-Cola's fresh, youthful appeal has been a key point-of-difference versus Coca-Cola. Moving away from its "Choice of a New Generation" slogan, Pepsi launched a new campaign with the slogan "Gotta Have It" during the 1992 Super Bowl. The ads, showing young and old Pepsi drinkers, were an attempt to expand the "Pepsi Generation" to include older age groups. With little indication of sales success, Pepsi returned to its more familiar and powerful positioning, introducing new ads with the snappy tagline "Be Young. Have Fun. Drink Pepsi" (McCarthy, 1993). Subsequently, Pepsi perhaps again ran the risk of straying away from a key source of equity with the introduction of the ad theme "Nothing Else Is a Pepsi." More recently, they have returned to the youth appeal of "Generation Next," and its creative follow-up, "Joy of Cola."

Another example of a too hasty departure from advertising equity occurred with Miller Lite light beer. Miller Lite was advertised for years with the slogan "Tastes Great. Less Filling" in humorous ads featuring famous retired athletes. In part to revive fading brand sales, a new ad campaign was launched in 1992. A dramatic departure from previous advertising, the new campaign, featuring fashionable young people, contained the slogans "C'mon, Let Me Show You Where It's At" and "It's It and That's That." When the slide in brand sales continued, Miller reversed their field to create a new campaign, much more faithful to their original positioning. The "Combinations" campaign showed Miller Lite drinkers disagreeing over which of two completely different events to watch on TV. After banging their TV set with a bottle of Lite beer, the two events became combined into one "wacky" spectator sport such as "Sumo High Dive," "Recliner Chair Ski Jump," and "Wiener Dog Winter Nationals." The new ad tagline, echoing the past, became "Great Taste. Less Filling. Can Your Beer Do This?" More recently, Miller Lite adopted yet another slogan, "Life is Good," although retaining some of the stylistic characteristics of the Combinations campaign. The return to advertising form saw a comeback in sales, although Miller chose in 1997 to introduce a quirky, controversial ad campaign featuring a fictitious copywriter, Dick, in explicitly targeting 21- to 25-year-olds that was eventually abandoned at the end of 1998.

Significant repositionings may be dangerous for other reasons. Brand images can be extremely sticky, and once consumers form strong brand associations, they may be difficult to change. Consumers may choose to ignore or just be unable to remember the new positioning when strong, but different, brand associations already exist in memory (Keller et al., 1998). Club Med has attempted for years to transcend its image as a vacation romp for swingers to attract a broader cross-section of people.

For dramatic repositioning strategies to work, convincing new brand claims must be presented in a compelling fashion. One brand that successfully shifted from a primarily non-product-related image to a primarily product-related image is BMW. Uniformly decreed as the quintessential "yuppie" vehicle of the 1980s, sales of the brand dropped almost in half from 1986 to 1991 as new Japanese competition emerged and a backlash to the "Greed Decade" set in. Convinced that high status was no longer a sufficiently desirable and sustainable position, marketing and advertising efforts switched the focus to BMW's product developments and improvements, such as the responsive performance, distinctive styling, and leading-edge engineering of the cars as the "Ultimate Driving Machine." These efforts, showcased in well-designed ads, helped to diminish the "yuppie" association, and sales by 1995 approached their earlier peak (Serafin, 1994).

Revitalizing Brands

Sometimes even the best-designed and implemented brand reinforcement strategies may fail. As noted above, changes in consumer tastes and preferences, the emergence of new competitors or new technology, or any new development in the marketing environment could potentially have a profound effect on the fortunes of a brand. In virtually every product category, there are examples of once prominent and admired brands that have fallen on hard times or, in some cases, completely disappeared. Nevertheless, a number of these brands—such as Harley-Davidson, Mountain Dew, and Chrysler—have managed to make impressive comebacks in recent years as marketers have breathed new life into their customer franchises.

To revive their fortunes, brands sometimes have had to "return to their roots" to recapture lost sources of equity. Adidas, once the standard of athletic footwear, saw its leading market position overtaken by rivals Nike and Reebok as the company became mired in outdated business practices and internal squabbles. New management, headed by a former chief executive at Saatchi & Saatchi ad agency, began efforts to turn the brand around in 1993. Adidas decided to concentrate their efforts on the lucrative, but fickle, teenage market with the hope that this group might choose to reject brands adopted by their parents and others to create their own identity. New performance-oriented products, advertising, and athlete sponsors targeted a young, urban audience. Additional promotional efforts capitalized on the World Cup soccer tournament in the U.S. Complementing this "pull" effort, Adidas also attempted to increase their share of shelf space in stores. As a result, Adidas increased their share of the $8 billion athletic shoe market to 5 percent from 2 percent in just four years, and has become the number four sneaker company in the U.S., challenging number three Fila (Goldman, 1994a; Levine, 1996).

In other cases, the meaning of the brand has had to fundamentally change to regain lost ground and recapture market leadership. Hush Puppies' suede shoes—symbolized by the cuddly, rumpled, droopy-eyed dog—was a kid's favorite in the 1950s and 1960s. Changes in fashion trends and a series of marketing mishaps, however, eventually resulted in an out-of-date image and diminished sales. Wolverine World Wide, makers of Hush Puppies, made a number of marketing changes in the early 1990s to reverse the sales slide. New product designs and numerous offbeat color combinations (bright shades of green, purple, and pink) enhanced the brand's fashion appeal. Increased expenditures backed an ad campaign featuring youthful, attractive people wearing the shoes and the tagline "We Invented Casuals." Popular designers began to use the shoes in their fashion shows. As a result of all these developments, and a concerted program to engage retailer interest, the brand has now reappeared in fashionable department stores and sales and profits have sky-rocketed (Suris, 1993a; Naughton, 1995; Miller, 1996).

General Approach

Reversing a fading brand's fortunes thus requires either that lost sources of brand equity are recaptured or that new sources of brand equity are identified and established. Regardless of which approach is taken, brands on the comeback trail have to make more "revolutionary" changes than the "evolutionary" changes to reinforce brand meaning. Often, the thing to do in turning around the fortunes of a brand is to understand what the sources of brand equity were to begin with. That is, in profiling brand knowledge structures to guide repositioning, it is important to accurately and completely characterize the breadth and depth of brand awareness and the strength, favorability, and uniqueness of brand associations held in consumer memory. Of particular importance is the extent to which key brand associations are still properly positioning the brand. Are positive associations losing their strength or uniqueness? Have negative associations become linked to the brand (e.g., due to some type of changes in the marketing environment)?

To answer these questions, a brand audit is often conducted. A brand audit is a comprehensive examination of the health of a brand in terms of its sources of brand equity from the perspective of the firm and the consumer. Decisions must then be made as to whether or not to retain the same positioning or to create a new positioning. Positioning considerations relate to desirability and deliverability of different possible brand associations—salient attributes and/or benefits—based on company, consumer, and competitor considerations.

With an understanding of the current and desired brand knowledge structures in hand, the customer-based brand equity framework again provides guidance as to how to best refresh old sources of brand equity or create new sources of brand equity to achieve the intended positioning. According to the customer-based brand equity model, two such approaches are possible:

- Expand the depth and/or breadth of brand awareness by improving consumer recall and recognition of the brand during purchase or consumption settings.
- Improve the strength, favorability, and uniqueness of brand associations making up the brand image. This approach may involve programs directed at existing or new brand associations.

Strategically, lost sources of brand equity can be refurbished and new sources of brand equity can be established in the same three main ways that sources of brand equity are created to start with—by changing brand elements, changing the supporting marketing program, and leveraging new secondary associations.

Expanding Brand Awareness

With a fading brand, often it is not the *depth* of brand awareness that is a problem—consumers can still recognize or recall the brand under certain circumstances. Rather, the *breadth* of brand awareness is the stumbling block—consumers only tend to think of the brand in very narrow ways. Therefore, one useful means of building brand equity is to increase the breadth of brand awareness, making sure that consumers do not overlook the brand and think of purchasing or consuming it in those situations where the brand can satisfy consumers' needs and wants.

Assuming a brand has a reasonable level of awareness and a positive brand image, perhaps the most appropriate starting point to creating new sources of brand equity is by employing tactics that increase usage. In many cases, approaches to increase usage represent the "path of least resistance" because they do not involve potentially difficult and costly changes in brand image or positioning as much as potentially easier-to-implement changes in brand salience and awareness. Usage can be increased by either

- increasing the level or quantity of consumption (i.e., "how much the brand is used") or
- increasing the frequency of consumption (i.e., "how often the brand is used").

In general, it is probably easier to increase the number of times a consumer uses the product than it is to actually change the amount used at one time. Consumption amount is more likely to be a function of the particular beliefs that the consumer holds as to how the product is best consumed. A possible exception to that rule is for more "impulse" consumption products whose usage increases when the product is made more available (e.g., soft drinks, snacks) (Wansink, 1996).

Increasing frequency of use, on the other hand, involves either identifying additional or new opportunities to use the brand in the same basic way or identifying completely new and different ways to use the brand. Increasing frequency of use is a particularly attractive option for large market share brands that are leaders in their product category.

Identifying additional or new usage opportunities

In some cases, the brand may be seen as useful only in certain places and at certain times, especially if it has strong brand associations to particular usage situations or user types. In general, to identify additional or new opportunities for consumers to use the brand more—albeit in the same basic way—a marketing program should be designed to include both

- communications to consumers as to the appropriateness and advantages of using the brand more frequently in existing situations or in new situations, and
- reminders to consumers to actually use the brand as close as possible to those situations.

For many brands, increasing usage may be as simple as improving top-of-mind awareness through reminder advertising (e.g., as with V-8 vegetable juice and its classic "Wow! I Could Have Had a V-8" ad campaign). In other cases, more creative types of retrieval cues may be necessary. These reminders may be critical as consumers often adopt "functional fixedness" with a brand such that it can be easily ignored in nontraditional consumption settings. Increased usage applications may also require more than just new ad campaigns. Often, increased usage can arise from new packaging. Maxwell House Filter Pack Singles and Folgers Coffee Singles were both an attempt to accommodate consumers' desires to drink ground roast coffee without brewing an entire pot.

Another potential opportunity to increase frequency of use is when consumers' *perceptions* of their usage differ from the *reality* of their usage. For many products with relatively short life spans, consumers may fail to replace the product in a timely manner because of a tendency to underestimate the length of productive usage (Cripps and Meyer, 1994). One strategy to speed up product replacement is to tie the act of replacing the product to a certain holiday, event, or time of year. For example, several brands have run promotions tied in with the springtime switch to daylight-savings time (e.g., Oral-B toothbrushes). Another strategy might be to provide consumers with better information as to either when the product was first used (or would need to be replaced) or the current level of product performance. For example, batteries now offer built-in gauges that show how much power they have left.

Finally, perhaps the simplest way to increase usage is when actual usage of a product is less than the optimal or recommended usage. In this case, consumers must be persuaded of the merits of more regular usage, and any potential hurdles to increased usage must be overcome. In terms of the latter, product designs and packaging can make the product more convenient and easier to use (Aaker, 1991). For example, a shampoo designed to be gentle enough for daily use may alleviate concerns from those consumers who believe that frequent hair-washing is undesirable, thereby eliminating their tendency to conserve the amount of product they use.

Identifying new and completely different ways to use the brand

The second approach to increase frequency of use for a brand is to identify completely new and different usage applications. For example, food product companies have long advertised new recipes that use their branded products in entirely different ways. After years of sales declines of 3 to 4 percent annually, sales of Cheez-Whiz rose 35 percent when the brand was backed by a new ad campaign promoting the product as a cheese sauce accompaniment to be used in the microwave oven (Alsop, 1989b).

Perhaps the classic example of finding creative new usage applications for a product is Arm and Hammer baking soda, whose deodorizing and cleaning properties have led to a number of new product introductions for the brand (such as toothpaste, deodorant, and rug cleaners). Other brands have taken a page from Arm and Hammer's book: Clorox has run ads stressing the many benefits of their bleach (how it eliminates kitchen odors); Wrigley's chewing gum has run ads touting their product as a substitute for smoking; and Tums has run ads for their antacid promoting its benefits as a calcium substitute.

Improving Brand Image

Although changes in brand awareness are probably the easiest means of creating new sources of brand equity, more fundamental changes are often necessary. A new marketing program may be necessary to improve the strength, favorability, and uniqueness of brand associations making up the brand image. As part of this repositioning—or recommitment to the existing positioning—any positive associations that have faded may need to be bolstered, any negative associations that have been created may have to be neutralized, and additional positive associations may have to be created.

In some cases, repositioning the brand requires establishing more compelling points-of-difference to better differentiate the brand. Other times a brand needs to be repositioned to establish a point-of-parity on some key image dimensions to "break even" with respect to other brands. For example, a common problem for established, mature brands is that they must be made more contemporary by creating relevant usage situations, a more contemporary user profile, or a more modern brand personality. Heritage brands that have been around for years may be seen as trustworthy but also as boring, uninteresting, and not that likable. Updating a brand may involve some combination of new products, new advertising, new promotions, and new packaging.

Sometimes negative product-related associations emerge because of changes in consumer tastes. Del Monte (makers of canned fruits and vegetables) found that their sales steadily declined after a peak in 1969. Even worse, their loyal buyers were aging (the typical buyer was a female over the age of 55) and were not being replaced by younger ones. The problem was that younger consumers saw Del Monte products as being old-fashioned, inconvenient, and laden with additives and preservatives. As a result, in the mid-1990s, the company launched their first ad campaign in ten years to dispel the negative associations that had been created. Attempting to make canned foods more relevant and contemporary, the campaign targeted "emerging families"—those consumers beginning a career, starting a household, getting married, and having children—who would presumably be more likely to re-evaluate their eating habits (Goldman, 1994b).

Positioning decisions require a specification of the target market and nature of competition to set the competitive frame of reference. The target market for a brand typically does not constitute all possible segments that potentially make up the entire market. In some cases, the firm may have other brands that target these remaining market segments. In other cases, however, these market segments represent potential growth targets for the brand. Effectively targeting these other segments typically requires some changes or variations in the marketing program—especially in advertising and other communications—and the decision as to whether or not to target these segments ultimately depends on a cost-benefit analysis.

Retaining vulnerable or recapturing lost customers

In some cases, simply retaining existing customers who would eventually move away from the brand or recapturing lost customers who no longer use the brand can be a means to increase sales. Brands such as Kellogg's Frosted Flakes cereal, Oreo cookies, and Keds tennis shoes have run ad campaigns targeting adults who presumably quit using the product long ago. Some of these ads use themes and appeals to nostalgia or heritage. Others attempt to make the case that the product's enduring appeal is still relevant for users today. The importance of retaining current customers can be recognized by calculating the lifetime value of customers. For example, one research study noted that the cost of selling an automobile to a new customer is five times greater than selling it to a satisfied existing customer. This is significant since a purchaser of automobiles will spend more than $500,000 on cars during his or her lifetime (Stewart, 1994).

Identifying neglected segments

Segmenting on the basis of demographic variables and identifying neglected segments is thus one viable brand revitalization option. To grow the brand franchise, many firms have reached out to new customer groups to build brand equity. One classic example of this approach was with Procter & Gamble's Ivory soap that revived their brand franchise by promoting it as a pure and simple product for adults instead of just for babies. Johnson & Johnson baby shampoo achieved success by virtue of a similar strategy, promoting the gentleness and everyday applicability of its shampoo to an adult audience. After a century of fighting tooth-and-nail with arch-rival Arrow, Van Heusen was finally able to take over the top spot in the dress shirt market in 1991. By devoting half of its $8 million budget to advertising directly to women in women's magazines, Van Heusen was able to influence the key decision makers in the men's dress shirt purchase since women buy an estimated 60 to 70 percent of men's shirts.

Attracting a new market segment can be unexpectedly difficult. Nike, Gillette, and other marketers have struggled for years to find the right blend of products and advertising to make their brands—which have more masculine-oriented images—appear relevant and appealing to women. Creating marketing programs to appeal to women has become a priority of makers of products from cars to computers. Marketers have also introduced new marketing programs targeted to different racial groups, age groups, and income groups. Attracting emerging new market segments based on more cultural dimensions may require different messages, creative strategies, and media (Stewart, 1994).

Attract new customers

Of course, one strategic option for revitalizing a fading brand involves simply more or less abandoning the consumer group that supported the brand in the past and targeting a completely new market segment. For example, Gillette decided Dippity-Do hair gel carried too much negative baggage to appeal to those women who used it in the 1960s but who now associated it with out-of-fashion bouffant hairdos and flips. Rather than targeting middle-aged consumers, Gillette chose to start with a clean slate by targeting a new generation of younger consumers and repositioning the brand as a fun, hip product through advertising in teen magazines (Alsop, 1989b). Similarly, the hair conditioner Brylcreem, which gave teenagers the slicked-back look in the 1950s, saw its sales go limp in the 1960s when the Beatles popularized a "mop-top" look and bangs. To revive the brand, product packaging has since been modernized and a clear Brylcreem Power Gel introduced to appeal to a younger audience (Horovitz and Wells, 1995).

Balancing New and Old Target Markets

Firms have multiple market segments they can target to grow their sales. All firms face tradeoffs in their marketing efforts to attract new customers versus their efforts to retain existing ones. In mature markets, building loyalty and retaining existing customers is generally more important. Nevertheless, a certain amount of customers inevitably leave the brand franchise, even if only by natural causes. Consequently, it is imperative that the firm proactively develops strategies to attract new customers, especially younger ones.

The marketing challenge in acquiring new customers, however, lies in making a brand seem relevant to customers from sometimes vastly different generations, cohort groups, and lifestyles. This challenge is exacerbated when the brand has strong personality or user image associations that tie the brand to one particular consumer group. Unfortunately, even as younger consumers age, there is no guarantee they will have the same attitudes and behaviors of the older consumers who preceded them.

The response to the challenge of marketing across generations and cohort groups has taken all forms. Some marketers have attempted to cut free from the past. Procter & Gamble's Old Spice has had to wrestle with the problem of being seen as "your father's after-shave" to young male consumers. As one P&G marketing executive notes, "We recognize the need to change and bring in a new generation of young users. At the same time, we don't want to alienate the users we already have." To revitalize the brand, a new campaign backed by heavy spending was launched in 1993. The new TV ads eliminated the trademark "whistling sailor" character to show—via rapid-fire editing—active, contemporary men. Old Spice also became a sponsor for several AVP volleyball tournaments. On the product side, P&G put heavy support behind their fast-selling and more youth-positioned Old Spice High Endurance deodorant (Goldman, 1993).

Perhaps the brand that attempted the cleanest break from their past in recent years was Oldsmobile with their lavish, $100 million-plus ad campaign in 1988. With the theme "This is Not Your Father's Oldsmobile," each ad featured an icon from the 1960s (such as Star Trek's William Shatner, TV game-show host Monty Hall, the Beatles' Ringo Starr, astronaut Scott Carpenter, and actress Priscilla Presley) paired with one of their children. The ads showed the celebrity parent being driven away in an Oldsmobile by their child. With the average age of an Oldsmobile buyer at 51 years old, the purpose of the ads was to redefine user and usage imagery and make the brand relevant for a new market. Although the ads were among the best-remembered of the year—especially among the target consumers aged 35 to 44—sales continued to slide even after the campaign was introduced. Ultimately, it was withdrawn from the air. Critics faulted the campaign for drawing attention to the dowdiness of the brand's image. Others defended the campaign by noting that auto sales were generally soft during that period; Oldsmobile's models were relatively high-priced for younger buyers and, most importantly, Oldsmobile's models really hadn't changed all that much anyway. Subsequent efforts to revive the brand similarly stuttered, and Oldsmobile sales have shrunk from 1.1 million cars and trucks in 1986 to under 400,000 in 1995. The company announced plans in 1996 to cut the number of dealers selling Oldsmobiles in half.

General Motors has experienced similar problems with their Buick and Cadillac divisions. Cadillac sales, which reached a peak of over 350,000 cars in 1978, dipped to roughly 175,000 in 1995. The average age of Cadillac buyers at that time was 65 years old but the average age of the entry-level luxury car owner was about 44 years old.

This younger market segment did not view Cadillac as a symbol of American affluence and success as much as their parents did. To attract younger consumers, Cadillac introduced the entry-level Catera, a clone of the Opel Omega MV6 sold by GM in Europe. Cadillac also targeted younger consumers with their older Seville models. To retain existing older customers, however, Cadillac only did a modest makeover of their Sedan de Ville models (redesigned primarily to satisfy their most loyal customers) and retained the expansive Fleetwood models. Similar demographic problems have plagued the Buick line too, causing one dealer to complain, "Our customers are going out the back door and nobody's coming in the front door" (Suris, 1993b; Stern, 1995a, b).

Multiple marketing communication programs

One approach to attracting a new market segment for a brand while satisfying current segments is to create separate advertising campaigns and communication programs for each segment. For example, Dewars launched the "Authentic" and "Profiles" campaigns, each directed to a different market segment. The "Authentic" campaign focused on the brand heritage in terms of its product quality and Scottish roots and was focused on an older segment, including existing customers. The "Profiles" campaign took a completely different tact, profiling younger users of the brand to make the brand seem relevant and attractive to a younger audience. Different media buys then attempted to ensure that the appropriate campaign was seen by the relevant market segment.

Similarly, Anheuser-Busch's popular Spuds Mackenzie and Budweiser "frogs" campaigns targeted to young adults have been balanced by a more "mature" product quality message featuring company president August Busch III. The increased effectiveness of targeted media makes multiple targets more and more feasible. The obvious drawback to this approach is the expense involved and the potential blurring of images if there is too much media overlap among target groups and if the respective ad positionings are seen as incompatible.

Brand extensions and sub-brands

Another approach to attract new customers to a brand and keep the brand modern and up-to-date is to introduce a line extension or establish a new sub-brand. Häagen-Dazs successfully introduced its ingredient-laden Exträas sub-brand (with flavors like Cappuccino Commotion and Carrot Cake Passion) to give its brand a more youthful appeal and to better compete with Ben & Jerry's, whose products had a stronger draw with younger consumers (Liesse, 1994). Similarly, Aqua Velva introduced their Ice Sport after-shave sub-brand to appeal to a younger audience.

New distribution outlets

In some cases attracting a new market segment may be as simple as making the product more available to that group. For example, the sunglasses industry, which grew sales from $100 million in 1972 to $2.5 billion only 15 years later, benefited not only from social and fashion trends, but also from a shift in distribution strategies. Sunglasses used to be sold mostly by opticians, but in the 1970s, Sunglass Hut and other companies moved into malls, sporting-goods stores, and campuses, building strong loyalty with teenagers and college students in the process.

Retiring Brands

Finally, it should be recognized that because of dramatic or adverse changes in the marketing environment, some brands are just not worth saving. Their sources of brand equity may have essentially "dried up" or, even worse, damaging and difficult-to-change new associations may have been created. At some point, the size of the brand franchise—no matter how loyal—fails to justify the support of the brand. In the face of such adversity, decisive management actions are necessary.

Several options are possible to deal with a fading brand. A first step in retrenching a fading brand is to reduce the number of its product types (e.g., package sizes or variations). Such actions reduce the cost of supporting the brand and allow the brand to put its "best foot forward." Under these reduced levels of support, a brand may more easily hit profit targets. Relatedly, if a sufficiently large and loyal enough customer base exists, marketing support can be virtually eliminated altogether as a means to milk or harvest brand profits from these "cash cows." Unilever's Lux Beauty Bar, despite not having received any advertising support for 15 years, still retains almost 3 percent market share from sales to consumers who became loyal to the brand in years past. As a result, Lux contributes over $10 million in gross profits to Unilever (Aaker, 1991).

In some cases, on the other hand, the brand is beyond repair and more drastic measures have to be taken. On possible option for fading brands is to consolidate them into a stronger brand. Procter & Gamble merged White Cloud and Charmin toilet paper, eliminating the White Cloud line in 1992. P&G also merged Solo and Bold detergents. With shelf space at a premium, brand consolidation will increasingly be seen as a necessary option to create a stronger brand, cut costs, and focus marketing efforts (Reingold, 1993). Finally, a permanent solution is to discontinue the product altogether. The marketplace is littered with brands that either failed to establish an adequate level of brand equity or found their sources of brand equity disappear because of changes in the marketing environment.

Obsoleting Existing Products

How do you decide which brands to attempt to revitalize, which to milk, and which to obsolete? Beecham chose to abandon such dying brands as 5-Day deodorant pads, Rose Milk skin care lotion, and Serutam laxative but attempted to resurrect Aqua Velva after-shave, Geritol iron and vitamin supplement, and Brylcreem hair-styling products. The decision to retire a brand depends on a number of factors, related to the strength of the brand, the market, and competitors.

Fundamentally, the issue is the existing and latent equity of the brand. As the head of consumer package goods giant Unilever commented in explaining his company's decision to review about 20 percent of their brands and lines of business for possible sell-offs: "If businesses aren't creating value, we shouldn't be in them. It's like having a nice garden that gets weeds. You have to clean it up, so the light and air get in to the blooms which are likely to grow the best" (Parker-Pope, 1996).

SUMMARY

Effective brand management requires taking a long-term view of marketing decisions. A long-term perspective of brand management recognizes that any changes in the supporting marketing program for a brand may, by changing consumer knowledge, affect the success of future marketing programs. Additionally, a long-term view necessitates proactive strategies designed to maintain and enhance customer-based brand equity over time in the face of external changes in the marketing environment and internal changes in a firm's marketing goals and programs. Figures 14-1 and 14-2 summarize the process for reinforcing and revitalizing brands.

Reinforcing Brands

Brand equity is reinforced by marketing actions that consistently convey the meaning of the brand to consumers in terms of what products the brand represents, what core benefits it supplies, what needs it satisfies, and how the brand makes those products superior. The goal should be creating strong, favorable, and unique brand associations in the minds of consumers. The most important consideration in reinforcing brands is the consistency of the marketing support that the brand receives, both in terms of the amount and the nature of that support. Consistency does not mean that marketers should avoid making any changes in the marketing program and, in fact, many tactical changes may be necessary to maintain the strategic thrust and direction of the brand. Unless there is some change in the marketing environment, however, there is little need to deviate from a successful positioning. In such cases, the critical points-of-parity and points-of-difference that represent sources of brand equity should be vigorously preserved and defended.

Reinforcing brand meaning depends on the nature of the brand association involved. For brands whose core associations are primarily product-related attributes and/or functional benefits, innovation in product design, manufacturing, and merchandising is critical to maintaining or enhancing brand equity. For brands whose core associations are primarily non-product-related attributes and symbolic or experiential benefits, relevance in user and usage imagery is critical to maintaining or enhancing brand equity. In managing brand equity,

FIGURE 14-1
Brand reinforcement strategies

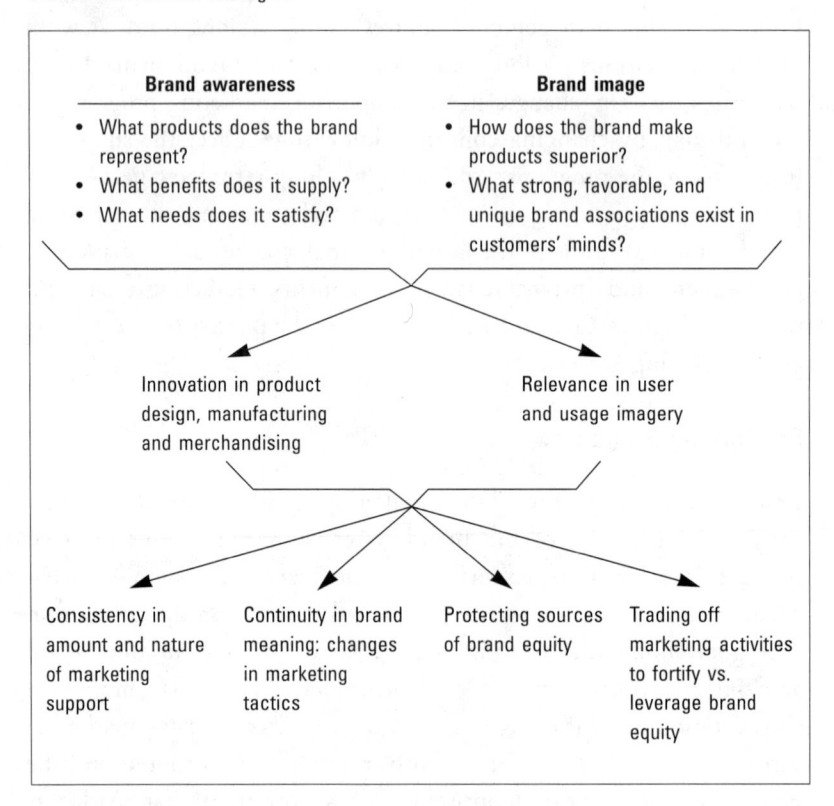

```
┌─────────────────────────────────────────────────────────────────────┐
│         Brand awareness                    Brand image              │
│  • What products does the brand     • How does the brand make       │
│    represent?                         products superior?            │
│  • What benefits does it supply?    • What strong, favorable, and   │
│  • What needs does it satisfy?        unique brand associations     │
│                                       exist in customers' minds?    │
│                                                                     │
│          Innovation in product          Relevance in user           │
│          design, manufacturing          and usage imagery           │
│          and merchandising                                          │
│                                                                     │
│  Consistency in    Continuity in brand   Protecting sources  Trading off │
│  amount and nature meaning: changes      of brand equity     marketing activities │
│  of marketing      in marketing                              to fortify vs. │
│  support           tactics                                   leverage brand │
│                                                              equity         │
└─────────────────────────────────────────────────────────────────────┘
```

it is important to recognize the tradeoffs that exist between those marketing activities that fortify the brand and reinforce its meaning and those that attempt to leverage or borrow from its existing brand equity to reap some financial benefit. At some point, failure to fortify the brand will diminish brand awareness and weaken brand image. Without these sources of brand equity, the brand itself may not continue to yield as valuable benefits.

Revitalizing Brands

Revitalizing a brand requires either that lost sources of brand equity be recaptured or that new sources of brand equity be identified and established. According to the customer-based brand equity framework, two general approaches are possible: expanding the depth and/or

FIGURE 14-2
Brand revitalization strategies

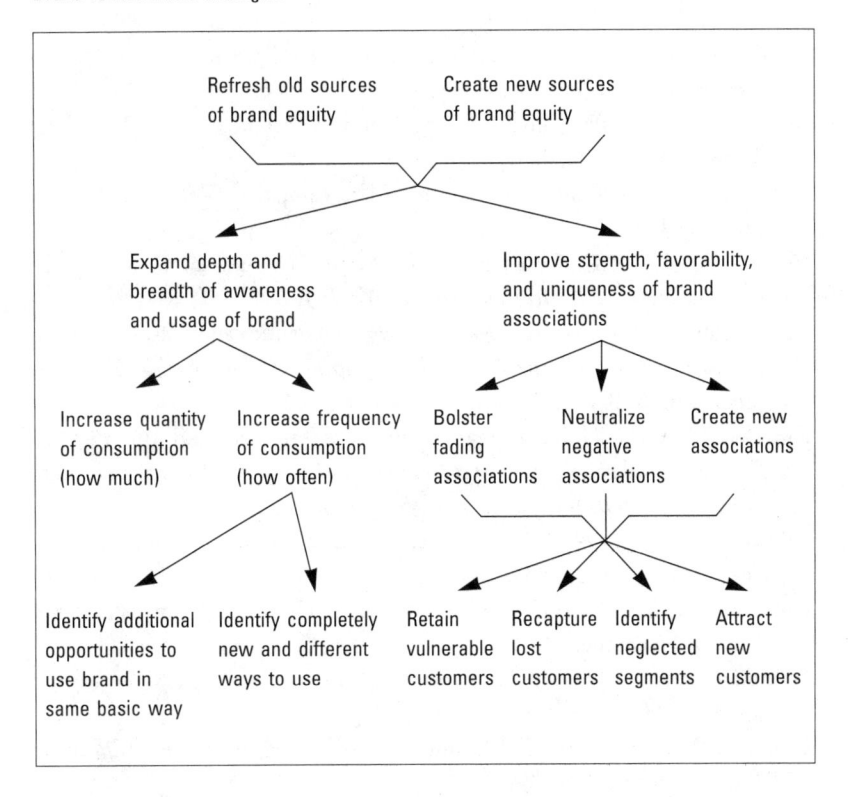

```
                Refresh old sources      Create new sources
                of brand equity          of brand equity
                              \         /
                               \       /
                                \     /
                         ┌──────────────────┐
                         ▼                  ▼
              Expand depth and          Improve strength, favorability,
              breadth of awareness      and uniqueness of brand
              and usage of brand        associations

         ┌──────────┴──────────┐     ┌────────┬────────┬────────┐
         ▼                     ▼     ▼        ▼        ▼
   Increase quantity    Increase frequency  Bolster   Neutralize   Create new
   of consumption       of consumption      fading    negative     associations
   (how much)           (how often)         associations associations

         ┌────┴────┐         │
         ▼         ▼         ▼              ▼        ▼        ▼        ▼
   Identify      Identify completely   Retain     Recapture  Identify   Attract
   additional    new and different     vulnerable lost       neglected  new
   opportunities ways to use           customers  customers  segments   customers
   to use brand in
   same basic way
```

breadth of brand awareness by improving brand recall and recognition of consumers during purchase or consumption settings; and improving the strength, favorability, and uniqueness of brand associations making up the brand image. This latter approach may involve programs directed at existing or new brand associations.

With a fading brand, the depth of brand awareness is often not as much of a problem as the breadth—consumers tend to think of the brand in very narrow ways. Although changes in brand awareness are probably the easiest means of creating new sources of brand equity, a new marketing program often may have to be implemented to improve the strength, favorability, and uniqueness of brand associations. As part of this repositioning, new markets may have to be tapped. The challenge in all of these efforts to modify the brand image is to not destroy the equity that already exists.

References

Aaker, David A. (1991). *Managing Brand Equity*. New York: Free Press.

Alsop, Ronald (1989a). Enduring brands hold their allure by sticking close to their roots. *Wall Street Journal Centennial Edition*.

Alsop, Ronald (1989b). Giving fading brands a second chance. *Wall Street Journal*, January 24: B-1.

Bird, Laura (1993). Tambrands plans global ad campaign. *Wall Street Journal*, June 22: B-8.

Charlier, Marj (1994). Coors pours on Western themes to revive flagship beer's cachet. *Wall Street Journal*, August 2: B-6.

Cripps, John D. and Robert J. Meyer (1994). Heuristics and biases in timing the replacement of durable products. *Journal of Consumer Research*, 21 (September): 304–18.

Farquhar, Peter H., Julia Y. Han, Paul M. Herr, and Yuji Ijiri (1992). Strategies for leveraging master brands: How to bypass the risks of direct extensions. *Marketing Research*, 4 (September): 32–43.

Gibson, Richard (1994). Classic Cheerios and Wheaties reformulated. *Wall Street Journal*, August 31: B-1.

Goldman, Kevin (1993). Old Spice's familiar sailor is lost at sea. *Wall Street Journal*, September 10: B-2.

Goldman, Kevin (1994a). Adidas tries to fill its rivals' big shoes. *Wall Street Journal*, March 17: B-5.

Goldman, Kevin (1994b). Del Monte tries to freshen its market. *Wall Street Journal*, October 20: B-4.

Horovitz, Bruce and Melanie Wells (1995). Long after their sales stop sizzling, some brand names linger in ... product purgatory. *USA Today*, May 2: B1.

Keller, Kevin Lane, Susan Heckler, and Michael J. Houston (1998). The effects of brand name suggestiveness on advertising recall. *Journal of Marketing*, 62 (January): 48–57.

Levine, Joshua (1996). Adidas flies again. *Forbes*, March 25: 44–45.

Liesse, Julie (1994). Häagen-Dazs spoons up a revival. *Advertising Age*, August 22: 38.

McCarthy, Michael J. (1993). Pepsi is returning to younger generation. *Wall Street Journal*, January 22: B-6.

Miller, Cyndee (1996). Hush Puppies: All of a sudden they're cool. *Marketing News*, February 12: 10.

Naughton, Keith (1995). Don't step on my blue suede Hush Puppies. *Business Week*, September 11: 84–86.

O'Brien, Timothy L. (1992). Beleaguered Schwinn seeks partner to regain luster. *Wall Street Journal*, May 20: B-2.

Parker-Pope, Tara (1996). Unilever plans a long-overdue pruning. *Wall Street Journal,* September 3: A-13.

Reingold, Jennifer (1993). Darwin goes shopping. *Financial World,* September 1: 44.

Roush, Chris (1993). At Timex, they're positively glowing. *Business Week,* July 12: 141.

Serafin, Raymond (1994). BMW: From yuppie-mobile to smart car of the '90s. *Advertising Age,* October 3: S-2.

Stern, Gabriella (1995a). Buick confronts its fuddy-duddy image. *Wall Street Journal,* June 19: B-1.

Stern, Gabriella (1995b). As old Cadillac buyers age, the GM division fights to halt slippage. *Wall Street Journal,* August 25: A-1.

Stewart, David W. (1994). Advertising in a slow-growth economy. *American Demographics,* 16 (September): 40–46.

Suris, Oscar (1993a). Ads aim to sell Hush Puppies to new yuppies. *Wall Street Journal,* July 28: B1, B6.

Suris, Oscar (1993b). Cadillac's Sedan de Ville spurns youth. *Wall Street Journal,* August 10: B-1.

Wansink, Brian (1996). Can package size accelerate usage volume? *Journal of Marketing,* 60 (July): 1–14.

CHINESE CONSUMERS' PERCEPTION OF ALPHA-NUMERIC BRAND NAMES

Swee Hoon Ang

This paper investigates what letters and numbers are perceived favorably by Chinese consumers and how they influence brand-name perceptions for different product categories. It then discusses the theoretical and managerial implications arising from the findings, as well as directions for future research.

INTRODUCTION

Developing effective brand names is critical as it helps to give new products a head start in facilitating consumer recall and conjuring favorable images of and attitude toward the product (Aaker, 1990; Charmasson, 1988; Keller, 1993). More recently, Howard et al. (1995) found that recall of name facilitated compliance with a purchase request. Research on brand naming has identified several qualities of an effective brand name. For instance, Robertson (1989) espoused nine qualities of a strategically desirable brand name, including simplicity, distinctiveness, meaningfulness, and association with the product class. These qualities have also been suggested as important even when naming a service (Berry et al., 1988). Given these findings, the sound, spelling, and meaning of a brand name are thus important as they affect its effectiveness. Yet, evidence has shown that brand naming is

Reproduced with permission from *Journal of Consumer Marketing*, Vol. 14, No. 3, 1997, pp. 220–31. © MCB University Press.

not performed on the basis of consciously linguistic criteria (Bergh et al., 1987). One possible reason is that the ever shortening of product life cycles does not justify the cost incurred in researching and identifying proper brand names for new products (Boyd, 1985). This, among other reasons, has therefore seen increased interest among both practitioners and academics in the use of alpha-numeric brand names.

Alpha-numeric brand names are those containing letters and numbers that do not carry literal meanings. Examples include WD40, Didi 7, and RX7. They can be used as abbreviations to the proper name, as inventory code numbers, as name extensions, or as symbolism of the technicality or a specific image that the product desires (Boyd, 1985). Besides short product life cycles, other reasons accounting for the proliferation of alpha-numeric brand names include the emergence of technology, lack of new words, variations in product models, and the need for a brand name that can be used when marketed internationally (Boyd, 1985). Although such brand names do not carry literal meanings, consumers impute meanings to them. In a study of nonsense words, Peterson and Ross (1972) observed that plural and one-syllable words were more remindful of cereals than singular and multiple-syllable words. Similarly, alpha-numeric brand names can likewise be used to infer qualities about the product. Indeed, certain letters have been observed to appear more frequently as the first letters of the top brand names than others (Schloss, 1981). More recently, Pavia and Costa (1993) found that the influence of letters and numbers on consumer understanding and expectations of the product varied depending on whether the product was technical or non-technical.

Although some progress has been made to help identify effective brand names, especially those of the alpha-numeric type, such research has been conducted in Western culture using mainly North American subjects. As noted by Pan and Schmitt (1995), brand names as linguistic labels are subjected to structural differences between language systems as well as sociocultural differences alluded to in a name. As such, there may be subtle but important cross-cultural differences in brand-name perceptions. Indeed, McDonald and Roberts (1990) underscored the importance of brand naming in Asia when they said, "In contemplating the symbolic impact of a brand, prudent marketers in the Asia Pacific region would be well advised to probe folklore, taboos, and superstitious and religious connotations by colors, numbers, or symbols." It has also been suggested that aesthetics, linguistics, and superstition influence corporate and brand naming (see Schmitt, 1994; Schmitt and Pan, 1994). In a study of localized Chinese names of international brands, it was found that they contain dissimilar connotations to those of the original names (Chan, 1990).

Likewise, alpha-numeric brand names may have letters and numbers that have different connotations in a non-Western environment. For instance, Boyd (1985) suggested that X and 7 are commonly used in alpha-numeric brand names because X is related to Christianity and has favorable connotations, while 7 is perceived to be a lucky number. Though this may be true in the Western culture, the non-Western culture such as Chinese is less familiar with Christianity and therefore members of such cultures are less likely to associate X with that religion. Instead, X may be perceived as negative since it is associated with a cross marked next to an error. In terms of numbers, the Chinese consider 3, 6, and 8, but not 7, to be lucky (Lip, 1992, 1995). These differences are important to international marketers as they enter the fastest growing economic region of Asia and the competition among such companies intensifies. Indeed, anecdotal evidence shows that numbers are used in brand names in Asia to create brand awareness (Simmons, 1979, 1983).

The objective of this research is therefore to investigate what letters and numbers are perceived favorably by Chinese consumers and how they influence brand-name perceptions for different product categories. In this connection, favorable perception of a letter or number is defined in terms of whether it will bring good fortune. The Chinese concern with fortune and luck is well documented. The Book of Records[1] shows that fortune telling was an official function during the Shang and Zhou dynasties (from the 18th to the 12th century B.C.), while anecdotal evidence of the Chinese concern with luck is given by Chan (1990).

Two studies were conducted. The first aims to identify letters and numbers that are considered lucky by Chinese and whether they vary depending on consumers' *locus of control*. Locus of control is the degree to which an individual perceives an event to be contingent on his or her own behavior (Rotter, 1966). Individuals with a low locus of control believe in fate, tend to think they are under the control of

---

[1] The Book of Records, also called *Shi Ji*, is a 130-page record of the Han period (104 to 91 B.C.).

others, and are more superstitious. This may influence their perceptions of the luckiness of certain letters and numbers. Reasons for why these letters and numbers are lucky will also be examined.

Based on the results of the first study, the second study seeks to determine how alpha-numeric brand names influence Chinese consumers' perceptions of different product categories. In so doing, this research extends current research by investigating the influence of product usage and product technicality on the effectiveness of alpha-numeric brand names. Further, following Leong's (1993) suggestion, this study provides an opportunity for cross-cultural validation of previous findings to ascertain their robustness.

In the following pages, the literature review is provided and hypotheses advanced. The two studies are explicated and the results furnished. Finally, a discussion of the theoretical and managerial implications arising from the findings is provided, followed by directions for future research.

Literature Review

Juliet vs. Joyce Principles

Two conflicting principles have been advanced concerning the efficacy of brand names on product success. The Juliet Principle suggests that as in Shakespeare's *Romeo and Juliet*, "that which we call a rose, by any other name would smell as sweet," all brand names are the same and do not influence consumer perceptions about product quality (Collins, 1977). In contrast, the Joyce Principle states that brand names have linguistic qualities that can serve to distinguish them from others and impute certain qualities about the product. The literature review that follows essentially uses the Joyce Principle because it identifies letters and numbers that carry different connotations to the consumer about the product.

Alpha-numeric Names

Alpha-numeric brand names are considered to be more suited for products that are technical. Boyd (1985) observed that as products become technologically advanced, scientific codes are increasingly used as product names. This observation was empirically supported by Pavia and Costa (1993). They found that consumers rated alpha-numeric brand names to be more fitting for technical than nontechnical products (e.g., insecticide vs. lingerie).

In terms of letters, Pavia and Costa (1993) found that *Z* was perceived to be a more favorable brand name than *A* for technical products because it is believed to be an indicator of high technology, speed, and complexity. It is also a masculine letter because of its sharp visual appearance, harsh spoken sound, and placement at the end of the alphabet. However, Schloss (1981) observed that among the top brands, some 65 percent began with letters *A, B, C, K, M, P, S,* or *T.* Based on this observation, it would appear that *A*, in general, is a preferred letter to *Z*.

Chinese Beliefs

The Chinese believe that numbers represent the direction and orientation affecting an individual. Chinese numerals are classified as either *yin* (feminine) or *yang* (masculine). Even numbers are *yin* while odd numbers are *yang*. When there are multiple digits to a number, a balance of *yin* and *yang* is preferred. These numbers are believed to influence an individual's fortune. The Chinese attach superstitious significance to these numbers and interpret their auspiciousness according to how they sound. Lip (1992) provides a description of how Chinese interpret each number and it is summarized in Table 15-1.

The favorable numbers to Chinese are 3, 6, 8, and 9, while the unlucky number is 4. As an example, 8 is considered lucky because in the Chinese dialect of Cantonese, it sounds like *fa*, meaning "succeed and prosper." Juxtaposed with selected numbers, it can also give auspicious meanings. There are also other origins of why the Chinese consider 8 to be a lucky number. Standing in the center of the universe, an individual can face eight directions—north, northeast, east, southeast, south, southwest, west, and northwest—thus suggesting omnipotence. There are also the legendary *Eight Immortals* in the Chinese literature, who are said to have achieved immortality through meditation. Chinese also believe that an individual's personality and fate can be interpreted based on the eight characters attached to one's year, month, day, and time of birth. Also, as a symbolic gesture for possessing the eight precious things in life, the Chinese feed on eight types of grains. In contrast, 4 is considered unlucky because it sounds like "death" in Cantonese. In the written

TABLE 15-1
Numbers and their meanings to Chinese

Number	Meaning
1	Represents unity and the beginning of all things.
2	Symbolizes complementary duality like sun and moon, man and woman. It also symbolizes reinforcement as when two similar words are combined, e.g., double happiness. When pronounced in Cantonese, 2 sounds like "easy."
3	Represents growth and is therefore considered as a lucky number. Chinese culture involving 3 includes the three precious elements of heavens (sun, moon, and stars), earth (water, fire, and wind), and man (spirit, breath, and vitality). Many Chinese classics are written in volumes of three, e.g., the *Three Classics of Confucius*.
4	Sounds like "death" in Cantonese. Therefore, it is not a popular number.
5	On the one hand, it is considered a balanced number because it is in a central position. But when spoken in Cantonese, it sounds like "nothing."
6	An auspicious number because it sounds like "wealth" in Cantonese.
7	It means "sure" and is associated with the cult of life after death and death festivities.
8	Represents luck because it sounds like "prosperity" in Cantonese.
9	Represents longevity. Phrases and things associated with 9 are mostly auspicious and significant to man.
10	Symbolizes completeness because it is the last number. However, it is not auspicious unless it is combined with 6 or 8.

Chinese form, 4 looks like 8 (prosperity) being overcast by clouds. Therefore, to the superstitious, 4 does not augur well as it suggests prosperity is entrapped. Further illustrations of the Chinese culture indicating the misfortunes associated with 4 include the four bad habits of wine drinking, women chasing, money chasing, and smoking; and the four kings who were of ill-repute before being converted to Buddhism.

Applications of these beliefs to marketing in Asia are plentiful. For instance, the Bank of China in Hong Kong opened its doors on the eighth day of August 1988 because it was considered to be the luckiest day of the century. The Hong Kong stock exchange once closed their index at 11,888 at the end of December so that Chinese investors will view this as a sign of further prosperity and good fortune in the new year. In Singapore, the treasury departments of most banks are located on the 8th or 18th floor. The Singapore dealer for the German car BMW is located at an address with the auspicious number 128, while the telephone number for Singapore Airlines ends with 8888.

Little is known, however, about Chinese responses to letters. According to Lip (1995), letters in the English alphabet can also be categorized as *yin* or *yang*. Those written with an even number of strokes are *yin* while those written with an odd number of strokes are *yang*. Examples of *yin* letters are *A, B, D,* and *E*; while *yang* letters include *C, F, S,* and *Z*. In general, *yang* characters are preferred over *yin* characters. However, it would seem intuitive that the letter *A* would be well received as it is the first letter in the alphabet and, in academic terms, an *A* grade signifies excellence. The association of letters with educational grades among Chinese is based on the strong emphasis Chinese place on education. The Imperial Examination for selecting scholars is an example of the Chinese passion for education. Another testimony of the importance of education is that scholars have long been recognized as occupying the highest rung of the Chinese social ladder. Correspondingly, letters *Z* and *F* would be less appealing as, respectively, they are the last letter in the alphabet and represent failure in education.

It is also hypothesized that Chinese consumers will be more influenced by numbers than letters. As Lip (1992) noted, Chinese are influenced by numbers. Further, regardless of whether it is written in Chinese or English, the same number carries the same numeral value. For instance, a 2 in English has the same numeral value as a 2 in Chinese. Thus, there is a corresponding matching in numbers between the English and Chinese writing systems. In contrast, there is no such equivalence between English letters and Chinese characters. English letters are different from the ideographs on which Chinese characters are based. For example, the English alphabet consists of 26 letters, while Chinese characters are pictorial representations of objects or ideas. There are about 50,000 characters, averaging 10 to 15 strokes. Thus, unlike numbers, there is no corresponding Chinese character to an English letter. Based on this difference in equivalence between the English and Chinese systems for letters and numbers, we predict that Chinese consumers will be more influenced by numbers than by letters.

Based on the above discussion, three hypotheses are advanced. *H1* replicates a hypothesis by Pavia and Costa (1993), while *H2* concerns the influence of lucky brand names over unlucky brand names. *H3* hypothesizes the effects of lucky numbers over lucky letters. Formally, the hypotheses are as follows:

H1: Alpha-numeric brand names will be perceived to be more fitting for technical than nontechnical products.

H2: Brand names with lucky letters and numbers will be perceived by Chinese consumers to be luckier in their marketing strategies, more successful, and have better quality than brand names with unlucky letters and numbers.

H3: Brand names with lucky numbers will be perceived by Chinese consumers to be luckier in their marketing strategies, more successful, and have better quality than brand names with lucky letters.

Study One

Method

Using a seven-point very unlucky (1)/very lucky (7) scale, 69 Chinese working adults rated how lucky each letter in the alphabet is. Similarly, they also rated how lucky each number from 0 to 9 is. These letters and numbers were randomly ordered. After which, subjects were asked to indicate on a six-point strongly disagree (1)/strongly agree (6) scale their responses to eight items from Rotter's (1966) locus of control instrument. These concerned how much their life is controlled by accidental happenings, whether there is a chance to protect their personal interests from bad luck, whether one is usually lucky, whether what is going to happen will happen, whether getting into a car accident is a matter of luck, whether things turn out as a matter of good or bad fortune, whether there is such a thing as being in the right place at the right time, and whether it is fate as to the number of friends one has. Finally, their age, sex, and Chinese dialect group were obtained. A follow-up was conducted a week later. Subjects were told the letters and numbers they had rated as lucky and unlucky. They were asked to give reasons why they thought these letters and numbers were considered lucky or unlucky.

Results

Preliminary analyses. Reliability test on the locus of control scale showed that when the item on protection of personal interest was deleted, the alpha was 0.79. Hence, an average score was computed across the remaining seven items. Using the median score of 2.86, subjects were split into two equal groups according to high versus low locus of control.

Letters. The ratings on perceived luckiness of each letter ranged from 3.50 to 5.67. Table 15-2 shows the mean ratings. The least lucky letters were *F* and *Z* at 3.50 and 3.58 respectively, while the luckiest letters were *A* and *S* at 5.67 and 4.61 respectively. To determine whether there were significant differences in perceived luckiness among these letters, *t*-tests were conducted. The results showed that *A* and *S* were significantly luckier than *F* and *Z* ($t > 4.30$, $p < 0.01$). Further, *F* and *Z* were perceived to be similarly unlucky ($t = 0.40$, $p > 0.10$). Letter *A* was considered to be significantly luckier than *S* ($t = 5.54$, $p < 0.01$). MANOVA tests were also conducted to determine whether perceptions of luckiness varied according to demographic characteristics or locus of control. None was significant (Hotelling $F < 0.33$, $p > 0.10$). Therefore, perception of luckiness of *A*, *S*, *F*, and *Z* did not vary according to demographic characteristics or locus of control.

Numbers. The luckiness ratings of numbers ranged from 3.03 (for the number 4) to 6.10 (for the number 8). The *t*-test showed they were significantly different ($t = 9.55$, $p < 0.01$). Moreover, no differences were observed among demographic groups or locus of control, suggesting that 8 was perceived to be a luckier number than 4 regardless of subjects' demographic and locus of control characteristics.

Open-ended findings. In the open-ended responses, subjects indicated that the letter *A* was considered lucky because it is the first letter in the alphabet. Also, it reminded them of an *A* grade in education that signifies excellence. *S* was lucky because subjects thought it implied superiority, special, success, and status (positive words beginning with S), as well as money (*S* becomes a dollar sign if a vertical line is drawn on the letter). Several reasons were cited for *F* as an unlucky letter, the chief of which is its connotation of failure. *Z* was unlucky because it is the last letter in the alphabet and therefore signifies being last in

TABLE 15-2
Perceived luckiness of letters and numbers

Letter/number	Perceived luckiness	Letter/number	Perceived luckiness
A	5.67 (1.28)	S	4.61 (1.23)
B	4.36 (1.16)	T	4.18 (0.96)
C	3.62 (1.38)	U	4.06 (1.01)
D	3.82 (1.07)	V	4.38 (1.05)
E	3.94 (0.88)	W	3.99 (0.92)
F	3.50 (1.26)	X	3.74 (1.62)
G	4.42 (1.11)	Y	3.91 (1.09)
H	4.05 (0.79)	Z	3.58 (1.35)
I	4.02 (1.12)	0	3.52 (1.64)
J	4.17 (1.15)	1	4.47 (1.63)
K	4.18 (1.21)	2	4.81 (1.28)
L	4.29 (0.99)	3	4.74 (1.65)
M	4.52 (1.11)	4	3.03 (2.00)
N	4.06 (0.84)	5	4.17 (1.15)
O	3.80 (0.98)	6	4.31 (1.68)
P	4.08 (0.92)	7	4.54 (1.55)
Q	4.11 (0.96)	8	6.10 (1.17)
R	4.11 (1.13)	9	4.99 (1.65)

Numbers in parentheses indicate standard deviations.

whatever venture an individual undertakes. Other reasons given for *Z* as an unlucky letter were that it sounds like "zzzz" for sleeping and therefore one is not alert; difficulty in forming words beginning with *Z*; and that it looks like the number 4, an unlucky number. Indeed, 4 was considered unlucky because it sounds like death in Cantonese, while 8 sounds like prosperity and is therefore a lucky number.

Study Two

Method

A 2 × 2 between-subject experiment was conducted. The independent variables were product technicality (technical vs. nontechnical) and product usage (personal vs. nonpersonal). The products used to represent personal usage were shower cream and sunblock lotion, with the latter being a more technical product. The products for nonpersonal usage were household liquid detergent and engine oil, with the latter corresponding to a technical product. Subjects were 73 Chinese working adults. They were randomly assigned to each condition, with cell sizes ranging from 17 to 20. Based on the findings to Study One, the lucky/unlucky letters and numbers were combined to give a list of eight alpha-numeric brand names—*A4, A8, F4, F8, S4, S8, Z4,* and *Z8*. For the product category they were in, subjects were asked to rate on a six-point disagree (1)/agree (6) scale whether each of these brand names is suitable for the product, whether they suggested that the product will be lucky in its marketing strategies, whether they suggested that the product will be successful in the market, and whether they suggested that the product has superior quality. Their opinions of the product on technicality were asked using three six-point semantic scales based on Pavia and Costa's (1993) study. They were technical/nontechnical, formulated/nonformulated, and chemical/nonchemical. Manipulation checks on perceived luckiness of the letters and numbers were asked on a six-point scale. Finally, demographic characteristics were obtained.

Results

Preliminary analyses. Reliability test on the three-item technical product scale was conducted, yielding a high alpha of 0.67. Hence, the average score of the items was used to conduct the manipulation check on product technicality. As expected, sunblock lotion was perceived to be more technical than shower cream ($x = 4.39$ vs. 2.75; $t = 4.92$, $p < 0.01$), while engine oil was more technical than household detergent ($x = 4.65$ vs. 2.76; $t = 5.16$, $p < 0.01$). No significant interaction was observed. Thus, the manipulation of product technicality was successful.

Tests on perceived luckiness of the letters and numbers yielded similar results as in Study One. *A* and *S* were considered luckier than *F* and *Z* ($x = 4.72, 4.18, 2.31,$ and 3.56 respectively; $t > 2.65$, $p < 0.01$). Number 8 was considered luckier than 4 ($x = 5.49$ vs. 2.19; $t = 12.90$, $p < 0.01$). Thus, for purposes of analyses, *A8* and *S8* are considered lucky brand names while *F4* and *Z4* unlucky brand names. These were used to test H2. *F8* and *Z8* are brand names with lucky numbers but unlucky letters, while *A4* and *S4* have lucky letters but unlucky numbers. Thus, they were used to test H3. Table 15-3 provides the descriptive statistics for each experimental condition.

H1 predicted that alpha-numeric brand names will be perceived to be more fitting for technical than nontechnical products. The average

TABLE 15-3
Descriptive statistics for each experimental condition

	Technical product		Nontechnical product	
Brand names	Personal use	Nonpersonal use	Personal use	Nonpersonal use
Suitability				
A4	3.50 (1.76)	2.55 (1.32)	2.47 (1.50)	2.67 (1.81)
A8	3.67 (1.53)	3.15 (1.81)	2.71 (1.40)	2.94 (1.73)
F4	2.82 (1.51)	2.68 (1.38)	2.00 (1.06)	2.47 (1.50)
F8	4.47 (4.85)	3.55 (2.09)	3.00 (1.75)	2.44 (1.29)
S4	4.47 (1.46)	0.40 (1.35)	3.19 (1.72)	3.00 (1.75)
S8	5.00 (1.33)	4.30 (1.78)	4.47 (1.59)	3.61 (1.88)
Z4	3.22 (1.22)	3.00 (1.65)	2.71 (1.40)	3.65 (1.84)
Z8	3.33 (1.50)	4.15 (1.79)	3.53 (1.97)	4.11 (1.68)
Luckiness				
A4	3.17 (1.42)	2.60 (1.27)	2.35 (1.66)	2.47 (1.50)
A8	4.06 (1.47)	4.55 (1.70)	3.76 (1.71)	4.78 (1.52)
F4	2.24 (1.25)	2.00 (1.03)	1.76 (0.75)	1.94 (1.09)
F8	3.61 (1.79)	3.65 (1.98)	3.29 (1.61)	3.78 (1.86)
S4	3.28 (1.45)	2.50 (1.36)	2.35 (1.58)	1.94 (1.11)
S8	4.83 (1.34)	4.40 (1.76)	4.47 (1.33)	4.78 (1.56)
Z4	2.50 (1.15)	2.30 (1.34)	2.31 (1.01)	2.67 (1.46)
Z8	3.83 (1.54)	4.05 (2.01)	3.94 (1.30)	4.61 (1.72)
Market success				
A4	3.61 (1.46)	2.85 (1.46)	2.24 (1.44)	2.78 (1.59)
A8	3.89 (1.53)	4.11 (1.56)	3.59 (1.66)	3.83 (1.92)
F4	2.78 (1.48)	2.30 (1.49)	1.94 (0.75)	2.61 (1.46)
F8	2.98 (1.39)	3.20 (1.70)	3.18 (1.94)	2.59 (1.54)
S4	3.76 (1.35)	2.63 (1.64)	2.71 (1.21)	2.59 (1.18)
S8	4.56 (1.46)	4.00 (1.75)	4.18 (1.42)	4.33 (1.50)
Z4	3.00 (1.28)	2.70 (1.34)	2.82 (1.59)	3.33 (1.78)
Z8	3.50 (1.58)	3.80 (1.85)	3.76 (1.56)	4.72 (1.67)
Quality				
A4	3.28 (1.60)	2.85 (1.31)	2.76 (1.44)	2.94 (1.89)
A8	4.00 (1.64)	3.80 (1.61)	3.41 (1.42)	3.78 (1.56)
F4	2.72 (1.36)	2.26 (1.41)	2.47 (1.12)	2.61 (1.38)
F8	3.28 (1.74)	3.26 (1.33)	3.47 (1.55)	2.63 (1.50)
S4	4.00 (1.33)	3.10 (1.77)	3.00 (1.75)	3.31 (1.62)
S8	4.67 (1.37)	4.30 (1.53)	4.00 (1.58)	3.47 (1.59)
Z4	3.17 (0.99)	3.05 (1.61)	2.65 (1.50)	3.89 (1.81)
Z8	3.67 (1.19)	4.05 (1.88)	3.71 (1.83)	3.72 (1.81)

Numbers in parentheses indicate standard deviations.

score on suitability across the eight brand names was used. ANOVA test showed a significant main effect for product technicality. Alpha-numeric brand names were rated more suitable for technical than nontechnical products ($x = 3.61$ vs. 3.02; $F = 7.54$, $p < 0.01$). No other significant effects were observed. Thus, *H1* was supported.

H2 hypothesized that brand names with lucky letters and numbers will be perceived to be luckier in their marketing strategies, more successful, and have better quality than brand names with unlucky letters and numbers. Within-subject *t*-test showed that lucky brand names were rated to be luckier in their marketing strategies than unlucky brand names ($x = 4.41$ vs. 2.21; $t = 12.46$, $p < 0.01$). As expected, subjects rated lucky brand names to have more success in the market than unlucky brand names ($x = 4.06$ vs. 2.69; $t = 6.20$, $p < 0.01$). Finally, subjects also rated lucky brands to have better quality ($x = 3.94$) than unlucky brand names ($x = 2.84$; $t = 5.87$, $p < 0.01$). Thus, *H2* was supported.

H3 stated that brand names with a lucky number will be considered luckier, more successful, and have better quality than brand names with a lucky letter. Within-subject *t*-test indicated that subjects thought that brands with a lucky number will be luckier in their marketing strategies than those with only a lucky letter ($x = 3.88$ vs. 2.59; $t = 4.91$, $p < 0.01$). Moreover, subjects rated brand names *F8* and *Z8* to be more successful than *A4* and *S4* ($x = 3.43$ vs. 2.88; $t = 2.28$, $p < 0.05$). However, no significant difference was observed in terms of perceived quality. Brand names *F8* and *Z8* were rated as of similar quality as *A4* and *S4* ($x = 3.44$ vs. 3.16; $t = 1.25$, $p > 0.10$). Therefore, *H3* was partially supported for perception of luckiness and success, but not for perceived quality.

Discussion

Two studies were conducted to test the perceived luckiness of alpha-numeric brand names and their influence on brand perceptions among Chinese consumers. The results to *H1* supported Pavia and Costa's (1993) finding that alpha-numeric brand names were deemed more fitting for technical than nontechnical products. Further, using Chinese consumers as subjects, the present study shows that Pavia and Costa's (1993) findings were not culture-bound, thus attesting to their robustness (see Leong, 1993). Additionally, alpha-numeric brand names were found to suit technical products regardless of whether such products were for personal use or to be used on objects. Thus, as long as they were technical in nature, even when used on an individual, alpha-numeric brand names were considered more suitable. However, as shown by the reported mean values, Chinese consumers seemed to favor proper brand names over alpha-numeric brand names. The highest score on suitability was 5.00 (out of 6 points), accorded to only one name—*S8*—while scores for most other alpha-numeric names hovered on the 2.50 to 3.50 band. Firms should therefore think twice before using alpha-numeric brand names.

The results also showed that the Joyce as opposed to the Juliet Principle of brand naming holds. Chinese consumers consistently regarded *A* and *S* to be lucky letters and *F* and *Z* to be unlucky letters. The lucky number was 8 while 4 was considered unlucky. These findings are consistent with anecdotal evidence that certain numbers are perceived to be luckier than others among the Chinese (Lip, 1992), and that some letters imply greater success (Schloss, 1981). Further, the results also showed that the attribution of luckiness to selected letters and numbers was prevalent in the Chinese community regardless of the individual's locus of control and demographic characteristics.

H2 found that brand names with lucky letters and numbers were perceived more favorably than those with unlucky letters and numbers. The ramifications of a lucky brand name were wide, ranging from perception that the brand is lucky, to being successful, and to having superior quality. Thus, in the absence of other information, Chinese consumers made inferences about product characteristics and success based on the brand name. Managerially, this suggests that the use of alpha-numeric brand names in a Chinese community has far-reaching implications beyond that of merely enhancing brand-name recall. Qualities of the product can be imputed by the brand name. Thus, the use of a lucky brand name is particularly important in a Chinese community to provide a head start to the business. There are also implications on location of outlets, dates for official opening and signing of important business contracts, interior décor, and pricing. For instance, a retail outlet may be located at an auspicious address, opened on a lucky day, have an auspicious number of columns and racks in the décor, and price its merchandise auspiciously at, say, $8.88. Industrial product manufacturers entering the Chinese market may also bear in mind their model number. Those with the number 4 may not be as well received as those with the number 8. In particular, pharmaceutical products or products that may inflict death (e.g., cars) should not bear the number 4. Further, in communities where literacy is low such as in some rural Asian regions, the use of alpha-numeric brand names may have an edge over proper names in generating consumer attention, recall, and favorable perceptions. Marketers may do well to consider the use of alpha-numeric names particularly for such markets.

Interestingly, the results to *H3* showed that Chinese consumers were more influenced by numbers than letters. A possible explanation is that Chinese are more familiar with numbers because numbers are not culture-bound as opposed to Romanized letters, which belong to a different system from the Chinese characters. This suggests that when marketing to Chinese consumers, auspicious numbers can be inserted to proper brand names to enhance perceptions. Thus, a restaurant called Paradise can be perceived more favorably if it were called Paradise 8. It also implies that when decisions have to be made between choosing a lucky number or a lucky letter (e.g., addresses such as 8-*F*), marketers should place more weight on the significance of the number than the letter. The results also showed that where quality perception is concerned, Chinese consumers were similarly influenced by letters and numbers as no significant difference was observed between brand names with lucky number *F*8 or *Z*8 and those with lucky letter *A*4 or *S*4. This means that the superiority of lucky numbers over lucky letters is limited to certain brand perceptions.

The present research studied the impact of lucky/unlucky alpha-numeric brand names on technical versus nontechnical products and those for personal use versus use on objects. Future research may investigate other characteristics such as product involvement on perceptions of brand-name success. For instance, it may be that lucky brand names play a more important role when the product is highly involving. A Chinese consumer buying a house or a car may well consider the number or model code more than one who is buying, say, a pen. The present study also used single-digit numbers. As noted by Lip (1992), the juxtaposition of the numbers also conveys different meanings. Future research may thus investigate multiple-digit numbers and their impact on brand perception. Pavia and Costa's (1993) work on large numbers imputing more power to the product can then be tested with a different consumer pool. The impact of the *yin* and *yang* characteristics of these letters and numbers can also be studied.

As the Asian region is an emerging economy, this research can also be replicated in several countries to identify the perceived luckiness of various letters and numbers. For instance, it has been documented that numbers 1, 3, 5, and 8 are considered by the Japanese to be favorable while 4 and 9 are unfavorable (Simmons, 1979, 1983). It may be prudent to identify similarities and differences among Asian countries as such information will help the international marketer enter this region. Finally, the present study focused on the perceived luckiness of alpha-numeric brand names. Besides letters and numbers, other forms of communication are also used to convey brand names. This includes pictorial symbols (e.g., bamboo, dragon) and colors in logos. Future research may investigate the perceived favorability of various colors and symbols to help marketers in their logo design.

References

Aaker, D. (1990). Brand extensions: The good, the bad, and the ugly. *Sloan Management Review*, 31 (Summer): 47–56.

Bergh, B.V., K. Adler, and L. Oliver (1987). Linguistic distinction among top brand names. *Journal of Advertising Research*, August–September: 39–44.

Berry, L.L., E.F. Lefkowith, and T. Clark (1988). In services, what's in a name? *Harvard Business Review*, September–October: 28–30.

Boyd, C.W. (1985). Point of view: Alpha-numeric brand names. *Journal of Advertising Research*, 25 (5): 48–52.

Chan, A.K.K. (1990). Localization in international branding: A preliminary investigation on Chinese names of foreign brands in Hong Kong. *International Journal of Advertising*, 9 (1): 81–91.

Charmasson, H. (1988). *The Name Is the Game*. Homewood, IL: Dow Jones–Irwin.

Collins, L. (1977). A name to conjure with. *European Journal of Marketing*, 11 (5): 340–63.

Howard, D.J., C. Gengler, and A. Jain (1995). What's in a name? A complimentary means of persuasion. *Journal of Consumer Research*, 22 (September): 200–11.

Keller, K.L. (1993). Conceptualizing, measuring, and managing customer-based brand equity. *Journal of Marketing*, 57 (1): 1–22.

Leong, S.M. (1993). Consumer decision making for common, repeat-purchase products: A dual replication. *Journal of Consumer Psychology*, 2 (2): 193–208.

Lip, E. (1992). *Chinese Numbers: Significance, Symbolism, and Traditions.* Singapore: Times Books International.

Lip, E. (1995). *The Design and Feng Shui of Logos, Trademarks and Signboards.* Singapore: Prentice Hall.

Pan, Y. and B.H. Schmitt (1995). What's in a name? An empirical comparison of Chinese and Western brand names. *Asian Journal of Marketing*, 4 (1): 7–16.

Pavia, T.M. and J.A. Costa (1993). The winning number: Consumer perceptions of alpha-numeric brand names. *Journal of Marketing*, 57 (July): 85–98.

Peterson, R.A. and I. Ross (1972). How to name new brands. *Journal of Advertising Research*, 12 (December): 29–34.

Robertson, K. (1989). Strategically desirable brand name characteristics. *Journal of Consumer Marketing*, 6 (4): 61–71.

Rotter, J.B. (1966). Generalized expectancies for internal versus external control of reinforcement. *Psychological Monographs: General and Applied*, 80 (1): 1–27.

Schloss, I. (1981). Chickens and pickles. *Journal of Advertising Research*, 21 (6): 47–49.

Schmitt, B. (1994). Managing brands in Asia. *Asian Manager*, July: 18–20.

Schmitt, B. and Y. Pan (1994). Managing corporate and brand identities in the Asia-Pacific region. *California Management Review*, 36 (Summer): 32–48.

Simmons, J.C. (1979). Adapting export packaging to cultural differences. *Business America*, December 3: 3–7.

Simmons, J.C. (1983). A matter of interpretation. *American Way*, April: 106–11.

ASIA'S GROWING SERVICE SECTOR

Jochen Wirtz and Christopher H. Lovelock

Growth in the service sector can be seen across the world in nearly all developing and developed countries. This paper first documents the growth of the service sector in Asia by showing the diversity in the stages of growth among the different Asian economies, and how services impact on these economies. Second, it discusses the key drivers of this growth, and proposes that the rapid growth mainly is driven by industrial services, and only secondarily by consumer services. One of the main reasons for the explosive growth of industrial services is globalization, which causes entire economies to restructure toward higher levels of specialization. Asian firms increasingly outsource noncore activities and focus on their core competencies to improve competitiveness and profitability. Other factors include the reduction of transaction costs due to the advancement of information technology (IT) and telecommunications, and the opening up of many hitherto closed or restricted sectors across many Asian countries. Together, these trends lead to increasing specialization of Asian economies. Growth in consumer services is suggested to be driven mainly by shifts in the socioeconomic and demographic environments. The paper ends with a discussion of the benefits a large service sector can bring to an economy.

....
Jochen Wirtz is Associate Professor at the Department of Marketing, Faculty of Business Administration, National University of Singapore. Christopher H. Lovelock is Principal of Lovelock Associates and holds various teaching appointments with leading business schools around the world.

The authors gratefully acknowledge the suggestions and feedback provided by Anna Mattila on earlier drafts of this paper, and the research assistance provided by Adrian K.L. Tan and Patricia Y.P. Chew. This paper is based on an earlier condensed version by Jochen Wirtz entitled "Growth of the services sector in Asia," published in the *Singapore Management Review*, Vol. 22, No. 2, 2000.

Introduction

With the progress of the world, the economic activities of mankind have been undergoing vast transformations. The farming and harvesting activities associated with the agricultural age gave way to manufacturing activities that characterized the industrial age and, finally, services, a characteristic of the current information age (Getzen, 1997). Income and wealth that were initially built on resources in agriculture were transferred to manufacturing prowess. With the growth in demand for a better quality of life, resources from manufacturing activities have moved to service-related activities (Euromonitor, 1992), and service activities are at the heart of the economic revolution taking place all around us. Growth in the service sector can be seen in nearly all developing and developed countries across the globe. In fact, all advanced economies are moving toward predominantly service-producing activities (McRae, 1994; Riddle, 1986) (see Table 16-1).

With the increasing importance of the service sector, efficiency in service industries has been predicted to be among the major drivers of future growth. Competitiveness in services rather than in manufacturing will drive economic growth in developed countries for years to come (McRae, 1994). The creation of value is increasingly knowledge-based—"the central wealth-creating activities will be neither the allocation of capital to productive uses, nor 'labor' ... value is now being created by productivity and innovation, both applications of knowledge to work" (Drucker, 1994: 8). Many services are knowledge-based. The information age has led to an explosion of industries like telecommunications, e-commerce, and financial services (Fingleton, 1999), and more and more people are earning their living by working in the service sector. Competitiveness in manufacturing is now seen as necessary, but not sufficient, for creating wealth. Services are no longer considered as peripheral activities supporting the manufacturing sector. Rather, they have become the dominant drivers in developed economies. The remainder of this paper discusses key developments in the service sectors of Asia's economies.

TABLE 16-1
History of the world's economic development

World's developmental stage	Stone Age	Agricultural age (preindustrial)			Industrial age			Information age (postindustrial)		
	5 million–10,000 B.C.	4000 B.C.	A.D. 1	A.D. 1200	1800	1900	1950	1975	2000	2050
Social/population development										
World population	Beginning to 4 million	8 million	250 million	400 million	950 million	1.6 billion	2.5 billion	4 billion	6 billion	20 billion
Growth rate in % (time to double in years)	0.0007% (100,000)	0.01% (7,000)	0.09% (800)	0.04% (varies)	0.1% (500)	0.5% (130)	0.9% (80)	1.9% (50)	1.9% (50)	0% (no growth)
Life expectancy	20 years		24 years			35 years			80 years	
Organization	Family/tribe		Fief–city–empire			Nation-states			Global village	
Economic development										
Economy (dominant sector)	Hunter-gatherer		Farming and harvesting			Manufacturing			Services	
Equivalent US$ per capita	$200		$300			$300 rising to $5,000			$10,000 rising to $30,000	
% of income spent on food	All		Almost all: 90%			80% falling to 30%			10–15%	
Information (dominant medium)	Oral		Written			Statistics			Electronic/networked	

The data provided in this table refer to developed economies, and developed areas within developing countries. A large proportion of the data in this table were taken or adapted from Getzen (1997: 324).

Asia's Service Sector

Culture of Service

Many parts of Asia are still very traditional and service is an integral part of the culture. Service in Asia is often people-oriented and ritualistic, and is crucial in determining the overall quality of a firm's offerings. The graciousness of the Thai service personnel, the young and courteous Singapore Girl of Singapore Airlines, the ritualized gift-wrapping service of the Japanese salesperson, are all examples of the hospitality of Asians, and part of their service excellence (Kotler et al., 1996).

The service sector is characterized by its diversity. Service companies range from large multinational corporations to locally owned and operated small and medium enterprises (SMEs). Business services, retailing, wholesaling, financial services, insurance, real estate, communications, utilities, transportation, and government and personal services are just some examples of common service organizations (Nusbaumer, 1987; Shugan, 1994). High growth rates of the service sector are expected to continue in the U.S., with business services being the fastest growing service category, followed by health care and entertainment (Dortch, 1996), and many Asian countries seem to be following suit.

Diversity in Stages of Development

Asia's economies, and with them their service sectors, are in diverse stages of economic development. Japan is a highly developed and mature economy, whereas South Korea, Taiwan, Hong Kong, and Singapore can be better described as newly industrialized economies (NIEs). The four NIEs have been called the "Four Tigers" because they have been experiencing sustained growth averaging almost 8 percent per year for the past three decades, unparalleled in history. For example, it took just one generation for Singapore to move from developing to developed world status. Malaysia and Thailand have also made impressive economic progress and poverty has been reduced (ILO, 1998). As such, they are being classified as "near" NIEs. Some economies, such as China, India, Vietnam, and Cambodia, are emerging economies with high growth potential.

The size of a country's service sector is to a large degree a function of its developmental stage. Societal development can be divided into three stages: preindustrial, industrial, and postindustrial (Fitzsimmons and Fitzsimmons, 1994; Reynoso, forthcoming). These three stages correspond to the agricultural age, industrial age, and information age suggested by Getzen (1997). Most developed Asian countries like Singapore, Hong Kong, and Taiwan are moving toward the postindustrial era. They have a good infrastructure, a highly literate and skilled workforce, and a generally high standard of living. This has fueled demand for high technology services, and these countries have a sizable information- and knowledge-intensive service sector, with strong sectors like financial services, insurance, real estate and business services, medical and health services, distribution and transportation, and communications (ILO, 1998). In contrast, some developing countries like Thailand, Indonesia, China, and India have the three different stages of economic development coexisting in the same economy. Comparatively, these economies have a smaller service sector that is partially characterized by more low-skilled, labor-intensive occupations. Within these economies, there also exists an informal ("underground") employment sector, most of which belongs to the service sector. Erosion of real incomes, high unemployment levels, and the contrast between income extremes have increased the number of informal service jobs (Reynoso, forthcoming). Unable to work in formal markets, workers have turned to self-employment, or work in micro-enterprises which typically have fewer than five to ten employees. These typically low-income jobs include domestic services, casual laborers, and street vendors (ILO, 1998).

GDP and Employment in Asia's Service Sector

The U.S. is the world leader in the transformation to a service economy. In 1996, services accounted for 74 percent of GDP (OECD, 1998) and 79 percent of jobs (U.S. Census Bureau, 1998). Service-sector employment expanded by more than 20 percent over the five-year period from 1987 to 1992 (Du et al., 1995), with more than eight in ten U.S. workers currently working in the service sector.

The Asian economies are clearly following the U.S. in the services bandwagon. As shown in Figure 16-1, for most Asian countries, the percentage of GDP accounted for by the service sector has been increasing since 1975. However, this percentage varies across Asian

Figure 16-1
Proportion of the service sector as a percentage of GDP in selected Asian countries

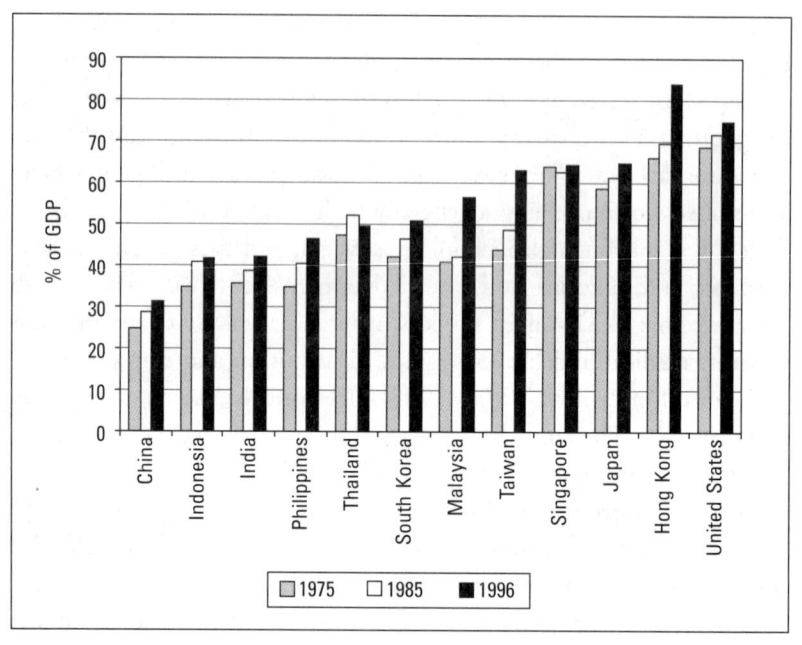

[Bar chart showing % of GDP for years 1975, 1985, and 1996 across countries: China, Indonesia, India, Philippines, Thailand, South Korea, Malaysia, Taiwan, Singapore, Japan, Hong Kong, United States]

Sources: Asian Development Bank (1997: 20); U.S. figures: OECD (1998).

countries as they are in different stages of economic development. Hong Kong has the most developed service sector, accounting for more than 80 percent of GDP as well as employment (see Figure 16-2). However, other countries are catching up. The proportion of services as a percentage of GDP and employment is in excess of 60 percent in Japan, Singapore, and Taiwan. Services represent a smaller portion of the GDP and total employment in Thailand, Indonesia, and China, where less than 40 percent of the workers are engaged in the service sector (see Figure 16-2).

The growing importance of the service sector reported in Asia's national statistics is impressive, given that growth or output is notoriously hard to measure when it comes to services. For services, even defining the unit of output is often a difficult task, partly because higher output frequently comes in the form of quality improvement, wider consumer choice, better customer service, time saving, and convenience. All these generators of higher output are important to consumers, but hard to estimate by traditional measures of GDP and productivity that were developed for the industrial society. There is

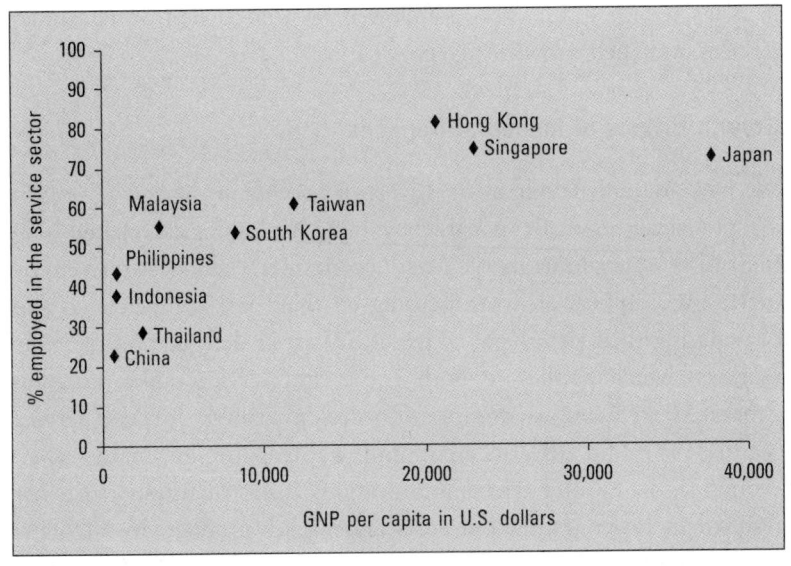

FIGURE 16-2
Percentage of economically active population employed in the service sector versus GNP per capita in U.S. dollars

[Scatter plot showing % employed in the service sector vs. GNP per capita in U.S. dollars for Asian countries: China (~20%, low GNP), Thailand (~30%), Indonesia (~40%), Philippines (~45%), Malaysia (~60%), South Korea (~55%), Taiwan (~60%), Hong Kong (~80%), Singapore (~75%), Japan (~75%, ~$40,000).]

Sources: U.S. Census Bureau, International Data Base, *www.census.gov/ipc/www/idbnew.html*; World Bank (1997).

little doubt that conventional methods of measuring an economy are no longer up to the task. However, economists do not seem to agree on how to improve them to better fit today's service-based economies. The proportion of services in the employment statistics may actually be underrepresented since a "hidden service sector" is not included in the employment figure for services (Rust et al., 1996). It has been estimated that as many as three-quarters of the workers classified in the manufacturing sector in the U.S. are engaged in support services. Similar figures could be estimated for the Pacific Rim countries. The service content of goods over time must be taken into account to measure the contribution of services. In fact, services have such a great impact on production, trade, and distribution of goods that they have become the major determinant of the overall economic performance of almost any country (Nusbaumer, 1987).

In sum, Asian countries are becoming increasingly dependent on the service sector for their economic well-being, and this trend is likely to continue in the foreseeable future. Next, key drivers for the growing Asian service sectors are examined.

Key Growth Drivers of Asia's Service Sector

In this section we first identify the growth drivers of industrial services in Asia's service sector. This is followed by a discussion on consumer services and their growth drivers.

Growth Drivers of Industrial Services

We have identified four main drivers of growth in the service sector: (1) globalization made possible by rapid technological change; (2) increasing specialization of Asian economies, which is driven by increasing numbers of firms focusing on their core competencies and outsourcing their peripheral activities; (3) rapid deregulation of many markets, which applies to both goods and services alike, and has generated tremendous competition-driven growth for the service sector; (4) rapid advancement and leapfrogging of many Asian economies in IT and telecommunications infrastructures, which has resulted in lower transaction costs and higher productivity of many service-based activities.

Globalization

The world economy is being transformed by globalization and rapid technological development. Globalization encompasses moves toward trade liberalization, increasing freedom in the movement of capital across national boundaries, and advances in communications (ILO, 1998). To deal with the new competitive pressures resulting from liberalization of the local marketplace, and the need to exploit global markets for newly developed and developing economies, many of Asia's best companies are focusing on R&D, especially in the high technology sector. Service industries like the financial and advertising services are responding to the pressures of liberalization by striving for new levels of innovative thinking and development. An example is Hong Kong's retail banking, which has been competitive in terms of service, and is now gearing up for intense wars on service quality (Hamlin, 1998). Services are becoming international, and there is a growing trade in knowledge- and information-intensive business services.

Increasing specialization of economic activity

Figure 16-3 shows the transactions in an economy, with the manufacturing activity in the center. The classification of jobs as service or manufacturing depends largely on the degree of specialization of that economy. For example, a canteen staff employed by a manufacturing firm that runs its canteens in-house would be classified as a manufacturing worker in the national statistics. The reason is that national statistics only reflect answers to "Whom do you work for?" and not "What do you actually do?"

Consider the following example. A large electronics manufacturing firm in Taiwan runs its own canteen with 50 workers, who in the national statistics are all classified as "manufacturing employees" who produce "manufacturing output" (their output is captured in the added value created by the manufacturing firm). However, how good is a manufacturing firm in buying ingredients for cooking, designing and running kitchens, supervising chefs, and conducting quality and cost control in a canteen? The general answer is that they would probably neither produce fantastic food, nor be very cost effective. The reasons for this are threefold. First, the operation lacks economies of scale and

FIGURE 16-3
Interaction between the service and manufacturing sectors

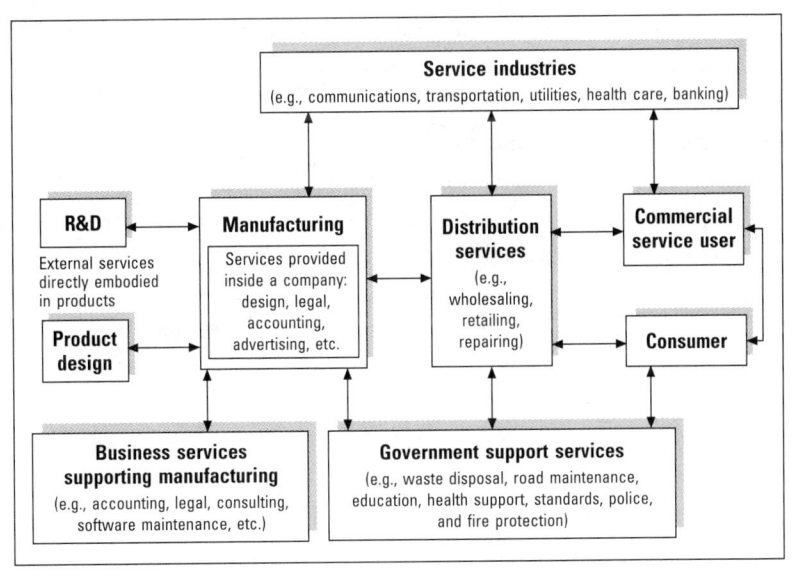

Source: Adapted from Quinn et al. (1988).

is high on the learning curve. Second, related to the first point, the manufacturer does not have a lot of experience catering to many sites, which makes management, cost and quality control, and benchmarking difficult. Third, the firm has little incentive to improve processes or conduct R&D on that aspect of their business, mainly because of the low volume and low criticality of canteen operation to the overall operation. Therefore, the canteen operation would neither justify much management attention nor significant investments in process improvements or R&D. The manufacturing firm may realize this and want to outsource the canteen operation, most likely via a tender process with a renewal every few years. The winning firm is likely to be a large catering firm or a firm that specializes in running canteens or kitchens across many sites. For that winning firm, running the canteen is its core competency, so the operation is managed with full attention and with powerful management control on service quality and costs (sites can internally be benchmarked across canteens run by the firm), has economies of scale, and is way down the learning curve. It thus makes sense for the firm to invest in process and service design and R&D as the benefits can be reaped for the entire firm across multiple sites. Experience has shown that the likely outcome is a steep reduction in unit costs with simultaneously increasing quality.

Outsourcing can be seen across many noncore functions and activities. Examples in many Asian economies include market research; advertising; inventory management; custodial services; facilities management of PCs, copying machines, and communications networks; Website design; processing of back-end operations for e-commerce transactions; payroll functions; and so on. This has resulted in the growth of "electronic-manufacturing services (EMS) providers," serving as efficient and high-quality suppliers of such services. These service providers like to see their customers as long-term partners, and constantly strive to improve their quality and services to keep their loyalty. Largely due to the Internet, financial and technical integration between firms in the value chain is growing, as these firms can work together and exchange real-time information at rapidly declining costs (*The Economist*, 2000). More and more companies have begun to realize that by outsourcing, they will also be able to obtain specialist services with high quality at lower costs. For example, it is easier for companies to commission a market research study with specialized research firms than to conduct this work themselves. The large firms can then concentrate on R&D and marketing, to keep up with the latest innovations, which is what matters these days. Outsourcing has occurred to such a large extent that some traditional manufacturing firms are now "virtual" organizations (*The Economist*, 2000). As discussed earlier, specialized firms have the expertise, economies of scale, and a steeper learning curve, which lead to higher quality and lower unit-cost output.

There are two implications of this increasing specialization of economies. First, the economy as a whole becomes more competitive, as the production inputs (mostly business-to-business services) get cheaper and better. In other words, the higher the specialization of an economy, the more competitive the firms that are operating in it.

The second implication is that the service sector grows rapidly whereas the manufacturing sector shrinks. In the canteen example, the manufacturing sector lost 50 jobs when the firm decided to outsource the canteen operation, and the service sector gained some 40 jobs (assuming the canteen specialist firm is more efficient and runs it with fewer staff), as all the employees in the canteen are now employed by a service firm. It is crucial to understand that this restructuring of economies is really the true motor of the growth in the service sector, and may continue until there are very few "true" manufacturing jobs left. In short, we propose that the service sector is not going to dominate our economies because we eat more fast food, go to movies more, go on holidays, and use child-care centers—that explains only a small part of that massive restructuring we are seeing in our economies (and is discussed later in this paper)—the main driver is the increasing specialization and restructuring of our economic activities.

This process toward increasing specialization of economic activities is also fostered by increasing deregulation of many markets and rapidly declining transaction costs (especially IT and telecommunications costs), which are discussed in the following sections.

Deregulation

A wave of deregulation has hit the Pacific Rim countries in many service industries. In 1991, for instance, Hong Kong Telecom lost its domestic monopoly position when the government announced that it would open up the telecommunications market by adding three new fixed telephone network service providers, who began operations in

1995. In 1999, the international phone traffic was also completely opened to competition. Other countries such as Malaysia (Razak and Siraj, 1993) and Singapore (Lim et al., 1997) followed the liberalization path. With the privatization of national phone companies and opening of their markets, the competition has intensified tremendously. The liberalization of the telecommunications market has resulted in the entry of many competitors. The Philippines alone now has five cellular service providers, eight operators of international gateways, and ten fixed line/local exchange providers (Hamlin, 1998). Singapore Telecom is responding to this increasing competition by operating subsidiaries and having joint ventures with partners throughout Asia and in other parts of the world. By expanding its communications network globally, its competitive advantage lies in its ability to service clients anywhere in the world (Hamlin, 1998).

This liberalization process has recently been accelerated by International Monetary Fund (IMF) stipulations drawn up in response to the 1997/98 Asian economic crisis, leading to more competitive markets, better and lower-priced services, and exploding markets in terms of volume, value, and types of services offered. Examples include mobile phone, Internet access, and financial services. This means consumers (businesses and end users) in these markets today can buy better-quality and lower-priced services, and because of the wider range of services offered, they can now select services that are better suited to their specific needs. As a result, businesses have become domestically and internationally more competitive, which is likely to result in a combination of higher profitability for these firms and lower prices for consumers. In other words, the benefits of deregulation trickle down the entire economy, ultimately leading to a better standard of living for the people in that economy.

Asian countries are also expected to adopt a more liberal attitude toward foreign direct investments and trade (see Figure 16-4). Together, these developments have greatly facilitated the growth of the service sector across many Asian countries.

Rapid advancement in information technology

Being at the leading edge of technological development is a prerequisite for competitiveness in today's increasingly integrated world economies. As one of the leaders in the region has put it: "It is no

FIGURE 16-4
Liberalization index of selected Asia Pacific countries

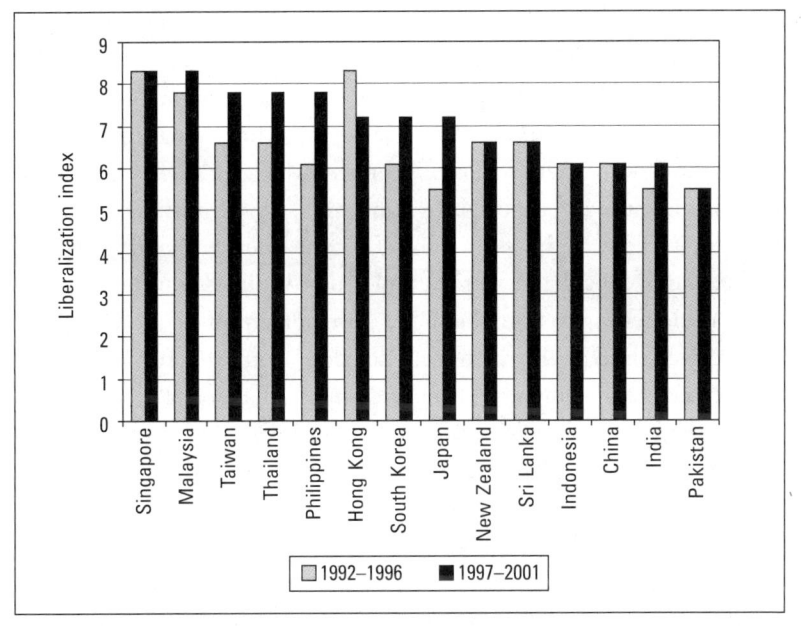

This chart is compiled based on quantitative data and EIU (Economist Intelligence Unit) country analysts' qualitative judgments. The liberalization index is measured on a scale of 1 (worst) to 10 (best).

Source: EIU (1999).

accident that there is no wealthy developed country that is information-poor, and no information-rich country that is poor and undeveloped" (Mahathir, 1991). New technologies, mainly information processing and telecommunications, have created massive restructuring in most economies. Up-to-date IT and infrastructure are critical for national and regional development. Many Asian economies are thus rushing to establish electronic networks between offices, factories, public and service sectors, and homes, using PC and fiber-optic cables, and these national IT policies can enhance their competitiveness. This has resulted in the burgeoning of services like electronic data exchange (EDI), teleshopping, electronic banking, telecommuting, and so on (Menkhoff and Wirtz, 1999).

Singapore, a leader of the region in IT, had recognized back in the early 1970s that "brain services" and "brain industries" were critical to the country's economic development (Hon, 1972). The Singapore government has recently rolled out a national broadband network called Singapore ONE, which offers high speed Internet access, online shopping, government services, and many other services to almost all households in Singapore. Singapore is also the country with the highest PC and Internet penetration outside Japan. Similar efforts to carefully plan a country's IT development have been pursued in other Asian countries. For example, Malaysia is pushing hard toward an information-rich society by Prime Minister Mahathir's "Way Forward" leadership with a flagship program called the Multimedia Super Corridor project, and Hong Kong Telecom is experimenting with a wide range of broadband services targeted at businesses and end users.

It is interesting to note that rapid development of IT industries has been driven heavily by increased demand from the service sector. Services are getting more and more complex (Bateson and Hoffman, 1999), therefore technological innovations are needed to handle the more sophisticated demand. It is thus no wonder that service industries have invested proportionally more in IT than manufacturing industries. A simple example of IT application is provided by the banking industry. Automated teller machines (ATMs), telephone banking with interactive voice response systems (IVRs), and Internet delivery have taken over almost to the point where customers do not have to speak to anybody in the bank anymore.

Consequently, manufacturing companies are now focusing on their core competencies and outsourcing peripheral activities, mainly supporting services. IT in the form of e-mail, the Internet, the fax machine, and computerized billing has greatly reduced transaction costs as well as the production costs of many business-to-business services, thereby increasing the attraction of buying these services from outside. Furthermore, outsourcing is less and less limited by geographic boundaries, since any activity that can be conducted through a screen and a telephone can be carried out anywhere in the world.

For example, Singapore Airlines has moved its computer software development to India, where these services can be produced more cost-effectively than in Singapore itself. We see more and more firms in the "rich" world and the wealthier Asian economies outsourcing low-skill and/or labor-intensive activities such as data processing, routine programming, and accounting to low-cost Asian countries.

One important factor that has fueled the trend toward outsourcing is rapidly falling transaction costs. Technology allows companies to specialize in specific service activities, automate them, create higher value-added services at lower costs, and, thanks to low-cost telecommunications services via corporate networks and/or the Internet, stay in close contact with their clients. An example is Automatic Data Processing's flexible and low-cost payroll-handling system that can serve clients anywhere in the world (Quinn et al., 1990).

The capacity of a submarine cable has increased 200 times in a short time span of only 13 years because of the rapid development of transmission technology (Table 16-2). Improved technology allows higher and higher transmission capacity at largely the same cost, as much of the cabling costs are fixed. For example, the costs of laying and burying such cables deep into the seabed close to shores or shipping lines are virtually independent of the capacity of the cable. Table 16-3 provides a rough estimation of the costs of connecting two distant continents with a telephone line using submarine cables. The cost per telephone line for long distance transmission is less than a fifth of a cent per minute[1] (excluding the switching costs in the local loops at both ends of the line, which would be approximately half of the cost of a local call at each end). The convergence of various forms of communications (i.e., through unified messaging and Internet telephony) and competition will drive costs down further. These developments make it foreseeable that the cost of a local call will not be much different from that of an intercontinental call, and that distance will not matter for the provision of services via telecommunications infrastructures. This again will have profound impacts on international specialization, provision, and consumption of services. For example, call centers and help desks can then be located wherever the required language capabilities and skills are available at the lowest cost. This is in contrast to today's situation where, for example, Citibank has a call center in virtually every country where it is offering retail banking services. Such operations will change drastically in the foreseeable future.

Advances in telecommunications technology and the Internet have increased the speed and ease at which services are crossing national

---

[1] We acknowledge that these cost-based calculations presently have little to do with actual telecommunications costs. However, with increasing deregulation, we can expect competition to drive down prices, which then are likely to reflect costs more closely.

TABLE 16-2
Capacity improvement and expansion of the Southeast Asia–Middle East–Western Europe (SEA–ME–WE) fiber-optic submarine cable

Cable name	Year of operational launch	Capacity (in number of simultaneous telephone conversations)
SEA–ME–WE1	1986	1,500
SEA–ME–WE2	1995	15,000
SEA–ME–WE3	1999	300,000

Source: *Sunday Times* (1998).

TABLE 16-3
Current cost of communications infrastructure based on fiber-optic submarine cables

	Costs (US$)
Cost of cable	1.3 billion*
Operational costs for 10 years	1.3 billion**
Total cost over 10 years	2.6 billion
Cost/day	712,300
Cost/day/line	2.37
Cost/minute/line	0.0016

* From *Sunday Times* (1998); ** authors' estimate.

borders. This is especially true for professional knowledge and expertise services such as legal, engineering, and management consulting, which would no longer be constrained by domestic boundaries (Lovelock et al., 1998).

Summary: Growth drivers of industrial services

It is advanced here that there are four key drivers of growth of business services. First, globalization puts pressure on Asian service providers to increase their competitiveness. Services are becoming international, and there is a growing trade in knowledge- and information-intensive business services. Second, focus on core competencies pushes firms to outsource, and service jobs in manufacturing firms that formally were classified as manufacturing jobs suddenly become part of the service sector. Third, deregulation drives competition, leading to lower prices, better quality, a wider variety of services on offer, and exploding volume. Fourth, rapid technological advances and falling prices in telecommunications and IT services drastically reduce transaction and communications costs. This fuels the outsourcing and specialization trend further and even brings it to an international level.

Growth Drivers of Consumer Services

After discussing drivers of industrial services, we now focus on several main drivers of consumer services. They are (1) rising levels of income and education, (2) demographic shifts, and (3) women in the workforce.

Rising levels of income and education

The mid-1970s saw the influx of foreign capital and investments into Asia, especially to Southeast Asia. It created jobs, and resulted in less poverty and a broader middle class in Asia. Asia's growing middle class enjoys the privileges of unencumbered credit, and the luxury of home and car ownership. The credit card market and all its connected services are doing a roaring trade. With growing demand for improvement in the quality of life, resources have moved from manufacturing to services. After-sales services, guarantees, and increasingly demanding government regulations dictate that firms include a larger service component in their operations (Euromonitor, 1992).

At the same time, the population has become more educated and prosperous, resulting in increasing demand for more sophisticated services (Wirtz, 1998). These include private banking, hair and body salons, and fitness centers. Many private bankers have set up shop in Singapore to tap the region's burgeoning wealth. Growing demand for galleries and other cultural services has come with a rising quest for aesthetics and art appreciation, which is generally seen as a function of affluence (Naisbitt, 1995).

However, rising income drives growth of the service sector only to a certain level. As income goes up, consumers spend less on agricultural products and more on services and manufactured goods (Shugan, 1994). When the economy approaches the level of an NIE, the price of personal services escalates (assuming only a limited amount of low-cost labor being brought into the country). This leads to a stagnated or even falling demand for such now relatively expensive services as consumers increasingly resort to do-it-yourself (DIY) solutions (e.g., do their own wall painting and gardening) and/or labor-substituting goods (e.g., dishwashers and ready-to-cook meals). In short, increasing income drives the growth of consumer services mainly in the early stages of economic development, but less so in more mature economies (Shugan, 1994).

Demographic shifts

As an economy advances, birth rates tend to fall, and people live longer because of improving health conditions and more and better food. In fact, countries such as Japan and Singapore are already approaching age structures comparable to those in North America and Europe. With low birth rates and among the most rapidly aging populations in the world, Japan and Singapore are set to overtake Europe with the proportion of senior citizens in the population surpassing 20 percent in 2020 (Pecotich and Shultz, 1998). The rest of Asia, especially the richer nations, mirrors this development. This aging phenomenon has led to an increase in demand for services targeted at older people, who consume a disproportionate share of services (Shugan, 1994). Examples include leisure, health-care, financial planning, and other retirement services.

Women in workforce

Traditionally, Asian women are not encouraged to work. However, because of the rising cost of living and the increasing demand for labor, more and more women enter the workforce. In fact, women across Asia form at least 35 percent of the labor force, with South Korea and Singapore having some of the highest female labor participation rates in the world at over 40 percent (Wirtz and Lee, 1999; French and Crabbe, 1998). As women are now more involved in business outside, they increasingly need help to cope with their dual role at home and at work (Kau et al., 1998). This leads to a growing demand for services, ranging from babysitting, catering, and laundry services to restaurant and tuition services. Women have become a potent consumer group as they become wealthier, more educated, and have more diverse choices (French and Crabbe, 1998). For example, women are enjoying their newfound independence and are powerful consumers of luxury services such as travel, beauty treatments, and entertainment services.

Other reasons driving consumer services

A number of other growth drivers of consumer services have been discussed in the literature. They include more leisure time leading to more demand for travel services, adult education, and the like; and greater complexity of products resulting in related services such as repair and maintenance for products such as cars and PCs (Schoell and Ivy, 1981). Furthermore, the Asia Pacific region is forecasted to account for 40 percent of the world's international air passengers by the year 2000. A low currency exchange rate, brought on by the recent currency crisis, has made the region more attractive to European and American tourists; and this is expected to push growth in Asia's tourism industry further.

Having discussed some key reasons behind the phenomenal growth of the service sector in Asia, the next section examines the implications of a large service sector on a country's economic well-being.

Is It Good to Have a Large Service Sector?

A simple answer to that question is yes if the large service sector is a reflection of a more specialized economy. As illustrated earlier, the increased level of sophistication and competitiveness in the world economies has pushed goods-producing firms to focus on their core activities and R&D as opposed to also trying to provide supporting services in-house (McRae, 1994). Firms specializing in specific services, such as accounting and tax advice, can perform these services more efficiently. As the unit costs of these services fall and quality improves, manufacturing firms are better off outsourcing them, thereby increasing their margins and/or passing on the cost savings to the consumer. In any case, these firms, and with them the economies they are operating in, become more competitive and wealthy. Kierzkowski (1984) pointed out that the service sector has become the most important source of employment and national income in advanced economies, and that this has also become the case in many developing countries. However, the role of the service industries is even more than that. Many services are seen as a prerequisite for development rather than a result of it. "Their adequate provision then becomes a crucial element in launching the economy on a dynamic growth path" (Kierzkowski, 1984: 29).

Furthermore, high-quality products are no longer enough to ensure high margins, mainly because product quality by itself is becoming increasingly common. Everybody expects high quality, thus making it harder and harder for manufacturing firms to differentiate their offerings. That is where service fits in, and it has become an integral part of many products (Tocquer and Cudennec, 1998). Unique and powerful strategies are likely to increasingly come from hard-to-duplicate, value-adding services rather than from the goods themselves (Quinn et al., 1990). For example, car dealers are using their after-sales and maintenance services as selling points in their advertising strategies rather than a wide selection of brands or models. Consequently, service is everybody's business, and understanding and managing services has now become the forefront of priorities (Walker, 1995; Wirtz et al., 1998).

Conclusion

With Asian economies developing rapidly, services have become the major driver of economic growth in the region. The growing importance of the service sector is clearly reflected in two economic indicators: GDP and employment. Services account for the largest share of economic activity in most Asian countries. The proportion of services in total employment in Asia's most advanced economies is reaching levels similar to those of the U.S. and Europe. Even for countries that have an important agricultural sector, such as India and the Philippines, services still account for more than 40 percent of GDP. The growth of the service sector has mainly been fueled by dynamic changes in the manufacturing environment toward outsourcing and specialization, which in turn have created a strong demand for business services. Deregulation of services and advances in IT further contribute to the fast growth of industrial services in Asia. In addition, shifts in the socioeconomic environment drive the growth of Asian consumer services. In sum, the trend toward service-dominated economies seems inevitable not only in the U.S. and Europe, but also in Asia.

References

Asian Development Bank (1997). *Key Indicators of Developing Asian and Pacific Countries.* Manila.

Bateson, J.E.G. and D.K. Hoffman (1999). *Managing Services Marketing*, 4th edition. Orlando, FL: Dryden Press.

Dortch, S. (1996). Metros at your service. *American Demographics*, 18 (5): 4–6.

Drucker, P.F. (1994). *Post-Capitalist Society.* New York: HarperCollins.

Du, F.L., P. Mergenhagen, and M. Lee (1995). The future of services. *American Demographics*, 17 (11): 30–45.

The Economist (2000). Have factory, will travel. February 12: 65, 66.

EIU (1999). *Country Forecast,* various countries. London: Economist Intelligence Unit.

Euromonitor (1992). *The World's Emerging Markets.* London.

Fingleton, E. (1999). The new economy's troubling trade gap. *Harvard Business Review*, 77 (6): 25–26.

Fitzsimmons, J.A. and M.J. Fitzsimmons (1994). *Service Management for Competitive Advantage.* New York: McGraw-Hill.

French, P. and M. Crabbe (1998). *One Billion Shoppers: Accessing Asia's Consuming Passions and Fast-moving Markets after the Meltdown.* London: Nicholas Brealey Publishing.

Getzen, T.E. (1997). *Health Economics: Fundamentals and Flow of Funds*, Chapter 15. New York: Wiley.

Hamlin, M.A. (1998). *Asia's Best: The Myth and Reality of Asia's Most Successful Companies.* Singapore: Prentice Hall.

Hon, K. (1972). *Singapore: Economic Pattern in the Seventies.* Singapore: Ministry of Culture.

ILO (1998). *World Employment Report, 1998–99: Employability in the Global Economy—How Training Matters.* Geneva: International Labour Office.

Kau, A.K., S.J. Tan, and J. Wirtz (1998). *Seven Faces of Singaporeans: Their Values, Aspirations and Lifestyles.* Singapore: Prentice Hall.

Kierzkowski, H. (1984). *Services in the Development Process and Theory of International Trade.* Geneva: Graduate Institute of International Studies.

Kotler, P., S.H. Ang, S.M. Leong, and C.T. Tan (1996). *Marketing Management: An Asian Perspective.* Singapore: Prentice Hall.

Lim, S.C., J. Wirtz, and S. Mohan (1997). *Singapore Multimedia Markets.* Singapore: Northern Business Information, McGraw-Hill.

Lovelock, C.H., P.G. Patterson, and R.H. Walker (1998). *Services Marketing: Australia and New Zealand.* Sydney: Prentice Hall.

Mahathir, M. (1991). Malaysia: The way forward. Working paper presented at the inaugural meeting of the Malaysian Business Council, Kuala Lumpur.

McRae, H. (1994). *The World in 2020.* Boston, MA: Harvard Business School Press.

Menkhoff, T. and J. Wirtz (1999). Local response to globalization: The case of Singapore. Faculty of Arts and Social Sciences Working Paper Series, No. 142, National University of Singapore.

Naisbitt, J. (1995). *Megatrends Asia.* London: Nicholas Brealey Publishing.

Nusbaumer, J. (1987). *Services in the Global Market.* Boston, MA: Kluwer.

OECD (1998). *Labour Force Statistics, 1977/1997,* 1998 edition. Paris.

Pecotich, A. and C.J. Shultz II (1998). *Marketing and Consumer Behavior in East and South-east Asia.* Sydney: McGraw-Hill.

Quinn, J.B., J.J. Baruch, and P.C. Paquette (1988). Exploiting the manufacturing-services interface. *Sloan Management Review,* 29 (4): 45–46.

Quinn, J.B., T.L. Doorley, and P.C. Paquette (1990). Beyond products: Service-based strategy. *Harvard Business Review,* 68 (2): 58–68.

Razak, D. and M. Siraj (1993). The Malaysian experience. Paper presented at the International Symposium on Videotext Development in the Asia Pacific: Policy, Marketing and Implications, National University of Singapore, Singapore.

Reynoso, J. (forthcoming). The evolution of services management in developing countries: Insights from Latin America.

Riddle, C. (1986). *Service-led Growth: The Role of the Service Sector in World Development.* New York: Praeger.

Rust, R.T., A.J. Zahorik, and T.L. Keiningham (1996). *Service Marketing.* New York: HarperCollins.

Schoell, W.F. and T.T. Ivy (1981). *Marketing: Contemporary Concepts and Practices.* Boston, MA: Allyn and Bacon.

Shugan, S. (1994). Explanations for the growth of services. In R. Rust and R. Oliver (eds.), *Service Quality: New Directions in Theory and Practice,* pp. 223–40. Thousand Oaks, CA: Sage.

Sunday Times (Singapore) (1998). 600,000 people talking—All it takes is a 17mm cable. February 15: 24.

Tocquer, G.A. and C. Cudennec (1998). *Service Asia: How the Tigers Can Keep Their Stripes.* Singapore: Prentice Hall.

U.S. Census Bureau (1998). *Statistical Abstract of the United States, 1998.* Washington, DC.

Walker, J. (1995). Service encounter satisfaction: Conceptualized. *Journal of Services Marketing,* 9 (1): 5–14.

Wirtz, J. (1998). Singapore: An analysis of changes in the marketing environment and their implications for marketing management. In A. Pecotich and C.J. Shultz II (eds.), *Marketing and Consumer Behavior in East and South-east Asia,* pp. 585–632. Sydney: McGraw-Hill.

Wirtz, J. and M.C. Lee (1999). Marketing in Singapore: Macro trends and their implications for marketing management—1999 update and extension. Faculty of Business Administration Research Paper Series, No. 99-79 (Mkt), National University of Singapore.

Wirtz, J., M.C. Lee, and A. Mattila (1998). Services in Asia: Macro trends. In *Asia-Pacific Advances in Consumer Research*, Vol. 3, p. 2. Provo, UT: Association for Consumer Research.

World Bank (1997). *World Bank Atlas, 1997*. Washington, DC.

NEW VS. OLD

The Rise of Full-service Superstores and the Demise of Traditional Wet Markets

Jan Selmer and Corinna T. de Leon

In most of Asia, it is customary to purchase fresh food from neighborhood wet markets. In Hong Kong, traditional Chinese markets have increasingly lost customers to two major chains of modern supermarkets. Recently, superstores or hypermarkets have been introduced, with extensive retail space that includes specialty sections offering fresh meat, fish, and produce. An exploratory study on customer preferences showed the overwhelming success of full-service superstores, as compared to traditional wet markets.

FOOD RETAIL OUTLETS

Food retailing is a lucrative business in Asia, especially so in Hong Kong where there is a relatively high standard of living and large household disposable income. Good food is not only a source of well-being but also the key to social networking in most Asian societies where shared meals are of central importance. Similar to ethnic

---

Jan Selmer is Professor at the Department of Management, School of Business, Hong Kong Baptist University, Hong Kong. Corinna T. de Leon is a consultant in management training and research, having previously taught at the City University of Hong Kong and the National University of Singapore.

The authors would like to extend their gratitude to Minako Kwong for data collection and preliminary data analysis.

Copyright © 2000 by Jan Selmer and Corinna T. de Leon.

Chinese in other countries, the Hong Kong Cantonese regard eating as a significant daily activity as well as the main mechanism for celebration. What food is partaken with whom imparts a myriad of cultural meanings. Consequently, price consciousness has declined rapidly in modern times, replaced by increasing interest in innovative Chinese cuisine with nontraditional prime-quality ingredients.

Traditional Wet Markets

In most of Asia, it is customary to purchase food from wet markets and small shops within the neighborhood. The Hong Kong Chinese maintain a particular preference for live seafood, fresh meat, and newly picked vegetables bought daily. Consumers expect to touch, smell, and inspect ingredients which are displayed accessibly and unpackaged. Usually housewives buy a very small quantity of each item, as Chinese meals usually consist of several dishes and are intended to be consumed completely within the day.

The daily ritual of marketing establishes a strong relationship between housewives and market stallholders. The market experience is characteristically a personal interaction, made lively by chit-chat, bantering, and good-natured haggling. Product quality is ensured by an implicit acknowledgment that unsatisfactory goods are returnable and complaints are entertained. Each stallholder usually offers specific specialties in goods, to minimize competition with nearby stalls; but, on the whole, there is a wide variety of products throughout the market. The seller–buyer relationship is largely based on the personal reputation of the vendor-owner, which is made evident by the stall's popularity.

Traditional fresh food distribution is dominated by small-business enterprises, comprised of many specialized wholesalers providing supplies to a proliferation of market vendor-owners. The system of neighborhood markets creates a network of personal relationships between the various wholesalers and the numerous vendors, each of whom relies on a steadfast set of regular customers. The price mechanism is driven by the daily routine of wholesale and retail transactions, which fluctuate on seasonal, holiday, and weekend demand.

Western-style Supermarkets

In the early 1950s, the Western-style supermarket was introduced in Hong Kong. A supermarket can be defined as a self-service outlet that provides the customer with a wide assortment of household commodities at the lowest possible prices. These stores were the first to offer an attractive shopping atmosphere and emphasize customer convenience. At that time, the supermarket was small and mainly targeted at the high-income Chinese and foreigners. Since most of the inventory was imported, the supermarket provided limited varieties of expensive, exotic food (Mun, 1974).

The supermarket industry started to develop fully after 1974, when the Hong Kong government finally allowed supermarkets to sell rice (Cheung and Fang, 1994). There were about a hundred supermarkets in 1975. As the basic staple of the Chinese diet, the availability of rice attracted more of the average Hong Kong Chinese. In time, the supermarket provided a larger retail space, promoted self-service, and sold a wide range of household provisions (Ho, 1994). The supermarket won customers from the small neighborhood groceries by providing a larger assortment of major household items and dry, nonperishable foodstuffs.

By the mid-1980s, the supermarket industry had grown rapidly to more than 500 outlets throughout Hong Kong. Sixty percent of middle-income housewives and 40 percent of low-income housewives shopped in supermarkets at least once a week (Lau and Lee, 1988). But the modern supermarket could not compete directly against the traditional wet market because of the lack of fresh, unpackaged seafood, meat, and vegetables.

In 1990, the number of supermarkets increased to around 800; and about half of nonrestaurant food sales went through supermarkets (Hong Kong Census and Statistics Department, 1991). The quality and variety of products were substantially improved, mainly through the addition of fresh food. Park 'N Shop established its own multistory, refrigerated storage centers to distribute fresh produce and meat to their numerous outlets (Williams, 1992). After a price war, wet markets lost market share to supermarket chains with good meat and produce sections. It became evident that the Hong Kong supermarket industry could anticipate faster growth (Kawahara and Speece, 1994).

The two major supermarket chains in Hong Kong are Wellcome and Park 'N Shop, which dominate the middle-class sector, who generally value good food quality at reasonable prices. Their strength in the industry is augmented by their being also the largest food importers in the territory. Another chain, the China Resources Group, is the main purveyor of goods from the People's Republic of China for decades, and has developed about 30 stores which specialize in ordinary and specialty Chinese foods for price-conscious consumers. The smaller local chains Kitty & Kettie (K&K) and Dah Chong Hong (DCH) each has fewer than 50 outlets in high-density neighborhoods.

As in the rest of Asia, Japanese retail giants expanded into the Hong Kong supermarket sector (Kawahara and Speece, 1994; Lok, 1986; McGoldrick, 1992). The largest organizations (two to four outlets each) competed against Park 'N Shop and Wellcome for middle-class Chinese customers by establishing large supermarkets in residential areas. Usually part of large department stores (Daimaru, Sogo, Seibu, Tokyu) located in major shopping districts, smaller Japanese food boutiques cultivated an international image through high prices, imported food, and a focus on expatriates. On the whole, Japanese supermarkets and food boutiques have had limited success in Hong Kong. Most (including Yaohan and Daimaru) had ceased operations in Hong Kong by the late 1990s or have recently downsized their operations substantially (e.g., Seibu and Seiyu).

Full-service Superstores

A *superstore* or *hypermarket* is defined as a supermarket with a minimum retail space of 30,000 square feet with annual sales volume of at least quadruple that of an average supermarket (Reece and Lynch, 1990; Yip, 1997). It offers an expanded selection of nonfoods as well as a vast perishables department, with extensive service from trained personnel. Superstores are characteristically low-priced, with the volume per transaction higher than that of a regular supermarket (Yip, 1997). The retail chains enjoy the advantages of wholesale discounts afforded by large-volume orders and worldwide sourcing.

In Hong Kong, superstores have been introduced gradually in recent years (Williams, 1992). Carrefour operated large French-style hypermarkets in Hong Kong, alongside its branches in Singapore, Taiwan, Indonesia, and South Korea (Yip, 1997). In late 2000, Carrefour closed all four outlets, which were located in outlying districts, citing restricted access to prime retail property as the main reason for its low sales. However, Carrefour's failure may also be due to the unpopularity of bulk purchases of dry goods among Hong Kong consumers, who typically have little storage space in their small flats.

In the meantime, Park 'N Shop has rapidly converted existing stores and opened new outlets with extensive space and expanded services. It now operates 24 superstores. Wellcome has attempted to go with the trend with branches called Xtra, which are comparatively smaller in size and limited in product lines.

A superstore's requirement for large retail space is hampered by high rental costs in Hong Kong. Nonetheless major outlets are now located in accessible shopping complexes in densely populated residential districts at major crossroads or hubs of public transportation. Customers usually visit once or twice a week (Yip, 1997). Although superstores provide free parking in dedicated car parks, automobile ownership is very low in Hong Kong. Most customers rely on the excellent system of bus, mini-bus, train, and underground train services. Although a typical customer can easily go to several superstores, the preferred outlet is usually within the home–work commuting route. Customer convenience is substantially enhanced by free home-delivery service for dry goods.

Self-service is the main retailing method for the numerous household commodities. The wider aisles encourage browsing along the well-stocked shelves displaying an extensive assortment of products and brands. The colorful materials of regular in-store promotions create a lively atmosphere.

The main innovation of superstores is the inclusion of specialty sections dedicated to a particular type of fresh food. A customer is served by a bakery with food freshly cooked from in-store ovens, a delicatessen with large containers of numerous prepared foods, aquariums with swimming fish, ice-packed counters with chilled seafood, refrigerated glass displays with unpackaged slabs of fresh meat, as well as large bins of fruits and vegetables. Uniformed shopping attendants put bread and pastries into custom-made bags or boxes, scoop ready-to-eat dishes into meal packs, cut fresh meat to order, gut and scale live fish, and weigh and pack produce.

The main selling proposition of the superstore is one-stop shopping, where the widest possible assortment of household commodities is offered. Also, many checkout counters with express lanes emphasize purchase speed for the busy customer. Hygiene is very evident in all areas, with the fresh food section kept meticulously clean and dry. Good lighting, professional interior design, and more than adequate air-conditioning envelop the customer with a pleasant and comfortable environment. Professional marketing management supports flexible adjustments to customer tastes.

Superstore chains practice strict product quality control. All fresh food sections encourage customers to inspect goods before packaging. Stock beyond its expiry date and nonfresh perishables are removed on a regular basis. The reputation of main superstore chains of Park 'N Shop and Wellcome stems from intensive activities to promote the corporate image, augmented by frequent advertisements in several media.

Exploratory Study on Customer Preferences

Previous Research

In a survey among Hong Kong consumers, Lum (1990) found that product quality, product assortment, and store location were the most important criteria for choosing supermarkets. Contrary to expectations, price ranked only fourth in importance. Heavy shoppers at department stores were even more likely to rate product quality, service, atmosphere, and image before price. The survey of Kawahara and Speece (1994) showed that local Chinese shoppers at Japanese supermarkets ranked price significantly lower in importance than shoppers at local stores, preferring food freshness and quality.

Cheung and Fang (1994) investigated the shopping behavior in Hong Kong supermarkets. The typical consumer shopped mostly for dry goods, such as beverages, snacks or candy, canned food, rice, noodles, and household cleaning products. Supermarket visits averaged one to two times per week, with an expenditure of about HK$51–$100 each time. Before going to the supermarket, the customer had decided on which products to purchase but had not chosen particular brands. Consumers reported that they always made more purchases than they had planned, and that they shopped with other family members.

Research Objectives

For the present discussion, an exploratory study was conducted in Hong Kong on consumer preferences between full-service superstores and traditional wet markets. The superstore has expanded its domain to include products usually found in traditional wet markets, especially the preferred unpackaged seafood and vegetables. Such an innovative style of food retailing may offer other attractive features not found in traditional wet markets. On the other hand, customers may persist in their view that wet markets provide advantages which superstores cannot replace.

The main rationale of the empirical investigation was to measure the attitudes of a typical customer toward a typical superstore and a typical wet market. Attitude is a mental state used by individuals to structure the way they perceive the environment, which guides emotional, cognitive, and behavioral responses (Aaker et al., 1998). Attitude also can be defined as a learned predisposition to behave in a consistently favorable or unfavorable way with respect to a given specific consumption-related concept (Schiffman and Kanuk, 1997). Measurements of the favorability of attitudes would yield comparisons on the relative success of the two types of food retail outlet.

As the intent was to study customer preferences, the specific objectives were the following: first, to determine and compare purchase patterns in a wet market and a superstore; second, to determine the importance of several criteria for choosing a wet market and those for selecting a superstore; and third, to determine and compare unfavorability or favorability of several attitude items on a wet market and those for a superstore. Purchase pattern was investigated in terms of expenditure per visit, time spent in the store, and products bought and their quantities. Several criteria for outlet selection were studied, namely, price, product quality, product variety, service, personnel, hygiene, reputation, environment, location, purchase speed, and one-stop shopping. The attitude scaling explored the favorability of the same criteria as for outlet selection.

Methodology

The questionnaire comprised close-ended questions. The section on purchase patterns consisted of multiple-choice items. Five-point Likert scales were used for measuring the importance of the various criteria for outlet selection, with the score of "1" meaning "not important at all" and "5" meaning "very important." Attitudes toward the outlet features were measured through five-point semantic-differential scales, with the score of "1" given to the negative/unfavorable pole and "5" to the positive/favorable pole of each item.

There was a total sample of 150 respondents who answered the questionnaire through personal interviews. A convenience-sampling method was used by interviewers, who accosted customers at the entrances of superstores or wet markets. Fifty interviews were conducted in each of the three major areas of Hong Kong (Victoria) Island, Kowloon, and the New Territories. Before proceeding with the questionnaire, the respondents were asked screening questions to include only those with prior experience of shopping in a superstore as well as a wet market.

In this exploratory study, eight out of ten respondents were female. Six out of ten were 21 to 40 years of age, and three out of ten were older. Only a minority of the respondents were housewives (19 percent), while more than half (56 percent) were white collar workers, professionals, and executives. More than half of the respondents earned more than HK$5,000 a month, while one-third (35 percent) earned less than HK$5,000 per month. Most of the respondents (73 percent) had completed secondary education.

SUPERSTORES VERSUS WET MARKETS . . . .

Purchase Patterns

The results are shown in Table 17-1. Almost all the respondents (94 percent) said that they spent about HK$150 per visit to a wet market. The average time spent shopping there was 30 minutes. More than half of the respondents (64 percent) said that they frequently bought food for one day's consumption. A large majority reported that they usually purchased fresh fruits and vegetables, fresh meat, and fresh seafood from the wet market. On the other hand, the typical Hong Kong customer *rarely* bought beverages, household commodities, prepared meals, groceries, or baked food from neighborhood stallholders.

In reference to a superstore, nine out of ten (93 percent) respondents said that they spent about HK$250 per visit. A large majority (88 percent) said that their average shopping time was 45 minutes. About half reported that they bought on impulse, not necessarily the things they had planned or needed to purchase. The most frequently purchased products were beverages and grocery items. A large majority of respondents said that they did *not* usually buy from superstores fresh meat, live seafood, baked food, fresh vegetables and fruits, prepared meals, nor prepared food items.

TABLE 17-1
Purchase patterns in wet markets and superstores

	Wet market	Superstore
Expenditure	HK$150	HK$250
Duration	30 minutes	45 minutes
Products	Fresh food	Dry goods
Quantity	One-day use	On impulse

Criteria for Outlet Choice

As shown in Table 17-2, the two most important criteria for choosing a food retailing outlet were product freshness and price. The store's location and product variety were next in importance. The least important factors were the environment and the reputation of the outlet.

TABLE 17-2
Importance of the criteria for outlet choice

Criterion	Mean*
Product freshness	4.45
Price	4.29
Location	4.13
Product variety	3.95
Hygiene	3.79
One-stop shopping	3.79
Personnel	3.78
Service	3.71
Purchase speed	3.63
Environment	3.14
Reputation	3.06

* 1 = not important at all, 5 = very important.

Customer Attitudes

None of the features was given a score higher than the neutral point of 3.0 on the semantic-differential scale (Table 17-3). Customer attitudes toward the traditional wet market were most favorable in reference to product freshness and purchase speed. The worst features were its dirtiness, poor reputation, and unpleasant surroundings. In summary, the average score of 1.90 over 11 items shows that Hong

Kong customers presently have an unfavorable image of wet markets.

In contrast, the respondents had a more favorable image of superstores, as shown by the average score (2.75) that approached the neutral point (Table 17-4). In 8 out of the 11 outlet features, the superstore was viewed neutrally (rounded-off scores). The best feature of the superstore was reported to be hygiene. The three lowest scores were given to product freshness, price, and purchase speed; but all were still within the range of customer acceptability.

TABLE 17-3
Favorability of attitudes toward wet markets

Outlet feature	Mean*
Product freshness	2.66
Purchase speed	2.55
Price	2.27
Location	2.20
Product variety	2.14
Staff	1.87
Service	1.75
One-stop shopping	1.62
Environment	1.53
Reputation	1.17
Hygiene	1.15
Average score	**1.90**

* 1 = negative/unfavorable, 5 = positive/favorable.

TABLE 17-4
Favorability of attitudes toward superstores

Outlet feature	Mean*
Hygiene	3.22
Product variety	2.94
Convenient location	2.93
Reputation	2.88
Environment	2.87
Service	2.80
Staff	2.77
One-stop shopping	2.64
Product freshness	2.50
Price	2.43
Purchase speed	2.31
Average score	**2.75**

* 1 = negative/unfavorable, 5 = positive/favorable.

Success of Superstores versus Wet Markets

Further statistical analysis assessed the relative success of the full-service superstore versus the traditional wet market. For each outlet feature, success scores for the superstore and the wet market were computed by weighting the unfavorability/favorability scores (Tables 17-3 and 17-4) with the score on criterion importance (Table 17-2). As such, a less favorable evaluation of an outlet feature that is considered more important is commensurate with a more favorable evaluation of a less important feature.

The findings in Table 17-5 show that superstores (total score = 115) were substantially more successful than wet markets (total score = 81). The overall success of superstores can be mainly attributed to hygiene, location, product variety, product freshness, and personnel. The glaring failures of wet markets were in reputation, hygiene (the most successful feature of superstores), and environment.

To verify the statistical significance of differences in customer attitudes toward the superstore and the wet market, paired sample t-tests were computed. There were significant differences for 8 out of the 11 outlet features ($p < 0.05$), as shown in Table 17-5. The responses show that the superstore was viewed more favorably than the wet market in all of these eight features: Superstores offered wider product variety, a higher standard of hygiene, better service, more capable personnel, more pleasant environment, and more positive reputation.

TABLE 17-5
Success of superstores versus wet markets

Outlet feature	Superstore	Wet market
Product freshness	11.13	11.84
Price	10.42	9.74
Location	12.10	9.09*
Product variety	11.61	8.45*
Hygiene	12.20	4.36*
One-stop shopping	10.01	6.14*
Personnel	10.47	7.07*
Service	10.39	6.49*
Purchase speed	8.39	9.26
Environment	9.01	4.80*
Reputation	8.81	3.58*
Total	**114.54**	**80.82**

* t-test: $p < 0.05$.

Also, superstores had more convenient locations, in which customers had more opportunities to buy all that they needed in one visit (one-stop shopping). These findings provide strong evidence that superstores are perceived by customers to have many unique benefits not offered by wet markets.

However, the respondents thought that the price, product freshness, and purchase speed of a superstore and a traditional wet market were similar. As these three features were viewed as the most favorable features of wet markets, it is evident that wet markets are perceived as lacking in any distinct advantages over superstores. In comparison, these three features were seen as the weakest attractions of superstores. Furthermore, these observations should be considered in view of the finding that price and product freshness were the two most important criteria for outlet selection. On the other hand, it is ironic that wet markets were seen as being as successful (if not more so) in purchase speed, a feature promoted by superstores as one of their winning attractions.

Conclusion

The exploratory study has shown strong evidence of the overwhelming success of full-service superstores in Hong Kong, as compared to traditional wet markets. Customers spend more money and time in superstores, with impulse buying of goods that are not immediately needed. The respondents had a positive image of superstores but viewed wet markets negatively. Consumer attitudes toward wet markets are so unfavorable that their best features of product freshness and low prices are seen to be only as good as the worst features of superstores.

Despite good performance in most features, superstores have not yet achieved a winning edge on the most important criteria of product freshness and low price. It is a critical point that most customers do not usually buy fresh food from superstores. Vast operating expenses are incurred for the supply and manpower requirements of the specialty sections in fresh food. If serious losses are to be controlled, superstores should take massive efforts in promoting the quality, variety, and price of their perishables departments. To compete against the customary bias and habit of buying fresh food only from wet markets, superstores need to focus on their impeccable hygiene and attractive environment.

A unique benefit of superstores and supermarkets in Hong Kong is the free home-delivery service. This may explain the frequent purchases of beverages and other grocery items. However, since delivery service is restricted to dry goods only, customers may be hesitant to buy fresh food from superstores because of the inconvenience of carrying them on public transportation. Fruits and vegetables are bulky and heavy, fresh fish and meat are wet and smelly. Unless more superstores are located within a short walking distance from customers' homes, fresh-food sales may remain limited. A cheaper but more complicated alternative would be to devise a delivery service for chilled seafood, meat, and produce.

As customers believe purchase speed in wet markets is faster, long queues in superstore counters should be avoided. Checkout is slowed down by the larger volume of goods purchased per customer, clearance for credit-card payments, and home-delivery orders. More checkout counters should be opened during high traffic periods. Better organization of checkout procedures should enable small-volume shoppers, who usually pay in cash and do not need delivery service, to proceed swiftly.

Despite the strong preference for superstores, wet markets still have the franchise on product freshness and low prices, the most important criteria for outlet selection in food retailing. Another plus point for wet markets is the impersonal nature of the limited social interaction in superstores. Market vendor-owners should capitalize on their personal reputations, presenting themselves as food experts and fair tradesmen. The personal network found in wet markets can be rejuvenated as a lively community activity, a refreshing respite from the hustle and bustle of the modern Hong Kong lifestyle.

However, the survival of traditional wet markets depends on substantial improvement in hygiene and environment. More of the older ones should be renovated to meet the standards of the few newly built wet markets, some of which even have air-conditioning facilities. Drainage should be more than adequate, mechanical ventilation should eliminate foul odors, lighting should be brighter, sanitation procedures should be regularly scheduled, and hygiene regulations should be strongly enforced. Market stalls should be built larger to eliminate the need for goods to overflow to the aisles. Corridors should be widened to facilitate customer movement. As the government administers neighborhood markets as a public service, the upgrade of neighborhood markets should not be hindered by the lack of funds nor the difficulty of organization.

Superstores are privately owned by enterprises that also control food importation and the extensive supermarket chains in Hong Kong. The dominance of a few business organizations in food trade and distribution has serious implications for the industry. With the small population of Hong Kong, the major retail giants have succeeded in easing out the smaller competitors in the supermarket sector. The proliferation of Park 'N Shop and Wellcome outlets throughout the territory, without nearby alternative food outlets, is seriously detrimental to the best interests of Hong Kong consumers, who spend a substantial portion of their income on food. Furthermore, the lack of competition from wet markets could seriously restrict product variety and inflate prices.

The prevalence of negative attitudes among modern Hong Kong customers forewarns of the inevitable demise of the traditional wet market. The rapid decrease in the popularity of the market system is jeopardizing the livelihood of small food wholesalers and market stallholders. As these vendors comprise a significant sector among small-business operators, less than adequate government support for neighborhood markets would suffocate the legendary entrepreneurial spirit of Hong Kong.

References

Aaker, D.A., V. Kumar, and G.S. Day (1998). *Marketing Research*, 6th edition. New York: Wiley.

Cheung, W.L. and K.T. Fang (1994). The comparison of shopper purchasing behavior and demographic profiles of two supermarket giants: A Hong Kong perspective. Working Paper Series No. WP94007, Business Research Centre, School of Business, Hong Kong Baptist University.

Ho, S.C. (1994). *Report on the Supermarket Industry in Hong Kong*. Hong Kong: Hong Kong Consumer Council.

Hong Kong Census and Statistics Department (1991). *Hong Kong Annual Digest of Statistics*. Hong Kong.

Kawahara, Y. and M. Speece (1994). Strategies of Japanese supermarkets in Hong Kong. *International Journal of Retail and Distribution Management*, 22 (8): 3–12.

Lau, H.F. and K.H. Lee (1988). Development of supermarkets in Hong Kong: Current status and future trends. In E. Kaynak (ed.), *Transnational*

Retailing, pp. 321–29. New York: de Gruyter.
Lok, W.H. (1986). A study of the adaptation of marketing policies of Japanese department stores in Hong Kong. MBA thesis, Chinese University of Hong Kong.
Lum, Y.C. (1990). Exploring the reasons of success of Japanese department stores in Hong Kong: A consumer survey approach. MBA thesis, Chinese University of Hong Kong.
McGoldrick, P.J. (1992). International positioning: Japanese department stores in Hong Kong. *European Journal of Marketing*, 26 (8/9): 61–73.
Mun, K.C. (1974). Opportunities for supermarket development in Hong Kong. *Journal of the Chinese University of Hong Kong*, 11: 183–96.
Reece, B.L. and R.L. Lynch (eds.) (1990). *Food Marketing*, 2nd edition. New York: McGraw-Hill.
Schiffman, L.G. and L.L. Kanuk (1997). *Consumer Behavior*, 6th edition. Upper Saddle River, NJ: Prentice Hall.
Williams, M. (1992). Hong Kong sees a new age of supermarketing. *Asian Advertising and Marketing*, February: 18–20, 45.
Yip, C. (1997). What is a hypermarket? *Direction: Journal of the Hong Kong Institute of Marketing*, August/September/October: 2–4.

18

E-TAILING IN ASIA PACIFIC
A BCG Perspective

David C. Michael, Greg Sutherland, and Scott R. Ohman

This article provides an overview of the online retail market in Asia Pacific. It examines the growth and structure of the market, as well as opportunities and challenges confronting e-tailers in the region. Key lessons for online retailers in Asia Pacific are outlined.

INTRODUCTION

E-commerce has revolutionized existing business practices around the world. Asia Pacific is no exception. Success in today's cybermarket goes well beyond merely establishing a Web presence. It involves a carefully articulated and executed strategy which includes a clear view of the dynamics underway in the business environment.

To obtain insights into the online retail market in Asia Pacific, the Boston Consulting Group conducted 482 in-depth interviews involving most major online retailers in the region. The information gathered was supplemented with publicly available data for all other online retailers of consequence. This article summarizes the major findings of the resultant report, "E-tail of the Tiger: Retail E-commerce in Asia-Pacific." Specifically, it documents the growth and structure of

---

David C. Michael and Greg Sutherland are vice presidents and directors of the Boston Consulting Group, where Scott R. Ohman is a manager. This article is based on a March 2000 Boston Consulting Group NetBizAsia report entitled "E-tail of the Tiger: Retail E-commerce in Asia-Pacific."

Copyright by The Boston Consulting Group 2000.

the region's online retail market, highlights several opportunities and challenges associated with it, and outlines key lessons for online retailers in Asia Pacific.

Market Growth

Online retail revenue in Asia Pacific rose to US$2.8 billion in 1999. Online retailers from Asia Pacific accounted for US$2.4 billion, while sales from nonlocal sites accounted for the remaining US$400 million. Compared with the US$36 billion recorded in 1999 in the U.S., however, business-to-consumer sales in Asia Pacific are still small. Nonetheless, the Asia Pacific online retail market witnessed an overall growth of 200 percent from 1998 compared with 145 percent observed in the U.S. Despite this rapid growth, overall online retail penetration in Asia Pacific is still low at 0.1 percent, lagging far behind the 1.2 percent in the U.S.

Table 18-1 provides data regarding the online retail market in various Asia Pacific countries. The three leading markets of Japan, South Korea, and Australia/New Zealand account for 94 percent of the total online retail market in the region. Other Asian markets, including Hong Kong and Singapore, are very small. This might reflect the difficulty online retailers have in developing compelling offerings in urban environments with convenient bricks-and-mortar shopping venues.

Table 18-1
E-tailing in Asia Pacific: 1999 vital statistics

Country	Internet penetration (%)	Online retail expenditure (US$ million)	Annual online retail revenue per capita (US$)	Largest online category
India	0.3	2	< 0.01	Music/video
Southeast Asia	0.5–24	48	0.13	Travel
China	1	13	0.01	Stockbroking
Hong Kong	27	39	5.90	Stockbroking
Taiwan	20	48	2.30	Stockbroking
Australia	31	380	20.00	Computerware
New Zealand	19	30	7.90	Computerware
South Korea	11	720	15.30	Stockbroking
Japan	19	1,520	12.00	Computerware

Source: "E-tail of the Tiger," a BCG NetBizAsia strategy report, Yankee Group, Access Media International and BCG analysis, March 2000.

Market Structure

Two aspects of market structure are of particular importance in any strategic analysis. The first relates to product category characteristics and the second to the nature of competition in the market.

Product Category Sales

Table 18-2 lists the 1999 online retail market size in Asia Pacific by product category. Mirroring the U.S., Table 18-2 indicates that the three largest categories in the region are computer hardware and software, online broking, and travel.

Computer-related products lead online retail sales in the region. Asia Pacific's early Internet shoppers tend to be technology-focused. Foreign players such as Dell, Gateway, and Compaq are leveraging their extensive online selling experience in their home markets, as well as their strong brand names, to aggressively penetrate this region. Online broking constitutes the next largest category. Growth has been aided by the strong retail orientation of Asia's stock markets, recent deregulation in stockbroking commissions, and market rebounds from

TABLE 18-2
Asia Pacific online retail market size by category in 1999

Category	Market size (US$ million)
Computer hardware and software	780
Financial brokerage	700
Travel	320
Books/magazines	200
Event tickets	120
Consumer electronics	120
Collectibles (person-to-person auctions)	110
Apparel/accessories	110
Food/wine	70
Automotive	40
Real estate	40
Health/beauty	40
Music/video	40
Toys/games	30
Others	80

Source: "E-tail of the Tiger," a BCG NetBizAsia strategy report.

the Asian crisis. Similarly, travel, the third largest category, also requires little physical fulfillment. The Internet provides shoppers with a wider selection than traditional travel information and booking options.

However, national variations are evident in this regional pattern. Computers and travel are the two largest categories in Japan, while online broking is still small. In South Korea, online broking is by far the largest category. Computers lead by a wide margin in Australia, while online broking edges travel for second place.

Concentration

The second dimension of market structure relates to the extent of concentration among competitors. Except for Japan, all of Asia's online retail markets are highly concentrated. The 10 leading players in each market typically account for more than 50 percent, and the top 50 retailers for more than 80 percent, of online retail revenue. By contrast, the more mature U.S. market is less concentrated, with the leading 10 and 50 players accounting for 43 percent and 71 percent, respectively, of online retail revenue.

Certain Asian markets are highly concentrated because they have just a few early categories and consequently just a few players. For example, the five leading South Korean online broking firms control 95 percent of the market. In Malaysia, computers are the largest segment, driven primarily by Dell. But Japan, with several thousand online retailers, is less concentrated. The 10 and 50 leading players there occupy 26 percent and 54 percent of the market respectively. This lower concentration, compared with the U.S., implies that many current online retailers could be subscale and the online market might face consolidation.

Such consolidation may come about given the flood of startups and traditional retailers going online. With competition intensifying and major players establishing their positions, many small firms could be forced out of business or acquired by larger online retailers. Indeed, most of Asia Pacific's online retailers are unprofitable today. Many will find they are not targeting a segment of sufficient size, that their value proposition is not compelling, or that their economics do not generate future profitability. Further, competition from strong multichannel and foreign players has yet to begin in earnest.

MARKET OPPORTUNITIES

While the current retail e-business market is still relatively small, Asia is on the threshold of a consumer revolution. According to the Yankee Group, as many as 230 million new Internet users are expected to move online in the next three years. As they start to spend, businesses able to quickly exploit the opportunity will prosper in this significant new area of wealth creation. Some of the major opportunities in the marketplace are described in this section.

Moving from Early Adopters to Mainstream Shoppers

With so many people coming online, the Internet will become available and acceptable to a wider spectrum of potential customers. Demographics will change fundamentally, and retailers must prepare for this shift in their customer landscape. For example, online retailers may be serving more women in future, in contrast to men who currently comprise 75 percent of users in Japan and China. Female-oriented sites such as *machiko.or.jp* in Japan and *ebabycare.com* in China will increase as more women use the Internet.

Wireless Internet Access

Multiple forms of Internet access will be common across Asia. Wireless access, in particular, is likely to be the most common non-PC-based medium because cellular technology already enjoys high penetration levels across Asia and mobile phones are less expensive and more portable than set-top boxes. Given the present access speed and display limitations of wireless technology, online retailers will need to streamline their sites for simplicity and efficiency to satisfy this user segment.

Integrated Business Models

Modern consumers use a variety of channels during the purchasing process. They might perform online search to obtain price information, test a product in a retail outlet, and buy wherever they obtain the best service guarantee. This process favors multichannel retailers, who are represented both online and in the physical marketplace. Existing retailers may acquire or partner an online provider to provide multichannel access to customers. A version of this clicks-and-mortar model is already emerging in Asia Pacific. For example, Flying Pig in New Zealand has taken over the online operations of bookseller Whitcoulls.

Online Killer Categories

Killer categories, those with large offline revenue and strong online growth potential, are likely to emerge in the future. Financial services, and online broking in particular, are currently the killer category in Asian online retailing. Some of the most visible online players in key Asian markets, such as *Boom.com* in Hong Kong, Philip Securities in Singapore, Polaris Securities in Taiwan, and Sejong Securities in South Korea, are online brokerages. However, the travel, automotive, and real estate sectors represent significant opportunities and growth possibilities in the region. Moreover, several strong offline regional and global players with undervalued assets are waiting in the wings. Thus, regional airlines such as Cathay Pacific, Singapore Airlines, Japan Airlines, and Qantas could dominate the lucrative travel market by focusing on the online segment.

Online Enablers

Information technology firms, Web-design companies, payment gateway providers, and distribution businesses will emerge to serve a growing demand for their services as the number and size of e-businesses increase. Companies with these capabilities can benefit from the boom by servicing Internet retailers' core needs while avoiding some of the risks.

CHALLENGES

Despite these opportunities, several challenges confront online retailers in Asia. These include cost and availability of Internet access, delivery infrastructure problems, installation of payment systems, and public policy issues.

Internet Access

Low telephone penetration rates are a problem in several Asia Pacific markets. According to the International Telecommunications Union, China, Southeast Asia (excluding Singapore), and India have penetration rates ranging from 5 to 20 lines per 100 people. Low PC penetration is also an issue for some markets. In terms of PC penetration, countries in the region fall into three groups: those that are close to the U.S. level of nearly 50 percent (Australia and Singapore), those that are half to two-thirds the U.S. level (Japan, Hong Kong, New Zealand, Taiwan, and South Korea), and others with less than 5 percent penetration.

Access costs also vary. Those of more wealthy Asia Pacific nations such as Japan and Australia are higher than in the U.S. In Japan, a high per-minute charge is the main cause, while the high price of PCs is the main factor in Australia. Among Asia's developing countries, access costs are similar to those of the U.S. However, given lower wealth levels, these costs still represent a significant barrier. For example, Internet access costs represent as much as 48 percent and 35 percent of monthly household incomes in China and India respectively, far more than the 1 percent in the U.S.

However, these barriers are being overcome. For example, Japan's NTT (Nippon Telegraph and Telephone Corporation) recently launched a new rate plan offering a 60 percent discount. Moreover, Asia Pacific users often use the Internet at work rather than at home. New game machines such as Sony's PlayStation 2 can be used as access platforms. Further, countries such as Hong Kong, Singapore, and Australia have broadband networks to support high-speed Internet access, while others such as China are developing television-based Web access.

Delivery Infrastructure

Efficient, convenient delivery poses one of the greatest challenges to e-tailers in Asia. Currently, delivery companies in many Asian countries are fragmented and have limited reach. Many also cannot provide adequate customer support. National postal systems provide cheaper and greater coverage, but not necessarily door-to-door service. The cost of shipping quickly into and around the region is also high. For example, for a parcel of books weighing about 4.5 kilograms and valued at US$100, the cost of in-country delivery is typically 5 to 15 percent of the cost of the parcel (for delivery in three to five days). For delivery within the region (e.g., Hong Kong to Bangkok), delivery cost rises to 30–50 percent of the parcel's value, while shipment from the U.S. 110 percent of the parcel's value.

Payment System

Most Asians do not use credit cards to settle transactions. According to Lafferty Cards Databank Asia-Pacific, while Australia and Hong Kong have credit card penetration approaching U.S. levels, those in other countries like Taiwan and Malaysia are low at about 30 percent. Recent surveys have shown that many Asian consumers still worry about security and vendor reliability over the Internet. Moreover, many traditional bankers are reluctant to assume fledgling e-tailers' merchant accounts as they cannot easily assess their credit worthiness.

Thus, other options have developed, including bank transfers, cash on delivery, and third-party settlement. For example, Chinese customers settle their bill with a local post office before delivery of goods. However, the payment issue will evolve, especially as consumers become more comfortable with credit card security. Regional banking systems are also beginning to adapt. For example, China Merchant Bank recently launched an online payment solution for local merchants.

Public Policy

Internet policies of Asian governments vary considerably. While nearly all express support for e-business, tangible support is inconsistent. Among the more proactive are Hong Kong and Singapore with their Cyberport and Singapore ONE projects respectively. Online retailers suggest some practical ways governments can become constructively involved in e-business.

First, Asian governments can embrace practical e-government. Government procurement could go online, as could such government services as school enrolment and tax returns. Operating standards could be established for online retailers as well. Second, Asian governments could avoid penalizing domestic e-tailers. For example, some governments have local sales taxes which goods mailed from abroad escape. Third, Asian governments could encourage foreign investment and capability transfer by creating a stable and attractive investment environment. Fourth, Asian governments could modernize their postal systems and make them e-business friendly. Offering value-added services such as inventory and returns management could in fact prove profitable for postal systems. Fifth, Asian governments could open up their telecommunications markets to lower Internet access costs.

KEY LESSONS

While Asian governments can help the growth of e-tailing in the region, online retailers in Asia Pacific will have to earn their success by careful planning and timely execution. Among critical success factors are the following.

Convert Visitors to Buyers

Online retailers must build trust and credibility with potential customers who are more attuned to person-to-person transactions. Hence, a strong brand image and fulfillment of price and delivery promises are essential. For example, the success of Hansol CS in South Korea is built on its reputation as a leading mail order business. It has also implemented a real-time system that confirms customers' orders almost immediately, a delivery tracking system, and a promise of rapid delivery backed up by customer compensation for late delivery. Thus, the trust and reputation of the online retailer enhance conversion of visitors to buyers.

Learn from Customers Daily

As e-business is rapidly evolving, the mix of customers, their behavior, and their choices will change. Quick responses to these changes are necessary for success, and the use of online surveys and data-mining techniques provide important insights into online consumer behavior. For example, China's *Stockstar.com* is a successful finance portal that has developed a large and loyal user base. It conducted an online survey that progressed from basic demographic information, to preferences regarding the site's services, and to preferences relevant to potential advertisers. Focus groups were employed to augment the findings, and the results have provided new insights into building the site and the business model, as well as attracting advertisers.

Build the Brand and Offer Customer Service

Online retailers must encourage customers to return to their site and "imprint" on it. Beyond getting the basics right (timely and reliable order fulfillment, friendly and responsive customer support, good selection, and competitive prices), e-tailers can introduce functions that engage customers, such as chat rooms and customer product reviews. For example, Kyobo Books is a leading online and offline bookseller in South Korea. Kyobo has leveraged a strong offline brand to build a loyal online customer base. It focuses on creating a strong reader community by hosting interactive chat rooms and promoting other book-related social events. It also has a team that creates targeted e-mail promotions and book recommendations based on past buying patterns.

Address Offline Compromises

Asian e-tailers must have a clear value proposition that beats traditional retailers. This will be difficult in major cities with well-developed retail sectors and in countries where various e-business enablers are not in place. E-tailers should explore where traditional shopping experiences leave consumers dissatisfied and exploit the situation. For example, General Motors in Taiwan started to sell cars online in 1999. It noticed that one area where the offline auto buying experience fell short was convenience. Thus, GM enhanced its site's convenience by designing a virtual online test drive and offering door-to-door delivery of a test-drive vehicle.

Get Talent

Successful online businesses require a wide range of capabilities. Beyond technical competence, skills are needed in management, business development, partnership formation, sales and marketing, fund raising, and corporate finance. All Asian markets are short of such expertise, despite the migration of talent from traditional companies into e-businesses. Offering nontraditional compensation, a flexible working environment, and an entrepreneurial atmosphere help to encourage creativity and retain employees.

Form Partnerships

Creating everything internally is unlikely, and undesirable, for most Asian online retailers. Partnerships with content and service providers are important to gain access to capabilities, industry experience, and fixed assets. For example, Japan's 7-Eleven plans to establish a joint venture to sell a wide variety of goods on its site *7dream.com*, whose major partners include NEC, Nomura Research Institute, and Sony. NEC will design and operate the site and produce the multimedia terminals, NRI will house the servers and data center, while Sony will furnish music data downloading for the Minidisc platform, among other technologies.

Create Defensibility

Successful e-tailers must avoid easily replicated "me-too" business models. A strong brand and solid relationships with customers, suppliers, and other e-business players raise entry barriers. Heavy traffic also creates a network effect that creates defensibility, as new users add to the value of the service for all other users. For example, such supplementary services as chat rooms and product ratings that allow a site's users to communicate with each other become more valuable as more people participate.

Target New Customer Communities

New communities, free of geographic constraints, form rapidly on the Internet. They are defined by interest (e.g., golfers), experience (e.g., frequent travelers), and culture (e.g., overseas Chinese). The Internet allows retailers to reach groups previously closed to them, particularly for those retailers operating in smaller markets with a small local customer base. E-tailers must thus identify the appropriate Internet community for their offerings. For example, a stamp collector in Tawau in East Malaysia did not realize there were international collectors interested in North Borneo stamps until he offered them for sale on e-bay. He has now turned his hobby into a small Internet business.

Secure Early Options

E-tailers must balance between seeking out potential growth areas and rushing into a market before it is ready. They should build flexibility in their business models which allow rapid movement into new categories or markets when they see the opportunity. Observing changing demographics to anticipate category and market shifts is important. But e-tailers must also assess the total size and opportunity of the target markets. For example, The Spot is an umbrella brand for multiproduct specialist sites in Australia. By creating new Spot sites (e.g., ToySpot, BookSpot, CDSpot, etc.), the company plans to gain quick results in these categories before strong competitors emerge.

Create a Scaleable and Flexible Supply Chain

Strong supply chain capability is the engine that powers a successful e-business, as online customers are sensitive to supply chain breakdowns. Late or unfulfilled orders are a leading source of customer complaints. Many systems are manual and paper-based in developing Asian countries, and are thus not scaleable to handle demand growth. E-tailers in the region must thus invest time and money to improve their supply chains. They should also encourage their partners (e.g., courier services and front-end suppliers) to enhance their own internal processes.

CONCLUSION

Success of e-tailing in Asia Pacific is by no means assured. The development and durability of four factors are crucial to the region. First, Asia Pacific needs a critical mass of potential online buyers. Most now tend to be wealthy, young, and educated. Large groups of such individuals may not appear any time soon in all Asia Pacific countries or in all product categories. Second, Asia Pacific e-tailing needs sellers. This appears to be accelerating in the region. Third, Asia Pacific e-tailing requires an attractive value proposition to bring online buyers and sellers together. This requires building sophisticated online businesses with a deep understanding of customer needs. Last, e-tailing in Asia Pacific needs enablers to supply the building blocks of successful online businesses. Venture capitalists, incubators, Website designers, banks offering credit card validation, and new government policies are also rapidly emerging, albeit unevenly across the region. As these four elements emerge across Asia Pacific, the region will be set for the continued growth of e-tailing, a phenomenon which will bring dramatic changes in the Asian consumer environment.

ETHICAL ISSUES ACROSS CULTURES
Managing the Differing Perspectives of China and the U.S.A.

Dennis A. Pitta, Hung-Gay Fung, and Steven Isberg

U.S. marketers know the U.S. standard of ethics. However, that standard can lead to ethical conflict when Americans encounter the emerging market giant, China. As smaller U.S. companies enter China, the potential for ethical conflict increases. Reducing that potential requires knowledge. Knowing the nature and history of the two cultures can lead to an understanding of the foundation of their ethical systems. Ethics and the expectations within cultures affect all business transactions. It is vital for Western marketers to understand the expectations of their counterparts around the world. Understanding the cultural bases for ethical behavior in both the U.S.A. and China can arm a marketer with knowledge needed to succeed in cross-cultural business. Implementing that knowledge with a clear series of managerial guidelines can actualize the value of that understanding.

INTRODUCTION

Western businesspeople often concentrate on the fundamentals. In the business and marketing sense, the fundamentals are

---

Dennis A. Pitta is Professor of Marketing at University of Baltimore, Baltimore, Maryland, U.S.A. Hung-Gay Fung is Dr. Y.S. Tsiang Professor of Chinese Studies at University of Missouri, St. Louis, Missouri, U.S.A. Steven Isberg is Associate Professor of Finance at University of Baltimore, Baltimore, Maryland, U.S.A.

Reproduced with permission from *Journal of Consumer Marketing*, Vol. 16, No. 3, 1999, pp. 240–56. © MCB University Press.

- sound marketing strategy;
- professional marketing research;
- world-class product development;
- effective pricing;
- motivating promotion; and
- appropriate distribution.

Focusing on the basics makes success in competitive markets possible. However, serious problems can materialize in business practice between the West and the emerging market giant, China.

The difficulty lies in more fundamental issues than product, price, promotion, and place. With the transition from domestic-focused operations to a true worldwide view, other factors are essential for success. One pervasive factor is culture. Culture and the expectations within cultures affect all business transactions. It is vital for Western marketers to understand the expectations of their counterparts around the world. Even at the threshold of the millennium, inability to master the basic cultural factors still leads to failure.

To be accurate, culture is one of the factors that affect business ethics. The *Random House College Dictionary* defines ethics as, "the rules of conduct recognized in respect to a particular class of human actions or a particular group, culture, etc." Different cultures have different rules of conduct and therein lies the issue addressed in this paper. That issue is understanding the roots of ethics across the two cultures.

Primary cultural values are transmitted to a culture's members by parenting and socialization, education, and religion. There are also secondary factors that affect ethical behavior. They include differences in the systems of laws across nations, accepted human resource management systems, organizational culture, and professional cultures and codes of conduct.

Our objective is not to point out which practices are ethical and which are unethical. Our objective is to understand the differences and outline a means of managing them. What is important is that some cultures might view these practices with different levels of condemnation. Therein lies the problem for managers engaged in cross-cultural transactions. How do they anticipate and manage differences in ethical behavior rooted in differences in culture?

The following discussion concentrates on the differences in the cultures of the U.S.A. and China, in an attempt to clarify potential sources of ethical discrepancy.

Ethical Behavior in Different Cultures

For Americans, the 1980s and 1990s marked the realization of the global economy. Even ordinary consumers know more about the national origin of the products they consume. The biggest impact seems to have been on small businesses. The U.S. government and many states offer global business help to all businesses. As smaller firms enter the global marketplace, they encounter different ethical frameworks than those of their domestic markets. Smaller firms may be less well-equipped to deal with the differences. This trend has highlighted the need to manage potential ethical conflict before it becomes a problem. Supporting that end, research into the ethics of international management has become a growing field (Jeurissen and van Luijk, 1998; Jackson and Artola, 1997; Honeycutt et al., 1995; Armstrong and Sweeney, 1994).

Cultural Conflict

Newspapers contain stories highlighting the domestic unethical behavior of managers. The behavior includes

- illegal campaign contributions;
- bribery;
- knowingly selling defective goods;
- hiding information; and
- other troubling acts.

These instances represent individual or organizational misconduct; there is an ethical framework that is not followed. The more serious problem entails two different ethical standards meeting in a business transaction. This situation is characterized as a cultural conflict.

Even in the West, ethical differences can lead to contrasting business practices. The Foreign Corrupt Practices Act, enacted in the U.S.A., is the source of a glaring comparison. U.S. companies, in their worldwide operations, are forbidden to engage in activities that are illegal in the U.S.A. As a case in point, bribery to obtain business is strictly forbidden for a U.S. company, no matter where in the world it takes place. Company officers can face jail terms and hefty fines are common.

In some countries, bribery is part of the fabric of life and no business can be transacted without it. Without knowing whom to pay to grease the wheels, companies face frustration and failure. If a U.S. company resorts to bribery, it faces great pressure to hide it, including hiding it in financial statements. In contrast, other countries have a more tolerant or pragmatic view of bribery. As a case in point, at this writing, bribes are explicitly tax deductible in another Western country, Germany.

When considering countries that do not share a common cultural heritage, the challenges can be even greater.

Culture, the Basis for Business Ethics

There is common agreement that a country's culture is directly related to the ethical behavior of its managers. The behavior is exhibited in two main ways: first, by overt actions such as public or corporate statements and actions about ethical behavior; second, by the collection of the group of ethical attitudes and values.

One problem in dealing with culture is that it is difficult to define universally. It represents the values and patterns of thinking, feeling, and acting in an identifiable group. While many nations possess the infrastructure of modern, developed civilization, culture represents how people in the civilization interact with one another.

A view that may help understand culture is to look at its levels (Schein, 1985). Schein proposed that culture has three levels. The most obvious concerns the works of culture, its artifacts. These are apparent and portray some of the values of the culture. Public works, works of art, museums, hospitals, and universities can reveal the value that the culture places on the arts and sciences. The Coliseum, in ancient Rome, and its purpose in entertaining the public revealed how Romans valued individual human life.

A deeper and less obvious level comprises those things which individuals hold dear and which guide their behavior. They serve as rules of conduct and can be important guidelines for how individuals should or ought to behave. The Japanese elevation of politeness in behavior may reflect the limited physical space in the island nation. However, politeness to others is clearly how the Japanese should behave toward one another. Violations of the norm cause others surprise and anger and sometimes lead to sanctions against the offender.

The third and hidden level represents values, and specifically represents the assumptions we use to perceive and deal with reality. For example, some cultures perceive people as essentially good while others tend to take a more pessimistic view. It is difficult to separate the lower two levels since attitudes and values tend to overlap. However, they form the underpinnings of individual and business interactions.

Dimensions of Culture

The goal of identifying a nation's value assumptions can be achieved by studying the dimensions of its culture. Kluckhohn and Strodtbeck (1961) compared a number of cultures across six dimensions, which have been studied by scholars in nonbusiness fields for many years. The six dimensions can be articulated as the following six questions:

1. What are society's assumptions about the essential goodness of people? Does the society assume that people are essentially good, bad, or both?
2. What does the society emphasize in interpersonal relations, the individual or the group? Should an individual feel free to act as an individual or should he consider the group before acting?
3. What is the value of personal space in a society? In some societies, people feel comfortable standing very close to one another. In others, there is an accepted physical distance, a buffer, which should not be entered. In those cultures, people are very uncomfortable standing too close.
4. What does the society assume about the relationship of man and nature? Is man meant to live in harmony with nature or to dominate it?
5. What is the role of change in society? Does the culture value stability, and preserving the status quo? In contrast, does the society value progress and change?
6. Finally, what is society's orientation toward time: past, present, or future?

Kluckhohn and Strodtbeck (1961) found that each society has a cultural orientation that can be described in terms of these six questions. Knowing the dimensions of culture can help in anticipating potential sources of conflict.

Types of Ethical Conflict

Managers like clear guidelines to aid their decision making. A list of rules citing prohibitions and allowed practices is often helpful. Unfortunately, such lists are too simple to guide cross-cultural ethical interaction. For example, gift-giving is not usually prohibited in most cultures. However, in a given culture, giving a gift may be ethical or unethical. In some societies, like China, presentation of a small, carefully chosen business gift conveys a great deal of respect and is a sign that the business relationship is valued by the giver. If there is a problem, it may rest with the receiver who may not trust the giver's motives. In this case, the issue can be understood as one of business etiquette.

Conversely, gifts whose purpose is to influence a decision maker's judgment is actually or essentially a bribe. They are more universally recognized as such. This leads to a second issue involving basic values. What is the proper place of a bribe in the business context? In Western cultures, bribes are usually not considered "right" or fair and are often against the law. In this case, the conflict deals with fundamental standards of fairness (Kohls and Buller, 1994).

There is a continuum of ethical conflict ranging from simple, rather innocuous practices like giving token gifts to serious issues like employing sweatshop or political prisoner labor. Judging the seriousness of the differences requires a look at the aspects of both the American and Chinese cultures.

The Cultural Foundation of American Ethics

To understand the impact of differences in ethical attitudes toward the conduct of business between the U.S.A. and China we should start with the ethical foundations in the U.S.A. There are several key questions to address:

- What constitutes ethics in business?
- What issues and behaviors are important?
- What constitute the ethical standards of business conduct?

Answers to these questions are important to our ability to reconcile differences in the way business agents in each country think and act.

Ethical roots in the U.S.A. date back to the country's Puritan origins. They tend to be based on a foundation of traditional Judeo-Christian and Western sociotheological laws and principles. Underlying this system is the belief in an intrinsic underlying truth. This belief is central to the biblical system of ethics and morality. Here, moral and ethical bases are provided through the decrees of a sovereign moral authority, God. As a sovereign, God declares right and wrong, providing a general moral and legal framework for organizing a society.

Separately, enlightenment philosophers reached similar conclusions. While Christianity was the predominant religion among the nation's founders, enlightenment philosophy and its focus on "natural law" led to their affirmation of an individual's "inalienable rights." The founders identified three basic "self-evident" truths regarding the "inalienable" rights of mankind to

1. life,
2. liberty, and
3. the pursuit of happiness,

exercised in an environment in which people are equal under the law.

Equality under the law does not imply equality in the endowment of natural talents, intelligence, and abilities. Rather, it means that there exist no *a priori* claims against one's life, liberty and/or ability to dispose of one's personal property in the pursuit of his or her personal life goals and activities. Limits on such freedom of choice are imposed only in two important cases. The first is when the individual voluntarily agrees to be bound by such a claim as part of a voluntary contract. The second case involves criminal or civil activity resulting in the harm to another's life, liberty, or property. That activity has led to the imposition of legal penalties as a result of a claim enforced under due process of law. As a result, the U.S.A. has become a place where the individual's rights are emphasized, contracts are important, and order in society is a goal.

The importance of an individual's right to choice is the foundation of the belief that competitive markets are the best way in which to organize an economy. The economy's role is to provide the greatest degree of satisfaction to the needs and desires of society. Laws enabling this process to function are designed to deny others the opportunity to deprive an individual of his or her freedoms of choice and property rights via the use of fraud or force. In the absence of fraud and force, any "heads-up" transaction in which property or time is exchanged is perfectly legal if not ethical.

The functioning free market economy has often been described as a "nexus of contracts," whereby individual and corporate economic agents voluntarily agree to exchange money, time, resources, and other goods and services in the pursuit of their own economic well-being. Since individual and corporate agents are principally responsible for their own well-being, they play the role of an advocate whose motivation and behavior are self-interested. As long as that behavior is absent the use of fraud or force, it is possible to engage in virtually any transaction that does not adversely affect the rights of others. There are both benefits and costs to such a system.

The principal benefit of the market system is that resources are allocated in an "optimal" fashion. The principal cost of this system is that it is designed to best satisfy the needs of overall society, but not necessarily the specific needs of any given individual or group within that society.

Adam Smith, who is given credit for contributing to the design of this system, argued that while it was important to allow the market economy to function freely, other social mechanisms would need to function in such a way as to make up for its deficiencies. In his book *The Theory of Moral Sentiments*, Smith outlined the importance of the role played by "institutional society," which is, in essence, charged with the responsibility to teach and encourage the practice of civic virtue in society. Whereby behavior in the market economy is dictated by self-interest, that in the civic society should be driven by the principle of self-control. The three main elements of institutional society,

1. home,
2. church, and
3. school,

are thereby responsible for instilling principles of ethical behavior in society, seeing to it that the practice of such behavior is socially rewarded. Self-controlled behavior in civic society may serve to mitigate the adverse effects of self-interested behavior in the commercial markets (Muller, 1993).

The integration of behavioral and ethical codes taught within civic and commercial society serves to make the overall society "decent." In the ideal setting, the civic virtue of self-control will influence commercial transactions in such a way as to maintain a high degree of ethical standards of conduct. While individuals acting out of self-interest in commercial transactions will play the part of advocates, transactions will be negotiated in an environment in which participants will be bound by the truth, and will represent themselves "in good faith." This brings us back to the importance of the traditional ethical foundations of the U.S.A. and the way in which transactions are negotiated and completed.

In the U.S.A., business transactions revolve around the contract. The contract, most often a written document, spells out the nature of the business relationship and the obligations of each party to the business transaction(s) covered by the contract. While many transactions are conducted on an informal or noncontractual basis, virtually any significant transaction will be based on a fairly detailed contract to which and by which the parties are bound both legally and ethically. Contracts are negotiated between parties acting as advocates but in good faith. It is generally accepted that commitments made will be honored to the letter if not the spirit of the agreement. The contract becomes the *a priori* vehicle for resolving disputes. If the parties to the contract cannot reach agreement, an arbitrator or other third party may be called on to interpret the contract. In either case, however, the contract becomes the principal document governing the relationship.

The importance of the absolute nature of the truth and its role in commercial transactions governed by contracts can be seen in some of the teaching of the Judeo-Christian tradition. Once an agent freely enters into a contract he or she agrees to be bound by its points. This is not only a legal but a socially ethical commitment made by the individual to other parties involved in the contract. Ethically speaking, individuals are bound to negotiate in the context of the truth, "saying what they mean" and "meaning what they say."

To summarize the impact of this ethical context on the conduct of commercial transactions, business agents in the U.S.A. can be expected to act as personal (or corporate) advocates, attempting to engage in transactions that maximize their own well-being. The process of negotiation, however, is intended to be in good faith, where the truth is represented in the words and actions of those participating. Once agreements are reached in this context, the participants are both legally and ethically bound to carry out their obligations and commitments as outlined in the contract. While this type of behavior can, if followed to the letter, be predatory in certain cases, the teaching of the value of self-control in institutional society will moderate the adverse effects of self-interested behavior in the environment where the terms of the transaction are carried out.

Comparison of Business Culture between China and the U.S.A.

Business culture is built from time-tested and conventional practices. Business practices and ways of thinking over a long period of time lasting hundreds or even thousands of years mold the business culture of a country. China and the U.S.A. have different business cultures, in part because of their differences in history. After the Chinese economic liberalization policies implemented by Deng Xiaoping in 1978, U.S. multinationals have substantially increased their investments in China through joint ventures, setting up subsidiaries and offices. With the increase in partnership business, it is of critical importance that executives in both countries understand each other's business culture. To this end, we will explain and contrast the various aspects of business culture for the two countries in the following section. A caveat is in order in the following generalizations about China, which should be taken with a grain of salt. China is a nation with a diverse and complex culture with contradictory characteristics. For example, the Chinese people are diligent yet they tend to be content with their lot. With respect to religion, they do not believe in one God but they believe in sages. This contrasts significantly with the U.S. view of one God and the importance of organized religion in the country.

It is important to discuss several notions that define Chinese culture and influence business ethics.

Notion of Harmony

The Chinese believe that everything should be in harmony, and they take a long-term view of things. Change can be viewed as disruptive, in particular if the change is sudden and substantial. As a result, nonaction will be better than action. This line of thinking is derived from the teachings of Confucius and Taoism, which, over a long period of time, have a profound impact on the Chinese people.

The notion of harmony is easily understandable for several reasons. First, there are many people in China. Conflict among people who live closely together is inevitable. Without paying proper attention to harmony, the Chinese society would be chaotic. Thus, scholars, philosophers, and rulers have to emphasize the importance of harmony in order to have peace and order in society. Second, dominant religions prevailing in China, such as Taoism and Buddhism, stress peace and nature and clearly have an impact on how the Chinese people behave and think.

Americans, however, believe in efficiency and effectiveness. Thus, competition and action that will contribute to the end result are regarded as critical and important. Americans believe in logical reasoning that is based on facts and are usually straight with them. They value the desired end result, which may be disruptive to relations and the normal existing patterns.

Importance of Relationship

The Chinese believe that they are dependent on four social groups, which include relatives, schoolmates, personal friends, and the indirect relationship from the three. The Chinese people attach special importance to human feelings. Human relationship is very important to them. In the Chinese language, human relationship is called *guanxi* or connection.

The importance of human relationship is primarily derived from the fact that China has been an agricultural state, where a small and closed community is a normal form of social structure. As a result, the Chinese mentality is to work in groups to accomplish a common goal. As a result, individualism is not singled out to be important in the process. In the Chinese culture, privacy is not so highly valued as in the American culture, whose value judgment is entirely based on individualism. This can be explained in two ways. First, the U.S. Constitution guarantees the rights of an individual, which is the building block of U.S. law. Second, the U.S.A. has a relatively short history, and thus old styles and ways of thinking that constrain the spirit of individualism in China do not burden daily life in the U.S.A.

Another reason why the Chinese value human relationship so much is their belief that the "rule of man" is more important than the "rule of law," which can be subject to manipulation and interpretation. This is particularly true because different emperors in different dynasties in the Chinese history designed laws that fit their needs or circumstances.

With this emphasis on man, in China, executives and entrepreneurs work constantly to maintain and expand their networks of *guanxi*. The connections can extend to other companies and individuals, to Hong Kong, Taiwan, and even abroad. Thus, the network of *guanxi* can be very powerful.

Americans gain their identity through their individual achievements and behaviors, although relationship does play a role. The American network of relationship exists and is important for business transactions but appears to be relatively more subtle. Because Americans come from different cultural backgrounds, they are diverse people from various races and cultures. Thus, there are relatively few norms in the U.S.A. It is not unusual to view the U.S.A. as the "melting pot" of all cultures. In reality that image is inaccurate. The melting pot never worked completely or immediately. In most cases, English is the glue that holds the nations together. Numerous subcultures coexist and even second and third generation Americans remember their immigrant heritage. With the freedom and money to travel and relocate anywhere in the country, Americans representing individual immigrant groups can be found all over the nation.

That effect has forced an increased tolerance of diversity. Thus, the U.S.A. tolerates all kinds of subcultures. However, at the same time, English as the major language represents the essence of what can be called "Anglo-Saxon American" culture, which is the dominant U.S. culture.

To Americans, business relationships can be separated from personal relationships because business transactions are bounded by legal contracts. Friendships are formed very quickly and can be dissolved as they are formed. In general, Americans are open and easy to make friends with, but the relationship is somewhat superficial, and, for many, it is short term. Most Chinese view relationships as lifetime commitments, and thus do not make close friends easily unless there is a well-respected third party from both sides who links the two parties together.

Subtlety and Explicitness

The Chinese culture is built on subtlety. For example, the Chinese language is not as precisely structured as the English language. It is based on an abstraction of ideas. Typically, the Chinese people do not usually want to confront each other even if there is disagreement. When the Chinese people are confronted in a situation where they do not like the outcome, they do not usually explicitly indicate how they feel. Outspokenness is not the norm and direct questioning is viewed as rude. The Chinese people do not easily reveal their true feelings to other people. Thus, outsiders have to be insightful in their listening. The expression "read the tea leaves" can refer to paying attention to words, body language, and the speaker's tone of voice.

Courtesy is important in Chinese culture; it is the leading virtue among righteousness, ethics, and honor. It is important for the Chinese people to save face for other people, and they are afraid of losing face themselves. Thus, the Chinese do not normally put someone in an uncomfortable position. They do not criticize or ridicule what other people are doing. If someone loses face as a result of other people's action, the situation is serious. Sometimes those who lose face at the hands of another seek revenge. This has important lessons for Western managers. Disagreements with a Chinese manager must not lead to loss of face and extraordinary efforts to preserve face may be necessary.

The Chinese people do not like saying "no" directly. Instead, they may say, "I will see what I can do." If they say something like "it is not convenient," this basically means either "no" or "it will take time and permission to do."

The Chinese typically give hints to others about what they really want. This contrasts with the frankness in American culture. The Chinese get used to hinting because they try to learn self-control; its importance has been rooted in ancient times. Self-control tends to make people appear shy in revealing their ideas and thoughts in public places. To illustrate the importance of subtlety, here is an example. If a Chinese person wants to borrow a book or money from a friend, the person would not ask for the book or money directly. Instead, he or she will give hints about the book or his or her need for the financial matters. A sincere friend will directly offer the book or money; otherwise, the hint will be ignored.

In many cases, the Chinese people speak openly and directly, especially if an important principle or a critical matter is at stake. In addition, if they are dealing with close friends or if the situation is not hurting people, they will be willing to speak more openly.

Communication Style

The Chinese people value silence, which is considered to be important in daily activities; silence is reserved for reflection and careful thinking. The Chinese people are strong believers of the English proverb: Speech is silver but silence is golden.

It is important for Chinese individuals to have their speech consistent all the time. Thus, the Chinese do not usually talk too much because they believe that the more they talk, the more mistakes they will make. Americans like to talk and tend to be uncomfortable when there is a gap of silence in the conversation. Some Americans view the silence as a tough negotiating technique. It seems like a stone wall that frustrates communication. In fact, it is a cultural value that is different from the corresponding American cultural value.

Another difference centers on the use of exaggeration. Steeped in a tradition of the "tall-tale" of the frontier, Americans know about larger-than-life folk heroes like Paul Bunyan and Casey Jones. Thus, some Americans believe it is all right to exaggerate. Fluency and the "gift of the gab" are generally viewed as admirable and desirable. American political figures often gain office on the strength of their eloquence. This sharply contrasts with the derogatory notion of eloquence in Chinese customs. This is a bit surprising since the Chinese language is colorful and expressive.

The fact that the Chinese prefer not to talk too much has implications for the advertising business, which is growing more important in China. After Deng Xiaoping began to implement economic reforms in China, corporations have utilized many marketing tools such as advertisements to sell their products. This difference in cultural preferences is the source of potential conflict. Explicitly, exaggeration, called trade puffery, is allowed in U.S. advertising. In fact, consumers and regulators alike expect it.

The essence of advertising is to promote a product and it is useful to create fantasy in showing the needs the product satisfies. However, this may not fit comfortably with the Chinese culture if it is not done properly. Chinese people in general value inner beauty or substance more than the look or style. Therefore, they would frown on the advertisements that contain extravagant accounts of products and services. Some still think advertisements are ways to cheat people. Thus, it is important to select appropriate words in promoting the products on TV and other media in China. That is, the focus of advertisements should be on delivery of product education and knowledge. Coupled with the desire not to create loss of face, comparative advertisements may create problems for the advertiser and should be avoided.

Another difference between the two cultures is in the way the two peoples think. Thinking is quite different from talking. In terms of the thinking process, the Chinese people are pragmatic and take actions that fit the existing patterns. Thus, they prefer the actions that are not too disruptive. In general, the Chinese do not think linearly, that is, from one point to another in a straight line. In many ways, Americans, like the Chinese, are pragmatic. Americans differ because they think in a linear fashion proceeding from point A to B to a final conclusion at C. Americans look toward a solution, which may be innovative, disruptive, or revolutionary. Americans believe that most productive thinking is linear and rational. In problem solving, the results or outcome should be based on concrete facts. For Americans, problem-solving thinking behavior is different from the trade puffery of advertising.

Most cultures have an ingrained sense of physical space and how people should interact. Western culture has developed several traditions that have implications in business. The handshake is a common, expected ritual when meeting someone. The right hand is chosen as the hand to shake. The ritual and the choice of hand stem from interactions during the days of knights and swords. Most people are right-handed, so are most warriors. Shaking the right hand shows that there is no hidden weapon, ready to be used. Thus, handshaking was originally an expression of trust. In essence, the handshake says, "I meet you weaponless, trusting you."

In terms of physical contact, the Chinese people do not like touching. This contrasts with the meaning of touching in Western culture. Between same-sex individuals, a touch on a shoulder, hand, or arm may be a statement of polite affection between friends. Some Americans touch business acquaintances politely to express the sentiment, "We are friends."

In contrast, Chinese do not like to be touched physically. In addition, they avoid direct eye contact with another person out of respect of the other's private space. When two strangers meet, they have to maintain a physical distance to avoid touching.

This differs markedly in the U.S.A. Direct eye contact is very important for showing sincerity in the American society. This may also have its origins in the days of knights and armor. Looking someone directly in the eye implies that you are not looking for a vulnerable area to use a weapon. Thus, you send a message, "I mean no harm."

Americans like to stand at about an arm's length away from each other, defining their comfort zone. This also conveys a sense of trust because the two individuals stand in a mutually vulnerable space. In certain areas, like Japan, the physical space is about three to four feet, the space needed for two people to face each other and bow politely. In the Middle East, physical space may be as little as a foot—conveying a heightened sense of trust. An American meeting with a Saudi colleague may feel very uncomfortable with the limited separation space and even back away to increase it. This is analogous with the discomfort a Chinese manager might feel toward an American's comfort zone.

When the Chinese say "yes," it basically means that they are listening to what you are talking about. It does not necessarily mean that they agree with you. However, Americans are open and straightforward to deal with. Therefore, when they say "yes," it really means positive and affirmative.

American people usually greet others (relatives, friends, and strangers) by saying "Hi!" In the Chinese culture, strangers will consider this greeting as shockingly inappropriate. In this case, you are supposed to be quiet when you meet a stranger. In contrast, friends and relatives expect, "How are you?" Using "Hi" as a greeting to them will be considered to be "cold."

Negotiation

Business typically involves negotiation and bargaining. Different cultures have different models of thinking and ways to solve problems. Negotiation with Chinese people clearly is different from negotiation in the Western countries.

In China, negotiations and contracts should link the association between people by confirming the strong human bond instead of resorting to legal binding. Traditional Chinese culture advocates that benevolence should be the guiding principle of association among people. This principle, admittedly limited, does influence many Chinese people.

Many Americans view negotiation and the signing of a contract as the final stage of association for a business. However, for Chinese managers, it is the first step to a deeper relationship. Continued negotiation is common because a legal contract does not necessarily give one the upper hand. This way of doing business is closely related to the "rule of man" principle discussed earlier.

Many Westerners believe that the Chinese businesspeople use banquets as a means to get a better bargaining position. Banquets are a mechanism for learning a bit more about the other side before the start of formal negotiations. Moreover, expect the Chinese to conduct business while all are eating and drinking at the banquet table.

Americans in negotiations usually openly discuss advantages, disadvantages, and alternatives. The Chinese would discuss and bargain as well, but the key in the negotiation process is to establish common feelings or bonds between the parties. The strategy is to achieve a win-win goal situation. That is, both sides can win. This contrasts with the one-sided negotiations where the winner takes all. Many Chinese people would consider the win-loss strategy immoral. However, the Chinese may use the feelings of friendship that they have built to their advantage to get some concessions in the negotiation process.

Because the Chinese people in general do not like to speak too much, it is important in the negotiation process to present objective facts without subjective feelings. There is a common saying in China—facts speak louder than eloquence. This principle of presenting indisputable facts is important on the negotiation table.

The Chinese prefer contracts that do not have too many details and prefer all issues to be subject to further negotiation afterwards, even after the signing of the contracts. However, they are meticulous note-takers and will exploit verbal comments made during negotiation that are not part of the written contract. In contrast, Americans are very legalistic and like to spell out all the details in the contracts, which will be backed fully by the U.S. legal system.

Rule of Banquet

As mentioned above, the Chinese pay much attention to eating and drinking. Generally speaking, Western food is not as meticulously prepared as Chinese food. The Chinese people have a lot of excuses for eating. In a business trip to China, the banquet is inevitable. American managers should learn the characteristics of banquets diligently, before visiting China. Both banquet customs and the cuisine will be unfamiliar. China, like the U.S.A., has regional differences in cuisine. All the different versions will each be different from American "Chinese food." Moreover, hosts tend to order expensive delicacies that are even more exotic. The result is that most of the food will be a surprise. The prepared manager will learn what to expect so that he or she can be a gracious guest.

Banquets are usually held in restaurants, in private rooms that have been reserved for that purpose. All members of the business delegation should arrive together and on time. As a guest, you have to wait until your Chinese hosts invite you to sit at a seat according to their arrangement. It is not polite to select your own seat because the prearranged seating chart is based on rank and seniority. Usually, the banquet table is round to accommodate eight to ten people sitting together.

At the banquet table, one can use chopsticks or forks to reach the main course. If you cannot reach the courses on the opposite side of the table, it is unwise to stand up and stretch your arm across to reach the food. In the American style, it is quite natural to ask someone to pass the food. In China, it is not desirable, and this is considered to be impolite. Instead, you can talk to the Chinese friends beside you and give hints. The Chinese people are very sensitive to the hints.

After your Chinese associates invite you for a banquet, it is proper to return the favor unless time or other constraints make it impossible. If possible, a third party should relay your invitations to the Chinese. If for some reason the Chinese must refuse the invitation, they will feel more comfortable telling the third party than speaking directly to you.

Although many people consider that the use of banquets in China is uniquely designed as such for better negotiation and networking, it should be noted that Chinese do observe the American style of network by using club members to achieve similar purposes. The difference between the Chinese and the American networking is only in style.

Taboos

China has many taboos, which, if violated, may hurt one's friendship or business. These taboos are primarily based on religious beliefs, superstition, and certain social norms.

The Chinese people are concerned with numbers, which may signal fortune to them. As a result, using a lucky number such as 1688 for a business phone number or house number is important for the Chinese people. The reason for using 1688 is because it means "all the way to riches" when pronounced in Cantonese.

In addition, the Chinese people are superstitious about their business success. If someone accidentally says something bad about their business, the bad signs will trigger future bad luck, which in turn may be believed to cause the downfall of the business. There is a well-known saying in China that for one's success, it depends on the following factors in the order of importance:

1. fate;
2. luck;
3. *feng shui*;[1]
4. accumulation of good deeds;[2] and
5. knowledge.

The list clearly reflects the importance of uncontrollable factors, which are believed to be critical in contributing to one's success. Thus, it is not difficult to see that the Chinese people have many taboos.

Americans, by and large, believe that hard work will pay off and one can achieve anything one desires. Because of the scientific mentality, Americans are relatively less superstitious than the Chinese people, especially in the running of business. To be successful, Americans should be knowledgeable about and sensitive to Chinese beliefs.

STRATEGIES FOR RESOLVING ETHICAL CONFLICT

We have shown some of the relevant differences between American and Chinese managers. They have the potential for several types of conflict and misunderstanding. Kohls and Buller (1994) list seven pragmatic

---

[1] *Feng shui* (wind-water) is the existence of harmony that combines the environment setting for successful and happy outcomes. For example, when Donald Trump opened up his business office in New York City several years ago, he hired several experts in the application of *feng shui* principles to design his office and made necessary changes for the office's design and furniture arrangement.

[2] The belief that previously performed good deeds affect future events is rooted in Buddhism, which believes the cause–effect relationship.

approaches to resolving ethical differences. The authors note that the approaches are not meant to be exhaustive or mutually exclusive. They do provide a useful range of possible options that managers might employ to avoid problems.

One response to cross-cultural ethical differences is avoiding. Avoiding has use in many general business content areas, not just the realm of ethics. For example, avoidance is often used in families and business relationships. In this case, the partners may choose to ignore the problem in the hope that it will go away. Too often the problem continues until it surfaces in an outburst. Avoidance is a potentially useful strategy for the stronger of two parties. It is especially useful when the costs of confrontation are high. The boss, for example, may prefer the status quo. In numerous examples, he may ignore complaints or requests for improvement of pay, working conditions, benefits, or other costly changes. Power may allow him to maintain the status quo.

In a cross-cultural business relationship, avoiding is sometimes used when one party is stronger than the other. A supplier or agent may engage in unethical conduct, but confronting the activity may result in loss of sales or market share. Thus, the costs of confrontation may be too high. Avoiding results in a kind of "do not ask, do not tell" posture.

Another resolution strategy is forcing. Forcing simply means that one party forces its will on the other. As with avoiding, power is necessary for this strategy. The stronger party can demand its way. For example, importers with controlled access to domestic markets can demand concessions or specific behavior of their suppliers. Markets in some economies are or have been essentially closed to outside firms. In the past it has been close to impossible for a U.S. company to set up a business operation in Japan, without a strong domestic partner. This situation manifests itself in the large number of joint ventures in Japan. In such a relationship, the Japanese partner can demand that things be done in a particular way that might conflict with U.S. practices.

A third possibility is to use a combination of education and persuasion. U.S. companies with operations in foreign countries have the opportunity of communicating the benefits of employee safety and human resources management policy. This strategy has the advantage of benefiting from communication.

Fourth on the list is infiltration. This refers to the spread of an idea or principle in a society. Marketing ideas, such as a consumer orientation or an emphasis on product quality, serve as examples of ideas that were introduced from the U.S.A. into several other cultures.

A strategy somewhat related to education and persuasion is negotiation and compromise. It is based on communication and leads to some kind of settlement. However, in this case, both parties may have to give up something—the compromise. This procedure may result in one or both parties feeling dissatisfied with the resulting outcome. The implication may be that nothing has really been resolved.

Another strategy, accommodation, results when one party adapts to the ethic of the other. A foreign company may agree to the ethical view of a U.S. partner because, otherwise, no business may be possible.

The last strategy, collaboration and problem solving, may result in the best outcome. Under a collaboration and problem-solving strategy, both parties may work together to reach a mutually beneficial and acceptable solution. Of all the listed strategies, this one offers the highest probability of actually bridging the difference separating the parties. The example of the U.S.A. and the People's Republic of China (PRC) agreeing on the Shanghai accords follows this strategy. The accords contained numerous articles. In this example, the U.S.A. agreed not to recognize "two Chinas—the PRC and Taiwan." Instead, the U.S.A. agreed to maintain diplomatic relations with the PRC government only. This feature represented a deep-seated desire on the part of the PRC government to be recognized as the sole government of the Chinese nation. Conversely, the agreement that the U.S.A. could supply the defense needs of Taiwan, if it did not escalate the quantity and quality of arms, represents a need on the part of the U.S.A. not to abandon a long-time ally completely.

On the surface, the collaboration and problem-solving strategy looks a lot like a negotiation and compromise solution. However, the focus is more on uncovering problems in the ethical relationship and solving those problems to mutual satisfaction.

The seven strategies form a series of strategic alternatives that can be selected to deal with a particular ethical conflict. Kohls and Buller (1994) are clear that no single conflict reduction strategy is really better than another. Each may be appropriate in a specific situation.

That said, the collaboration and problem-solving strategy has another advantage in U.S.A.–China managerial cooperation. It lays the foundation for establishing a relationship of trust that is a part of the *guanxi* concept.

SUMMARY

Culture forms the foundation for ethical behavior and determines what is ethical and what is considered unethical. We have shown some of the crucial differences between the business and ethical cultures of the U.S.A. and China. The differences include a context versus content orientation. In China, *guanxi*, the set of connections or relationships, form the context of business. Within that context exist a series of expectations and a level of trust. When Chinese managers negotiate a contract, they rely not on the content of the contract but the context in which it was negotiated. What is important is the relationship among the individuals. If a sticky detail comes up, Chinese managers feel that communication and relationships will solve it. There is less concern about meeting contract conditions, since the contract is viewed as a symbol of the relationship among partners.

In contrast, Western managers view the content of a contract as most important. The specific wording, the dates, the amounts, the responsibilities are spelled out clearly. To an American manager, negotiating the details implicitly means striving to meet the demands of the contract. Failure to do so would embarrass an American, a loss of face. The situation is even more pronounced when German managers are involved. German culture is even more high content than U.S. culture. Every point, value, date, and article in a German contract would be gospel.

Other potential ethical conflicts arise simply from the different values inherent across cultures.

MANAGERIAL IMPLICATIONS

Several important implications can be drawn from the paper. Perhaps the most important one revolves around the importance of respecting the terms of a contract. Americans will do so and also expect others to. Chinese managers do not regard a contract with the same degree of importance.

Numerous cross-cultural interactions have resulted in frustrated Americans who did not understand that deadlines would not be met, even though they were spelled out clearly. In addition, some Chinese managers are irate to learn that their American partners had no intention of modifying an agreement after signing. Worse, the common business practice of adding a penalty or fee for the modifications seems like thievery.

Chinese and American societies place different emphasis on interpersonal relations, the individual, and the group. In the U.S.A., the rights of individuals are safeguarded and individual uniqueness and diversity are valued. In China, the individual is less important. In human resources decisions, Chinese managers may attach less importance to individuals' rights. Conversely, Chinese managers may attach great importance to their network of connections. Outsiders may have difficulty in penetrating the network. Even lower cost, higher quality, higher-profit proposals, essentially "better" offers, from outsiders may not be accepted in China. This may lead to the impression of unethical favoritism. In fact, it is just an honored system of working.

We considered the question of society's assumptions about the relationship of man and nature. Chinese managers live in harmony with nature. Americans feel that man should dominate it. This difference in orientation may lead Americans to be perceived as unethical polluters and destroyers of old artifacts. It is important to understand the Chinese position and insure that it is respected. Otherwise, business dealings may be difficult.

A potential clash of cultures revolves around the role of change in society. The Chinese culture values stability, and preserving the status quo. Changes, if necessary, should be evolutionary. In business dealings, change, especially an increase in prosperity, is valued. However, too rapid change upsets balance. In contrast, U.S. culture values progress and change even at the expense of traditional values. The implication is that U.S. managers must respect the values of their Chinese counterparts. This will require Americans to have great patience.

Other problems may be rooted in society's orientation toward time. Chinese revere the past and pray to elders and deceased relatives for help. The concept of time has a longer duration for most Chinese. In contrast, most Americans have little concern for the past and live in a youth culture. They live in the present and plan for the future. Americans also have a shorter conception of time; things must happen quickly since "time is money." American managers cannot underestimate the accommodations necessary to deal with this difference.

In short, knowing the differences in culture between the two societies can help avoid costly problems and failure. Employing an expert in the other side's culture and business practice can be the best insurance of success.

References

Armstrong, R.W. and J. Sweeney (1994). Industry type, culture, mode of entry and perceptions of international marketing ethics problems: A cross-cultural comparison. *Journal of Business Ethics*, 13: 775–85.

Honeycutt, E., J. Siguaw, and T. Hunt (1995). Business ethics and job-related constructs: A cross-cultural comparison of automotive salespeople. *Journal of Business Ethics*, 14: 235–48.

Jackson, T. and M. Artola (1997). Ethical beliefs and management behaviour: A cross-cultural comparison. *Journal of Business Ethics*, 16: 1163–73.

Jeurissen, R.J.M. and H.J.L. van Luijk (1998). The ethical reputations of managers in nine EU-countries: A cross-referential survey. *Journal of Business Ethics*, 17: 995–1005.

Kluckhohn, F.R. and F. Strodtbeck (1961). *Variations in Value Orientations*. Evanston, IL: Row Peterson.

Kohls, J. and P. Buller (1994). Resolving cross-cultural ethical conflict: Exploring alternative strategies. *Journal of Business Ethics*, 13: 31–38.

Muller, J.Z. (1993). *Adam Smith in His Time and Ours: Designing the Decent Society*. New York: Free Press.

TAKE A CONSERVATIVE APPROACH WHEN ENTERING THE CHINA MARKET

Allen Appell, Richard Jenner, and Len Hebert

Economic growth in China over the past two decades has resulted in many companies making substantial financial commitments in China, typically with a Chinese joint venture partner. Many additional companies are contemplating entering China in the same way. Serious problems and high risks argue for a more conservative market entry strategy as an alternative approach.

This study presents the research results of in-depth interviews with heads of joint venture subsidiaries of major Western companies in China. Results indicate it is advisable to lower expectations of success in the China market. The time anticipated to achieve objectives should be extended, standards of quality may need to be modified, the size of entry may need to be streamlined, transferring obsolete technology remains a viable strategy, and the Western firm should maintain dominant control of the joint venture or enter without a partner. These findings reveal a more cautious entry strategy that reduces or eliminates the involvement of a Chinese joint venture partner may be the optimum way for many firms to enter the China market.

Allen Appell is Professor, Department of Marketing, San Francisco State University. Richard Jenner is Professor, Department of Management, San Francisco State University. Len Hebert is Assistant Professor, Department of Management, San Francisco State University.

Copyright © 1999 by The Haworth Press, Inc., Binghamton, NY. Reprinted from *Journal of Global Marketing*, Vol. 12, No. 4, pp. 65-78.

A Global Market Strategy Involving Significant Commitment versus a Conservative Market Strategy in China . . . .

At first glance, China appears an ideal candidate for a major commitment global entry strategy. The popular business press and many theorists present China as an emerging market with unlimited opportunity (Overholt, 1993). It has been likened to a gold rush consisting of a market of a billion two hundred million people to be mined. Make a profit of one dollar on only 1 percent of the population and you stand to make a profit of 12 million dollars. Thousands of foreigners have flooded China since the beginning of its "open-door" policy in 1978, reportedly investing $6.5 billion by 1992 and $20 billion by 1993, and the amount grows as China continues to privatize and encourage foreign investment. In fact, some economists predict that China will be the world's third largest economy by the year 2000 (Osland, 1994).

During the 1980s more international joint ventures were formed in China than in any other nation and market entry continues through the 1990s (Beamish, 1993). However, there is little knowledge about the actual performance of international joint ventures in China (Anderson, 1990; Geringer and Hebert, 1989; Osland and Cavusgil, 1996). Many economists who analyze China find the economic outlook for the country far from clear because the current growth rate assumes the present trend will continue without major problems arising. In addition, there is a great deal of variance and disagreement among economists as to how to calculate the data on China (Gelb, 1996). Like much data from single-party communist systems where political considerations override economic objectivity, official reports of such growth are suspect. For example, "Official statistics show that in the past 45 years China has grown at about 7 percent per year which is greater than Japan and Germany. These numbers suggest that China's per capita income should be about $8,000 per year ... not $480" (Lee, 1996). Official Chinese government statistics show that GDP per capita reached $579 in 1995 (Xue, 1997). In fact, the World Bank has revised downward its estimates on the size of the Chinese economy by 25 percent and says the proportion of the population living in poverty is closer to 33 percent rather than the 7 percent previously reported (*The Economist*, 1996b).

Paul Krugman, an economist at MIT, in a controversial article, "The myth of Asia's miracle," argues that China's growth is transitory because it has been achieved primarily through temporary heavy investment and a shift of labor from farms to factories. He predicts that, like the Soviet Union, diminishing returns will result in slow growth once inputs are exhausted and capital-to-output ratios approach developed country levels (Krugman, 1994). While there is disagreement from other economists concerning Krugman's findings, there is sufficient question as to the validity of statistics and the notion of unbridled growth of the China market to support a more careful market entry approach (*The Economist*, 1997).

China faces innumerable problems which threaten to significantly undermine its economic progress. Communism is the biggest problem; a system that has fundamental flaws demonstrated by its collapse in most countries around the globe. Two destabilizing factors of communism include a lack of an orderly political succession process and a dysfunctional economic system that misallocates resources. Among China's 100,000 state enterprises, "losses and bad debts are reaching staggering new levels. Some 40% are spilling red ink, whether they make paper, chemicals, steel, or TVs" (*Business Week*, 1996).

On the positive side, there is a minority of the population, primarily in the industrial centers of the East Coast, that is experiencing economic improvement in contrast to the rest of the country. However, this has resulted in a great and growing discontinuity in wealth distribution that threatens political and social stability. While some urbanites have experienced increasing income, a large urban underclass is developing and the rural, primarily agriculturally oriented population is growing poorer. Exacerbating the problem is the mass migration from farms to cities. As a result, land planted in the primary Chinese crops was reduced by 4.4 million hectares from 1992 to 1993. Since it is estimated that China is already 20 million hectares short of the amount needed to feed its growing population, any loss of farmed land is a critical problem (Weil, 1995). Economic statistics vary significantly concerning China. For example, economist Robert Weil says 1993 urban GDP per capita was $269 and rural GDP was $106, while Chinese government data doubles these figures (Weil, 1995). However, there is little disagreement that China is a poor country.

At the firm level, prior studies of joint venture profitability in China have shown profits to be typically illusive (Beamish, 1993; Campbell, 1989; Stelzer et al., 1992). Previous research of international joint ventures in China shows low profitability because manufacturing costs were significantly greater than expected due to low labor productivity and inadequate infrastructure (Shapiro et al., 1991). While a global market entry strategy may well work for some companies, the problems inherent in China's economy as a poor country with a per capita GDP of even the official $579, and significantly less in rural areas, support the need for an alternative strategy that adjusts to local market conditions.

The Research Project

The following analysis results from a research project in which Western managers of ten joint ventures between Western and Chinese companies were interviewed in depth about their experiences doing business in China. In addition, administrators at three Chinese universities and two government agencies were part of the survey. Interviewees were heads and key managers of joint ventures of large Western companies located in Hong Kong, Guangzhou, Shanghai, and Beijing. Firms were selected primarily because they are major players in their particular industries. The sales of seven Western parent companies ranged from $2 billion to $18 billion in 1997. Three companies were mid-sized with sales between $1 million and $10 million. There were eight American companies, one Canadian, and one Danish. Structured, in-depth interviews were conducted for one to two-and-one-half hours each. In order to preserve the anonymity of interviewees, their companies will be referred to by descriptions rather than their actual names. Their insights, presented below, frequently contradict the conventional wisdom that depicts China as an unbridled booming market with unlimited opportunities.

How can one go wrong in such a gold rush where the economy is supposedly growing dramatically each year and there is such a large market desiring the products of the West? Like a gold rush, there is money to be made, but only some do so; many are not so fortunate. The difficulties of entering the China market will be discussed and an alternative strategy for maximizing market entry will be presented.

LOWER YOUR EXPECTATIONS OF SUCCESS IN THE CHINA MARKET . . . .

While China has experienced growth in the last two decades, the prior discussion points to potential present and future weaknesses. Other fundamental factors upon which successful market entry is based are also problematic.

There is no real legal system upon which one can rely to enforce contracts and property rights. The bureaucracy is powerful, intrusive, and erratic. For example, McDonald's had its Tiananmen Square lease canceled by one government entity after it was agreed to by another.

The infrastructure in the cities is barely adequate, with massive congestion of roads and frequent brownouts in the electrical system. Outside the cities the infrastructure is one of the most underdeveloped in the world.

Not everything is as successful as portrayed. The supposedly booming new enterprise zones that we visited in Guangdong Province were full of empty buildings with little traffic or business activity. According to the food processing equipment company executive we interviewed, the prime market in China is other Western companies because the Chinese do not have sufficient purchasing power. He added, "Western companies are in China because their competitors are here and they don't want to be left out. But there is not much of a market outside of Westerners because the Chinese have little money." Fundamental to economics, basic demand is driven by not only population, but per capita income as well. In many market sectors, private citizens are forbidden from doing any international business so international trade must be done with state-owned monopolies. This factor further limits the market and profits (Lee, 1996).

Most of the interviewees agreed that U.S. firms should lower their expectations of profitability because costs will be significantly higher than anticipated. It would seem that costs would be lower in a developing country, but just the opposite is true if you attempt to maintain developed country standards. For example, the head of the farm equipment manufacturer joint venture we interviewed said costs of maintaining expatriates in China are $330,000 per year per person. His rent for a three-bedroom condominium in downtown Shanghai was $15,000 per month. The manager of the food processing equipment company paid rent of $7,000 per month for a condominium outside of Shanghai, and $35,000 per year for private kindergarten education for his two children. The Jeep vehicle he drives costs his company $60,000, instead of the $19,000 it would cost in the U.S. Real estate costs have soared as urban China has become a landlord's market. From 1991 to 1994 rent for premium office and residential space in Beijing and Shanghai increased approximately 40 percent every year as a multitude of foreign as well as domestic firms crowded into these markets (Ness, 1995).

Adjust Your Standards of Quality and TQM

Executives at the delivery service company noted that Chinese worker culture emphasizes risk avoidance, avoiding mistakes, and avoiding individual accountability. This was affirmed by the head of the farm equipment manufacturer, who noted that for thousands of years if one was wrong one was severely punished by a feudal system of dictatorial rule headed by an emperor. This system persists today in the form of a communist bureaucracy.

A committee decision-making orientation in Chinese management impedes progress. In 1987, the farm equipment manufacturer sold technology for diesel engines and tractors in the form of a ten-year-old turnkey assembly line. While everything was set out for them, the Chinese management refused additional consultation and could not get the line running because committee decision-making completely bogged down implementation. Ultimately the Chinese contributed the line back to the farm equipment manufacturer as their contribution to the present joint venture and it has finally begun production under Western management. According to the Associate Dean of a school of business in Shanghai, the problem with Chinese management is that top managers have not yet learned to be CEOs and tend to be mere information conduits for a central authority. They are not decision makers and risk takers. He believes they must first learn to be true managers in a hierarchical format and then learn to shift to the modern more flat organizational style.

Training was found to be difficult in China. The printing forms company found employees difficult to train and prone to return to their old low-quality methods immediately after training. The industrial equipment manufacturer brought in a trainer for two years to instruct their JV partner's employees. According to the Western head of the JV, the trainer worked hard and "did everything right." Although the Chinese listened attentively and took notes, they implemented nothing of what they had learned. He asserts that "greenfield" (starting from scratch) operations are the only successful ones and "the only thing his company adopted from the Chinese is patience." His was the only company interviewed that was currently profitable, as most others projected profitability to be a decade away.

The head of the farm equipment manufacturer found training for equipment maintenance to be a great problem. He cited the example of employees draining the coolant from engines and others who would start them without replacing it, so engines burned up at great cost to his company. He said, although it is easy to get good young people on the shopfloor and intelligent young engineers, they don't know how to implement what they have learned. Chinese schools teach theory but not "hands-on" dealing with machinery. Fear of failure and making mistakes creates problems in training because it is difficult to teach that progress comes by making mistakes.

Younger workers, less than 30 years old, were found to be the best by the farm equipment manufacturer, as they are ready for change and can be more readily trained. For these reasons, the industrial equipment manufacturer wants people in their thirties, and the food processing equipment company will not hire anyone older than 25.

Corruption was another detrimental factor. The printing forms company, which established a joint venture with an existing small printing company, found their partner's existing sales force preferred calling on accounts that paid them bribes. They avoided calling on the new foreign companies in their market that refused to pay bribes, even though they represented a great source of new business.

Employee motivation is undermined by the state bureaucracy, even in Western companies. The delivery service company found motivating employees difficult because all its employees are required to be hired through a government agency that retains responsibility for paying them and appropriates half the employees' salaries in the process. This takes away the ability of the joint ventures' foreign managers to give incentives to Chinese employees.

Education Is Below the Level of Quality in Developed Countries Resulting in Lower Employee Productivity and Higher Personnel Costs . . . . . .

Chinese students demonstrate intelligence and quality work in their studies, and Chinese culture, reflecting Confucian philosophy, places high value on education. However, the Chinese education system is not up to developed country standards making it difficult to obtain qualified employees without the expense of significant additional training. Western students interviewed at a Hong Kong university said their classes were of significantly lower quality than their American and Canadian ones. A visiting American professor at a major university in Beijing confirmed that Chinese higher education was weak. We looked through the books in the small library at a university in Guangzhou and found no books with copyrights newer than the mid-1980s. Business students in a seminar we put on there had great difficulty understanding the concept of a contract, and had never heard of the *Asian Wall Street Journal* even though the school is only a hundred miles from Hong Kong.

The head of a software company we interviewed shared his disappointment in Chinese higher education. He said the problem must be addressed by the government, but now universities are no longer subsidized and are left on their own to raise funds. He asserted that "nothing is going on in academia." The hope for the future lies with the many students that China has overseas who will ultimately return home to fill managerial ranks. He lamented that only a few faculty members in Chinese universities are European or U.S. educated. We noticed that those faculty members who held Western degrees were a source of pride and status in the Chinese universities we visited.

Extend the Time to Meet Objectives . . . .

Most interviewees said that the time span for success in entering the Chinese market is a decade or more. The head of the farm equipment manufacturer said originally their target was 4 years, but he anticipates 10 to 15 years is a more realistic time frame in which to achieve profitability.

The manager at the delivery service company said it takes 200 "chops" (personal stamps, or chops, are used in lieu of signatures on documents) to set up a partnership. It requires approvals from as many as 200 bureaucrats at various levels to finalize a joint venture. It was pointed out that it is best to obtain approvals at all levels (frequently necessitating bribes) in order to have solid government backing. If only a top official is bribed for approval, excluding others, you run the risk of being shut down if that official is replaced. You must also make sure you secure permission to operate from a multiplicity of bureaucrats, some easily overlooked. For example, even though you get approval to ship by air from the administrator of airlines, you still need permits to buy fuel from another agency, and permits from the police department to have your trucks travel over roads to the airport.

Our contact at the American Consulate in Shanghai pointed out that China is a "consensus society" resulting in slow decision making and little accountability (Quistorff, 1996). In addition, a naïve Westerner might think a deal has been finalized after it has been signed by both parties, but Chinese characteristically continue to re-negotiate a contract for years after it has been signed. At the farm equipment manufacturer, after two years the Chinese joint venture partners are still negotiating on responsibilities, amount of investment, etc. In China, getting a contract signed only gives you the right to negotiate a license with the government, and your partners have a propensity for never ceasing to negotiate its terms.

There is no developed legal system of relatively consistent laws in China. Those rules of law that are in existence are open to interpretation and negotiation. It has been said that in China "the rule of man is stronger than the rule of law" (Roehrig, 1994). The multiplicity of bureaucrats prefer this because they can administer the law as they see fit. There always has been little commercial law in China where *guanxi*, or relationship marketing, is the substitute for legal contracts which Chinese may sign only to humor their Western counterparts (Ambler, 1995).

Transfer Older Technology

The advocates of global marketing, such as Levitt (1983), say that since the world is aware of, and wants, the latest technology, it will not settle for last year's models. On the contrary, we found many instances in which the old strategy of selling obsolete technology to developing countries remains viable in China. The printing forms company has brought its carbonless form process to China where the country presently has widespread use of carbon paper forms, and the life cycle of carbonless forms is just beginning. In the West, carbonless forms are at the end of their life cycle due to the growing use of computer laser printers. China cannot make the leap directly to widespread use of laser printers because of their significant cost. The head of the printing forms company predicts that the life cycle of carbonless forms in China will be another 10 to 15 years.

The head of the farm equipment manufacturer affirmed that the Chinese market is frequently not ready for Western quality products because the Chinese do not have the money to pay for quality. His joint venture is, therefore, producing an obsolete line of equipment with lower price points.

Price is not the only reason for selling obsolete technology; cultural norms are another. The farm equipment manufacturer found that introducing the latest, more powerful, diesel engines the Chinese requested was a mistake because of Chinese maintenance practices. The newer engines required more frequent filter changes because cleanliness and higher-quality fuel were more critical than in the older engines that could be operated with a less critical maintenance program. When Chinese workers could not bring themselves to put in new filters, or ineffectively tried to wash the dirty ones with gasoline, the new engines broke down. As a result the farm equipment manufacturer only markets older less powerful, but more tolerant, engines in China. The industrial equipment manufacturer brought in 1984 vintage technology because the latest is based on micro-chips which are difficult or impossible to service in China. They found it better to have hard wired circuits that Chinese can repair than circuit boards which they cannot. In addition, the company refuses to transfer newer technology until it buys out its partner and is wholly owned because of its concern with pirating.

Streamline the Size of Your Entry and Perhaps Go It Alone . . . . . .

Almost all of the interviewees emphasized the necessity of obtaining a controlling interest in the joint venture in order to operate effectively. The head of the farm equipment manufacturer joint venture recommends maintaining "at least 90 percent ownership because the Chinese want their Western partners to pay at least 90 percent of the costs." Capital contribution has been a more critical issue recently because the government-instituted credit crunch has resulted in Chinese partners not being able to obtain additional financing to make contributions to preserve their proportion of equity. The result is that Western partners are securing a larger ownership percentage as the Chinese equity portion is reduced, which has caused a great deal of resentment by Chinese joint venture partners.

The head of the printing forms company says that a 50/50 joint venture is the worst case because nothing happens in meetings but "gridlock." He prefers to enter with a wholly owned subsidiary. The industrial equipment manufacturer head, who is negotiating to increase ownership from 50 percent to 70 percent, said the downside of having a Chinese partner is that he eventually becomes more of a burden than a help. Contending with a Chinese joint venture representative who has a risk-averse, bureaucratic, non-decision-making orientation can tie up your company's progress in a series of unproductive meetings. This was affirmed by the film company manager who said that a wholly owned subsidiary is ideal because it is easier to operate with no conflict from a Chinese partner.

Another problem is that the typical Chinese joint venture partner is usually significantly overstaffed and will expect the Western partner to bear the cost of this. In the Otis joint venture in the Tianjin Economic/Technology Development Area there were 2,100 employees while only 700 were needed (Lee, 1996). The Chinese partner of the printing forms company was more than 50 percent overstaffed. The head of the industrial equipment manufacturer was given 300 Chinese personnel but insisted on setting up his own organization and took only 42 people.

Although the conventional wisdom is that the best way to enter the China market is with a well-connected Chinese joint venture partner, these results indicate there are significant reasons to consider the alternative of a wholly foreign-owned enterprise. In fact, this appears to be a growing trend (Vanhonacker, 1997).

Rather than a global approach, the American Commercial Consul in Shanghai, Ned Quistorff, recommends it is better to work in China on a regional rather than a national basis due to the significant differences in markets across the country (Quistorff, 1996). The head of the printing forms company took over a local government-owned small printing business and backed out of a much larger government state enterprise. The larger operation required them to take over many old, obsolete buildings and equipment, as well as problematic operations that were 100 percent overstaffed. Because projects over $30 million require approval from the central government in Beijing, involving rather onerous bureaucratic intervention, most contracts are written for less than this amount wherever possible.

Conclusion

Western companies entering China have traditionally found success in capitalizing on low labor costs and exporting products to other countries. Selling products in the China market is another matter. We have seen from this research that there are many discontinuities, as well as present and potential problems that do not make China a homogeneous market in which a high commitment global strategy always works best. This paper recommends a conservative strategy for many market entries in China. Reduced commitment and lower cost are relative to company size and capital requirements for different industries. A reduced commitment market entry strategy for a large capital-intensive company may take the form of initially marketing to a limited geographic or demographic target market. It may result in setting up a smaller wholly owned plant that can be tightly controlled rather than taking on a larger state-owned partner in a sizable joint venture. All types of companies may choose to limit their legal and financial commitment. For example, opening a representative office is an economical way of exploring the market and establishing a presence in China with minimum commitment. By law, officially sanctioned representative offices cannot engage in direct profit-making business activity in China, but they can promote products, do market research, contract administration, and negotiate on behalf of their head office. Average startup costs for such an office total approximately $10,000 (Rothstein, 1996), a significant saving over the hundreds of thousands and millions of dollars spent on full-scale market entry that may not return a profit for a decade or more. Such a conservative approach may be the optimum market entry strategy when confronted by severe risks and problems in a particular Chinese market segment.

References

Ambler, Tim (1995). Reflections in China: Re-orienting images of marketing. *Marketing Management*, 4 (1): 22–30.

Anderson, Erin (1990). Two firms, one frontier: On assessing joint venture performance. *Sloan Management Review*, 31 (2): 19–20.

Beamish, Paul W. (1993). The characteristics of joint ventures in the People's Republic of China. *Journal of International Marketing*, 1 (2): 27–48.

Business Week (1996). Time for a reality check in Asia. December 2: 66.

Campbell, Nigel C.G. (1989). *A Strategic Guide to Equity Joint Ventures in China*. Oxford: Pergamon.

The Economist (1995). China, not so miraculous? May 27.

The Economist (1996a). China, a funny-looking tiger. August 17.

The Economist (1996b). How poor is China? October 12: 35.

The Economist (1997). The Asian miracle. Is it over? March 1.

Gelb, Catherine (1996). Anyone's guess. *China Business Review*, 23 (3): 12.

Geringer, J. Michael and L. Hebert (1989). Control and performance of international joint ventures. *Journal of International Business Studies*, 20 (Summer): 235–54.

Krugman, Paul (1994). The myth of Asia's miracle. *Foreign Affairs*, November/December: 62–78.

Lee, George (1996). Chair, U.S.–Eurasia Institute, San Francisco State University. Personal interview, November 25.

Levitt, Theodore (1983). The globalization of markets. *Harvard Business Review*, May/June.

Ness, Andrew (1995). Hanging out your shingle in China. *China Business Review*, September/October.

Osland, Gregory E. (1994). Successful operating strategies in the performance of U.S.–China joint ventures. *Journal of International Marketing*, 2 (4): 53.

Osland, Gregory E. and Tamer S. Cavusgil (1996). Performance issues in U.S.–China joint ventures. *California Management Review*, 38 (2): 106.

Overholt, William H. (1993). *China: The Next Economic Superpower*. London: Weidenfeld & Nicolson.

Quistorff, Ned (1996). Commercial Consul, American Consulate General, U.S. Department of Commerce, Shanghai, China. Personal interview, June 4.

Roehrig, Michael F. (1994). The right time and place. *China Business Review*, 21 (5): 8–9.

Rothstein, Jay (1996). Easing your way into China. *China Business Review*, January–February: 30.

Shapiro, James E., J.N. Behrman, W.A. Fischer, and S.G. Powell (1991).

Direct Investment and Joint Ventures in China. New York: Quorum Books.

Stelzer, Leigh, C. Ma, and J. Banthin (1992). Gauging investor satisfaction. *China Business Review*, 19 (6): 54–56.

Vanhonacker, Wilfried (1997). Entering China: An unconventional approach. *Harvard Business Review*, March–April: 130–40.

Weil, Robert (1995). China at the brink: Class contradictions of market socialism. *Monthly Review*, 46 (8): 11.

Xue, Chun Shan (1997). Commercial Consul at the Consulate General of the People's Republic of China in Los Angeles. February.